FORMULAS,

METHODS,

TIPS and DATA

for HOME

and WORKSHOP

FORMULAS,

METHODS,

A POPULAR SCIENCE BOOK

BY KENNETH M. SWEZEY

TIPS and DATA

for HOME and

WORKSHOP

Popular Science Publishing Co.
Harper & Row
New York, London

Success and safety in the use of tools or in compounding or using formulas depend largely on the operator's skill and knowledge in handling tools and chemicals. To promote both success and safety, techniques in this book have been described in unusual detail, and precautions in handling chemicals that may be hazardous if improperly used have been explicitly pointed out. These instructions and precautions should be followed faithfully. Because the actual manipulation of the materials and processes described in the book are entirely in the hands of the operator, however, neither author nor publisher can guarantee the results of any instructions or formulas, and therefore each of them expressly disclaims any responsibility for injury to persons or property through their use.

A Word Of Thanks

The material in this book has been devised and adapted from literally thousands of sources. It began with a huge collection of notes, books, and personal experiences gathered during many years of preparing physics, chemistry, and home-workshop articles for *Popular Science Monthly* and other magazines and similar material for my books *After-Dinner Science, Science Magic, Chemistry Magic,* and *Science Shows You How,* published by McGraw-Hill. It has been expanded and brought up to date by further research in related literature, by the actual testing of many formulas, and by the kind and expert help of the following business, manufacturing, and Government organizations:

U.S. Department of Health, Education and Welfare
U.S. Public Health Service
U.S. Department of Agriculture
U.S. Forest Products Laboratory
U.S. Fish and Wildlife Service
U.S. Bureau of Mines
U.S. Department of Defense
U.S. Army Engineer Corps

U.S. Secret Service
U.S. Department of the Interior
National Bureau of Standards
N.Y. State College of Agriculture, Cornell University
N.Y. State College of Home Economics, Cornell University
University of Wisconsin, College of Agriculture
N.Y. Zoological Society
American Dental Association
American Red Cross
National Better Business Bureau
National Board of Fire Underwriters
National Fire Protection Association
National Safety Council
American Brush Manufacturers Association
American Gas Association
American Petroleum Institute
Best Foods
Bethlehem Steel Corporation
Borden Chemical Company
Calgon Corporation
Church & Dwight Company
Commercial Solvents Corporation
Diamond Crystal Salt Company
Dow Chemical Company
E. I. DuPont de Nemours & Company
Eastman Kodak Company
ESB, Inc. (formerly the Electric Storage Battery Company)
Esso, Inc.
Fisher Scientific Company
Ford Motor Company

General Aniline & Film Corporation
Heath Company
Humble Oil & Refining Company
International Nickel Company
International Salt Company
Walter Kidde & Company
Landers-Segal Color Company
Lead Industries Association
Mallinckrodt Chemical Works
Marble Institute of America
Morton Salt Company
National Flaxseed Processors Association
National Lead Company
National Lime Association
National Paint, Varnish and Lacquer Association
Pennsalt Chemicals Corporation
Pittsburgh Plate Glass Company
Portland Cement Association
Pyrofax Gas Corporation
Radio Corporation of America
Rose-X Chemical Company
Velsicol Chemical Corporation
Vermont Marble Company
Wool Bureau, Inc.
William Zinsser & Company

K.M.S.

CONTENTS

Cleaners for Metal • Cleaners and Polishes for
Special Problems

XII

Anti-Freeze Mixtures • Temperatures Useful to Know • Chemical Elements • Popular and Scientific Names for Chemicals • The Greek Alphabet

Introduction

This is a book of practical but often hard-to-find information for anybody who likes to do things for himself. Its purpose is to put at your fingertips the special technique, the needed table, the right formula to help solve all sorts of problems that crop up constantly around the home and in the workshop.

Some of the methods and formulas may save you money. Others may help you do a better job or make a special product you can't buy ready-made. Still others may just satisfy your curiosity or enable you to carry out a project you have always wanted to undertake but didn't know quite how.

As you can see from the table of contents, the book covers an exceptionally wide range. Included, of course, are the everyday basic and more familiar methods, hints, and tables you would expect to find in any comprehensive home and workshop data book. Beyond these, however, are hundreds of lesser known and more specialized techniques, uncommon tables, and useful formulas that have been selected and adapted from technical and professional literature as well as from personal experience, many of which appear in no other book of this type. If, therefore, you can't locate a wanted item by title in the table of contents, don't give up until you have double-checked it by subject matter in the index.

One help you should not overlook is the table of Conversions of Common Units beginning on page 603. In this table—compiled especially for this book—units of weight, area, volume, power, velocity, and so on are listed in simple alphabetical order, with the units you may wish to convert to, and the number you should use to make the conversion, immediately adjacent. Another table in the same chapter will enable you to convert from spoons, cups, and other household measures to more conventional ones. A third table will help you convert from specialized and unusual units, ranging from cubits and furlongs to Angstrom units and light-years.

In choosing formulas, the author has tried to include only those that might be actually useful around the home and shop, that are relatively easy to make with home equipment, and that are either better than, or cheaper but just as good as, proprietary products that serve the same purpose.

Most of the basic ingredients needed for preparing these formulas are well-known and are easily obtainable from the local grocery, hardware, paint, or drugstore, or from the supermarket. You may soon discover, however, that many others that were once readily available in such stores have either disappeared or are now sold only in disguise as specialty products under proprietary names and at a considerable markup in price. But don't give up! You can usually still get these products under their own names and at reasonable cost by sleuthing a little among sources that cater to special trades or industries.

Another complication may also at first discourage you. To protect inexperienced persons—especially children—from poisons and other products that may be hazardous if improperly used, Federal and State laws now prohibit the sale without prescription of many additional common chemicals that were once freely obtainable in drug and other stores that sell directly to the general public. Again, most of such chemicals can be bought by any responsible adult from chemical supply houses and from dealers to industry or to specialty trades in which the chemicals are routinely used.

To help you find some of the elusive materials, a list of sources is included in the back of the book, just before the index.

FORMULAS,

METHODS,

TIPS and DATA

for HOME

and WORKSHOP

1

Wood:
Selection, Finishing,
Preservation

HOW YOU ARE CHARGED FOR LUMBER

Lumber is sold by the "board foot" measure. A board foot is equal to a piece 1 inch thick and 12 inches square. If you know the board-foot price, you can find the cost of any size or shape of lumber by using this formula (thickness and width are in inches and length is in feet):

$$\frac{\text{Thickness x width x length}}{12} = \text{board feet}$$

Prices are based, however, on *nominal* or original rough sizes rather than *actual* dimensions as sold. In softwoods, thicknesses less than 1 inch are charged as a full inch, while in hardwoods the prices vary.

The following tables give the nominal and actual average sizes of commonly used lumber:

SOFTWOODS

THICKNESS		WIDTH	
Nominal (Rough)	Actual (Average)	Nominal (Rough)	Actual (Average)
1/2″	7/16″	2″	1-5/8″
1″	25/32″	3″	2-5/8″
1-1/4″	1-1/16″	4″	3-5/8″
1-1/2″	1-5/16″	6″	5-1/2″
2″	1-5/8″	8″	7-1/2″
3″	2-5/8″	10″	9-1/2″
4″	3-5/8″	12″	11-1/2″

HARDWOODS
Thickness (widths vary with grades)

Nominal (Rough)	Surfaced 1 Side (S1S)	Surfaced 2 Sides (S2S)
3/8″	1/4″	3/16″
1/2″	3/8″	5/16″
5/8″	1/2″	7/16″
3/4″	5/8″	9/16″
1″	7/8″	13/16″
1-1/4″	1-1/8″	1-1/16″
1-1/2″	1-3/8″	1-5/16″
2″	1-13/16″	1-3/4″
3″	2-13/16″	2-3/4″
4″	3-13/16″	3-3/4″

HOW WOOD IS GRADED

When a lumber dealer refers to "boards," he means stock less than 2 inches thick and usually more than 6 inches wide. Narrower boards are "strips."

Dimension lumber (also called *framing* lumber) includes structural pieces from 2 to 5 inches thick, used for studs, joists, and rafters. Lumber 5 inches thick or more is *timber*.

Each type is sold in various grades according to the size, number, and kind of defects found in them. Both boards and dimension lumber are graded by the same designations, but for different purposes. Boards are graded primarily for appearance—their faces show. Dimension lumber is graded for strength since it must support loads.

Here are the general designations:

B and better (also called No. 1 and No. 2 clear) is top quality and is almost completely free of knots. It is expensive, but is a good choice for the finest natural finishes.

C SELECT has some minor defects such as small, tight knots, but takes a good natural finish.

D SELECT, stocked by some lumberyards, has more blemishes.

NO. 1 COMMON (also Construction) may have many small, sound knots, none larger than about 2 inches and rarely on edges. Paint hides most but not all its defects.

NO. 2 COMMON (also Standard), an all-round utility grade, has same defects as No. 1, but knots up to 3½ inches and some on edges. Even paint won't hide everything.

NO. 3 COMMON (also Utility) allows loose, coarse, and missing knots, also splits and pitch. A No. 4 or Economy grade is also available at some yards.

By looking over lumber grades carefully, you can choose the cheapest one that will do for your purpose. Don't buy the most expensive clear grade if you're going to cover it up with paint. On the other hand, a low, knot-filled grade may be fine for rustic panelling.

If you're building a garage or addition to your house, you'll need a high grade that has good strength. Local building codes may specify grades that must be used; check these before starting construction.

CHOOSING THE BEST WOOD FOR THE JOB

Careful shopping will enable you to suit the wood you buy to the job you intend it for. Woods have widely different characteristics. Woods like redwood and cypress stand up well and are easy to work. But they are too soft to take a fine finish. Birch and maple finish beautifully, but aren't easy to work without power tools. They also are more susceptible to moisture damage and decay. The accompanying chart will help you choose the woods that have the qualities you need for each job.

Woods that sand smooth and take a high, hard finish are listed as "good." Those that require more work and take softer, duller finishes are listed as "medium" or "poor."

Strength won't matter much in woods used for paneling, or which are supported by a framework, but can be very important in structural woods or furniture parts such as table legs. Density, or hardness, can be roughly translated into "dentability." In general the hardest woods make the best cabinets and table tops.

HOW WOODS WEATHER

The accompanying chart shows how woods stand up under age and weather. Only those with very high decay resistance should be used unpainted outdoors. But many lower-rated woods will last well under outdoor conditions if treated with a preservative or are varnished or painted.

Woods with high shrinkage aren't necessarily a bad choice if you make sure they are dry. "Checking" (small cracks) and "cupping" (warping) are defects found in woods exposed to the weather. How much a wood cups or checks helps determine its suitability for exterior uses, as in house siding.

PICKING THE BEST IN PLYWOOD

Plywood is a highly versatile material. Depending on type and grade, it can provide weather resistance, beautiful grain, strength and toughness, flexibility, or a combination of these qualities. It can save work by eliminating or simplifying framing. It gives you broad surfaces ready-made.

Fir plywood is the most common type. For the finest finishes, you can get plywood faced with your

FACTS ABOUT WOOD PROPERTIES

Wood	Color	Strength	Weight	Density	Ease of Working With Hand Tools	Resistance To Nail Splitting	Base For Finishing	Cost
ASH, white	grayish brown	high	heavy	hard	hard	poor	medium	medium
BALSA	creamy white	low	light	soft	easy	good	poor	medium
BASSWOOD	creamy white	low	light	soft	easy	good	poor	medium
BEECH	light brown	high	heavy	hard	hard	poor	good	medium
BIRCH	reddish brown	high	heavy	hard	hard	poor	good	high
BUTTERNUT	light brown	low	light	soft	easy	good	medium	medium
CEDAR, red	red	medium	medium	medium	easy	poor	good	medium
CHERRY	reddish brown	high	medium	hard	hard	poor	good	high
CHESTNUT	grayish brown	medium	light	medium	easy	medium	poor	medium
COTTONWOOD	grayish white	low	light	soft	medium	good	poor	low
CYPRESS	yellowish brown	medium	medium	soft	medium	good	poor	medium
ELM	grayish brown	medium	medium	medium	hard	poor	poor	medium
FIR, Douglas	orange brown	medium	medium	soft	hard	medium	medium	medium
FIR, white	off white	low	light	soft	medium	poor	poor	low
GUM	reddish brown	medium	medium	medium	medium	medium	medium	medium

Wood	Color	Strength	Weight	Density	Ease of Working With Hand Tools	Resistance To Nail Splitting	Base For Finishing	Cost
HICKORY	reddish brown	high	heavy	hard	hard	poor	good	medium
MAGNOLIA	yellowish brown	medium	medium	medium	medium	medium	good	medium
MAHOGANY, Honduras	reddish brown	medium	medium	medium	easy	good	medium	high
MAHOGANY, Philippine	reddish brown	medium	medium	medium	easy	good	medium	medium
MAPLE, hard	light reddish brown	high	heavy	hard	hard	poor	good	high
MAPLE, soft	reddish brown	high	medium	hard	hard	poor	good	medium
OAK, red	flesh brown	high	heavy	hard	hard	medium	medium	medium
OAK, white	grayish brown	high	heavy	hard	hard	medium	medium	high
PINE, eastern white	cream to brown	low	light	soft	easy	good	medium	medium
PINE, ponderosa	orange to brown	low	light	soft	easy	good	medium	medium
PINE, sugar	creamy brown	low	light	soft	easy	good	poor	medium
PINE, yellow	orange to brown	high	medium	medium	hard	poor	medium	medium
POPLAR	yellowish brown	low	medium	soft	easy	good	good	medium
REDWOOD	deep reddish brown	medium	light	soft	medium	good	poor	medium
SPRUCE	off white	low	light	soft	medium	medium	medium	medium
SYCAMORE	flesh brown	medium	medium	medium	medium	good	good	medium
WALNUT	dark brown	high	heavy	hard	medium	medium	medium	high
WILLOW	brown	low	light	soft	easy	good	medium	low

HOW WOODS WEATHER

Wood	Resistance To Decay	Amount Of Shrinkage	CHANGES DUE TO WEATHERING		
			Color Becomes	Checking	Cupping
ASH, white	low	medium	dark gray	conspicuous	very high
ASPEN	low	medium high	light gray	inconspicuous	medium
BASSWOOD	low	high	light gray	conspicuous	medium
BIRCH	low	medium high	light gray	conspicuous	very high
CEDAR, red	very high	low	dark gray	inconspicuous	low
CHESTNUT	high	medium	dark gray	conspicuous	high
COTTONWOOD	low	medium high	light gray	conspicuous	very high
CYPRESS	very high	medium low	silvery gray	inconspicuous	low
FIR, Douglas	medium	medium	dark gray	conspicuous	medium
FIR, white	low	medium	dark gray	conspicuous	medium
GUM	medium	medium	light gray	conspicuous	very high
HEMLOCK, eastern	low	medium	light gray	conspicuous	medium
HEMLOCK, western	low	medium	light gray	conspicuous	medium
HICKORY	low	high	light gray	conspicuous	very high
LARCH	medium	medium high	dark gray	conspicuous	medium

CHANGES DUE TO WEATHERING

Wood	Resistance To Decay	Amount Of Shrinkage	Color Becomes	Checking	Cupping
MAPLE	low	high	light gray	conspicuous	very high
OAK, red	low	medium high	dark gray	conspicuous	very high
OAK, white	high	medium low	dark gray	conspicuous	very high
PINE, eastern white	medium	low	light gray	conspicuous	medium
PINE, ponderosa	low	medium low	light gray	conspicuous	medium
PINE, sugar	medium	low	light gray	conspicuous	medium
PINE, western white	medium	medium high	light gray	conspicuous	medium
PINE, yellow	medium	medium high	dark gray	conspicuous	medium
POPLAR	low	medium	light gray	inconspicuous	high
REDWOOD	very high	medium low	dark gray	inconspicuous	low
SPRUCE	low	medium	light gray	conspicuous	medium
WALNUT	high	medium	dark gray	conspicuous	high

choice of many hardwood veneers—mahogany, walnut, birch, cherry, gum, and other handsome woods.

Core construction. If you look at plywood edges,
you will find two main types. Lumber-core plywood
has a thick middle layer of solid wood. This is just the
thing for fine furniture.

For most jobs, the cheaper veneer-core plywood,
made up of many thin layers or plies, will do. It has
three, five, seven, nine or more plies depending on
thickness.

Some sizes also come in different numbers of plies
within the same thickness. You can buy ¼-inch plywood with either three or five plies. In general, the
more plies the stiffer the board and the less it will
warp. Where you need high rigidity, such as for loud-
speaker cabinets, ⅞-inch plywood with nine plies is a
better choice than ¾ inch with seven.

Sizes. Sizes in plywood are actual sizes as sold. A
⅞-inch piece is ⅞ inch thick. Common panel dimensions
are 3 by 8, 4 by 4, 4 by 6, 4 by 8, and 4 by 10 feet. A
special 5-by-9-foot panel is now made for table-tennis
tables.

Veneers. Veneers for plywood are cut three different ways. For fir plywood, they are rotary cut—
sliced off a log like peeling an apple. This gives them
a prominent, often wild, zig-zag grain.

Most hardwood plywood veneers are either flat-
sliced, which gives a milder but still prominent grain,
or quarter-sliced, which is the most expensive and
gives a fine striped pattern.

Grades. The quality of the two faces of a panel determines its grade. In softwood plywoods, a "good" face consists of a single sheet of smooth clear veneer. A sound face may consist of two plies perfectly joined but with small patches, stains, or sapwood. A 'utility" face may have knots, pitch pockets, knotholes, and small splits.

The most expensive grade has two good sides (designated as G2S). This is needed only for natural finishes when both sides will show. Where only one side will show, a "good-one-side" panel (G1S) will save you money.

For painted projects, the sound-two-sides (S2S) will do, or even the sound-one-side (S1S) when only one side shows. Wallboard grade (WB) has a sound face and utility back. Sheathing (SH) has two utility faces and comes unsanded.

Another grading system designates faces as A,B,C, and D. An A-A panel has two good faces, one marked A-C a good face and a utility back.

Hardwood plywoods are graded by still another system as is explained in one of the accompanying charts. The other charts describe special plywoods for decorative work, cabinet making, and boat building, and give further details on the plywoods already mentioned.

INTERIOR SOFTWOOD PLYWOOD (fir)

GRADE NAME*	TYPES AND USES	VENEER QUALITY			STOCK SIZES		
		Face	Back	Inner Plies	Width Length		Thickness
A-A	Best grade for all interior uses where both sides will show, such as cabinet doors and furniture.	A	A	D	3', 4'	8'	1/4", 3/8", 1/2" 5/8", 3/4"
A-B	Alternate for A-A grade for high-quality uses where only one side will show, such as cabinets, built-ins, paneling.	A	B	D	3', 4'	8'	1/4", 3/8", 1/2" 5/8", 3/4"
Plypanel	All purpose "one-side" panel for less expensive wall paneling, cabinets where only one side will show. Also for counters, backing, underlayment for floors.	A	D	D	3', 4'	8'	1/4", 3/8", 1/2" 5/8", 3/4"
B-D	Utility panel with lower grade face. If painted, a good substitute for A-B.	B	D	D	4'	8'	1/4", 3/8", 1/2" 5/8", 3/4"
Plybase	Underlayment grade for subfloors and base for tile, linoleum, carpeting.	C	D	D	4'	8'	1/4", 3/8", 1/2" 5/8", 3/4"
Plyscord	Unsanded grade for wall or roof sheathing, subflooring, rough or temporary construction uses.	C	D	D	4'	8'	5/16", 3/8", 1/2" 5/8", 3/4"
Plyform	For re-usable concrete forms, oiled and edge-sealed, but not as durable as exterior-grade Plyform.	B	B	C	4'	8'	5/8", 3/4"

HARDWOOD PLYWOOD

GRADES AND USES

(Sizes: widths from 24" to 48" in 6" multiples; lengths from 36" to 96", plus 10' and 12' on order.)

GRADE NAME*	
Custom Grade	For highest-grade natural finishes. Veneers are selected for clear, uniform and matching grain with practically no blemishes. Also includes architectural panels, technical types and special matched-grain panels. Expensive except for best cabinetwork or paneling.
Good Grade (1)	For fine natural and stained finishes on cabinets, built-ins, paneling and furniture. Veneer has typical species grain markings, occasional small burls, pin knots and slight color streaks, but is smooth, tight and matched in grain where two pieces join. Comes in both good-one-side and good-two-sides grades. (Some mills identify as A grade or 1 grade.)
Sound Grade (2)	For less-costly natural finishes or high-grade paint finishes. Veneers are not selected for color or appearance and may have sound, tight knots, small burls, patches, sapwood and mineral streaks. They are, however, firm, smooth and free from physical defects that would mar a paint finish.
Utility Grade (3)	For rough paint or natural finishes, such as for children's furniture, storage cabinets, shelves, playroom paneling. Has same defects as Sound Grade plus small splits not wider than 3/16", rough grain and knotholes up to 3/4".
Backing Grade (4)	Cheapest grade of hardwood plywood for construction uses where appearance does not matter or possibly as very rough, rustic paneling. Has knots, knotholes up to 2", splits and other defects that do not impair its strength.

*Grade names established by the Hardwood Plywood Institute

EXTERIOR SOFTWOOD PLYWOOD (fir)

GRADE NAME*	TYPES AND USES	VENEER QUALITY			STOCK SIZES		
		Face	Back	Inner Plies	Width	Length	Thickness
A-A	Permanent water-resistant plywood for exterior uses where both sides will show.	A	A	C	4'	8'	1/4", 3/8", 1/2" 5/8", 3/4", 1"
A-B	Alternate for A-A grade where appearance of back side is less important.	A	B	C	4'	4'	1/4", 3/8", 1/2" 5/8", 3/4", 1"
Plyshield	"Good-one-side" grade for uses where back side won't show.	A	C	C	4'	8'	1/4", 3/8", 1/2" 5/8", 3/4", 1"
Utility	All-around outdoor construction panel for less expensive farm buildings, summer cabins, fences, playhouses.	B	C		4'	8'	1/4", 3/8", 1/2" 5/8", 3/4"
Underlayment	Backing or subfloor for linoleum, tile, wall coverings, especially in high-moisture areas.	C	C	C	4'	8'	1/4", 3/8", 1/2" 5/8", 3/4"
Sheathing	Unsanded panel for rough construction exposed to weather or excessive moisture, such as sheathing, subfloors.	C	C	C	4'	8'	5/16", 3/8", 1/2" 5/8", 3/4"
Plyform	Oiled, edge-sealed panels for maximum re-use as concrete forms.	B	B	C	4'	8'	5/8", 3/4"

*Grade names established by the Douglas Fir Plywood Association.

SPECIALTY PLYWOOD

NAME	TYPES AND USES	STOCK SIZES		
		Width	Length	Thickness
Texture One-Eleven*	Exterior plywood with 3/8"-wide grooves for decorative siding, gable ends, carports, fences. Has shiplap edges.	16", 32", 48"	8', 10'	5/8"
Special Surfaces	Striated face to give comb-look, brushed face to accentuate grain, and embossed panels for decorative cabinets, paneling and siding.	4'	8'	5/16", 3/8"
Overlaid Plywood	Plastic-faced exterior plywood for high-grade paint finishes that won't show grain, for kitchen cabinets, exterior siding.	4' (also in 12", 16" and 24" siding)	8'	3/8", 1/2", 5/8", 3/4"
Hardboard-Faced Plywood	Combines smooth, paintable hardboard face with strength of plywood backing for cabinet doors, counter tops.	4'	8'	1/2", 5/8", 3/4"
Natural Finish N-N, N-D*	Special cabinet-grade panels for high-grade natural or stained finishes. N-N has two sides of select, all-heartwood veneers where both will show; N-D, one select side.	4'	8'	N-N: 3/4", N-D: 1/4"
Boat-Hull Grade	Exterior-type plywood with a special inner-ply construction for marine uses.	Standard sizes and special large sizes to order		

*Grade names established by the Douglas Fir Plywood Association

BLEACHING WOOD

To produce blond, champagne, lime, straw, or other popular light finishes, wood must generally first be bleached. This process removes the natural coloring matter in wood without damaging the fibers. Light-colored, even-grained woods are best for bleaching, though such dark woods as walnut and mahogany bleach successfully. Individual pieces of wood or veneer that are abnormally dark or that contain dark streaks known as mineral streaks may also be bleached to match the surrounding wood.

If varnish, stain, or other finishing material is present on wood surfaces to be bleached, it must be removed completely before bleaching is started. Even waxy materials left on the wood by varnish removers may interfere with the action of bleaching chemicals. A final sanding before bleaching is desirable in such cases.

In small-scale work, or in bleaching selected areas such as mineral streaks, the bleaching solutions are usually applied with a cloth swab, a sponge, or a brush. In large-scale production work, they are sometimes applied with a spray gun. In this case, the gun should be one with a glass solution container, and with all metal parts that come in contact with the solution made of stainless steel or other corrosion-resistant alloy.

(*Caution*: Many bleaching chemicals are injurious to the skin and eyes. Therefore goggles, rubber gloves, and aprons should be worn when applying them—particularly those containing oxalic acid. If any is spilled on your skin, wash the part thoroughly under running water. Also do large bleaching jobs outdoors over bare ground, or protect the floor and surroundings from spilled solutions.)

Oxalic Acid Bleach

Oxalic acid, which comes as white crystals, is one of the oldest bleaching agents. It is used where a comparatively mild bleaching action will suffice. Prepare this bleach as needed by dissolving from 3 to 4 ounces of the acid in each quart of hot water. Do this in glass, earthenware, or enameled steel vessels. Several applications may be made, until the desired color is reached. Then neutralize the acid by swabbing the surface with a solution of 3 ounces of borax per gallon of water. Finally rinse with hot water and wipe dry.

Bleach for Walnut

Black walnut may be bleached by first coating with a solution of 6 ounces of sodium bisulfite in 1 gallon of water. After this dries, apply a second coat consisting of 8 ounces of oxalic acid in 1 gallon water. After this dries, wash with hot water and neutralize with solution of 3 ounces borax in 1 gallon water. Rinse with hot water and dry.

Bleach for French Walnut Finish

This is a 2-solution specialty bleach to precede a French or a Huguenot walnut finish, though it may be used with other woods. Make the first solution by dissolving 1 ounce of potassium permanganate in 1 gallon of water. Apply this purplish liquid liberally.

While still wet, apply the second solution, which consists of 3 ounces sodium bisulfite in 1 gallon of water. The purplish tint will vanish and the wood will be considerably lighter than it was originally. Rinse the surface, let it dry, and then sand lightly.

Sodium Hydrosulfite Bleach

A simple bleach can be made by dissolving 3 ounces of sodium hydrosulfite in 1 quart of water. This chemical is commonly used for removing dyes from textiles, and is the color remover supplied with some brands of household dyes (read label). Repeatedly wet the wood with this solution until the desired bleaching is obtained. Rinsing is not necessary.

Bleaching with Laundry Bleach

Ordinary chlorine laundry bleach—a 5 to 6 percent solution of sodium hypochlorite—is the basis for a simple bleach suited to many woods. Mix 8 ounces with a gallon of water. Apply it liberally, then let it dry. Repeat, if necessary, and then rinse.

Bleach for Mineral Streaks

For dark spots in maple, one recommendation calls for the use of 4 pounds of oxalic acid and 4 pounds of sodium hypophosphite per gallon of water, used hot. Neutralize with a solution of 4 pounds borax in 1 gallon of water. Rinse with hot water, dry and sand lightly.

Some mineral streaks in oak or other woods cannot be removed with ordinary bleaches. Many finishers paint these out with material tinted to match the surrounding bleached surfaces.

Bleaching Iron Stains in Oak

Oak sometimes becomes discolored with greenish or black stains where it comes in contact with iron in the presence of moisture. These result from the reaction of iron rust with the tannic acid present in oak. Their composition is insoluble black ferric tannate, the coloring matter in some inks.

Oxalic acid will reduce this to the colorless, water-soluble ferrous tannate. Give the surface several applications of a solution of 4 ounces of oxalic acid per quart of hot water. After the stains disappear, wash the wood thoroughly with warm water to remove both the acid and all ferrous tannate which might in time be oxidized back to the colored salt.

Iron stains on oak may be avoided by keeping all uncoated iron or steel off the wet wood.

Bleaching Out Bluestain

Unslightly dark stains known as bluestain or sapstain often appear in the sapwood of woods of some species. They are caused by a type of fungi. Sodium hypochlorite laundry bleach (5 to 6 percent), diluted 8 ounces to 1 gallon of water, will reduce this staining if it is not too severe. This treatment is not recommended for oak or poplar.

Removing Glue Stains

Casein and vegetable glue stains can be removed almost entirely by swabbing them with a solution of 1 ounce oxalic acid in 12 ounces water. Rinse thoroughly with hot water and dry.

Bleached Effect without Bleaching

A finish lighter in color than the natural color of the wood can be obtained by first applying a white or light-colored paint of very thin consistency, made with opaque pigments of the desired color. Such paint can be made by mixing enamel undercoater, flat wall paint, or even ordinary house paint with about twice its volume of a mixture of equal parts of boiled linseed oil and turpentine or mineral spirits. Another suitable mixture is wood sealer with enough color-in-oil of color-in-japan to give the required color and opacity. For a fast-drying material, lacquer enamel may be mixed with twice its volume of a clear lacquer.

The coloring material should be spread on the wood with a mop, brush, or spray gun, allowed to stand 5 or 10 minutes, and then wiped with clean rags to remove excess and leave only what sinks into the grain. Lacquer must be wiped immediately after applying, before it has time to harden. Wipe first across the grain and then parallel with the grain. When dry, apply further protective finish, such as clear wood sealer, varnish, or lacquer, as desired.

To Produce a Limed Finish

A limed effect, not quite as light as that produced by bleaching, can be developed by either of the following methods:

1. Mix thoroughly 1 pound of unslaked lime in 2 quarts water. Apply this mixture to the surface of the smooth wood with a rough cloth, rubbing it into the pores of the grain as you would a wood filler. Wipe off excess by rubbing across the grain with another

cloth and allow the surface to dry. Then apply a wash coat of shellac. After this has dried, finish with varnish or lacquer.

2. Mix 1¼ pounds white lead paste with ½ pound of fine silex and apply this filler to the smooth wood as mentioned in the procedure above. After it has set slightly, force the filler into the pores and wipe off excess by rubbing with a rough cloth across the grain. When thoroughly dry, apply a wash coat of shellac. Then finish with varnish or lacquer.

STAINS FOR OUTDOOR USE

Stains used for wood shingles, rough siding, out-buildings, and fences are essentially greatly diluted linseed oil paints. In addition to ordinary paint ingredients, they often contain coal-tar creosote to kill microorganisms, and asbestine—a species of hydrated magnesium silicate or talc—as an extender.

On rough wood they are cheaper than paint and sometimes give service twice as long. Unlike stains for interior use, exterior stains contain only pure, finely divided opaque pigments, with iron oxide, chrome, and carbon pigments being the most durable. The following formulations all use the same basic medium with different combinations of pigment and asbestine to vary the color.

MEDIUM FOR ALL COLORS

Raw linseed oil	36 fl oz
Coal-tar creosote	16 fl oz
Turpentine	16 fl oz
Japan drier	8 fl oz

To make a stain of any of the following colors grind thoroughly the specified dry pigment and asbestine with one-half of the linseed oil in the above formula, adding the oil slowly and grinding continuously until it is uniformly mixed. Mix together the other ingredients, and then add them, with stirring, to the combined pigments.

DARK RED STAIN
    Indian red dry color   14½ oz
    Asbestine   1½ oz

LIGHT RED STAIN
    Venetian red dry color   14½ oz
    Asbestine   1½ oz

MAHOGANY STAIN
    Raw sienna dry color   13 oz
    Asbestine   2½ oz

DARK BROWN STAIN
    Burnt umber dry color   14½ oz
    Asbestine   1½ oz

BROWN STAIN
    Raw umber dry color   14½ oz
    Asbestine   1½ oz

GOLDEN OAK STAIN
    Raw sienna dry color   13 oz
    Asbestine   2½ oz

GREEN STAIN
    Chrome green dry color   15 oz
    Asbestine   ¾ oz

YELLOW GREEN STAIN
    Chrome green dry color   11 oz
    Yellow ochre dry color   4 oz

OLIVE GREEN STAIN
    Chrome green dry color   15 oz
    Lampblack   ⅛ oz
    Asbestine   ½ oz

GRAY STAIN
    Lithopone   9½ oz
    Whiting   4 oz
    Asbestine   2 oz
    Lampblack   ⅛ oz

Emergency Shingle Stain

To improvise a shingle stain of a special color, mix 1 gallon of outside paint with 1 gallon of turpentine or mineral spirits and 1 gallon of linseed oil.

Natural Wood Finish for Exterior Use

Owners of houses of western red cedar, redwood, or other woods of interesting color and grain figure, often desire a durable finish that will preserve the character of the natural wood. Commercially available finishes that form a clear film, however, do not bond well and are susceptible to cracking and peeling. They therefore must be renewed frequently.

The following oil-base penetrating stain was developed by the Forest Products Laboratory of the U.S. Department of Agriculture to overcome this disadvantage. Tests indicate that one application on planed surfaces of bevel siding of redwood or western red cedar fully exposed to the weather would last at least

3 years before renewal. The finish should last 1 or 2 years longer on siding that receives some shelter. As it merely wears or erodes away, it may then be reapplied without further treatment. The following formula will make slightly less than 5 gallons of finish.

Paraffin wax	1 lb
Zinc stearate	2 oz
Turpentine or mineral spirits paint thinner	1 gal
Pentachlorophenol, concentrate, 10:1	½ gal
Boiled linseed oil	3 gal

To the foregoing vehicle, the following pigments must be added to produce the colors mentioned:

LIGHT REDWOOD
Burnt sienna in oil	2 pints

CEDAR
Burnt sienna in oil	1 pint
Raw umber in oil	1 pint

DARK REDWOOD
Burnt sienna in oil	⅓ pint
Raw umber in oil	⅓ pint
Indian red iron oxide in oil	⅔ pint
Additional turpentine or mineral spirits	1 pint

By varying the proportions of the burnt sienna and raw umber colors-in-oil, other shades may be produced. Raw umber produces a dark brown, burnt sienna gives a red, and Indian red iron oxide gives a darker red. These components contain iron oxide pigments, which are the most durable of all pigments. By using other colors, or smaller amounts of those specified, the life of the present finish will be shortened.

Pentachlorophenol, commonly called "penta," is used widely as a preservative to protect a finish from mildew. It may be obtained at a paint store, lumberyard, or mail-order house. Zinc stearate may be bought at a drug store.

To prepare the finish, melt the paraffin and zinc stearate in the top unit of a double boiler. Stir until completely melted and combined. Then, with vigorous stirring, slowly add the mixture to the turpentine or mineral spirits.

Caution: Perform the latter operation outdoors or in a well-ventilated room, and far from sparks or flame. Turpentine and mineral spirits are flammable and their concentrated vapors are not healthful to breathe.

When the mixture has cooled to room temperature, add the penta concentrate and the linseed oil. Then gradually stir in the pigments until the color is uniform.

A single application of the finish by brush or spray is recommended. On a smooth surface, a gallon should cover 400 to 500 square feet; on rough, 200 to 250 square feet. It may be used over other penetrating natural finishes that have been worn until they need renewal. Varnish films must be removed before applying the finish. In good drying weather, it should dry to a low luster within 24 hours.

The finish was designed particularly for siding, but has been used satisfactorily on wood fences, lawn furniture, and sun decks. It does not provide sufficient protection for exterior millwork, such as frames, window sash, and doors, which should be painted.

Penetrating Stain for Rough and Weathered Wood

Simply by doubling the amount of pigment in the dark redwood finish mentioned above, forest products experts of the University of Wisconsin have developed a moisture resistant, long lasting, and economical finish for exterior surfaces that had always been difficult to paint.

The new finish is excellent for rough-sawn and weathered lumber with "fuzzy" surfaces. Because of its penetration, it also works well on dense, smooth woods, such as exterior plywood and knotty or flat-grained boards of oak, pine, and fir, from which paint peels. It is an effective finish for wood that has been neglected until the paint has fallen off and the raw wood is exposed to the weather.

One coat of the fortified stain properly applied to rough wood should last 8 to 10 years. Due to less penetration, it should last about 3 years on smooth planed surfaces. It will not blister, crack, peel, or scale, even if moisture penetrates into the wood.

You can make the finish from scratch by adding ⅓ of a pint each of burnt sienna and raw umber in oil, and ⅔ of a pint of Indian red iron oxide, to the formula given for the dark redwood stain in the previous unit

You can also make a satisfactory version by thinning premium-quality red barn paint with linseed oil and water-repellent wood preservative. The paint should contain about 55 percent pigment, at least one-third of which should be ferric oxide. The vehicle should contain about 85 percent linseed, soybean, or other "drying" oil. Thin this paint with 2 gallons of boiled linseed oil and 2 gallons of paintable water-repellent wood preservative to a gallon of paint.

Apply only one coat of the fortified stain, at the rate of 200 to 250 square feet per gallon on rough surfaces and 400 to 500 square feet on smooth surfaces, using a brush or spray gun. Apply immediately to rough wood, but let smooth wood weather several months before application. Apply when the wood is dry, and the temperature above 40 degrees F. To prevent lap marks, stain the full length of boards without stopping for more than 5 minutes.

INTERIOR AND FURNITURE STAINS

Pigment Oil Stains

These oil stains are easy to prepare and use. They work best on soft woods of close grain, such as poplar, gum, and basswood; they have little effect on hardwoods. Their disadvantages are that they dim the grain a little, and they usually need to be sealed with a thin coat of shellac to prevent bleeding.

To promote even absorption, first wipe on the wood a coat of 1 part boiled linseed oil mixed with 3 parts gum turpentine, or 1 pound cut shellac.

Medium for all colors

Boiled linseed oil	6 parts
Gum turpentine	2 parts
Japan drier	1 part

To this mixture, add the desired colors-in-oil, blended thoroughly with a little turpentine. The amount of the colors to be added will depend on the wood to be stained and on the shade desired. Test a stain for color on a sample or inconspicuous spot of the wood on which it is to be used. To see the true color, wait for it to dry.

General colors

Reds: Turkey red, rose madder, rose pink; burnt sienna

Yellows: Raw sienna; yellow ochre

Browns: Burnt umber, Vandyke brown, raw umber

Black: Lampblack or ivory black

Cherry

Dark: Burnt sienna	
Light: Burnt sienna	3 parts
Raw sienna	2 parts

Mahogany

Red: Burnt sienna	3 parts
Rose pink	2 parts
Burnt umber	½ part
Brown: Burnt sienna	3 parts
Rose pink or maroon lake	1 part
Vandyke brown or	
burnt umber	1 part

Maple

Yellow: Raw sienna	3 parts
Raw umber	1 part
Red: Burnt sienna	4 parts
Burnt umber	1 part
Reddish honeytone:	
Raw sienna	1 part
Burnt umber	1 part

Oak

Light: Raw sienna	4 parts
Raw umber	1 pint
Dark: Raw sienna	4 parts
Burnt umber	1 part
Antique: Raw sienna	8 parts
Burnt umber	2 parts
Lampblack	1 part
Mission: Ivory black	2 parts
Rose pink	1 part

Pine

Pumpkin pine: Raw sienna
    Small amount of ultramarine
Honey pine: Yellow ochre
    Small amount of raw sienna

Ebony

Coach black	20 parts
Prussian blue	1 part

Gray

Zinc oxide white
Lampblack, to get shade desired

WALNUT

Dark walnut: Vandyke	
brown	6 parts
Drop black	1 part
Rich dark brown: Burnt	
umber	4 parts
Vandyke brown	1 part
Yellowish brown: Burnt	
umber	3 parts
Raw umber	2 parts
Rich reddish brown: Burnt	
umber	8 parts
Burnt sienna	1 part

Apply the stain with a brush or cloth. Let it stand 2 or 3 minutes. Then rub it with a soft cloth. Let the stain dry for at least 36 hours before smoothing with fine sandpaper or steel wool.

Penetrating Oil Stains

An easy way to make oil stains that will penetrate more deeply into the wood surface is simply to replace up to half of the linseed oil in any of the preceding formulas with the solvent toluol.

Another way to make penetrating stains is to dissolve oil-soluble dyes in a mixture of 5 parts toluol to 1 part painter's naphtha. Ordinarily about 1 ounce of dye is needed for each quart of liquid dye. Because oil-soluble dyes are made in an almost endless variety of trade-named colors, combinations to produce specific effects must be obtained by experiment, or from suggestions by individual dye suppliers or manufacturers mentioned in the back of the book.

Caution: In using penetrating dyes containing toluol have plenty of ventilation. The vapor of toluol is toxic, and the vapor of both toluol and naphtha is flammable.

How to Mix and Apply Water Stains

Water stains are especially good for hardwoods such as walnut, birch, maple, cherry, rosewood, and mahogany. They do not obscure the grain and they produce clear, rich colors that do not fade or bleed. They are not recommended for use on veneer, however, because they might loosen the glue.

You can get water stains in powder form in standard wood colors at large paint and craft stores or you can compound your own. In the former case, follow the directions on the package for mixing and application; in the latter, follow these:

1. Moisten 1 ounce of dry aniline stain powder with hot water and stir to make a smooth paste. Use only soft or distilled water for mixing water stains, as hard water causes a change or loss of color.

2. Add the paste to 1 pint of hot water and stir well. Then add water to make 1 quart. Let stand for 24 hours.

3. Reduce the standard solution with a measured amount of hot water to make any lighter stain required. Test on wood similar to that to be stained. Mark the dilution ratio on the label.

4. Keep stock solutions of 1 ounce each of black, red, and yellow in 1-quart jars to use in shading new colors. Make a record of each mixture for future duplication.

Before application of water stain, sponge the wood with plain water and then dry it. This will raise tiny "whiskers" which you should remove with 3/0 or 4/0 steel wool or very fine finishing paper.

Use a rubber-set brush to apply the stain freely and evenly with the grain of the wood. Allow to dry slowly and thoroughly, away from heat, so that the wood will not warp or crack. Let it dry at least 24 hours. Then smooth very lightly once more with the finishing paper or steel wool. Be careful in smoothing edges as it is very easy to remove color at such places.

Tobacco Stain for Pine

To give new pine paneling and furniture an "old pine finish look," try this recipe suggested by the Home Economics College of Cornell University:

Break up 1 plug of chewing tobacco in a jar and add 1 pint of clear household ammonia. Cover the jar tightly and let stand for about a week. Wipe surface and end grain of wood with a damp cloth just before applying stain, to insure even penetration. Strain liquid though a piece of old but clean nylon stocking, and mop several coats of it on the wood with a lintless cloth. Allow to dry 24 hours. Then rub lightly with fine steel wool. Dust with dry cloth and finally with a tack rag.

This stain dries lighter than it appears when wet; it shows up darker again, however, after it has been shellacked, varnished, or waxed.

Stains for Maple

All maple finishes should be clean, thin, and transparent. Sand wood clean with 4/0 finishing paper; sponge with clean water, but avoid touching with the hands; dry; sand clean again with the finishing paper. Then use one of the following water stain formulas. The colors mentioned are standard water-soluble wood stains sold in powder form.

HONEY MAPLE

Canary yellow, concentrated	½ oz
Orange	¾ oz
Hot water	1 gal

AMBER MAPLE

Add to the preceding formula:

Jet black	¼ oz

COTTAGE MAPLE

Add to the amber maple formula:

Scarlet	¼ oz

New Stains with Household Dyes

Everyday household dyes used generally for textiles can not only be used to pinch-hit for regular water stains but to obtain exciting and off-beat decorator color effects on furniture, craft work, and other home projects in wood. If you are tired of such old standbys as oak, walnut, and maple, these dyes will enable you to try your hand with items in rose pink, tangerine, and Kelly green!

If your household dye is RIT, dissolve 1 package of a single color, or an equivalent amount of mixed colors, in 1 pint of hot—but not boiling—water. (If you use a different brand, experiment for yourself. Begin by trying twice the concentration of dye ordinarily used for textiles.) Test the color on hidden parts of the wood to be dyed. If the color is too light, add more dye; if too dark, add hot water.

As with all water stains, be sure the wood to be dyed is clean, free of grease, and sanded smooth. Sponge the surface evenly with water and wipe. When thoroughly dry, smooth with 3/0 or 4/0 steel wool or sandpaper. Apply the dye solution, while still warm, with a brush, sponge, or soft cloth. Let dry 24 hours, sand lightly with 4/0 finishing paper, and finish as you would any other water-dyed surface.

Wood Fillers

For a fine finishing job on open-grained woods such as oak, ash, butternut, chestnut and mahogany, or on medium-grained woods such as maple, birch, redwood, and cherry, a wood filler should be applied. This should be done after staining but before the application of other finishes. If you can wait from 12 to 24 hours for drying before you apply the next coat, this traditional type of filler has some advantages over newer quick-drying types:

Boiled linseed oil	12 parts
Drier	6 parts
Gum turpentine	1 part
Fine silex	enough for desired consistency

For medium close-grained woods make a thin paste; for open-grained woods a stiffer one. Cream color in this state, it is suitable only for very light finishes on naturally pale wood. You can easily color it, however, to match any wood or finish by mixing with it a small amount of suitable colors-in-oil. To accentuate the grain, the filler is generally made a little darker than the surrounding wood.

Vandyke brown and burnt umber are the most useful colors for almost any traditional wood finish. For suggestions for others, refer to the color combinations under "Pigment Oil Stains."

Apply filler with a brush or rough cloth, using a circular motion and rubbing it well into the pores. After the surface has dulled over from evaporation of the turpentine, carefully remove excess filler by scraping with the edge of a card followed by wiping the wood across the grain with burlap. After 24 hours, touch up lightly with 6/0 finishing paper.

Linseed Oil Finish

A rubbed linseed oil finish requires patience and "elbow grease" to apply, but develops a beautiful, durable, mellow luster on stained or raw wood that many consider the most attractive of all finishes. Although not highly water resistant, this finish will withstand hot dishes and is less likely to show scratches than a varnish finish. It may be kept in condition just by rubbing on more oil.

Use either straight boiled linseed oil, or 2 parts boiled linseed oil diluted with 1 part gum turpentine. Spread the oil liberally over the surface with a thick pad of folded cloth. Allow this to sink in until no more is absorbed. Then rub again with the same pad, making an effort to work additional oil into the pores of the wood. Use clean cloths to wipe off surplus oil, allow to dry overnight, and then repeat the whole process. The greater the number of coats, the more attractive and durable the finish will be. For most pieces, a minimum of three coats is recommended. (*Caution*: At the end of the day, burn used rags or store them under water. Otherwise they might catch fire spontaneously.)

WOOD FINISHING WITH SHELLAC

Although shellac has been used as a decorative and protective coat for centuries, it is still one of the most convenient, attractive, and useful finishes for the home handyman. It is easy to apply, is ready for a second coat in an hour or two, and may be washed from brushes and rollers with nothing but ammonia in warm water.

Shellac dries to a varnish-like transparent film. White shellac has only a slight toning effect on wood. Orange shellac is just as clear but with a decided amber cast to its film. The finish may be medium or high gloss, depending on the number of coats applied. It may be steel-wooled or rubbed with pumice and oil to a pleasing low sheen.

What "pound cut" means. This term describes the pounds of dry shellac dissolved in 1 gallon of alcohol solvent. For example, a standard 4-pound cut is made dissolving 4 pounds of bleached shellac in 1 gallon of alcohol. (In 1 gallon of 4-pound cut shellac there would be a little less than 3 pounds of dry resin.)

Thinning. A coat of 4- or 5-pound cut shellac would be too thick to penetrate and to develop a good bond with wood. For most end uses, shellac must be diluted to a 2- or 3-pound cut before application. For French polishing and for a wash coat under stains, it must be diluted to a 1-pound cut. As a thinner, use only denatured alcohol that is recommended on the label for this purpose.

To thin shellac, follow these ratios:

Basic cut	Desired cut	Alcohol per quart shellac
5 lb	3 lb	⅞ pint
5 lb	2 lb	1 qt
5 lb	1 lb	⅔ gal
4 lb	3 lb	½ pint
4 lb	2 lb	¾ qt
4 lb	1 lb	2 qt
3 lb	2 lb	¾ pint
3 lb	1 lb	3 pints

Storage and test for drying. Liquid shellac tends to deteriorate with long storage, so don't buy more than you need at a time. Also don't expose it to heat. Shellac is too old for use when it refuses to dry. If in doubt, test a sample by coating it on a scrap of clean wood. If the shellac dries to a hard film, it is still good. If it doesn't, throw it out. Adding alcohol won't help.

Surface preparation. On floors, shellac may be used over old shellac, varnish, and lacquers, as well as on bare wood. Just be sure the surface is clean, smooth, and dry, and free from oil and wax. In refinishing furniture, however, it is better to first remove all the old finish. Then smooth the wood with 2/0 steel wool, followed by 2/0 sandpaper, dust it, and bleach or stain as desired. Because they are easier to apply uniformly, and dry faster, water stains are here preferable to oil stains. If you do use oil stains, let them dry at least 12 hours before applying shellac.

New construction. It is wise to apply the first coat of shellac to floors in a new building just as soon as the floors are laid. It's a good idea, also, to coat stair treads and other exposed and unfinished woodwork. Then this new wood, covered further with building paper, will be protected against dirt, grease, and paint spots while construction goes on. As soon as this other work is over you can apply the final coats. If wood has raised grain fibers, the first coat of shellac will stiffen these so they can be sanded smooth with less effort.

Floors. Shellac gives a beautiful, long-wearing finish that often may be applied and walked on the same day. On both old and new floors, sand smooth, ending with a 2/0 (100) garnet paper, and remove all dust. Apply a 2-pound cut shellac by brush or applicator, following grain of wood. Do 2 or 3 board widths at a time, using a full brush and avoiding overlapping and excessive brushing.

Let dry 2 hours, hand-sand lightly with 2/0 garnet paper or fine steel wool and dust lightly with a barely damp rag. Apply second coat. In 4 hours, second coat should be hard enough to walk on. For heavy wear areas, apply a third coat 3 hours after second coat. Let dry overnight before subjecting it to traffic.

If floors have first been stained, be sure stain is thoroughly dry before applying shellac. On pine or other soft woods, a 1-pound cut wash coat of shellac is recommended before staining to give the wood uniform porosity.

Shellacked floors will have better water and wear resistance if they are waxed. Allow 24 hours' drying time after last coat, then apply a good paste wax and buff.

Bowling alley floors. Apply 6 to 8 coats, in not more than 2-pound cut. Several additional coats may be applied to parts receiving an unusual amount of wear—the pit end, and also the groove, from the foul line to a point some 20 feet down the alley. Allow plenty of drying time between coats.

In refinishing a well-maintained alley, sanding is usually not required before the first coat; but take great care that all old wax is removed. After dewaxing, rub down lightly with steel wool.

Furniture, wall paneling, woodwork. Sand smooth. Apply 3-pound shellac, with full brush, following grain of wood, and with minimum of brushing. After 3 hours sand lightly with extra fine paper and wipe free of dust. Apply second coat using same technique. Do not sand. Do not put heavy objects on surface for at least 48 hours.

If a semi-dull finish is wanted, gently burnish second coat with fine steel wool. For a flat finish, rub down with fine powdered pumice and oil.

Waxing will increase the water and wear resistance of any finish. Let last coat of shellac dry 24-48 hours. Then apply paste wax and buff.

Raw wood to be painted. On soft wood such as pine, 1 coat of 3-pound cut seals off pores of the wood, and so prevents finish coat from striking in to leave an uneven finish.

Undercoat for varnish. One coat of 3-pound shellac serves as an excellent undercoat for conventional varnishes. Shellac's quick dry shortens finishing cycle and reduces amount of varnish needed. Note: Do not use under urethanes.

Sealing knots and sappy streaks in new wood. Apply 1 or 2 coats of 3-pound cut.

Wash coat under stains. One coat of 1-pound shellac assures uniform surface and controls penetration of stain.

Undercoat for wax finish. Wood that is to have an all-wax finish should first be sealed with a coat of 3-pound cut. This prevents dirt from being ground into the wood.

French polishing. This is one of the most beautiful and lasting of finishes. Sanded and stained surface must be completely dry. Then wipe on a 1-pound shellac with a soft lintless cloth rolled into a ball. Dip the ball into the shellac and rub on the wood in rapid straight strokes, exerting only light pressure. On drying, rub the wood with 4/0 steel wool or 7/0 sandpaper. The surface can be sprinkled lightly with very fine powdered pumice before sanding. Continuous coats are applied with sanding or steel wooling every third coat until a light glow appears.

At this point add several drops of boiled linseed oil to the shellac mixture and continue application, but with a rotary motion. Add more oil by degrees with subsequent coats until a deeply glowing finish is achieved. Ordinarily 8 to 12 coats will be required.

Outside application. One or two coats of shellac spot seals knots and sappy streaks. Cover with exterior paint for protection against the weather.

HOW TO REPAIR WOOD FINISHES

Badly worn furniture may require complete refinishing. If, however, it is just soiled from everyday use, or it is marred merely by minor scratches, water marks, cigarette burns, and other local blemishes, it may be wonderfully improved by one of the following treatments.

Cleaning. This may be all that is needed to revive the luster and character of an oil, varnish, or lacquer finish. (Shellac must be given special treatment, which will be described separately.)

Here is a cleaning mixture suggested by the New York State College of Home Economics, at Cornell University:

Warm water	1 qt
Boiled linseed oil	3 tbs
Turpentine	1 tbs

Keep the mixture warm in a double boiler. Rub the finish with a soft cloth dampened with it. Then wipe the surface dry and polish with a dry cloth.

Dullness is difficult to remove from varnish or enamel of poor quality. To increase the luster, apply a thin coat of paste wax and buff well; or use the following mixture:

Boiled linseed oil	2 parts
Turpentine	1 part

Rub this polish well into the surface and buff briskly with a clean dry cloth until the finish is dry and shiny.

White spots on oil, varnish, and lacquer finishes are caused by heat, moisture, or alcohol. In most cases you can remove them by rubbing the finish carefully with a thin paste of finely powdered pumice in light mineral or machine oil.

Rub the mixture over the spot, using your fingertips or a piece of felt. Wipe the surface clean with a dry cloth. To remove any remaining oil, wash the surface with a cloth moistened with detergent suds. If the pumice leaves a dull spot, polish it with rottenstone and oil.

Repairing shellac. Ordinarily a shellac finish is easily maintained by cleaning with a damp cloth or waxing. For stubborn stains, use mild soap and water. Rinse and dry. Water spots can generally be removed by rubbing gently with a cloth moistened with alcohol. (If the surface is waxed, first remove the wax with turpentine.)

If damage is too severe for this remedy, or the finish is burned or scratched, remove the old film in the affected area with fine sandpaper or pumice and oil. Then apply two or more coats of spray shellac or 3-pound cut liquid shellac. When dry, buff with No. 00 steel wool until new finish blends with the old.

Scratches. The cleaning solution described above often makes scratches less noticeable. More serious scratches may require further treatment.

Fine scratches can often be removed by softening the finish and letting it flow together. Use alcohol for shellac, turpentine for varnish, lacquer thinner for lacquer. Dab the solvent on with a fine artist's brush.

Where the stain is damaged, it can be restored with fine-tipped touch-up applicators that come in many colors. Dark woods also respond to repeated rubbing with liquid shoe polish or stain waxes. You might also rub a small amount of oil color into the scratch to color it and then cover with a quick-drying varnish, or mix the varnish directly with the oil color before application. Here are some suggestions for matching colors:

> Reds: Turkey red, rose madder, or rose pink. Burnt sienna.
>
> Yellows: Raw sienna, French ocher.
>
> Browns: Burnt umber, Vandyke brown, raw umber.
>
> Blacks: Lampblack, ivory black.
>
> Walnut: Use either burnt umber or Vandyke brown. Raw umber, a yellowish brown, is sometimes added.
>
> Mission oak: Raw umber.
>
> Brown oak: Burnt umber alone or with a little raw sienna.
>
> Golden oak: Raw sienna, a little burnt umber.
>
> Maple: Burnt sienna for the redder maples; raw sienna for the yellow maples. Mix for blends.
>
> Red mahogany: Turkey red, rose madder, or rose pink; add a little burnt umber or black, if needed.

Brown mahogany: Burnt umber, with a very little red, if needed.

Dark mahogany: Use one of the mahogany reds with black added.

Cherry: Burnt sienna. Add a little burnt umber and one of the mahogany reds, if needed.

Deep scratches can be filled with stick shellac in the same way as for burns (see below). Build up the shellac to the height of the masking tape, then shave it down with a razor blade and polish with fine pumice.

A temporary scratch repair can be made with a wax crayon of a color to match the finish. Rub in, clean off the excess, then polish with wax. This works especially well on enamel.

Small dents can often be raised by steaming the wood, thus swelling the compressed fibers. Remove the surface wax with turpentine so moisture can penetrate the wood. Lay a blotter over the dent and keep it wet for several hours to saturate the wood.

Apply heat to the dent with an electric iron. Do this by placing a metal bottle cap on the blotter, directly over the dent, and resting the iron on the cap. This concentrates the heat, steaming the dent. If the dent won't swell, remove the finish and try steaming again. If this won't work use the filling method that follows.

Cigarette burns, scars, and cracks. These need more drastic treatment. If burned, clean out the burn thoroughly, scraping away all damaged fibers with a knife edge or razor blade. Then smooth the wood with a small piece of fine sandpaper or steel wool, feathering the edges into the good wood.

Fill deep scars with wood paste filler or stiff spackling compound until the recess is almost flush with the surrounding surface. Shallow burns can be built up with coats of varnish or shellac, depending on furniture's finish, without the filler.

Mask the area around the scar with masking tape. Cover the filler with stick shellac in a color to match the furniture. Melt the shellac in an alcohol flame and smooth it on with a small spatula. Remove the tape and shave the shellac flush with a razor blade. Rub gently with very fine steel wool, or pumice and oil, to smooth the patch and the surrounding surface. Apply wax or polish.

Instead of using shellac, you may fill large scars with spackling compound mixed with oil color to match the finish. Make the compound a little darker than the finish, however, because it lightens as it dries. When thoroughly dry, smooth down the patch with fine steel wool or very fine abrasive paper. Varnish or shellac.

Removing Silicone Polish

Modern liquid furniture polishes containing silicone compounds are often a blessing to the housewife. These tough chemicals, related to sand, effectively repel water and resist staining and oxidation. Because they also repel the liquids in many present-day paints and varnishes, however, they can be a bane to the retoucher or refinisher. Every trace of silicone must be removed before the new finish can be successfully applied.

The best way to do this is to wash the surface with a silicone solvent, such as turpentine, xylol, or toluol. After wiping the surface dry with a clean cloth, wash it again with a fresh cloth.

Even after washing, it is best to apply a barrier coat of shellac or other sealer before you apply the final finish.

If you intend to use an old-fashioned oil and resin finish, the washing need not be done. In this case the oil in the finish will dissolve and blend with the silicone.

Tack Rag for Furniture Finishing

In varnishing and enamelling furniture and other woodwork, it is important to keep the surface clean just ahead of the brush. A practical means for doing this is to use a so-called "tack rag." This may be purchased or made. To prepare one, use lintless cloth such as an old handkerchief, which is especially good because of its hemmed edges. Dip it in water, wring quite dry, then sprinkle it lightly with varnish from a brush. Refold and rewring so the varnish permeates the cloth. Keep it rolled in sheet plastic or waxed paper when not in use to prevent drying out. Should this occur, sprinkle with water and wring out again.

HOW TO PREVENT CRACKS IN NEW WOOD FLOORS

Cracks that develop within a few weeks or months in a new, well-laid floor are the result of changes in the moisture content of the wood either before or just after the floor is laid. By taking proper precautions, they can be prevented.

The well-informed manufacturer generally sees that floor stock is properly dried and delivered in good condition to the retailer. The good dealer, in turn, stores it under conditions that won't allow it to absorb moisture. Trouble usually starts, however, if the wood is delivered on a damp or rainy day, or if dry wood is laid in a cold, damp house in which the plaster or masonry has not thoroughly dried.

Boards swell when they absorb moisture and shrink when they dry. If flooring contains too much moisture when it is installed, cracks will open up soon after the house is occupied and heated. If, on the other hand, dry flooring is installed in a damp house, what is known technically as "compression set" will take place. As the boards swell, their edges press powerfully against each other, crushing the wood fiber and permanently compressing it; when they dry again, they leave cracks.

The cure for such cracks lies wholly in prevention. The rules are simple, but often overlooked:

1. Make sure the wood is dry when you lay it.
2. Do not lay it in a cold, damp house.
3. To retard moisture absorption, coat the floor with shellac, floor sealer, or varnish as soon as practicable.

Humidity control. To keep indoor dampness low enough to prevent swelling of newly-laid flooring, experts of the Forest Products Laboratory of the Department of Agriculture recommend that heat be maintained in a house from the time the workmen

leave until they return the next workday, even during
warm summer weather. If the heating plant has not
already been installed, then a temporary stove should
be used.

It is also good practice, they say, to open the
bundles of flooring so that all surfaces are exposed to
the air for at least 4 days. This allows time for the
flooring to reach a moisture equilibrium with the air
in the heated house before it is laid. The inside temperature should be kept at least 15 degrees F above
outdoor temperatures and should not be allowed to
cool below about 70 degrees during the summer or
62 to 65 degrees F when the outdoor temperatures
are below freezing. Slightly higher temperatures will
do no harm, but severe overheating should be avoided. After the floor has received its coating of protective finish, temperatures should be kept approximately what they will be when the house is occupied.

Besides preventing crack formation in the flooring, such heating will also permit better performance
from mechanical sanders. In addition, it will prevent
swelling and cracking of other interior woodwork and
finish, such as doors, trim, and cabinets.

How dry should flooring be? It depends on
where you live and to some extent what type of
heating system you will use. With conventional heating systems, using warm air or hot-water or steam
radiators, flooring should be laid at an average moisture content of 8 percent in most parts of the United
States. This value is about midway between the highest and lowest values the flooring will attain during
the different seasons.

The accompanying table gives moisture allowances for individual pieces and for other parts of the country.

RECOMMENDED MOISTURE CONTENT FOR WOOD FLOORING AT TIME OF LAYING
(For dwellings with conventional heating systems)

CLIMATIC REGION	MOISTURE CONTENT, PERCENT	
	Average	Individual pieces
Semidesert region (Nevada, parts of California, Utah, and Arizona)	6	5 to 8
Damp southern coastal regions (from North Carolina to eastern coast of Texas, and on the southern coast of California)	11	9 to 12
Remainder of United States	8	6 to 9

Exceptions to these figures should be made for dwellings with radiant heating systems in which heating pipes or coils are placed beneath the floor. Wood for flooring in such homes should be kiln dried and carefully protected from moisture absorption during both storage and installation. Its average moisture content should be about 2 percent lower than that indicated in the table.

Test for moisture content. Large lumber manufacturers test the moisture content of their lumber by means of electric moisture meters. You can make your own test with the help of a fairly accurate scale and your kitchen oven.

Cut a small specimen, preferably not smaller than 9 square inches, from the flooring. Weigh it accurately to find its original weight. Dry it in an oven maintained at a temperature of 212 to 221 degrees F until the wood stops losing weight. The lowest weight of the specimen is its oven-dry weight. You can then compute the original moisture content of the wood by this formula:

$$\frac{\text{Original weight} - \text{oven-dry weight}}{\text{Original weight}} \times 100$$

The answer is the moisture content in percent.

MILDEW TREATMENT FOR WOOD

Conditions that favor the growth of surface mold on unpainted wooden parts of buildings and on stored wood are warmth, dampness, and poor ventilation. Because new, unseasoned lumber contains considerable natural moisture, it should be avoided if possible where such conditions prevail.

Under similar conditions, the molds of mildew also feed on the oils and minerals in paint, causing a dirty-looking discoloration. Indoor wood surfaces coated with varnish, enamel, or hard-surfaced paints, if kept reasonably dry, resist these molds fairly well. Softer paints on outdoor surfaces mildew more readily, the molds even penetrating to the wood.

Mildew-resistant paints containing fungicides can be bought ready-made, as can fungicides which can be mixed with ordinary paints. Linseed oil paint containing zinc oxide, used as a top coat, also inhibits the mildew fungi.

To prevent and cure mildew on house paint, the Forest Service of the U. S. Department of Agriculture recommends these steps:

1. In warm damp climates where mildew occurs frequently, use a paint containing zinc oxide for top coats over the primer coat. (Zinc oxide, however, makes a paint too brittle for a priming coat.)

2. For mild cases of mildew, use a prepared paint containing a mildewcide (a poison for mildew fungi), or mix a mildewcide in regular paint.

3. Ideally, to cure mildew, remove the mildew from the old paint surface and apply a paint that contains zinc oxide or a mildewcide.

4. To kill the fungi and clean an area for repainting, scrub the paint surface with the following solution:

Trisodium phosphate	3 oz	(⅜ cup)
Household detergent	1 oz	(⅛ cup)
Sodium hypochlorite, 5% solution (household bleach)	1 qt	
Warm water	3 qt	

When clean, rinse thoroughly with fresh water from a hose. Avoid splashing the solution on shrubbery or grass; it may do harm. Repaint with a zinc-oxide paint or one containing a fungicide.

HOW TO COMBAT BLUE STAIN

Blue stain is a blue-black discoloration of wood that may also discolor paint applied over it. Blue stain is caused by certain fungi that grow in sapwood and use part of this wood for their food. It is not decay, although the conditions that lead to its growth may favor decay-producing fungi also. The main condition is an excess of moisture, produced by contact with moist ground or constant exposure to rain, dew, or water vapor.

If it does not penetrate too deeply, blue stain can be removed temporarily by sanding or by treating with a solution of household liquid chlorine bleach. Permanent cure, however, depends on keeping moisture out of the wood. Treat unpainted wood with a water-repellent preservative. Provide protection against excess water and water vapor for other wood.

PRESERVING WOODEN FENCE POSTS

The life of wooden fence posts and other outdoor timber can often be more than doubled by treating them with chemicals that inhibit decay. There are so many possible treatments, however, that it is hard to make a choice. The advertising of commercial or "patented" preservatives and processes makes the choice harder. Often the products with secret formulas are made to appear less expensive than they really are by recommending such sparing use that they are ineffective.

The two methods that follow are simple, proved, and inexpensive ones suggested by the Forest Products Laboratory of the Department of Agriculture.

Cold soaking. This consists in submerging posts for 1 to 2 days or longer in a solution of pentacholorophenol, or of copper naphthenate in fuel oil. A "penta" solution should contain 5 percent of this chemical by weight. A copper naphthenate solution should contain the equivalent of at least 1 percent of copper metal by weight. You can buy both of these preservatives in concentrated solutions, with accompanying directions for proper dilution. This treatment works best with round pine posts that are well seasoned. Posts so treated with the penta solution have averaged more than 20 years of service.

End-diffusion treatment. This is a simple and inexpensive method for use on green unpeeled posts. It consists in standing such posts, freshly cut, in a container of a measured quantity of a solution of zinc chloride or chromated zinc chloride. These chemicals are cheap, can be bought as dry powder or concentrated solution, and are not dangerous to people or animals.

Use a 15 to 20-percent solution of either. About 5 pounds, or about ½ gallon, is recommended for each cubic foot of post treated. Allow the posts to stand with butts down in the solution until approximately ¾ of the solution has been absorbed—which may take from 1 to 10 days. Then turn them over and let the tops absorb the rest of the solution. Store at least 30 days before setting in ground.

HOW TO STOP "DRY ROT"

The decay of wood is caused by decay fungi, and these microscopic plants can't work in wood without moisture. Although decayed wood may be dry in the final stages, it is not so while the fungi are doing the damage. For this reason, there is actually no such thing as "dry rot."

Often, however, the term is applied to decay that is found in house lumber many feet from the nearest possible source of moisture. When such decay occurs, it is apt to be caused by one of the water-conducting fungi. Between two layers of wood, such as a floor and subfloor, these fungi may produce thick rootlike strands that are capable of carrying moisture for considerable distances. Vapor barriers or ventilation may limit their spread, but may not stop their activity entirely.

The first thing to do to control these fungi is to trace them back to the source of their moisture and cut off the connection. Usually the moisture comes up from the ground, using a brace, frame, wooden concrete form, or a grade stake as a bridge to let the fungus climb from moist soil to a joist or sill. Sometimes a joist is in direct contact with a tree stump that has been left under the house. In other cases the source from which the fungus is bringing its moisture may not be so easily located. These special fungi sometimes get their moisture directly from the soil through strands of mycelium, or vegetative fibers, that may grow a foot or more over the surface of foundation walls, or through cracks in loosely built masonry.

If any wood has already been made useless by the decay, replace it with wood that is sound and dry. If you are sure you have eliminated the sources of moisture that started the decay, replace only the wood that has been weakened. If there is any doubt, however, it is safer to remove also the apparently sound wood 2 feet in each direction from the part obviously decayed, and to replace it with wood that has been thoroughly impregnated with a preservative (see paragraph on "cold soaking" in previous item on preserving fence posts). Before installing the new wood, give all adjacent old wood and masonry surfaces a heavy treatment with a similar preservative.

2

Paints and
Paint Removers

HOW TO PAINT YOUR HOUSE

The paint on your house will cost less, look better, and be far easier to maintain, if you choose and apply it according to a few tried-and-tested rules. When painting a new wood house or any other outside wood surfaces, there are three recommended steps:

STEP 1—TREAT WITH WATER-REPELLENT PRESERVATIVE
Protect the wood against penetration of rain and heavy dew by applying a water-repellent preservative solution before painting. If you'd rather not do this yourself, you can buy lumber already treated and retreat cut ends on the job with a preservative solution sold at most paint and building supply dealers. It is especially important that window sash and trim be treated.

Or you can apply the solution to untreated wood with a brush. Be careful to brush it well into lap and butt joints of trim and siding. Old houses can be treated effectively after paint has been removed. Allow 2 warm, sunny days for adequate drying of the treatment before painting.

Step 2—Apply a priming coat

The first or prime coat is the most important coat of paint to be applied to wood. For this coat, and for spot priming bare wood areas when repainting, experts at the U.S. Forest Products Laboratory find that a linseed oil-base paint adheres best to the wood and makes the best foundation for subsequent coats. It may contain lead or titanium pigments, but should not contain zinc oxide. Zinc oxide forms a hard and inflexible film that may crack itself and also crack later paint layers.

Apply the primer thickly enough so you can't see the grain of the wood. If you use ready-made paint, follow the spreading rates recommended by the manufacturer. This rate should be approximately 400 to 450 square feet per gallon with a paint that contains at least 85 percent solids by weight. The prime coat should not be porous, which would permit capillary flow of rain and dew through the paint film.

If the second coat is to be an exterior emulsion or latex paint, a primer of the type just mentioned is still necessary. The primer should be applied both to new wood and to painted surfaces that are badly weathered. It would be extremely unwise to apply emulsion-base paint directly to bare wood or to an undercoat that is chalking or deteriorated.

STEP 3—FINISH COATS OVER PRIMER

For a smooth and durable finish, keep the following points in mind:

1. Use a high-quality paint; cheap paints are more costly in the end. Finish coats can contain zinc oxide pigment and can be of the linseed oil, alkyd, or latex type.

2. Apply two topcoats, particularly to areas that are fully exposed to the weather such as the south side of the house. A two-coat job of low-quality paint may last only 3 years, but a three-coat job with good-quality paint may last as long as 10 years.

3. To avoid peeling of one coat of paint from another, apply topcoats within 2 weeks after the primer. Do not prime in the fall and delay topcoats until spring. It is better to treat with a water-repellent preservative and delay all painting until spring.

4. To avoid temperature blistering, do not apply oil-base paints on a cool surface that will be heated by the sun within a few hours. Follow the sun around the house.

5. To reduce the wrinkling and flatting of oil-base paint and watermarks on latex paint, do not paint late in the evenings of cool spring and fall days when heavy dews frequently form.

How to Repaint

A repaint job is only as good as the old paint beneath it. Here are some general rules to observe:

1. Before repainting, wash old, glossy, and un-weathered surfaces with a detergent, washing soda, or trisodium phosphate solution, or roughen it well

with steel wool to remove contaminants that may prevent adhesion of the next coat. Failure to do this is a common cause of intercoat peeling.

2. Repaint only when the old paint has weathered to the extent that it no longer covers or protects the wood. Where paint is peeling and wood surfaces are exposed, remove loose paint from adjacent areas. Treat with water-repellent preservative and spot prime with the house-paint primer described above. Remove excess chalk or old paint with steel wool. The paint in protected areas of the house may need only cleaning by washing.

3. For the topcoats, use any high-quality exterior paint reputed to give good service.

Other Outdoor Paint Jobs

Besides the wooden clapboard siding of a house, there will probably be wood trim, shingles, porch floors, metalwork, brick, concrete and other items to be decorated and protected. Each of these may require a different type of paint, varnish, or other coating material.

Shingles of various decorative woods may have a pleasing natural grain that you will want to preserve. These may be coated merely with a clear water-repellent preservative or with a pigmented stain. Wood trim, such as window sashes, shutters, and doors may be given finish coats of colored high-gloss or semigloss exterior enamel.

Masonry surfaces—brick, cement, stucco, cinder block—can be brightened and protected with a variety of paint products. One of the newest ideas in painting brick is a clear coating that withstands weather yet allows the natural surface of the brick to show through. Cement-based and rubber-based paints, as well as alkyd, vinyl, and emulsion coatings are also used on many types of masonry. Almost all exterior house paints may be applied to masonry, however, when surface preparations are made properly.

Metal surfaces of iron and steel should be primed with a rust-inhibiting paint such as red-lead, zinc chromate, or special aluminum paint. Finish coats may be of any good house paint or exterior enamel. Although copper building materials do not rust, they give off a corrosive wash that may discolor surrounding areas and so should be coated with a clear weatherproof varnish. Aluminum, like copper, does not rust in a conventional way, but gets oxidized and stained if not coated.

Porches, floors, and steps are subjected to unusually heavy traffic and so must be coated with a paint designed for durability. You can buy special porch and deck paints which will stand up well under this hard use. Wooden porches, floors, and steps can be primed with a thinned version of the top coat. Cement and concrete ones, however, may have to be primed with an alkali-resisting paint. Formulas for paints for wood and concrete floors may be found later in this chapter, and instructions for preparing a concrete floor for painting in the chapter on concrete.

The charts on pages 62, 63 will help you tell at a glance what outdoor paint you should use for what surface.

MIXING YOUR OWN HOUSE PAINT

For many generations, "house paint" to a paint-er meant simply white-lead paste, linseed oil, turpen-tine, a drier, and perhaps a few colored pigments-in-oil for tinting. With these basic ingredients—plus con-siderable elbow-grease—he could mix priming coats and finish coats, white paints and paints of any color he desired, right on the job.

He stuck to this combination for several good reasons. White lead is the oldest and one of the most durable white pigments known to man. (The ancient Egyptians, Greeks, and Romans made it by treating metallic lead with wine or vinegar.) Its hiding power is good and it brushes out easily. It improves the adhesion of paints, making it an excellent primer. On weathering, it chalks rather than checks or cracks, leaving a satisfactory surface for repainting. Linseed oil, with lead, dries to a tough, long-lasting film.

The do-it-yourself house owner of the day also used the combination because it was almost foolproof. Inaccuracy in thinning, variations in formula, and in-expert application have little or no effect.

Today white lead paint is still widely used for primer and finish coats on exterior surfaces, and is included in many government specifications. (It is no longer used indoors, however, because of the pos-sibility of lead poisoning if dust or flakes from the dry paint should be swallowed or inhaled.) You can buy it ready-mixed, or mix it yourself from white-lead paste and linseed oil according to the formulas on page 64. To color either ready-mixed or home-made paint, see tinting formulas on pages 65-66.

WHAT OUTDOOR PAIN

TYPE OF COATING

√. Black dot indicates that a primer or sealer may be necessary before the finishing coat (unless surface has been previously finished.) **APPLICATION**	House Paint (Oil)	Transparent Sealer	Cement Base Paint	Exterior Clear Finsh	Aluminum Paint	Wood Stain	
Clapboard Siding	√.				√		
Brick	√.	√	√		√		
Cement & Cinder Block	√.	√	√		√		
Asbestos Cement	√.						
Stucco	√.	√	√		√		
Natural Wood Siding & Trim				√		√	
Metal Siding	√.				√.		
Wood Frame Windows	√.				√		
Steel Windows	√.				√.		
Aluminum Windows	√.				√		
Shutters & Other Trim	√.						
Canvas Awnings							
Wood Shingle Roof						√	
Metal Roof	√.						
Coal Tar Felt Roof							
Wood Porch Floor							
Cement Porch Floor							
Copper Surfaces							
Galvanized Surfaces	√.				√.		
Iron Surfaces	√.				√.		

TO USE AND WHERE

TYPE OF COATING

Roof Cement	Asphalt Emulsion	Trim-And-Trellis Paint	Awning Paint	Spar Varnish	Porch-And-Deck Paint	Primer or Undercoater	Metal Primer	Latex Types	Water Repellent Preservatives
						√		√.	
						√		√	
						√		√	
						√		√	
						√		√	
				√					
		√.					√	√.	
		√.				√		√.	
		√.					√	√.	
		√.					√	√.	
		√.				√		√.	
			√						
									√
							√	√.	
√	√								
					√				
								√	
				√					
		√.		√			√	√.	
		√.					√	√.	

White-Lead Exterior Paints

The following are suggested proportions for making durable white-lead oil paints for use on houses and all other outside wood. If *heavy* white-lead paste is used, add 1 pint of turpentine to each formula. If *boiled* linseed oil is used, omit the drier.

FOR NEW WOOD, FIRST COAT:

White-lead soft paste	50 lb
Raw linseed oil	2 gal
Turpentine	1 gal
Liquid drier	½ pint

This makes a little more than 4 gallons, and will cover about 600 square feet per gallon. Pour the white lead into a strong bucket that will hold at least one fourth more than the amount of paint you intend to make. Add the oil, turpentine, and drier a little at a time. Blend with a heavy wooden paddle, each time producing a smooth paste before adding more.

SECOND COAT:

White-lead soft paste	50 lb
Raw linseed oil	3 qt
Turpentine	3 qt
Liquid drier	½ pint

THIRD COAT:

White-lead soft paste	50 lb
Raw linseed oil	6½ qt
Liquid drier	½ pint

The formulas for the second and third coats make more than 3 gallons each. Each gallon will cover about 700 square feet.

For previously-painted wood, first coat:

White-lead soft paste	50 lb
Raw linseed oil	1 gal
Turpentine	1 gal
Liquid drier	½ pint

For the finish coat, use the formula for the third coat for new wood.

Colors for Exterior White-Lead Paint

White-lead paint may be given a wide range of tints and hues by adding colors-in-oil. The following are recommended for their ability to stand up under exposure. The quantities are based on the use of Dutch Boy colors. One tube equals ⅛ pint. Colors of other makes may give approximately the same results.

COLOR DESIRED	COLOR-IN-OIL	QUANTITY PER GALLON
Lemon	C.P. chrome yellow—lemon	½ tube
Ivory	Raw sienna	½ tube
Cream	French ochre	2 tubes
Light maize	C.P. chrome yellow—medium	½ tube
Light buff	French ochre, and C.P. chrome yellow—medium	1 tube 1 tube
Medium buff	Raw sienna	½ pint
Dark buff*	Raw sienna	1 quart
Pearl gray	Lampblack	¼ tube
Medium gray	Lampblack	½ tube

COLOR DESIRED	COLOR-IN-OIL	QUANTITY PER GALLON
Slate gray	Lampblack	1 tube
Light tan	Burnt umber	½ tube
Putty	Raw umber	½ tube
Warm gray	Raw umber	2 tubes
Medium tan	Burnt umber	1 tube
Coral	Burnt sienna	1 tube
Terra cotta	Burnt sienna, and	1 tube
	burnt umber	1 tube
Light green	C.P. chromium oxide green	1 tube
Medium green**	C.P. chromium oxide green	1 pint
Olive green	Burnt umber, and	½ pint
	C.P. chrome green— light	¼ pint
Shutter blue*	Dutch Boy blue, and	1 quart
	raw umber	½ pint

     * Add 1½ pints of linseed oil per gallon of paint.

     ** Add ¼ pint of linseed oil per gallon of paint.

Back Primer for Unpainted Wood

On new construction—to help preserve the wood and seal out moisture—it is best to give a priming coat of paint to the back surfaces and edges of siding, plywood panels, and flooring before it is put in place. For such priming give one coat of the third coat formula for white-lead exterior paints.

White-lead Paint for Wood Floors

Primer for unpainted floors:

White-lead soft paste	10 lb
Boiled linseed oil	39 fl oz
Turpentine	26 fl oz

This amount covers about 500 square feet.

Second coat:

White-lead soft paste	10 lb
Boiled linseed oil	6½ fl oz
Turpentine	29 fl oz

Finish coat:

White-lead soft paste	10 lb
Boiled linseed oil	10 fl oz
Turpentine	9½ fl oz
Varnish	16 fl oz

Repainting Wood Floors

Touch up worn spots with second coat formula given above. Use same paint for first coat, and the finish coat formula for second coat.

INDOOR PAINT

With the dozens of new coating products now on the market, it is often difficult to decide which is the best suited for a specific application. The accompanying chart should help to give you a start. Emulsion paints include all rubber and synthetic resin paints (alkyd, vinyl, acrylic, etc.) that are thinned with water. Emulsion waxes are of the no-rub, self-polishing type.

WHAT INDOOR PAINT

✓. Black dot indicates that a primer or sealer may be necessary before the finishing coat (unless surface has been previously finished.)	Flat Paint	Semi-Gloss Paint	Enamel	Rubber Base Paint (not Latex)	Emulsion Paint (Including Latex)	Casein	Interior Varnish
Plaster Walls & Ceiling	✓.	✓.		✓	✓	✓	
Wall Board	✓.	✓.		✓	✓	✓	
Wood Paneling	✓.	✓.		✓	✓.		✓
Kitchen & Bathroom Walls		✓.	✓.	✓	✓		
Wood Floors							
Concrete Floors							
Vinyl & Rubber Tile Floors							
Asphalt Tile Floors							
Linoleum							
Stair Treads							
Stair Risers	✓.	✓.	✓.	✓			✓
Wood Trim	✓.	✓.	✓.	✓	✓.		✓
Steel Windows	✓.	✓.	✓.	✓			
Aluminum Windows	✓.	✓.	✓.	✓			
Window Sills			✓.				✓
Steel Cabinets	✓.	✓.	✓.	✓			
Heating Ducts	✓.	✓.	✓.	✓			
Radiators & Heating Pipes	✓.	✓.	✓.	✓			
Old Masonry	✓	✓	✓	✓	✓	✓	
New Masonry	✓.	✓.	✓.	✓	✓		

TO USE AND WHERE

Shellac	Wax (Liquid or Paste)	Wax (Emulsion)	Stain	Wood Sealer	Floor Varnish	Floor Paint or Enamel	Cement Base Paint	Aluminum Paint	Sealer or Undercoater	Metal Primer
									√	
									√	
√	√		√	√						
									√	
√	√	√.	√.	√	√.	√.				
	√.	√.	√			√				
	√	√								
		√								
√	√	√			√	√				
√			√	√	√	√				
√			√	√						
√	√		√						√	
								√		√
								√		√
										√
								√		√
								√		√
							√	√	√	
							√		√	

How to Mix Custom Colors

Special colors of interior paint to suit your exact taste can be made in two ways.

The first is to blend several different colors of ready-mixed paint. If you do this, be sure to use paints of the same brand and type. Never mix oil-base with emulsion or latex type paints. Don't mix gloss paint with flat or semigloss, unless you deliberately want to reduce the gloss.

The second way is to tint a light-colored base paint with concentrated colors-in-oil. These may be used with almost all opaque surface coatings except lacquers and those thinned with water. They should not be used in large quantities in flat paints as they may produce glossy streaks.

Colors-in-oil come in both liquid and paste form. If you use the latter, first mix it with enough paint thinner so that the mixture will pour smoothly.

When mixing special colors, be sure you mix enough for the whole job. If you intend to duplicate the color later, note down the amounts of the various colors used. Even if you do this, however, it is seldom possible to duplicate a batch exactly.

The accompanying table suggests combinations of basic colors from which you can make hundreds of others. The base paint should in all cases have an oil base.

COLOR	BASE PAINT	COLORS-IN-OIL
Apple green	White	Light chrome green and orange chrome yellow
Apricot	Medium chrome yellow	Venetian red and carmine lake. For light tint, lighten with white

COLOR	BASE PAINT	COLORS-IN-OIL
Browns	Venetian red	Ochre and lampblack in proportions according to shades of brown wanted
Cafe-au-lait	Burnt umber	Yellow ochre, Venetian red, and white
Canary	Lemon chrome yellow	White
Chartreuse	Lemon chrome yellow	Medium chrome green
Colonial yellow	White	Medium chrome yellow and a touch of orange chrome yellow
Copper	Medium chrome yellow	A little burnt sienna
Coral pink	Vermilion	White and medium chrome yellow
Cream and buff	White	For cream, add ochre. For buffs add also burnt umber
Crimson	Toluidine red	For very rich hue add crimson lake
Ecru	White	Ochre, burnt sienna, and lampblack
Electric blue	Ultramarine blue	White and raw sienna
Emerald	Light chrome green	

COLOR	BASE PAINT	COLORS-IN-OIL
Fawn	White	Medium chrome yellow, Venetian red, and burnt umber
French gray	White	Lampblack with touch of ultramarine blue and madder lake or carmine
Gray	White	Lampblack to obtain desired shade, plus color, if wanted
Ivy green	Ochre	Lampblack and Prussian blue
Jonquil	White	Medium chrome yellow and touch of vermilion
Lavender	White	Ivory black, ultramarine blue, touch of madder lake or carmine
Lemon	Lemon chrome yellow	
Marigold	Medium chrome yellow	White and orange chrome yellow
Maroon	Venetian red	Lampblack
Mauve	Ultramarine blue	White and madder lake
Navy blue	Ultramarine blue	Ivory black
Old gold	White	Medium chrome yellow, ochre, and a little burnt umber

COLOR	BASE PAINT	COLORS-IN-OIL
Olive green	Lemon chrome yellow	Prussian blue and lampblack
Peach	White	Pale Indian red and chrome yellow
Pink	White	Any red desired
Plum	White	Indian red and ultramarine blue
Robin's egg blue	White	Prussian blue
Scarlet	Pale English vermilion or any scarlet-toned vermilion reds	
Sea green	White	Prussian blue, raw sienna
Shrimp	White	Venetian red, burnt sienna, and touch of vermilion
Sky blue	White	Prussian blue
Tan	White	Burnt sienna and touch of lampblack
Terra cotta	Ochre	Venetian red and white. For some shades add also Indian red
Turquoise	White	Prussian or phthalocyanine blue and pale chrome green
Violet	White	Lake red and ultramarine

LIGHT REFLECTING POWER OF PAINTS

The average light reflecting power of various interior and exterior paint colors is as follows:

	Percent
White	70-90
Ivories and creams	55-90
Light yellows	65-70
Light buffs	40-56
Light greens	40-50
Medium greens	15-30
Oranges	15-30
Medium blues	15-20
Dark blues	5-10
Medium grays	15-30
Red and maroons	3-18
Medium and dark browns	3-18
Black	1-4

WHITEWASH AND COLD-WATER PAINTS

Although white or tinted lime "whitewash" is admittedly not as durable as most modern high-grade paints, its use has survived through the centuries for several good reasons: It is easy to make and to apply; compared with paint, it is fantastically cheap; and —at least when newly applied—it achieves a fresh, clean, chalk-white or delicate pastel effect unrivalled by any other coating material.

Today whitewash is used to protect and beautify brick or stone houses, outbuildings, fences, stones and curbs along driveways, trellises and arbors, basements, bases of trees. It is also used to protect tools and implements from corrosion (see Chapter 3 on Metals), and to control heat in greenhouses and on black roofs, pipes, and other surfaces. A type made with glue is used on inside walls and ceilings.

The basis for whitewash is calcium oxide or hydroxide—quicklime or hydrated lime. On exposure to carbon dioxide in the air, this gradually turns into calcium carbonate or ordinary chalk. Extra ingredients help keep it from rubbing off, increase its moisture and weather resistance, and help bind it to masonry surfaces.

Whitewash Formulas

Each of the following formulas will make 10 or more gallons of whitewash, depending upon how much it is thinned with water. For smaller quantities, reduce the formulas proportionately. Final whitewash mixtures should be thinned to a consistency resembling that of whole milk.

LIME PASTE

This is the foundation ingredient of all whitewash. You can start with quicklime if you want to go through the long and messy job of slaking it. It is easier, however, to begin with one of the more refined types of commercial hydrated limes that go under such names as chemical hydrate, agricultural spray hydrate, or finishing lime. To make 8 gallons of stiff lime paste, just soak 50 pounds of hydrated lime in 6 gallons of water.

UTILITY WHITEWASHES

These are the cheapest and easiest to make. The first two formulas are recommended for general utility use on wood, glass, or metal surfaces, such as fences, sheds, tree trunks, public service poles, greenhouse roofs, etc. The third should be used on masonry surfaces *only*—brickwork, concrete, cinder block, or stone masonry, stucco, for marking safety zones, traffic guide lines, and so on. It will help materially to dampproof interior basement walls.

1. Salt   15 lb
   Lime paste   8 gal

   Dissolve the salt in about 5 gallons of water and add this solution to the lime paste. Mix thoroughly and thin to desired consistency with plain water.

2. Calcium chloride (dry)   5 lb
   Lime paste   8 gal

   Calcium chloride, in place of the salt, makes a mixture that does not chalk and is more durable. Mix as above.

3. *White* portland cement   25 lb
   Hydrated lime   25 lb

   Add the dry cement and lime together to about 8 gallons of water. Mix thoroughly to form a thick slurry. Then add more water, with continued mixing, until the mixture has the consistency of heavy cream. Don't mix more than you can use in a few hours.

WEATHER-RESISTANT WHITEWASH

For any purpose where a no-rubbing, weather-resistant whitewash is needed, the following formula is superior to numbers 1 and 2:

4. Casein	5 lb
Trisodium phosphate	3 lb
Formaldehyde	3 pints
Lime paste	8 gal

Soak the casein in 2 gallons of hot water for about 2 hours, or until thoroughly softened. Dissolve the trisodium phosphate in 1 gallon of water, add this solution to the casein, and stir occasionally until the casein dissolves. When the casein solution *is thoroughly cool*, slowly add it to the *cool* lime solution, stirring constantly.

Dissolve the formaldehyde in 3 gallons of water, and just before applying the whitewash add the formaldehyde solution to the batch, stirring constantly and vigorously. Be careful not to add the formaldehyde too rapidly as this may cause the casein to gel and so ruin the batch. Do not make up more of this formula than can be used in a day.

SKIMMED-MILK WHITEWASH

Here skimmed milk supplies casein and most of the water. This formula is a favorite of dairy farmers for coating the walls and ceilings of barns.

5. Skimmed milk	7 gal
Formaldehyde	3 pints
Lime paste	8 gal

After mixing the skimmed milk with the lime paste, add the formaldehyde slowly, stirring vigorously. Add water to make desired consistency.

WHITEWASH FOR PLASTERED WALLS

Formula 4 makes a durable coating for interior plastered walls and ceilings. Although less water-resistant, the following is also good for this purpose and is easier to make:

| 6. Animal glue | 3 lb |
| Lime paste | 8 gal |

Dissolve the glue in about 2 gallons of water. Add this solution to the lime paste, stirring constantly, and then thin to desired consistency.

Colors for Whitewash and Cold-Water Paints

When choosing and mixing colors to be used to tint whitewash and cold-water paints, remember three things: They must not react chemically with the lime; they must be insoluble in water; they must be mixed as thoroughly as possible.

The following pigments may be bought as dry powders and added to any of the whitewash formulas just given. To be sure the desired tint or shade will be obtained, better mix a small sample with measured quantities of materials and let it dry before mixing a large batch.

Blacks—Black oxide of iron is safe. Ivory black and carbon black are, also, but they are lacking in strength.

Blues—Ultramarine, cobalt blue, and copper phthalocyanine blue are the only blues recommended.

Browns—Pure precipitated brown iron oxide or mixtures of black iron oxide with turkey or Indian red are recommended. Sienna and turkey umber are lacking in strength, but may give good results.

Greens—Chromium oxide green (not to be confused with chrome green, a mixture of chrome yellow and prussian blue, which is not limeproof) and copper phthalocyanine green are both recommended.

Reds—Indian red made from pure ferric oxide is highly recommended. Madder lake and toluidine vermilion are alkali-fast but have little strength and fade under light.

Violets—Cobalt violet and mixtures of the reds, whites, and blues suggested are satisfactory.

Whites—Lime itself is satisfactory. Titanium dioxide or titanium-calcium pigment and zinc sulfide or light-fast lithopones may also be used.

Yellows—Precipitated yellow iron oxides are best. Ochre, raw sienna, cadmium orange, and cadmium yellows are less suitable, as they lack strength, and may fade or change shade. Chrome yellow is not limeproof.

Applying the Wash

Whitewashes and lime paints should be applied thin, and the surface should be dampened so that the coating will dry gradually. *In fact, you will get best results if you apply the wash so thin that you can easily see through it to the surface beneath while the film is wet.* Although it may seem doubtful at the time, the coating will dry opaque. A second thin coat may be applied over the thoroughly dry first coat if a whiter or brighter surface is desired.

These cold-water preparations can be applied best with a large brush. Don't try to brush out the coating as is done with oil paint, but simply spread it on as evenly and as quickly as possible. Stir the whitewash frequently while applying it to prevent settling.

Special Uses for Whitewash

To decrease illumination. According to the British Building Research Board, whitewash decreases drastically the solar illumination of glass roofs. Tests revealed a decrease in illumination of 75 percent with one coat of whitewash and 92 percent with two coats. This material is used widely to control illumination in greenhouses and hotbeds.

To decrease heat in buildings. For many years, one large factory roof has been sprayed each June with waterproof whitewash. By reflecting heat away from the roof, this treatment has resulted in reducing the temperature in the factory by about 10 degrees during the hottest part of the day. Although whitewash is not as weather-resistant as other types of paint, its low cost makes it attractive as an insulator against summer heat.

To protect asphalt or tar coatings. Asphalt and tar coatings that are exposed to direct sunlight can be kept from sagging and wrinkling, or even from running, by applying a coating of whitewash to the black surface. The white coating reflects away the radiant heat that the black one would otherwise absorb. If the exposure is to be short, a plain lime and water mixture will do. For longer exposures, formulas 1 and 4 are recommended.

PAINTING EXTERIOR IRON AND STEEL

The following painting procedure is suitable for iron, steel, and rusted galvanized steel. For coatings to adhere and to continue to protect the metal beneath, the first important step is to clean the surface of rust, grease, oil, and dirt. Remove rust and scale by scraping and wirebrushing. Oil, grease, and dirt may be removed with mineral spirits, or with a strong solution of washing soda or trisodium phosphate.

For unpainted metal, use this red-lead primer:

Red-lead paste	25 lb
Raw linseed oil	60 fl oz
Turpentine	6 fl oz
Drier	6 fl oz

This formula makes a little more than a gallon, enough to cover about 600 square feet. Pour the paste into a strong bucket that will hold at least 1½ gallons. Stir in the oil, thinner, and drier a little at a time, each time producing a smooth paste before adding more.

For first regular coat, give a second coat of the primer or, if you prefer black, the primer to which you have added 3 ounces of lampblack color-in-oil.

For white or colored final coat, use white-lead paint formula (page 64) either alone or tinted with desired colors-in-oil.

For black final coat, use this:

Red-lead paste	3½ lb
Raw linseed oil	59 fl oz
Turpentine	7 fl oz
Drier	7 fl oz
Lampblack, color-in-oil	1 qt
Prussian blue, color-in-oil	11½ fl oz

For repainting metal, prime bare spots with primer above, then follow the same sequence as for unpainted metal.

Painting Galvanized Iron

New galvanized iron will hold paint better if it is first washed with a solvent to remove grease and then treated with a chemical wash that forms a coating of a zinc salt. Here are several suitable washes:

1. Ordinary vinegar.
2. A solution of 4 ounces of copper sulfate in 1 gallon of water.
3. A solution of 1 part hydrochloric acid in 4 parts of water.

Prepare solutions 2 and 3 in a glass or plastic container. Apply to the metal with a brush or a cloth swab tied on the end of a stick. Let dry and then rinse off the surface with plain water. To prevent further contamination, paint the surface as soon as possible with a rust-inhibitive primer. After this is dry, sand lightly and apply a finishing coat of exterior paint.

Finishing Radiators and Pipes

1. Clean surface with sandpaper and steel scratch brush. Wipe with clean rags wet with naphtha or mineral spirits to remove all traces of oil and grease.

2. If new and unpainted, radiators should receive a first coat of standard metal primer, which should be allowed to dry hard.

3. The finishing coats should be an eggshell or flat finish identical with that on the walls or woodwork of the room. Contrary to an opinion once popular, this type of paint permits the maximum radiation of heat. Aluminum and other metallic paints reduce radiation by reflecting heat into the radiator.

4. Allow the paint to dry completely before turning on the heat. Then bring the heat up slowly over a 12-hour period.

OIL PAINT FOR CONCRETE FLOORS

Before applying the paint, be sure the floor is clean and perfectly dry. The first two formulas make enough to cover about 330 square feet.

PRIMER COAT FOR UNPAINTED FLOORS:

White-lead soft paste	20 lb
Raw linseed oil	½ gal
Lead mixing oil	½ gal

SECOND COAT:

White-lead soft paste	10 lb
Boiled linseed oil	6½ fl oz
Turpentine	9 fl oz

FINISH COAT:
Use any high quality floor enamel.

Repainting Concrete Floors

Touch up worn spots with second-coat formula given above. When dry, use same paint for first regular coat. For second coat use high quality floor enamel.

SEALING SURFACES WITH SHELLAC

Raw or painted plaster walls and ceilings, wallpapered surfaces, and wallboard: One coat of 3-pound shellac seals these porous surfaces, prevents suction, and provides a smooth base for finish paint or enamel.

Dry wall to be papered: One coat of 3- or 4-pound cut seals pores for easy removal of wallpaper at a later time.

Patches in plaster: Patched cracks and spackled areas can be quickly sealed with shellac before painting.

TO PREVENT BLEEDING OF STAIN

When oil paint or enamel is applied over a surface already treated with oil stain or varnish stain, the oil in the new finish tends to dissolve the stain. This, in turn, discolors the new coating.

To find out if such bleeding will occur on a given project, make a test by painting a small area. The stain may bleed through immediately, but it is better to wait three or four days before deciding to continue.

If the stain does come through, it is best to first remove as much as possible by washing the surface with turpentine or benzine if it is an oil stain, or with denatured alcohol if it is an alcohol stain.

Next apply a 2-pound cut of shellac to the surface. Then repeat the paint test on a small area. If the color still bleeds, apply a coat of aluminum paint over the shellac. You can then apply the paint or enamel with confidence.

HOW TO BREAK IN A NEW BRUSH

A good paint brush will give better and longer service if you start caring for it as soon as you buy it. First flick it across one hand to remove dust and dirt. Then remove any loose bristles.

Unless it is to be used to apply lacquer, shellac, or water-based paints, a new brush should be preconditioned. To do this, suspend the brush so its bristles dip in linseed oil overnight. Don't let it stand on its painting tip. A hole drilled through the handle will make suspension easy. Just insert a piece of coathanger wire through the hole and rest the wire on the edges of the can containing the oil. After soaking, remove all excess oil by firmly stroking the bristles toward their tip with a smooth stick or the back of a comb.

If the brush is to be used in shellac, water-base, or latex paint, it should be washed in soap and water and then rinsed.

As soon as the brush is dry it is ready to use. Dip it into the paint about halfway to the ferrule. Then tap it lightly five or six times against the edge of the container to shake off excess paint (this is better for the brush than scraping it across the inner lip of the can). Now you are ready to begin a fine paint or varnish job.

BRUSH AND ROLLER CLEANING

The secret of cleaning your brushes easily is to get after them as soon as you stop working. If you have been using latex, alkyd, cement-based, or other paints that are thinned with water, give them a good washing with soap and water. Then rinse them thoroughly with water, straighten the bristles by pulling them between your fingers, and lay them flat, or hang them up, to dry. (Never leave a brush standing on its bristles!) When dry, wrap them in paper or aluminum foil to keep out dust.

For brushes loaded with other types of paint, start by wiping off as much paint as possible on old newspapers. If you plan to use these brushes the next day, follow the wiping with a rinse in turpentine or the proper thinner. Then leave them suspended in clean solvent, or wrap them tightly in aluminum foil and stored either by hanging from the handle or laid flat.

If brushes used with oil paints are to be stored for any time, they should be cleaned more thoroughly. After working out the paint, wash them in several rinses of thinner, or in the TSP brush cleaning solution described in the next item. If you use the latter, be sure to give the brush a final rinse in clear water. When a brush is clean, squeeze out the liquid and smooth out the bristles. If it has been cleaned with a water solution, first let it dry.

To clean paint rollers, run them over newspapers to remove as much paint as possible. Then slide the cover off and wash it in the proper thinner. Replace the cover, wrap the roller in sheet plastic or aluminum foil, and store it either suspended by the handle or on end.

If you let a roller lie on its side for any length of time it will develop a flat spot.

TSP Paint Brush Cleaner

A strong solution of trisodium phosphate makes an excellent cleaner for old brushes so hardened with paint they are no longer usable. The water should be hot and contain 4 ounces of TSP per quart (*Caution:* Wear rubber gloves and don't spatter the solution on surroundings). A squat 1-pound coffee can makes a good working container.

Start by pressing the bristles against the bottom of the can to work the cleaner up into the heel of the brush. Separate the bristles with a comb or the edge of a putty knife as the paint softens. Keep dunking the brush and combing it until all the paint has been removed. When the brush is clean, rinse it thoroughly in plain water to remove all the solution. Squeeze out excess water and smooth the bristles to their proper shape. Let dry thoroughly before wrapping for storage.

CARE OF SPRAYING EQUIPMENT

Paint-spraying equipment should be cleaned before the paint sets because otherwise it may be difficult or even impossible to remove the hardened paint from the operating mechanisms. With accelerated or catalyst-set types of paint (such as epoxy) now being used, cleaning must usually be done within a matter of minutes. If paints of the latter type are allowed to harden in the operating mechanism, they cannot be removed and valuable parts may have to be discarded.

When spray equipment is to be taken out of service, clean the paint pot thoroughly with an appropriate solvent and wipe it out. Then place clean solvent in the pot and force it through the gun until all paint has been removed.

The nozzles of small pressurized paint containers may be cleaned by turning the can upside down and pressing the valve until only propellant gas comes through the nozzle.

PAINT REMOVERS

Removing Hard Paint and Varnish With Lye

Many homeowners and do-it-yourself enthusiasts have discovered what professional painters and furniture refinishers have known for a long time—that the fastest and cheapest way to remove old, hard, and many-layered coatings of paint and varnish is with a strong solution of everyday household lye. The method can be used successfully on woodwork, metals (except aluminum), and old furniture. In many cases, a lye solution will do a stripping job as well as, or better than, a solvent-type cleaner costing 10 or 15 times as much.

Don't try lye, however, unless you can meet the following conditions:

1. Lye and the softened paint must be flushed off finally with a garden hose or buckets (literally) of water. This means that it must be used over an un-

painted concrete floor (say in a garage or a basement) provided with a drain, or outdoors over concrete or dirt where the run-off will not damage grass or plants.

2. Because lye solution works too slowly when cold, it must be used where the air temperature is at least 70 degrees.

3. As with other strong paint removers, you must wear rubber gloves (the best for this and similar uses are workmen's gauntlet type canvas gloves coated with neoprene, a synthetic rubber that resists acids, alkalies, and solvent) and protect from spatter any of the surroundings that might be damaged by it.

If you can meet these conditions, here is what you do: Measure a quart of cold water into an earthenware crock, or an enamel or stainless steel utensil. Do not use aluminum. Dissolve 1 can of household lye in the water, pouring it in slowly and stirring with a stick as you pour.

Next, measure 2 quarts of water into another container of similar material and stir in 4 heaping tablespoons of ordinary cornstarch. Then pour the lye solution into the cornstarch solution, stirring as you do so. The resulting mixture is of a jelly-like consistency which helps hold the lye against upright surfaces.

To remove paint or varnish, merely apply the solution to the surface with a scrubbing brush (remember the rubber gloves!). Let stand a few minutes, then flush off with water. If more paint remains, repeat the procedure. When all has been removed, flush off thoroughly with the hose.

When dry, metal surfaces are ready for repainting without further treatment. After thorough rinsing, wood surfaces should be dried with old rags or paper towels and then rinsed with a solution of 1 part vinegar to 1 part water—followed by a final rinse with plain water.

Lye solution will generally darken wood. If this is objectionable, you can lighten it again by applying a household liquid chlorine bleach (Clorox, Rose-X, Purex, etc.) as a neutralizer instead of the vinegar. Rinse finally, as in the other case.

If you prefer a straight liquid to a pasty remover, you can use the lye solution described above all by itself. You can apply it with a cotton dishmop or a wad of cotton waste or cloth tied to the end of a stick. Keep mopping on the solution, as the paint softens, until you are down to the bare wood.

Lye Paste Paint Remover

Except on flat, horizontal surfaces, the paste form of paint remover adheres better and is easier to apply. Here is another type of lye remover, containing soft soap and whiting to lend body, and pumice powder to help final removal of the paint:

	Parts
Sodium hydroxide (lye)	10
Soft soap	30
Whiting	20
Pumice powder	10
Water	30

Put the water in an earthenware, enamel, or stainless-steel vessel. Dissolve the lye in the water, pouring it in slowly and stirring with a stick. (*Caution*: Observe all the conditions in handling lye mentioned in the preceding item.) Next stir in the soft soap. Mix the whiting and the pumice powder thoroughly, and then stir this into the lye and soap mixture until it is uniformly distributed.

Apply thickly with a fiber-bristled brush (lye eats hair!). Let remain until paint has softened down to the wood. Then scrape off. Finally wash the surface thoroughly with plain water, and dry with rags or a dry mop.

Universal Paint Remover

The following preparation will remove most finishes, including paint, varnish, lacquer, and shellac:

Toluol	1 qt
Acetone	1 pint
Denatured alcohol	1 pint
Paraffin wax	4 oz

Warm the toluol slightly by placing a pan of it in another pan of warm water. (*Caution*: All the ingredients in this mixture are flammable, so do not mix or use near any open flame. Also mix and use in a well-ventilated room, as the vapors are somewhat toxic.) Melt the wax separately in a double boiler and pour it, with stirring, into the warm toluol. Then add the acetone and alcohol and stir until all are combined. Store it in a tightly capped metal or glass container.

To use, shake well and then flow on in a thick coat on the surface to be treated. Do not brush out. Leave undisturbed for about half an hour. Then test by pressing down one finger into it, using a small rotary motion. If by this test your finger touches bare wood, the remover has done its job; if not, apply more remover and wait until the test is positive. Then remove the softened finish with a putty knife. Before refinishing, wash off any remaining wax with paint thinner or turpentine.

TSP as a Paint Remover

Used in a much higher concentration than for *cleaning* paint, trisodium phosphate makes an excellent paint *remover*—one that is easier to handle than lye, yet cheap and effective if the paint coating is not too thick. Use it in the same proportion as for the cleaning of paint brushes—1 pound of TSP per gallon of hot water. Mop or brush on the solution and let it remain for about 30 minutes. Then remove the softened paint with a dull scraper or putty knife. Rinse the clean surface well with plain water, and dry it with rags or a dry mop to prevent excessive raising of the wood grain. (*Caution:* Wear rubber gloves when handling hot concentrated TSP solution, and do not spill it on surfaces from which you do not wish to remove paint.)

TSP Paint Remover for Walls

This paint remover for vertical surfaces is not quite as caustic as one made with lye, but be sure to wash it off with plain water immediately if you get any on yourself or your surroundings.

Trisodium phosphate	1 part
Whiting	2 parts
Water	sufficient

Mix the TSP thoroughly with the whiting and add enough water to make a thick paste. Apply with a trowel or putty knife to a thickness of about ⅜ inch. Allow to remain about half an hour. Then scrape it off, with the finish beneath it. Rinse with plain water.

Varnish Remover Practice

1. Apply paint and varnish remover freely with one-way strokes only. Leave until the old surface of-tens, wrinkles, or becomes blistered.

2. Peel off the material with a flexible putty knife. Wipe the knife on squares of newspaper. Burn all waste promptly, to reduce fire hazard, or keep it in tightly-covered metal containers until this can be done.

3. Recoat the surface as often as may be needed.

4. Use No. 2 steel wool and denatured alcohol for the final clean-up.

5. Wash thoroughly with alcohol and burlap or bagging. Wipe dry with clean rags. Use a wooden picking stick on all panel lines and moldings.

6. Use a scratch brush or a fiber brush carefully to clean any carvings that may be present.

3

Finishing, Plating, and Working Metals

HOW TO BUFF METALWARE

Few workshop operations are as satisfying as buffing. With little effort, dramatic changes take place right before your eyes.

Almost any metal object that was shiny once will respond. Wall-switch plates, decorative copper pots, silverware, door knobs and knockers, andirons, and golf clubs can all be restored to their original brilliant finish.

The process of buffing involves three operations. The first is *polishing*, which, surprisingly, is the term for a coarse preliminary operation done with a specially prepared *polishing wheel*. This removes the pits and scratches, and prepares the surface for the next operation, *cutting down*. This is actually buffing with sharp buffing compounds that remove the smaller imperfections and leave the metal bright. *Coloring* is the final buffing, done with soft compounds, to bring out the natural color and luster of the metal.

Selecting wheels. Before buying buffing wheels, consult the chart at the end of this section for the wheel diameter and thickness best suited to the horsepower and speed of your motor. Buffing wheels are made in various types for different operations.

Spiral-sewed wheels are stitched in a continuous circle from center to face, making them hard and well suited to cutting down. Cushion-sewed wheels have only two or three rows of stitching to provide a resilient, cushioning effect. Softest are the loose wheels, which are joined by a single circle of stitching around the arbor hole. Loose wheels are also made in flannel.

Preparing and using a polishing wheel. Mount several spiral-sewed wheels on a dowel and roll them in liquid glue poured on waxed paper. Smooth out blobs of glue with fingers and hang wheel to dry for 24 hours. Then sand smooth to remove loose or projecting threads.

To apply powdered grit, roll wheel again through abrasive, such as No. 280-grit silicon carbide. Roll wheel back and forth without pressing until entire surface is coated. For fast work, make a second wheel using a coarser grit, such as No. 120.

When glue dries, scrape off loose abrasive and tap face of wheel with ball end of ball-peen hammer to produce hundreds of tiny cracks, making the wheel flexible enough to follow contours. Ink an arrow on one side of the wheel so you can always mount it to turn in the same direction. Also mark on it the grit size. Properly made, an abrasive wheel will give long service.

This wheel cuts fast. Rust disappears almost immediately. Pits and scratches take a little longer. After good working over with abrasive wheel, metal is bright and smooth and ready for cutting-down and coloring.

Cutting down and coloring wheels are made by applying stick buffing compounds to uncoated wheels. Mark wheels with the compound used on them and use them only with that compound.

Buffing techniques. Knowing what wheel to use with what compound on what material is only half of your buffing education. The other, equally important half is knowing how to use your equipment. Here are some tips:

• Leave your necktie in the closet; it is dangerous around a buffing wheel.

• Wear gloves unless the work is so small or delicate that gloves are impractical. Much heat is generated when buffing and the work often becomes uncomfortably hot.

• Wear a shop coat and hat to catch the dust that will settle on you.

• Hold work firmly against the buffing wheel slightly below the spindle center and move it up and down—up to get the maximum cut, and down to blend the cuts together.

• Never take your eyes off the work—not even for a moment. The fast-moving wheel can snatch the work away from you, especially when it strikes an edge.

• Inspect the work frequently while cutting. When the many fine lines and scratches are blended out, you are ready for coloring.

BUFFING-WHEEL SELECTION CHART FOR VARIOUS SIZE MOTORS

MOTOR SIZE	RECOMMENDED WHEEL THICKNESS			
	4″ diam	6″ diam	8″ diam	10″ diam
1/6-1/8 hp	1″	1/2″		
1/4 hp	1-1/2″	1″	1/2″	
1/3 hp	2-1/2″	2″	1-1/2″	1/2″
1/2 hp	3″	2-1/2″	2″	2″

Formula for calculating surface feet per minute (s.f.p.m.)
(Ideal buffing speed is 5,000 s.f.p.m.)

$$\frac{\text{diam of wheel in inches}}{4} \text{ x r.p.m. of spindle} = \text{s.f.p.m.}$$

Example:

$$\frac{6''\text{-diam wheel}}{4} \text{ x 3,450 r.p.m.} = 5,175 \text{ s.f.p.m.}$$

COLORING METALS WITH CHEMICALS

The chemical coloring of metals isn't practiced in home workshops as often as it might be. In most cases the process is simple, while the results range from pleasing to spectacular.

TYPES OF BUFFS AND
COMPOUNDS FOR VARIOUS MATERIALS

MATERIAL	FOR CUTTING		FOR COLORING	
	Wheel	Compound	Wheel	Compound
Iron, steel, other hard metals	Spiral sewed	Emery or stainless	Cushion	Stainless
Brass, copper, aluminum, soft metals	Spiral sewed	Tripoli	Cushion or loose	Stainless or rouge
Brass or copper plate	Do not cut		Loose, cushion or flannel	Tripoli or rouge
Solid and plated gold or silver	Do not cut		Flannel	Natural rouge or jeweler's rouge
Nickel or chrome plate	Spiral sewed	Stainless	Cushion or loose	Stainless

Before applying any of the following formulas be sure the metal to be treated is absolutely clean. If lacquered, remove this finish with a lacquer solvent or a heavy-cutting buffing compound. Unlacquered brass, copper, and aluminum can be cleaned by rubbing with a good metal polish. Wash in hot water with a strong detergent and follow with a hot-water rinse.

Many of the processes are simply artificially induced corrosion. Others etch the metal bare. To prevent continued action, rinse them in very hot water. Brass, copper, and aluminum objects can then be waxed or coated with a clear metal lacquer. Colored steel tools and hardware should be coated with oil.

Black on brass. Dissolve 1 ounce copper nitrate in 6 ounces water and apply to the brass. Then heat the brass to change the copper nitrate to copper oxide, which produces a permanent black finish.

Instead of heating, you may apply this solution over the copper nitrate coating.

Sodium sulfide	1 oz
Hydrochloric acid, concentrated	½ oz
Water	10 oz

This changes the coating to black copper sulfide.

Dull black on brass. Dissolve copper scraps in concentrated nitric acid diluted with an equal amount of water in a glass container. (*Caution:* Nitric acid is extremely caustic.) Immerse brass object in solution until desired depth of black has been produced. Remove and wash well with water. If desired, the coating can be given a sheen by rubbing with linseed oil.

Golden matte on brass. Immerse in a solution of 1 part concentrated nitric acid (*Caution!*) in 3 parts water in a glass container. Rock the solution gently. Wipe the object clean under running tap. When dry, protect the surface with wax or lacquer.

Antique-green patina on brass

Potassium bitartrate (cream of tartar)	3 oz
Ammonium chloride	1 oz
Copper nitrate	7½ oz
Sodium chloride (table salt)	3 oz
Water, boiling	13 oz

Dissolve the salts in the boiling water and apply the hot solution to the brass with a piece of sponge or rag mounted on a stick. When the desired effect has been attained, wash and dry.

As another method, paint the object daily for three or four days with this solution:

Copper carbonate	3 oz
Ammonium chloride	1 oz
Copper acetate	1 oz
Potassium bitartrate	1 oz
Strong vinegar	8 oz

Yellow-orange, blue, red-brown on brass. You can get yellow through bluish tones by immersing the object in the following solution. Increase the concentration for bluish tone.

Sodium hydroxide (lye)	½ oz
Copper carbonate	1 oz
Hot water	24 oz

Get red-brown shades by brief dip in this solution:

Copper carbonate	¼ oz
Household ammonia	7½ oz
Sodium carbonate (washing soda)	¼ oz.
Water, near boiling	48 oz

Cold-rinse the object and dip for a moment in dilute sulfuric acid (*Caution*: caustic!), Experiment for different shades.

Black on copper

Potassium or sodium sulfide	¼ oz
Household ammonia	1½ oz
Water	32 oz

Do not heat this solution, as heat will drive off the ammonia gas.

Light matte on copper. Use same treatment as for golden matte on brass, above.

Antique-green patina on copper. Use same treatment as for similar finish on brass, above.

Yellow-green patina on copper. Swab the object for a few days with a mixture of equal parts of sugar, salt, and strong vinegar. Don't immerse the metal. Crush the salt and sugar to a fine powder before mixing the solution.

Bright blue on copper

Lead acetate	½ oz
Sodium thiosulfate (hypo)	1 oz
Water	32 oz

Immerse the object in this solution for about 15 seconds. (*Caution*: Lead acetate is poison!)

Bronze on copper

Ferric nitrate	1½ oz
Potassium thiocyanate	½ oz
Water	32 oz

Use this solution hot. Heat the metal object by first immersing it in hot water. Then dip in the hot chemical solution until the color is satisfactory. Rinse in running water and dry in breeze of a fan.

Red-bronze to brown on copper

Sulfurated potassium (liver of sulfur)	½ oz
Sodium hydroxide (lye)	¾ oz
Water	32 oz

Use this solution hot and dip the object in it.

Concentration and temperature of the solution, metals alloyed with the copper, and time of immersion will cause differences of color.

Steel-gray on aluminum

Zinc chloride	8 oz
Copper sulfate	1 oz
Water, boiling	32 oz

Immerse the objects until desired tone is obtained. Rinse in a 2% solution of lye (*Caution!*) in water, then thoroughly in clear water.

Near-white and matte colors on aluminum. A soft-etched, imitation anodized finish may be produced on aluminum by dipping it in a solution of 1 tablespoon or more of lye to a pint of water. To color the aluminum, then dip it in a solution of household dye. (*Caution*: Be careful with the lye. Caustic!)

Black on iron and steel. Heat red-hot and dip in heavy engine or linseed oil. Most cast irons, etched or blasted, will become bluish-brownish or blackish if soaked or painted with a solution of 6 tablespoons of tannic acid in 1 pint of water.

This formula is also good:

Copper sulfate	2 oz
Concentrated nitric acid	4 oz
Denatured alcohol	10 oz
Water	24 oz

Dissolve the copper sulfate completely in the water. Then stir in the nitric acid (*Caution*: Corrosive!) and the alcohol. Apply this solution uniformly to the metal and allow to air dry. If not black enough, apply again. When dry, rub on a coat of linseed oil.

Brown on iron and steel. The following is an old formula for coloring the outside of gunbarrels. It is especially popular because the ingredients can usually be obtained at the drug store.

Copper sulfate	¾ oz
Mercuric chloride	1 oz
Concentrated nitric acid	½ oz
Denatured alcohol	1 oz
Tincture ferric chloride	1 oz
Tincture ethyl nitrate (sweet spirits of nitre)	1 oz
Water	25 oz

Dissolve the copper sulfate and the mercuric chloride in the water, then stir in the other ingredients in the order named. Apply the solution uniformly with a pad of glass wool and expose to the air for 24 hours. Then wash in hot water, dry in air, and wipe with linseed oil. (*Caution*: Nitric acid, caustic; mercuric chloride, poison!)

Blue on iron and steel

Ferric chloride	2 oz
Antimony chloride	2 oz
Gallic acid	1 oz
Water	5 oz

Dissolve in the order given, and apply the same as the last formula. (*Caution*: Antimony chloride, poison!)

Antiquing Copper

When the natural color of copper or a highly polished finish is inappropriate, it is a simple matter to give it a more subdued "antique" or French finish.

Dissolve about 1 cubic inch of potassium sulfide (liver of sulfur) in 1 pint of water. Add 6 drops of household ammonia. Clean the copper thoroughly to remove all dirt and grease, and rapidly swab on the solution. The metal will gradually darken to black. With a cloth or toothbrush and clear water, rub off the outer black deposit immediately. If the metal is not then a deep brown-black, clean thoroughly and repeat the process. Wash well and dry with a cloth.

With very fine steel wool, rub to bring out the tone desired. The less rubbing, the deeper the tone. Excessive rubbing will restore the copper to its natural color. It is at this point that recessed parts can be left dark, while high parts are brightened to the amount desired. A smooth surface can be given an attractive mottled appearance by judicious use of steel wool, some spots being left darker than others.

The finish should be protected either with clear metal lacquer or by several coats of good-quality wax, each left to harden and then polished.

Apart from embossing, peening, crimping, and other worked effects that are set off by the treatment, considerable variation on a smooth surface is possible by scratch-brushing, sandpapering, or rubbing with coarse steel wool before treatment. The deeper the scratches, the more dark tones will remain, and the more "grain" and the deeper the tone the finish will have.

ANNEALING AND PICKLING COPPER AND ITS ALLOYS

When being shaped, copper, brass, and other alloys of copper become work-hardened and must be softened by annealing. They also become dirty and covered with an oxide, and must be cleaned, or "pickled," in an acid bath. During forming, annealing and pickling may be done in a single operation. When forming is completed, only pickling is necessary.

Annealing. Heat piece to dull red over a Bunsen burner, gas stove, or with torch. Move the piece in the flame to bring it slowly and evenly up to annealing temperature. Holding it with copper tongs or tweezers, *slide* it gently into pickling solution, avoiding splash. The solution will anneal (by quickly cooling it) and clean the metal at the same time. Remove the piece with tongs and rinse it under warm water.

Pickling solution for copper and alloys can be made by mixing 1 part of concentrated sulfuric acid with 9 parts of water. (*Caution*: Always pour the acid into the water, and not vice versa. Do not spill on skin or clothing as it is extremely caustic.) Mix and use in a glass or earthenware container. Cover when not in use and keep in a well-ventilated place, as concentrated fumes from it may rust nearby articles of iron and steel.

When object is completely formed, and does not have to be softened again, place in solution without heating. Let remain 5 to 10 minutes. Then remove with tongs, rinse, and dry with paper towels.

CLEANING METAL FOR PLATING

Before metals can be plated, all grease, corrosion, and scale must be removed so the plating solution can make perfect contact with the bare solid metal. Grease can be removed by organic solvents, such as a combination of 1 part trichloroethylene and 1 part naphtha, or by washing in a hot solution of washing soda or trisodium phosphate (*Careful*: Wear rubber gloves!). After degreasing, you can remove corrosion and scale from silver, copper, and copper compounds by dipping the objects in the pickling solution described in the preceding article. From iron and other base metals, you can do so by using a weaker solution: ½ part sulfuric acid to 9½ parts water (mixing and using, of course, with the same precautions!).

PLATING WITHOUT ELECTRIC CURRENT

Thin films of nickel or silver can readily be plated on copper or brass without the use of an external source of current, simply by local chemical or electrolytic action. These films are not as durable as those made by regular electroplating, but they may serve on objects that will not be subjected to hard use.

Plating with Nickel

When moistened with water, the following mixture will cause a plating of nickel to be formed on copper or brass:

Nickel ammonium sulfate	60 parts
Powdered chalk	35 parts
Powdered magnesium metal	4 parts

Mix the powders thoroughly together, and apply to the previously cleaned metal with a cloth pad kept wet with water. Zinc dust may be substituted for the magnesium powder if a little tartaric acid is added to the mixture.

Plating with Silver

Silver may similarly be plated out on copper or brass with the help of one of the following formulas:

No. 1

Silver nitrate	1 part
Salt (not iodized)	1 part
Potassium bitartrate (cream of tartar)	14 parts

Mix these ingredients thoroughly in a glass or ceramic vessel. Apply to the cleaned metal with a damp cloth pad. Keep the powder dry until immediately before use, however, as moisture causes it to decompose in the presence of light. (*Caution:* Silver nitrate is poisonous and corrosive and produces an indelible stain on the skin, cloth, and other materials. So be careful not to spill it; also wear rubber gloves when applying it.)

No. 2

Silver nitrate	4 parts
Salt (not iodized)	12 parts
Potassium bitartrate (cream of tartar)	7 parts
Powdered chalk	10 parts

Mix chalk, salt, and potassium bitartrate thoroughly, and then mix in the powdered silver nitrate. Apply as in formula 1, being sure to observe the precautions, and store the remaining powder in well-stoppered bottles.

No. 3

This formula is a solution, in which small objects can be immersed:

Silver nitrate	15 parts
Potassium hydroxide	15 parts
Water	50 parts

Dissolve the silver nitrate in half the water and the potassium hydroxide in the other. Use glass vessels for mixing and do not spatter either on yourself or your surroundings, as both are poisonous and caustic. Until ready to use, keep both solutions in opaque glass or plastic bottles with corrosion-resistant stoppers (do not use rubber stoppers on the silver nitrate bottle).

When ready to use, mix the solutions in equal quantity in a glass or plastic container, and immerse the well-cleaned object to be plated in the resulting combination, using a slight motion to remove air bubbles. Leave it for several minutes. Then remove, wash, dry, and buff lightly.

ELECTROPLATING

The plating of copper, chromium, silver, gold, or other superior metals on baser metals by means of an electric current can make a fascinating hobby, or even a profitable small business. To do a first-rate plating job with different metals on different sizes and types of objects, though, requires special equipment, plus a knowledge of techniques and of handling extremely corrosive and poisonous chemicals that cannot be adequately described in a few pages. If you would like to investigate further, consult a book on electroplating, or write to a manufacturer or dealer in electroplating supplies, several of which are listed at the end of this book under Sources of Supply.

To copper plate nonmetallic objects in a simple acid bath is, however, relatively safe and uncomplicated. By means of this process, you can encase small objects of wood, plaster, plastics, ceramics—or even baby shoes!—in a novel and permanent sheath of metal.

First of all, you will need a source of regulated d.c.—one that will deliver up to about 6 volts at up to 5, 10, or more amperes, depending upon the size of the object to be plated. This can be a storage battery, a battery charger, or a transformer-rectifier low-voltage power supply such as is used in radio. In any case, a rheostat must be connected in series with the output of the power supply and the tank electrodes to regulate the voltage. To check the current and voltage, an ammeter must be connected in series with the rheostat and a voltmeter connected in parallel with the tank terminals.

The plating tank should be large enough to handle your work. Allow at least 6 inches from the object to be plated to the anode plates, and at least 1 inch from the anodes to the tank sides. You can make it yourself from wood lined with sheet lead or sheet rubber, or you might use a one-piece rectangular glass fish tank or a container made of polyethylene.

Be sure that the finish on the object to be plated is as perfect as you can make it, as any flaws in the surface will be more conspicuous in the final metal coating.

To make the surface conductive you can coat it with copper bronzing powder held in place with thinned-down lacquer. Mix about 1 ounce of this powder with ¾ ounce of clear lacquer thinned with about 6½ ounces of lacquer thinner. Before applying this, test it on a piece of material similar to that of the object. When dry, a finger touched to the surface should show some of the copper powder. If it doesn't, add more thinner and test again.

Good electrical contact with the surface can be insured by drilling several tiny holes in inconspicuous spots in the work and wedging in them one end of the copper wires from which the object will be suspended, afterwards touching these spots with a brush dipped in the bronzing mixture. Then spray the mixture over the whole surface.

Make the plating solution, or electrolyte, by dissolving 27 ounces of copper sulfate crystals in enough warm water to make a gallon, using a glass or plastic stirrer. Then gradually and carefully stir in 6½ ounces by weight (about 3½ fluid ounces, by measure) of concentrated sulfuric acid (*Caution*: Always add acid to the water, and not vice versa. Do not spill on skin or surroundings as it is extremely corrosive). Increase or decrease the quantities proportionately to make enough solution to fill your tank.

With the tank filled, place two copper or brass rods across the top, about 1 inch away from the sides. Hang from these rods (by copper wires, or by bending one end and hooking it over the rods) strips of copper sheet having an immersed area at least equal to the area of the surface to be plated. These are the anodes and should be connected to the positive lead from the current source. Connect the negative lead to a "buffer," consisting of a small piece of copper or brass, suspended from a wooden bar across the center of the tank. Turn on the current and adjust the rheostat until the voltage is between 0.75 and 2 volts. Then connect the wires attached to your object to the negative lead and suspend it also from the center bar.

If plating is taking place properly, the lacquered surface will take on a pinkish glow. The buffer sheet may be removed as soon as this happens. After 15 minutes, remove the work and inspect it carefully. Color should be a light shade of pink. If it is darkish pink, the plate is "burning." In this case, the burned areas must be removed and the object recoated with the conductive coating. Then you must reduce the voltage and begin again. If the color is right, continue plating until about 1/32 inch of metal (determined by caliper comparison) has been deposited.

For best plating, keep the temperature of the solution from about 77 to 80 degrees F and agitate the object frequently. Professional platers generally keep the solution moving about the objects being plated by connecting a mechanical agitator to the rod on which they are hung or by bubbling air through the solution.

After plating, the work can be finished by very light and careful filing, buffing, and polishing. If desired, it may then be lacquered.

Baby shoes can be electroplated by the same method. Begin by removing wax and polish from the shoes and by treating them with lacquer to stiffen them and prevent the absorption of moisture. How to do this is explained in the article "To metallize baby shoes without electroplating" in the chapter on Arts and Crafts. Instead of the last coat of lacquer, however, apply the bronzing mixture, suspend the shoes in the center of the tank by means of copper wires, and plate as described above.

LOW-MELTING ALLOYS

Certain alloys of lead, tin, and bismuth have a lower melting point than that of any one of these metals. This curious fact was discovered by the famous Isaac Newton more than 200 years ago. Not long after that, the German chemist Valentin Rose and the French physicist Jean Darcet produced combinations of the same metals that have still lower melting points.

These and similar alloys are used today to make fusible links in automatic sprinklers, safety plugs for steam boilers, special electrical fuses, and other heat-triggered safety devices. They are also used for making molds and casts of wooden or other objects that might be damaged by molten metals of higher temperature.

Their low melting temperature makes such alloys especially useful to the home mechanic who would like to cast small metal objects but has no blast furnace. Because they have the unusual property of expanding when they cool, they make particularly sharp impressions. If he is a practical joker, the home mechanic can use them, too, to make fusible parts in spoons or other tableware. These parts will melt away when an unsuspecting friend tries to stir coffee or other hot liquid with the trick implements!

Here are the approximate formulas and melting points for the original alloys, all parts being measured by weight:

Alloy	Bismuth	Lead	Tin	Melting point, °F
Newton's	5	3	2	201
Rose's	8	5	3	200
Darcet's	2	1	1	199

As Darcet's alloy contains equal parts of lead and tin, you can make it rather easily by melting regular half-and-half solder, and mixing into this melt an equal weight of bismuth.

More recent investigators have found that by substituting cadmium for part of the tin, the melting point of low-melting alloys can be lowered still further. The following are two common examples:

Alloy	Bismuth	Lead	Tin	Cadmium	Melting point, °F
Wood's	4	2	1	1	149
Lipowitz's	15	8	4	3	154

In making fusible alloys, the lead and bismuth are generally melted together first. Then the tin is added, and stirred until melted and mixed. Cadmium, which comes in sticks, may catch fire if heated too hot in the open air. So add this metal by holding a stick of it in tongs and stirring it into the other molten metals which are kept just hot enough to melt the cadmium.

Alloy for Making Exact Castings

Most metals shrink when they solidify from a melted state; bismuth, contrariwise, expands. By combining bismuth in different combinations with tin and lead, low-melting alloys can therefore be produced that shrink, expand, or do neither, on cooling.

An alloy that melts at 248 degrees F and maintains its same dimensions when cold can be made by combining 57 percent bismuth with 43 percent tin. This alloy is used in making master patterns in foundry work and for soldering lead, tin, and zinc foils.

SOLDERS AND SOLDERING

The term "soldering" generally means "soft soldering," a method of joining two metals together with an alloy of relatively low melting point, usually composed of tin and lead.

Types of solder. Common soft solder comes in bar, ribbon, and wire form. Wire solder may be solid or it may be tubular with a core of either acid or rosin soldering flux. Bar solder is used with heavy irons and blow torches on plumbing and large sheet metal work, while ribbon and wire solder are used with light irons on electrical wiring and other small jobs.

When solder is designated by numbers, the first number represents the proportion of tin, the second of lead. A 40-60 solder, for instance, means a solder with 40 percent by weight of tin and 60 percent by weight of lead. One of the commonest solders for all-round use is 50-50, or "half-and-half." Soft solders for gold and silver and for copper and brass sheet generally contain more tin and melt at a lower temperature. Solders containing more lead are better for lead plumbing, but require more heat. Pewter is soldered with a special alloy to which bismuth has been added to lower the temperature below that of lead and tin alone.

So-called "liquid solders" or "cold solders," which are recommended by their manufacturers for joining all types of materials, are usually not really solders at all, but are cements or glues fortified with aluminum or other metallic powder. Although such preparations may be useful for sealing off small holes to stop leaks and for other minor patching jobs, they should not be used where real solder is required. They do not make a real metal to metal bond, they are not electrically conductive, and they may disintegrate in the presence of organic solvents or at temperatures considerably below the softening point of lead-tin solders.

Need for fluxes. For the solder to adhere firmly to the metals to be joined, the surfaces must be completely free of oxide. Because oxides form on most metals at room temperatures, and almost immediately when heated by a soldering iron, a coating material must be used that will remove the film already present and protect both solder and metal from further oxidation. Such a material is called a soldering "flux," from a Latin word meaning "to flow."

Except for electrical work, the fluxes most commonly used for soft soldering are solutions or pastes that contain zinc chloride or a mixture of zinc and ammonium chlorides. The heat of the soldering operation evaporates the medium containing the chloride flux. The flux then melts and partially decomposes with the liberation of hydrochloric acid, which dissolves the oxides from the metal surfaces. The fused flux also forms a protective film that prevents further oxidation.

Acid fluxes. The fluxes just mentioned, called "acid fluxes," come in both liquid and paste form, and as the core in acid-core wire solders. Zinc chloride and ammonium chloride (sal ammoniac) are also used dry, in the form of cake or powder.

A good liquid zinc-chloride flux can be made simply by adding scraps of zinc to hydrochloric acid until no more zinc dissolves. The resulting solution should be diluted with an equal amount of water before using.

A liquid flux that combines both chemicals can be made by dissolving 2½ ounces of zinc chloride and 1 ounce of ammonium chloride in 6 ounces of water.

To make a paste-type flux, dissolve 1 teaspoon of zinc chloride and 1 teaspoon of ammonium chloride in 4 teaspoons of hot water. Then stir in thoroughly 3 ounces of petroleum jelly, heating the combination until it boils. Let cool before use.

A small stiff brush is useful in applying either liquid or paste. When the liquid flux is applied, the soldering operation should follow immediately. The paste-type flux can remain on the work for as long as an hour before soldering, owing to its lesser activity at room temperature. At soldering temperatures, however, one type is as active as the other, and so once heat has been applied, soldering should be continued without delay. Otherwise, salt deposits will be formed which will make subsequent soldering difficult.

After soldering, excess flux should be removed immediately by using a large swab and hot water.

Rosin fluxes. Because acid fluxes do have a corrosive action, they should not be used in soldering electrical connections or on other types of work where the last traces of flux cannot be removed after the job has been completed. For such jobs, a noncorrosive flux is necessary. Rosin is the most commonly used flux of this type and is the only flux known to be noncorrosive in all soldering applications. Rosin may be mixed with alcohol in varying proportions to obtain any desired consistency. Paste rosin flux also can be made by using petroleum jelly as a base.

Other fluxes. Palm oil, olive oil, or rosin, or mixtures of these, have been recommended as suitable fluxes for pewter. Tallow is often used by plumbers in wiping lead joints. These mild fluxes are not corrosive, but for the sake of cleanliness and appearance are generally removed with naphtha or other organic solvent after soldering.

Soldering irons. Soft soldering is generally done with a copper-headed tool called an "iron." Nonelectric soldering irons that must be heated by a torch or other means come in sizes from ¼ to 5 pounds. Electric irons, however, are today more popular and are generally used wherever an electric circuit is available. They range from 25 to 300 watts.

In wiring radio or other electronic kits, the 25-watt size is the largest recommended for making connections to printed circuit boards, while the 50-watt size may be the largest ever needed for making chassis connections. A 150- to 200-watt iron will do for most home sheet-metal work, with the 300-watt size being required for only the heaviest jobs.

Soldering guns, which heat up almost instantly on the pull of a trigger, are used widely in electrical work, but many consider them too heavy and less convenient than a small regular iron for extensive kit wiring.

Tinning the iron. Before a soldering iron can be used, one or more faces of its tip must be filed smooth and coated with solder, or "tinned." For most work, the iron should be tinned on all four faces. For work where the iron is held under the object to be soldered, however, only one face should be tinned—the face to be held against the object. If all four sides were tinned in this case, solder from the top of the iron would flow down the sides and drip off the bottom. Untinned sides will prevent this flow.

To tin an iron, follow these steps:

1. File the tip faces bright while the iron is cold.

2. Plug iron into outlet (or heat over a burner, if non-electric). As the iron heats, rub flux-core solder (or flux followed by solder) over the tip faces every 15 or 20 seconds. As soon as the iron is hot enough, the solder will spread smoothly and evenly over the faces. The purpose of this caution is to coat the copper before it gets hot enough to oxidize.

3. As soon as the tinning is completed, wipe the tip with a rag or a paper towel while the solder is still molten. This will expose a mirror-like layer of solder on the tip faces.

Soldering a joint. First of all, the area to be soldered must be absolutely clean. If it is dirty or greasy, clean it with a solvent cleaner. If it is heavily oxidized, clean the surface with abrasive cloth until it is bright. Make sure the parts to be soldered are rigidly supported, so they won't move while the solder is setting.

Apply the proper flux to the entire surface to which the solder is to adhere. Too much flux, however, will interfere with soldering.

Heat the soldering iron to the proper temperature. Test this by touching solder to the tip: if it melts quickly, the iron is nearly hot enough. Then heat the metal to be joined hot enough with the iron so that solder touched to it will flow into the joint. If the metal is not hot enough to melt the solder, the solder will not adhere. Be particularly careful of this when

using rosin-core solder, or rosin and solder. If the
metal is not hot enough to vaporize the rosin and to
cause the solder to take its place, the result will be a
"cold-soldered" joint held together feebly and non-
conductively by rosin, rather than strongly by solder.

Hard Soldering

Hard solders are distinguished from soft solders
in that they have much higher melting points and
form joints of much higher strength. They are used for
joining such metals as copper, silver, and gold, and alloys such as brass, German silver, and so on, which require a strong joint and often solder of a color near
that of the metal to be joined. When used to join common metals, hard soldering is generally called "brazing," and the lower-melting alloys are known as
"spelter."

There are three general types of hard solders:
precious-metal alloy solders or "silver solders," ordinary brazing solders, and aluminum brazing solders.
Because of their high melting points, hard solders cannot be applied with a soldering iron, but require the
use of torches, furnaces, or dipping tanks. Since hard
solders also require special skills in their application,
they are seldom used by the homecraftsman or mechanic except in making jewelry or on other small
jobs that can be done with a small propane torch or
with a blowtorch.

Precious-metal solders. Silver solders for use with
a torch are supplied in the form of wire and powder.
They consist of alloys of silver, copper, and zinc, and
have melting points ranging from about 1,200 to 1,600

degrees F. Solders containing gold are used primarily for joining gold and gold alloys, and usually are alloys of gold with copper, silver, and zinc. Gold solders are generally designated by karat numbers to indicate the fineness, or karat number of the alloy with which they should be used. Soldered joints in platinum or platinum alloys may be made with fine gold or the higher karat gold alloys.

Common brazing solders are generally supplied in granular, lump, rod, or wire form. They are made from different combinations of copper, zinc, and tin, and have melting points from about 1,400 to 1,980 degrees F.

Aluminum brazing alloys are used almost exclusively by industry. They consist of special, and usually proprietary, alloys of aluminum and must be obtained from manufacturers of aluminum alloys.

Fluxes for hard soldering. For most purposes, borax, or mixtures of borax with boric acid, is a good flux for the precious metal and ordinary brazing solders. The chloride fluxes used for soft soldering would vaporize immediately under the high temperatures of hard soldering and so cannot be used here.

RUSTPROOFING METAL ARTICLES

In general, paints and lacquers give maximum protection, but these can be applied only to unmachined surfaces. Neutral oil, wax, and grease films provide protection for a limited period ranging from a few weeks to several months. Articles coated with such films may be wrapped in paper, plastic film, or cloth as an additional protection. Metals may be kept corrosion-free with no coating at all if they are packed in a moistureproof wrapping of plastic that contains a packet of the moisture absorbing chemical silica gel. The following substances may be applied as rust preventives on iron and steel:

Articles packed for storage or shipment

Petroleum jelly
High-viscosity oil (chemically neutral)
Petroleum jelly and oil mixtures

Articles subject to handling

Paint and lacquer
Commercial antirust preparations
Soluble-oil emulsions
Chemical films such as oxides and gun bluing
Paraffin wax

Rusty objects can first be cleaned by hand or power wire-brushing, with abrasive cloth, steel wool, abrasive powders and polishes, and by chemical rust solvents.

Rust Preventive for Stored Tools

Mechanical equipment, tools, etc., which are to be taken out of service and stored can be effectively protected from rust by using the following mixture: Heat 1 part of powdered rosin and 6 parts of lard slowly and with stirring until the rosin is completely melted. Then remove from the fire and thin to a flowing consistency with V.M.&P. naphtha (*Caution*: Flammable!).

Rub this mixture sparingly on the steel, after being sure that the metal is clean and that all rust spots have been removed. A leading manufacturer of chisels has found that tools rubbed lightly with this mixture will resist rust even when immersed for some time in salt water.

Rust Prevention with Whitewash

The rusting or corrosion of iron and steel may be retarded or prevented by applying a good coat of whitewash. This is particularly helpful for the farmer, homeowner, or building contractor who has tools, shovels, plowshares, structural shapes, reinforcing rods, and so on, exposed to the weather. If the tools or implements stand out in the open, use whitewash formulas 1, 2, or 4 given in the chapter on paint. If stored under cover and not disturbed, however, a simple slaked lime and water mixture will serve the purpose.

Rusting of the inside of furnaces will be greatly reduced if the surface is cleaned and whitewashed at the end of the heating season.

HOW SHEET METALS ARE MEASURED AND PURCHASED

Metal	How measured	How purchased	Characteristics
Aluminum	Decimal thickness	24 x 72" sheet or 12 or 18" by linear foot	Pure metal, or stronger and more ductile alloys
Copper	Gauge number (Brown & Sharpe or Amer Wire Gauge) or by weight per sq ft	24 x 96" sheet or 12 or 18" by linear foot	Pure metal
Brass	Gauge number (B & S or AWG)	24 x 76" sheet or 12 or 18" by linear foot	Copper and zinc alloy
Cold rolled steel sheet	Gauge number (US Standard)	24 x 96" sheet	Oxide removed and cold rolled to final thickness
Black annealed steel sheet	Gauge number (US Standard)	24 x 96" sheet	Hot-rolled mild steel with oxide coating left on
Galvanized steel	Gauge number (US Standard)	24 x 96" sheet	Mild steel plated with zinc
Tin plate	Gauge number (US Standard)	20 x 28" sheet 56 or 112 to a package	Mild steel plated with tin
Expanded steel	Gauge number (US Standard)	36 x 96" sheet	Metal is pierced and stretched to produce diamond-shape openings
Perforated steel	Gauge number (US Standard)	30 x 36" sheet 36 x 48" sheet	Here design is cut in sheet and many designs are available

Note: The actual thickness of steel sheet may be a shade less than that indicated by the United States Standard Gauge number, but is close enough for most practical purposes. The reason for this difference is given in the following discussion of wire and sheet-metal gauges.

WHICH METAL GAUGE MEASURES WHAT?

This is a question that can sometimes baffle expert as well as layman. When the wire and sheet-metal industries were young, systems of thickness gauging were devised by, and often named after, individual manufacturers. In attempts to establish greater uniformity, the United States and the British governments, late in the last century, established national standards. Because even these did not fit all the conditions in the manufacturing of iron and steel sheets, manufacturers jointly set industrial standards for such sheets. To complicate things still further, the dozen or so different metal-thickness gauges that were developed during this time have been variously assigned several times that many names and abbreviations.

To help you find your way through this maze, here follow the various names and abbreviations for the most commonly used gauges, what the gauges are used for, and a table of the thicknesses associated with the gauge numbers. A separate table giving additional information on copper wire can be found in Chapter 18.

American wire gauge (AWG), or
Brown and Sharpe (B&S)

This should cause you little trouble. It is the gauge commonly used in the United States for copper, aluminum, and resistance wires; also for copper, aluminum, and brass sheets.

Birmingham wire gauge (BWG), or
Stubs' iron wire gauge

An old gauge still used in the United States for brass wire, and used to a limited extent in Great Britain.

Steel wire gauge (SWG, StlWG, A(steel)WG), or
Washburn and Moen (W&M), or
American Steel and Wire Co.'s gauge, or
Roebling gauge

The gauge usually used in the United States for iron and steel wire. Watch out for the abbreviation SWG, as that is also one of the abbreviations for the British standard wire gauge!

British standard wire gauge, or
Standard wire gauge (SWG), or
New British standard (NBS), or
English legal standard, or
Imperial wire gauge

Since 1883 this has been the legal standard of Great Britain for wires of all metals. It is a modification of the Birmingham wire gauge.

United States standard gauge (US)

This gauge for sheet iron and steel was adopted in 1893 by an Act of Congress, and was formerly the legal standard for duties. It is a *weight* gauge based on the density of wrought iron at 480 pounds per cubic foot. As originally interpreted, a gauge number in this system represented a fixed weight per unit area. Steel, however, weighs about 9½ pounds more per cubic foot than wrought iron, and so a steel sheet would have a smaller thickness under this system than a wrought iron sheet of the same gauge number. In the face of this discrepancy, some manufacturers make sheets according to weight, others according to thickness, while still others settle on a compromise thickness of their own. In any case, however, thicknesses will not vary greatly from those shown in the table. If you are in doubt about gauge number, order your sheet metal by actual thickness.

COMPARISON OF SHEET-METAL AND WIRE GAUGES

(Dimensions are expressed in approximate decimals of an inch)

Gauge	AWG B&S	Birmingham or Stubs BWG	Steel wire gauge	British Imperial NBS SWG	United States standard US
0000000	——	——	0.4900	0.500	0.5000
000000	0.5800	——	0.4615	0.464	0.4688
00000	0.5165	0.500	0.4305	0.432	0.4375
0000	0.4600	0.454	0.3938	0.400	0.4063
000	0.4096	0.425	0.3625	0.372	0.3750
00	0.3648	0.380	0.3310	0.348	0.3438
0	0.3249	0.340	0.3065	0.324	0.3215
1	0.2893	0.300	0.2830	0.300	0.2813
2	0.2576	0.284	0.2625	0.276	0.2656
3	0.2294	0.259	0.2437	0.252	0.2500
4	0.2043	0.238	0.2253	0.232	0.2344
5	0.1819	0.220	0.2070	0.212	0.2188
6	0.1620	0.203	0.1920	0.192	0.2031
7	0.1443	0.180	0.1770	0.176	0.1875
8	0.1285	0.165	0.1620	0.160	0.1719
9	0.1144	0.148	0.1483	0.144	0.1563
10	0.1019	0.134	0.1350	0.128	0.1406
11	0.0907	0.120	0.1205	0.116	0.1250
12	0.0808	0.109	0.1055	0.104	0.1094
13	0.0720	0.095	0.0915	0.092	0.0938
14	0.0641	0.083	0.0800	0.080	0.0781
15	0.0570	0.072	0.0720	0.072	0.0703
16	0.0508	0.065	0.0625	0.064	0.0625
17	0.0453	0.058	0.0540	0.056	0.0563
18	0.0403	0.049	0.0475	0.048	0.0500
19	0.0359	0.042	0.0410	0.040	0.0438
20	0.0320	0.035	0.0348	0.036	0.0375
21	0.0285	0.032	0.0318	0.032	0.0344
22	0.0254	0.028	0.0286	0.028	0.0313
23	0.0226	0.025	0.0258	0.024	0.0281
24	0.0201	0.022	0.0230	0.022	0.0250
25	0.0179	0.020	0.0204	0.020	0.0219

Gauge	AWG B&S	Birmingham or Stubs BWG	Steel wire gauge	British Imperial NBS SWG	United States standard US
26	0.0159	0.018	0.0181	0.018	0.0188
27	0.0142	0.016	0.0173	0.0164	0.0172
28	0.0126	0.014	0.0162	0.0148	0.0156
29	0.0113	0.013	0.0150	0.0136	0.0141
30	0.0100	0.012	0.0140	0.0124	0.0125
31	0.0089	0.010	0.0132	0.0116	0.0109
32	0.0080	0.009	0.0128	0.0108	0.0102
33	0.0071	0.008	0.0118	0.0100	0.0094
34	0.0063	0.007	0.0104	0.0092	0.0086
35	0.0056	0.005	0.0095	0.0084	0.0078
36	0.0050	0.004	0.0090	0.0076	0.0070
37	0.0045	——	0.0085	0.0068	0.0066
38	0.0040	——	0.0080	0.0060	0.0063
39	0.0035	——	0.0075	0.0052	——
40	0.0031	——	0.0070	0.0048	——

TWIST DRILL SIZES

Above ½ inch, drills are available in fractional sizes only. Three sets of drills are commonly used for smaller sizes. One set is based on wire-gauge sizes—ranging from 80, the smallest, to 1, the largest. Letter sizes begin where wire-gauge sizes end. Fractional-size drills range from 1/64 inch to ½ inch, increasing by steps of 1/64 inch. The accompanying table includes all three sets. Notice that every drill is of a different size except the E and the ¼-inch drills.

NUMBER, LETTER, AND FRACTIONAL DRILL SIZES

Diam-eter	Decimal equivalent	Diam-eter	Decimal equivalent	Diam-eter	Decimal equivalent	Diam-eter	Decimal equivalent
80	0.0135	49	0.073	20	0.161	I	0.272
79	0.0145	48	0.076	19	0.166	J	0.277
1/64	0.0156	5/64	0.0781	18	0.1695	9/32	0.2813
78	0.016	47	0.0785	1/64	0.1719	K	0.281
77	0.018	46	0.081	17	0.173	L	0.290
76	0.02	45	0.082	16	0.177	M	0.295
75	0.021	44	0.086	15	0.18	19/64	0.2969
74	0.0225	43	0.089	14	0.182	N	0.302
73	0.024	42	0.0935	13	0.185	5/16	0.3125
72	0.025	3/32	0.0938	3/16	0.1875	O	0.316
71	0.026	41	0.096	12	0.189	P	0.323
70	0.028	40	0.098	11	0.191	21/64	0.328
69	0.0292	39	0.0995	10	0.1935	Q	0.332
68	0.031	38	0.1015	9	0.196	R	0.339
1/32	0.0313	37	0.104	8	0.199	11/32	0.34375
67	0.032	36	0.1065	7	0.201	S	0.348
66	0.033	7/64	0.1094	13/64	0.203	T	0.358
65	0.035	35	0.11	6	0.204	23/64	0.359
64	0.036	34	0.111	5	0.2055	U	0.368
63	0.037	33	0.113	4	0.209	3/8	0.375

Diameter	Decimal equivalent	Diameter	Decimal equivalent	Diameter	Decimal equivalent	Diameter	Decimal equivalent
62	0.038	32	0.116	3	0.213	V	0.377
61	0.039	31	0.12	7/32	0.21875	W	0.386
60	0.04	1/8	0.125	2	0.221	25/64	0.3906
59	0.041	30	0.1285	1	0.228	X	0.397
58	0.042	29	0.136	A	0.234	Y	0.404
57	0.043	9/64	0.1406	15/64	0.2344	13/32	0.4063
56	0.0465	28	0.1405	B	0.238	Z	0.413
3/64	0.0469	27	0.144	C	0.242		
55	0.052	26	0.147	D	0.246		
54	0.055	25	0.1495	1/4	0.250		
53	0.0595	24	0.152	E	0.250		
1/16	0.0625	23	0.154	F	0.257		
52	0.0635	5/32	0.15625	G	0.261		
51	0.067	22	0.157	17/64	0.2656		
50	0.07	21	0.159	H	0.266		

CUTTING SPEEDS FOR DRILLS

The most efficient cutting speed for drills varies with the material being worked, the rate of feed, and the cutting fluid used. Carbon-steel drills lose their temper at about one-third to one-half the temperature of high-speed drills, and so must be run slower. If they are used within their heat range, however, they will cut just about as well and last just about as long as their high-speed relatives. The following tables suggest conservative speeds for both types of drills under highly controlled industrial use and in ordinary hand use in the home shop. In hand work, the operator must, of course, be governed by the immediate action of the drill and be ready to adjust the speed accordingly.

SAFE DRILLING SPEEDS FOR MILD STEEL (R.P.M.)

DRILL SIZE IN INCHES	INDUSTRIAL USE, WITH MACHINE FEED AND COPIOUS LUBRICATION		HOME-SHOP USE, WITH HAND FEED AND INTERMITTENT OR NO LUBRICATION	
	Carbon	High-speed	Carbon	High-speed
1/16	1,830	6,110	920	3,060
3/32	1,220	4,075	610	2,050
1/8	920	3,060	460	1,530
3/16	610	2,040	310	1,020
1/4	460	1,530	230	760
5/16	370	1,220	180	610
3/8	310	1,020	150	510
1/2	230	764	115	380

SAFE DRILLING SPEEDS FOR OTHER METALS

To find the safe drilling speed for any of the following metals, just multiply the number of r.p.m. in the preceding table by the number given after the metal. For example, to find the safe drilling speed for aluminum, under home-workshop conditions and using a ¼-inch high speed drill:

760 r.p.m. x 2.5 = 1900 r.p.m.

Die castings (zinc base)	3.5
Aluminum	2.5
Brass and bronze	2
Cast iron, soft	1.15
Malleable iron	.85
Cast iron, hard	.80
Tool steel	.60
Stainless steel, hard	.30
Chilled cast iron	.20
Manganese steel	.15

CUTTING FLUIDS FOR DRILLING AND COUNTERSINKING

Cutting fluids applied at the point of contact between a drill or other cutting tool and the work perform several jobs at once. They reduce heat that would otherwise soften and ruin the cutting edge of a tool by direct cooling and by reducing friction. In this way they permit faster cutting speeds. They also help prevent the sticking of chips to tool or work.

Unfortunately there is no ideal cutting fluid that will serve all purposes. Many of the best cutting lubricants are not good coolants. On the other hand, water is probably the best coolant there is, yet on most materials it has almost no lubricating action.

The accompanying table shows recommended cutting fluids for use with specific materials.

CUTTING-FLUIDS GUIDE

MATERIAL	TYPE OF CUTTING FLUID
Aluminum and its alloys	Kerosene, kerosene and lard oil, or soluble oil
Brass and bronze	None
for deep holes	{ Kerosene and mineral oil, lard oil, or soluble oil
Copper	Mineral-lard oil and kerosene, soluble oil, or none
Monel metal	Mineral-lard oil or soluble oil
Mild steel	Mineral-lard oil or soluble oil
Tool steel or forgings	Sulfurized oil, mineral-lard oil, or kerosene
Cast steel	Soluble oil or sulfurized oil
Cast iron	None
Wrought iron	Soluble oil
Malleable iron	Soluble oil or none
Stainless steel	Soluble oil or sulfurized oil
Manganese steel	None
Titanium alloys	Soluble oil or sulfurized oil

Soda-Soap Cutting Fluid

One of the cheapest lubricant-coolants used for turning and milling steel is a soda-soap mixture you can make yourself. Here are the ingredients:

Sal soda (washing soda)	1½ oz
Lard oil	3 fl oz
Soft soap	3 fl oz
Water, enough to make	1 gal

Dissolve the sal soda in the water, which should be warm to make solution easier. Then stir in the soft soap and finally the lard oil. Boil slowly for about ½ hour, with occasional stirring. If the solution smells bad, you can correct this by stirring in about 3 ounces of unslaked lime.

TAP DRILL SIZES (Fractional)

Nominal Size	Commercial Tap Drill	Nominal Size	Commercial Tap Drill
1/16-64	3/64	18	37/64
72	3/64	27	19/32
5/64-60	1/16	11/16-11	19/32
72	52	12	19/32
3/32-48	49	16	5/8
50	49	3/4-10	21/32
7/64-48	43	12	43/64
1/8-32	3/32	16	11/16
40	38	27	23/32
9/64-40	32	13/16-10	23/32
5/32-32	1/8	12	23/32
36	30	7/8- 9	49/64
11/64-32	9/64	12	51/64
3/16-24	26	14	13/16
32	22	18	53/64
13/64-24	20	27	27/32
7/32-24	16	15/16- 9	53/64
32	12	12	55/64
15/64-24	10	1- 8	7/8
1/4-20	7	12	59/64
24	4	14	15/16
27	3	27	31/32
28	3	1-1/8- 7	63/64
32	7/32	12	1-3/64
5/16-18	F	1-1/4- 7	1-7/64
20	17/64	12	1-11/64

TAP DRILL SIZES (Fractional)

Nominal Size	Commercial Tap Drill	Nominal Size	Commercial Tap Drill
24	I	1-3/8- 6	1-7/32
27	J	12	1-19/64
32	9/32	1-1/2- 6	1-11/32
3/8-16	5/16	12	1-27/64
20	21/64	1-5/8 5-1/2	1-29/64
24	Q	1-3/4- 5	1-9/16
27	R	10	1-21/32
7/16-14	U	1-7/8- 5	1-11/16
20	25/64	2- 4-1/2	1-25/32
24	X	3- 3-1/2	2-23/32
27	Y	10	1-29/32
1/2-12	27/64	2-1/8 4-1/2	1-29/32
13	27/64	2-1/4 4-1/2	2-1/32
20	29/64	8	2-1/8
24	29/64	2-3/8- 4	2-1/8
27	15/32	2-1/2- 4	2-1/4
9/16-12	31/64	8	2-3/8
18	33/64	2-3/4- 4	2-1/2
27	17/32	8	2-5/8
5/8-11	17/32	8	2-7/8
5/8-12	35/64		

SELECTION OF GRINDING WHEELS

Abrasive. Fused alumina for materials of high tensile strength, silicon carbide for those of low tensile strength.

Grain size. Fine grain for hard and brittle materials, for small area of contact, and for fine finish; coarse grain for soft, ductile materials, for large areas of contact, and for fast cutting. The number that designates grain size represents the number of openings per lin-

TAP DRILL SIZES (Machine Screw)

Nominal Size	Commercial Tap Drill	Nominal Size	Commercial Tap Drill
0-80	3/64″	8-30	30
1-56	54	32	29
64	53	36	29
72	53	40	28
2-56	50	9-24	29
64	50	30	27
3-48	47	32	26
56	45	10-24	25
4-32	45	28	23
36	44	30	22
40	43	32	21
48	42	12-24	16
5-36	40	28	14
40	38	32	13
44	37	14-20	10
6-32	36	24	7
36	34	16-18	3
40	33	20	7/32″
7-30	31	22	2
32	31	18-18	B
36	1/8″	20	D

NOTE: The tap drills listed will produce approximately 75 percent full thread. The sizes given are National Form. National Fine (N.F.) comprises a series formerly designated as A.S.M.E. pitches and S.A.E. sizes and pitches. National Coarse (N.C.) comprises a series of former A.S.M.E. pitches and U.S. Standard sizes and pitches.

ear inch in the screen used to size the grain. Eight to 10 is very coarse; 12 to 14, coarse; 30 to 60, medium; 70 to 120, fine; 150 to 240, very fine; 280 to 600, flour sizes.

Grade. Hard wheels for soft materials; soft wheels for hard materials. The smaller the area of contact, the harder the wheel should be. Grade is often designated by letters: E to G, very soft; H to K, soft; L to O, medium; P to S, hard; T to Z, very hard.

Structure. Close grain spacing for hard and brittle, for small area of contact, and for fine finish; wide grain spacing for soft, ductile materials, for large area of contact, and for rapid removal of stock. Numerals are sometimes used to indicate spacing: 0 to 3, close; 4 to 6, medium; 7 to 12, wide.

Bond. Resinoid, rubber, and shellac wheels are best for a high finish. Vitrified can be used for speeds up to 6,500 surface feet per minute; rubber, shellac, or resinoid for speeds above that.

GRINDING-WHEEL SPEED

TYPE	SURFACE FEET PER MINUTE	
Cutlery wheels	4,000 to	5,000
Cutting-off wheels (rubber, shellac, resinoid)	9,000 to	16,000
Cylindrical grinding	5,500 to	6,500
Hemming cylinders	2,100 to	5,000
Internal grinding	2,000 to	6,000
Knife grinding	3,500 to	4,500
Snagging, off-hand grinding (vitrified wheels)	5,000 to	6,000
Snagging (rubber and resinoid wheels)	7,000 to	9,500
Surface grinding	4,000 to	6,000
Tool and cutter grinding	4,500 to	6,000
Wet tool grinding	5,000 to	6,000

To determine the number of revolutions per minute required, divide the surface speed in feet per minute by the circumference of the wheel you are using (measured in feet or fractions of a foot). You can find the circumference directly with a cloth tape, or calculate it by multiplying the diameter (also measured in feet or fractions of a foot) by 3.1416.

AVERAGE CUTTING SPEED AND RPM FOR METALS ON A LATHE

(Cutting speed is the distance the piece you are working on moves past the cutting point in 1 minute, as measured around the circumference of the piece.)

METAL	CUTTING SPEED, SURFACE FEET PER MINUTE	DIAMETER AND RPM			
		½ in	1 in	1½ in	2 in
Tool steel	50	400	200	133	100
Cast iron	75	600	300	200	150
Low-carbon steel	100	800	400	266	200
Brass	200	1600	800	533	400
Aluminum	300	2400	1200	800	600

HACKSAW BLADES FOR VARIOUS MATERIALS

HAND BLADES

14 teeth —Brass, bronze, cast iron, heavy angles, rails, soft steel

18 teeth*—Drill rod, high-speed steels

18 teeth —Light angles, small solids

24 teeth —Brass tubing, heavy BX, iron pipe, metal conduit

32 teeth —Flush pipe, light BX, sheet metal, thin tubing

LIGHT POWER BLADES

14 teeth —Bronze, copper, iron pipe, wrought iron

18 teeth —Cipper tubing, light angle iron, thin metals

HEAVY POWER BLADES

 4 teeth —Large solid stock and die blocks

 6 teeth —Machine steel, soft steel, solid stock

10 teeth —Brass, bronze, heavy angle iron, iron pipe, steel rails, tool steel

14 teeth —Hard materials, steel tubing, light angle iron

---

*A speed of 40 strokes per minute is recommended in this case, but 60 strokes per minute in all others. This speed, however, applies to tungsten alloy steel. If molybdenum or high-speed steel saws are used, the speed can be increased.

TEMPERING TEMPERATURES FOR STEEL

After hardening, steel is given a heat treatment which increases its toughness without reducing its hardness. As the steel heats up a film of oxide forms on its surface. The color of this oxide is an indication of the steel's temperature. On the facing page are some temperatures, with their corresponding surface colors, suited for different types of tools.

TEMP IN °F	COLOR OF OXIDE FILM	TYPE OF TOOLS
437-455	Light straw to straw	Scrapers for brass, steel-engraving tools, light turning tools, hammer faces, planer tools for steel, planer tools for iron, wood-engraving tools, drills, milling cutters
456-482	Dark straw to yellow-brown	Wire-drawing plates, boring cutters, screw-cutting dies, taps, rock drills, mill chisels and picks, punches and dies, reamers, shear blades, half-round bits, planer knives, and molding cutters (to be ground), gouges, plane irons
483-527	Yellow-brown to dark purple	Twist drills, flat drills, wood-boring cutters, drifts, cup tools, edging cutters
528-572	Dark purple to full blue	Wood bits and augers, cold chisels for steel, axes and adzes, gimlets, cold chisels for cast iron, needles, wood chisels, hack saws, planer knives and molding cutters (to be filed), circular saws for metal, springs, saws for wood

4

Working with Concrete, Brick, and Plaster

HOW TO MIX CONCRETE FOR DIFFERENT JOBS

Properly-made concrete is a strong and versatile building material made by combining portland cement and sand with pebbles, crushed stone, or other aggregate, and enough water to cause the cement to set and to bind the whole mass solidly together.

In mixing concrete, the most important proportion to remember is that between cement and water. As long as a mix is workable, the amount of aggregate may be varied considerably. For a given strength of concrete, the ratio between cement and water, however, is *fixed*. The relationship between strength of concrete and the relative quantities of water and cement is expressed more definitely by concrete experts:

For given materials and conditions of handling, the strength of the concrete is determined primarily by the ratio of the volume of the mixing water to the volume of cement as long as the mixture is plastic and workable.

In other words, if 6 gallons of water are used for each sack of cement in a mixture, the strength of the concrete at a certain age is already determined. The only extra provision is that *the mixture is plastic and workable* and the aggregates are strong, clean, and made up of sound particles. More water will mean less strength and less water greater strength.

Following this principle, modern practice is to state the amount of mixing water for each sack of cement to produce "pastes" of different strengths. Common combinations are 5-gallon paste, 6-gallon paste, and 7-gallon paste, to be selected according to the type of work to be done.

To help choose pastes and make trial mixes for different types of jobs, the accompanying table shows proportions recommended by the Portland Cement Association.

Choosing Materials

Portland cement is sold in sacks of 94 pounds each, or 1 cubic foot in volume. It should be free from all lumps when used. If it contains lumps that cannot be pulverized between thumb and finger, don't use it.

Water should be clean, and free of oil, acid, or alkali. As a general rule, you can use any water that is fit to drink.

HOW TO SELECT PROPER CONCRETE MIX

KINDS OF WORK	Add U.S. gal. of water to each sack batch if sand is			Suggested mixture for trial batch*			Materials per cu.yd. of concrete*		
	Very wet	Wet (average sand)	Damp	Ce-ment, sacks	Aggregates		Ce-ment, sacks	Aggregates	
					Fine cu.ft.	Coarse cu.ft.		Fine cu.ft.	Coarse cu.ft.
5-Gal. Paste for Concrete Subjected to Severe Wear, Weather or Weak Acid and Alkali Solutions									
One-course industrial, creamery and dairy plant floors, etc.	3½	4	4½	1	2	2¼	Maximum size aggregate ¾ in. 7¾	15½	17½
6-Gal. Paste for Concrete to be Watertight or Subjected to Moderate Wear and Weather									
Watertight floors, such as industrial plant, basement, dairy barn; watertight foundations; driveways, walks, tennis courts, swimming and wading pools, septic tanks, storage tanks, structural beams, columns, slabs, residence floors, etc.	4¼	5	5½	1	2½	3½	Maximum size aggregate 1½ in. 6	15	21
7-Gal. Paste for Concrete not Subjected to Wear, Weather or Water									
Foundation walls, footings, mass concrete, etc., for use where watertightness and abrasion resistance are not important.	4¾	5½	6¼	1	3	4	Maximum size aggregate 1½ in. 5	15	20

*Mixes and quantities are based on wet (average) aggregates and medium consistencies. Actual quantities will vary according to the grading of aggregate and the water actually used.

Aggregates are classified as fine or coarse. Fine aggregate consists of sand or other solid and clean fine material including rock screenings. Suitable sand will contain particles ranging uniformly in size from very fine up to ¼ inch.

Coarse aggregate consists of gravel, crushed stone, or other materials up to about 1½ inches in size. Material that is sound, hard, durable, and free from foreign matter is best for making concrete.

The maximum size of coarse aggregate depends on the kind of work for which the concrete is to be used. Aggregate up to 1½ inch, for example, may be used in thick foundation wall or heavy footing. In ordinary walls, the largest pieces should never be more than one-fifth the thickness of the finished wall section. For slabs the maximum size should be approximately one-third the thickness of the slab. Coarse aggregate is well graded when particles range uniformly from ¼ inch up to the largest that may be used on the kind of work to be done.

Allowance for moisture in the aggregates. Most sand or fine aggregates contain some water. Allowance must therefore be made for this moisture in determining the amount of water to be added to the mix. You can easily determine whether sand is damp, wet, or very wet by pressing some together in your hand. If the sand falls apart after your hand is opened, it is damp; if it forms a ball that holds its shape, it is wet; if the sand sparkles and wets your hand, it is very wet. If the sand is bone dry—an unusual condition—you should use the full 5, 6, or 7 gallons of water called for in the table.

Measuring Materials

All materials, including water, should be accurately measured. For measuring water, a pail marked on the inside to indicate quarts and gallons will prove handy. On small jobs a pail may also be used for measuring cement, sand, and pebbles. In mixing 1-sack batches merely remember that 1 sack holds exactly 1 cubic foot. Sand and pebbles are then conveniently measured in bottomless boxes made to hold exactly 1 cubic foot, or other volumes desired.

If you can buy concrete aggregates in your community by weight, you may assume, for purpose of estimating, that a ton contains approximately 22 cubic feet of sand, or about 20 cubic feet of gravel. For closer estimates on local aggregates, consult your building material dealer.

How to Obtain a Workable Mixture

A workable mixture is one of such wetness and plasticity that it can be placed in the forms readily, and that with light spading and tamping will result in a dense concrete. There should be enough portland cement mortar to give good dense surfaces, free from rough spots, and to hold pieces of coarse aggregate into the mass so that they will not separate out in handling. In other words, the cement-fine-aggregate mortar should completely fill the spaces between the coarse aggregate and insure a smooth, plastic mix. Mixtures lacking sufficient mortar will be hard to work and difficult to finish. Too much fine aggregate increases porosity and reduces the amount of concrete obtainable from a sack of cement.

A workable mix for one type of work may be too stiff for another. Concrete that is placed in thin sections must be more plastic than for massive construction.

Mixing and Placing the Concrete

Mixing should continue until every piece of coarse aggregate is completely coated with a thoroughly mixed mortar of cement and fine aggregate. Machine-mixing is preferable, if you have the equipment available, and should continue for at least 1 minute after all the materials have been placed in the mixer.

The concrete should be placed in the forms within 45 to 60 minutes after mixing. It should be tamped or spaded as it goes into the form. This forces the coarse aggregate back from the face or surface, making a dense concrete surface.

How to Estimate Materials Required for 100 Square Feet of Concrete of a Given Thickness

The accompanying table will give you the approximate quantities. Actual quantities used may vary 10 percent, depending upon the aggregate used. It is good practice to provide 10 percent more fine and coarse aggregates than estimated, to allow for waste.

To Prevent Concrete From Sticking to Forms

To prevent concrete from sticking to wooden forms, the forms must be treated with a suitable oil, varnish, or other coating material. This oil should also prevent absorption of water from the concrete.

ESTIMATING MATERIALS FOR CONCRETE

Thickness of concrete, in.	Amount of concrete, cu. yd.	Proportions								
		1:2:2¼ mix			1:2½:3½ mix			1:3:4 mix		
		Cement, sacks	Aggregate		Cement, sacks	Aggregate		Cement, sacks	Aggregate	
			Fine, cu. ft.	Coarse, cu. ft.		Fine, cu. ft.	Coarse, cu. ft.		Fine, cu. ft.	Coarse, cu. ft.
3	0.92	7.1	14.3	16.1	5.5	13.8	19.3	4.6	13.8	18.4
4	1.24	9.6	19.2	21.7	7.4	18.6	26.0	6.2	18.6	24.8
5	1.56	12.1	24.2	27.3	9.4	23.4	32.8	7.8	23.4	31.2
6	1.85	14.3	28.7	32.4	11.1	27.8	38.9	9.3	27.8	37.0
8	2.46	19.1	38.1	43.0	14.8	36.9	51.7	12.3	36.9	49.3
10	3.08	23.9	47.7	53.9	18.5	46.2	64.7	15.4	46.2	61.6
12	3.70	28.7	57.3	64.7	22.2	55.5	77.7	18.5	55.5	74.0

Almost any light-bodied petroleum oil will do. Fuel oil is satisfactory for use with normal gray concrete except in very warm weather, when it should be thickened with 1 part of petroleum grease to each 2 parts of oil. When making pastel-colored concrete or concrete using white portland cement, use white mineral oil to prevent staining.

Before applying oil, be sure the form is clean and smooth. Rough wood surfaces may cause the concrete to stick. Apply the oil evenly with a brush, spray, or swab. Wipe off excess so it does not soften or discolor the concrete.

Several coats of shellac applied first to plywood is better than oil alone in preventing moisture from raising the grain and so marring the finished surface of the concrete. Forms that are to be used repeatedly should be coated with asphalt paint, varnish, or several coats of boiled linseed oil rubbed in and allowed to dry. Forms so coated may be used just as they are, or oiled as usual for extra ease in removal.

If oil is not available, wetting the forms with plain water just before placing the concrete may help prevent absorption and sticking, but this method is not so effective and should be used only in an emergency.

FINISHING CONCRETE

Concrete can be finished in many ways, depending on the effect desired. Walks and floors may require only screeding to proper contour and height. In other cases you may wish to give surfaces a broomed finish or trowel them smooth. Here are the basic operations in finishing horizontal slabs:

Screeding. The term "screed" comes from an old Anglo-Saxon word meaning "strip" or "band." To the cement mason, screeds are the side strips of a concrete form that mark the height at which the concrete is to be leveled off. Screeding, then, is simply leveling off the concrete by drawing along it a straight-edged or contoured board whose ends ride on the screeds.

Screeding should be done just as soon as possible after the concrete has been dumped and spread—before free water in the concrete has had time to rise to the surface, or "bleed." This is one of the most important rules of successful concrete finishing. *Screeding or any other operation performed on a concrete surface when bled water is present may result in subsequent severe scaling, dusting, or crazing.*

Do your screeding with a "strikeboard," which can be simply a 2-by-4 or 2-by-6, a foot or so longer than the width of the form. The working edge should be straight, unless you are making a walk or other surface that you want higher in the middle to provide better drainage. In the latter case, contour the edge as desired.

Move the strikeboard back and forth across the concrete with a sawing motion, advancing it a short distance along the length of the slab with each motion. Keep a surplus of concrete against the front face of the strikeboard as a supply to fill depressions as the board is moved forward.

Floating. If you want a smoother surface than that obtained by screeding, the surface should be worked sparingly with a "float." This can be a flat rectangle of wood, 12 to 18 inches long and 3½ to 4½ inches wide, provided with a handle on its upper face. Use the float to remove high or low spots or ridges left by the strikeboard, also to imbed the coarse aggregate so the surface is smooth enough for subsequent troweling. This operation must be done immediately after screeding, being careful not to overdo it and so bring an excess of water and mortar to the surface. Concrete is often floated a second time, after the surface water has disappeared and just before troweling.

Troweling. If a dense, smooth finish is desired, floating must be followed by steel troweling at a time after surface water has disappeared and the concrete has hardened enough so that no fine material and new water will be worked to the top. This step should be delayed as long as possible, but not so long that the surface is too hard to finish properly. Troweling should leave the surface smooth, even, and free of marks and ripples. If there are wet spots on the surface, do not trowel these spots until the water has been absorbed, has evaporated, or has been mopped up. Never sprinkle dry cement on such spots to take up the water; this will only produce a surface that will later scale off.

Brooming. A nonskid surface can be produced by brushing or brooming. The brushed surface is made by drawing a soft-bristled push broom over the slab just after it has been steel-troweled. For coarser textures, a stiffer bristled broom may be used.

CURING CONCRETE

The first requirement for strong, high-quality concrete is the proper proportion between water and cement; the second, and more often neglected, requirement is proper curing.

Concrete hardens because of a chemical reaction between cement and water. This reaction starts immediately they are mixed and causes the concrete to set solid in a matter of hours. Hardening, however, does not stop with this setting. If you do not let the concrete dry out, it will continue to harden for about a month. Tests have shown that if you keep concrete warm and moist during a curing period as long as 28 days, it will be more than twice as strong as it would have been if you had kept it that way only 3 days. Concrete that is allowed to dry before it is fully cured is relatively soft, porous, and of poor appearance.

For concrete to cure thoroughly, it must be protected so that little or no moisture is lost during the curing or hardening period. Newly placed concrete must not be allowed to dry out too fast and so must be protected from the sun and from drying winds. This may be done in the beginning with burlap or canvas coverings kept constantly wet.

One method of moist curing that is applicable to horizontal surfaces after the concrete has become surface hard is called "ponding." This is accomplished by building an earth dike around the edges of the concrete slab and keeping the slab covered with an inch or so of water. Another method that may be used under the same conditions is to first wet the surface thoroughly with a fine spray of water and then keep it covered during the entire curing time with a sheet of plastic film. The plastic sheet should be large enough to cover the width and edges of the slab. If several sheets must be used, lap them at least 12 inches. Weight down the joints and edges to keep the sheets moisture-tight and in place.

The barest minimum of curing time should be 3 days, though 14 days would make the concrete much stronger. A curing period of 28 days at 70 degrees F is considered standard for greatest strength.

How the proportion of water to cement and the length of proper curing both affect the strength of the resulting concrete is shown in the accompanying graph.

CONCRETES FOR SPECIAL PURPOSES

Air-entrained concrete. By adding to the concrete mix a small amount of a chemical called an air-entraining agent, billions of microscopic air bubbles are formed in the resulting concrete. These change the basic structure of the concrete, making it more workable during mixing, laying, and finishing, and stronger and more durable after it has set. Air-entrained concrete also has superior resistance to scaling caused by alternate freezing and thawing as well as that caused by salts used to melt snow and ice.

You can buy ready-mixed air-entrained concrete from producers in the colder parts of the country.

EFFECT OF WATER AND CURING TIME ON CONCRETE

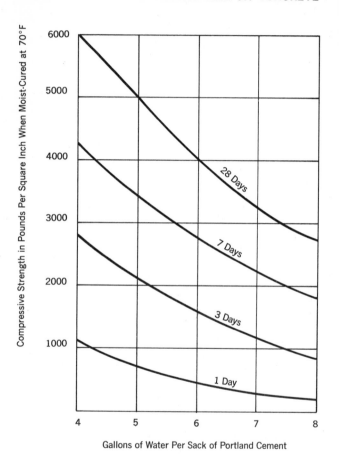

Gallons of Water Per Sack of Portland Cement

Or you can buy cement by the bag with the air-entrained chemical already incorporated in it. This is designated as Type IA portland cement, and the bag is so labeled. Less water should be mixed with air-entrained concrete than with ordinary concrete for an otherwise similar mix.

Lightweight concrete. Normal portland-cement concrete weighs about 145 pounds per cubic foot. By using special lightweight aggregates, concrete can be made weighing only 40 to 110 pounds per cubic foot. Such concretes are used for concrete blocks, for filler material where high strength is not necessary, for fireproofing steel, and for concrete that can be nailed. Lightweight concretes possess good insulating properties and they also have good fire-resistance, especially those made from burned clay or shale.

Aggregates for lightweight concrete are produced by crushing pumice, infusorial earth, lava, or tufa, a porous rock formed as a deposit from springs or streams. Others are made from cinders, by burning clay and shale, and by expanding molten slag with steam.

Because lightweight aggregates vary in their uses and mixing proportions, buy them only from reliable dealers who understand their characteristics and can give you definite instructions for making concrete with them.

Another type of lightweight concrete can be made by adding a chemical compound to standard concrete. This compound causes a gas to form in the mix, expanding it and thus reducing its weight.

Porous concrete through which water can easily pass can be made by omitting sand and using coarse aggregate only. Such concrete is frequently used for drain tile, in which the mix proportions are 5 parts of pea gravel by weight to 1 part of cement. The maximum size particle in the pea gravel should be ⅜ inch and the smallest 3/16 inch. Porous concrete is put in place without much tamping, since tamping tends to overconsolidate it and so reduces its porosity. If cured for about 7 days under conditions recommended for standard portland-cement concrete, the compressive strength of porous concrete should be at least 1,000 pounds per square inch.

Grout is a special sand-cement mortar made for such uses as sealing cracks, sealing the joints of precast pipe and filling the space between the bed plates of machinery and foundations. The primary requisite of grout is that it should not shrink. To meet this requirement, mortar used for grouting should be as dry as possible. Shrinkage can also be reduced by prolonged mixing and by the addition of a small amount of aluminum powder.

Aluminum powder mixed in concrete causes the concrete to swell. Thus, by blending in just the right amount, the natural shrinkage of a mortar can be balanced. Only extremely small amounts of aluminum are needed. One teaspoon per sack of cement has been found satisfactory in many cases. The aluminum powder should be mixed thoroughly with fine sand first, because unmixed powder tends to float. One pound of sand-aluminum powder mixture should contain enough aluminum for a batch of mortar that you can place completely in not more than 45 minutes after mixing.

Watertight concrete must be as dense as possible and must be moist-cured for a longer period than would be necessary if watertightness was not important. Here are the main requirements:

1. Do not use more than 6 gallons of water per sack of cement.
2. Use aggregates that are sound and of low porosity.
3. Place the concrete properly and compact it thoroughly.
4. Keep the concrete moist and at a temperature of more than 50 degrees F for at least 7 days.

The most effective way to prevent entirely the passage of water through concrete is to sandwich a membrane of waterproof material between two concrete layers. On horizontal surfaces, the method ordinarily used is to first coat the surface to be waterproofed with hot roofing asphalt. This can be applied with a mop as soon as the concrete surface is dry enough to allow the hot asphalt to stick. One layer of roofing felt is placed on this coating while it is still hot. The felt is then mopped with hot asphalt and a second layer of felt is applied which is then also coated with asphalt.

On vertical surfaces a thick coat of fibrous tar or asphalt cement is trowelled on and a layer of flexible tar or asphalt-treated burlap is imbedded in this coat.

On either horizontal or vertical surfaces, the membrane should be protected with an outer coating of either 3 inches of concrete or 1 course of brick.

Waterproofing compounds are sometimes added to the concrete mix or applied as a surface wash to the finished concrete. As they do not affect the strength, setting, or curing of new concrete, and may also be applied to old concrete, the washes are generally preferable. These include tar coatings, asphalt emulsions, and special portland cement paints. For best results, surface washes should be applied on the surface where the water enters. Because they vary so in nature, they should be applied according to the manufacturer's specifications.

HOT WEATHER CONCRETING

Making concrete in hot weather poses special problems, among which are reduction in strength and the cracking of flat surfaces due to rapid drying. Concrete also may harden before it can be consolidated because of rapid setting of the cement and excessive absorption of mixing water. This makes it difficult to finish flat surfaces.

The most important considerations in hot weather concreting are to keep materials and mixed concrete cooler than 90 degrees F, to prevent absorption, to protect against too rapid evaporation, to place the concrete without delay, and to begin curing immediately. Here are a few specific suggestions:

1. During extremely hot weather, start jobs in the late afternoon.

2. Sprinkle stockpiles of coarse aggregate with water to cool the material by evaporation. Chill the mixing water by refrigeration or with ice—making sure, however, that the ice has all melted before placing the concrete.

3. To prevent absorption of water from the mix, sprinkle the wood forms and the surface on which the concrete is to be placed with water just before the concrete is laid. Sprinkle coarse aggregates just before they are added to the batch.

4. Erect windbreaks of canvas or polyethylene sheet to prevent strong, hot winds from drying exposed surfaces while they are being finished.

5. Place concrete as soon after mixing as possible. Level it immediately. Then cover it with a temporary cover of burlap kept continuously wet. When hard enough for final finishing, uncover and finish only a small area at a time, protecting it again after finishing by replacing the wet cover.

6. Start curing as soon as the surface is hard enough to resist marring. In extremely hot weather use the "ponding" method described under "Curing" for at least the first 12 hours. After that, keep the concrete *continuously* wet to avoid alternate wetting and drying. Cure for at least 7 days.

COLD WEATHER CONCRETING

Concrete may be placed in winter provided it is protected against freezing. A single cycle of freezing and thawing during the first few days may not lower the eventual strength of the concrete, but it will decrease its watertightness and reduce its resistance to weathering. Several such cycles at an early age, however, will permanently affect its strength, water resistance, and wearing qualities. This is the reason why walks and driveways placed late in the fall often deteriorate within a few years. Below are some of the steps to follow to avoid cold weather problems:

1. When the air temperature is very low, you must heat the materials. The temperature of the concrete as it is placed in the forms should be between 50 and 70 degrees F. If the air temperature is between 30 and 40 degrees, heat the mixing water, If the temperature is below 30 degrees, heat the sand also, and sometimes the coarse aggregate. Be sure no lumps of frozen aggregate are in the concrete when it is placed. To prevent flash setting of the concrete do not, however, overheat the materials. Water temperature should be kept below 140 degrees F. Do not place concrete on frozen ground. Thawing will produce unequal settling.

2. Accelerators to speed the setting of the concrete may be used with care. About 1 pound of calcium chloride per sack of cement will hasten hardening safely. Add it in the form of a solution, considered as part of the mixing water. Never use more than 2 pounds per sack because of the danger of flash set. Never use antifreeze compounds or other materials to lower the freezing point of concrete. The amounts required will seriously reduce the strength and wearing qualities of the concrete.

3. When using normal portland cement, keep the temperature at 70 degrees F for the first 3 days, or 50 degrees F for 5 days. Do not let concrete freeze for

the next 4 days. Then let concrete cool gradually at the rate of 1 to 2 degrees per hour until it reaches the outside temperature.

4. In many cases a thick blanket of straw or other insulating material is sufficient protection during curing for slabs on the ground. At very low temperatures, however, housings of wood, insulation board, waterproofed paper or tarpaulins over wood frames, plus artificial heat, may be necessary. Moist, warm air should be circulated between slab and housing. If the concrete is indoors, and heating units are used, be sure to keep the concrete moist by sprinkling it or evaporating water into the air.

PREVENTING SURFACE DEFECTS

Many defects that soon develop on the surface of new concrete are caused by improper construction techniques, or by these combined with unsuitable weather. Here are some of the most common defects, with suggestions on how to prevent them:

Scaling

In this the surface of a hardened slab breaks away in scales up to about 3/16 inch thick.

Causes	*Preventive measures*
Cycles of freezing and thawing right after concrete has been placed.	Keep the temperature of newly placed concrete above 50° F for at least 5 days when using normal portland cement.

Causes	*Preventive measures*
Later cycles of freezing and thawing in normal portland cement concrete, also the use of de-icing salts in connection with them.	Coat cured concrete with linseed oil mixture described later in this chapter, or use air-entrained concrete in place of regular concrete in the first place.
Performing any of the finishing operations—such as screeding, floating, or troweling—while free water is on the surface. By mixing this water into the top of the slab, these operations will bring to the surface a layer of cement that is not bonded to the concrete under it. This layer will scale off after the concrete sets.	Don't perform any finishing operation while free water is present. First let the water evaporate from the surface, or remove the water by dragging a rubber garden hose over it.

Crazing

Crazing is the formation of an overall pattern of fine cracks on newly hardened concrete due to surface shrinkage.

Causes	*Preventive measures*
Rapid drying of the slab surface generally caused by hot sun, high air tem-	Cover with burlap or canvas immediately after screeding or leveling the

Causes	Preventive measures
perature, drying winds, or any combination of these.	surface of the newly placed concrete. Keep this cloth damp until ready for floating and troweling. Begin the moist cure of the concrete as soon as possible without marring the surface.
Second floating and troweling while there is too much moisture on the surface or while the concrete is still too plastic. Doing this will bring too much water and fine materials to the surface. If the surface water then evaporates too fast, the result may be shrinking and crazing.	Don't start second floating and troweling until excess moisture has evaporated, and the concrete has begun to set. To avoid excess moisture, increase the amount of fine and coarse aggregate in the mix or use air-entrained concrete.

Dusting

This is the appearance of a powdery coating on the surface of newly hardened concrete.

Causes	Preventive measures
Too much clay or silt in the concrete. These harmful materials degrade the cement at the surface, causing it later to dust off.	Use only clean and well-graded coarse and fine aggregate.

Causes	*Preventive measures*
Second floating and troweling while there is still excess surface water on the concrete slab.	Delay these operations until all free water has disappeared from the surface and the concrete has started its initial set.
Dry heat from winter-protection heaters may lower the relative humidity around the concrete excessively, causing the concrete to dry out too fast. This will produce weak concrete as well as dusting by preventing proper hydration of the cement.	Place water jackets on the heaters to increase the relative humidity, and employ any of the previously described methods for moist curing. Move the heaters periodically so that no area will become overheated.
No curing or insufficient curing.	Proper curing for sufficient time is necessary. Uncured concrete will be weak and its surface easily worn off by foot traffic.

COLD WEATHER TREATMENT FOR CONCRETE

Winter damage to driveways, sidewalks, steps, patios, and other structures of exposed concrete is caused by repeated cycles of freezing and thawing of water entrapped in the pores of the concrete. It takes the form of scaling and pitting known to the cement trade as "spalling." The process is aggravated by the use of salt and other de-icing chemicals.

You can largely prevent spalling by the application of an inexpensive compound you can make from linseed oil and mineral spirits. This compound has been endorsed by the Bureau of Public Roads of the U. S. Department of Commerce and has been used successfully for some years on highways, bridge decks, parking lots, and other outdoor concrete installations throughout the country.

To make it, simply mix together equal quantities of mineral spirits (obtainable in paint and hardware stores under either this name or as "turpentine substitute" or "paint thinner") and boiled linseed oil. The linseed oil reacts with oxygen in the air to form a tough film through which moisture and destructive salt solutions cannot penetrate. The mineral spirits makes the oil easier to spread and enables it to penetrate deeper into the concrete.

The compound is most effective if applied to new concrete at the end of the curing period, which is about 28 days. It has been successfully applied, however, after 7 to 10 days' curing. It will also inhibit damage to old concrete where spalling has already begun.

The compound dries and cures best if the atmospheric temperature is 70 degrees F or above, although it has been successfully applied at temperatures as low as 35 degrees F. The surface to be treated should be dry and free from dirt and debris.

On highways and other large areas the compound is generally applied by spraying. The best means of application for the small user is a cheap short-nap paint roller that can be thrown away after use. A long handle will make the work easier. A brush is not recommended, except to touch up edges, because with a brush the rate of application is hard to control and too much compound is left on the surface.

Two coats should be applied. The first at the rate of about 40 square yards per gallon; the second at about 67 square yards per gallon. The first coat should be completely dry before applying the second. At 70 degrees F or above, drying should be complete within a few hours.

Under moderate weather conditions and ordinary usage, the first application may last up to 3 years. Under severe conditions, reapplication may be required each year for the first 3 or 4 years. After that, every third or fourth year should suffice.

The treatment leaves no greasy residue after drying. At first the concrete may be slightly darkened, but this tends to bleach out and become unnoticeable with time.

HOW TO COLOR CONCRETE

By adding color to concrete you may be able to create many pleasing decorative effects around your home and garden. Stepping stones, patios, swimming pool decks, floors, walks, and driveways, and so on, may all readily be livened by this means.

To color concrete you have four methods to choose from: (1) mix dry color through the whole material; (2) place a foundation layer in the usual way, and then top this with a layer of colored concrete; (3) sprinkle the concrete before it hardens with a special "dry-shake" mixture of pigment, cement, and sand; (4) color a finished slab with stain, dye, or paint. The first three methods are outlined below, the fourth is described in the chapter on paint.

Pigments for concrete. Only commercially pure mineral pigments should be used, as other pigments are apt to fade or to reduce the strength and wearing qualities of the stucco, mortar, or concrete in which they are used. You may buy them as "cement colors" or "limeproof colors" under brand names, or you may get them under their chemical names as listed here:

Blues	Cobalt oxide
Browns	Brown iron oxide
Buffs	Synthetic yellow iron oxide
Greens	Chromium oxide green
Reds	Red iron oxide
Grays or Slate effects	Black iron oxide or carbon black. Common lampblack should not be used

These pigments may be blended to get intermediate colors or tones. Red, yellow, and brown dry pigments are the least expensive, blues and greens may cost up to three times as much. Use the smallest amount of pigment necessary to get the tint or shade required. Always weigh the amount you use, so you can duplicate or alter a future mix. Never, however, add more than 10 percent of the weight of the cement.

Concrete colored all the way through costs the most for pigment, but is the easiest to make. Full-strength pigments will usually produce a deep color when 7 pounds are mixed with 1 bag of cement. Extra deep shades may take 10 pounds, while 5 pounds will do for medium shades, 3 pounds for light shades, and 1½ pounds for a pleasing pastel tint. For cleaner, brighter colors use white portland cement instead of the normal gray type and also white sand. Regular cement will do for black or dark grays. To prevent streaking, blend the dry cement thoroughly with the pigment before adding to the mix. Mix longer than usual to further distribute the color, then place, finish, and cure as you would ordinary concrete.

Colored top layer concrete begins by placing a base layer of uncolored concrete in the usual manner. As soon as this layer has stiffened and the surface water has disappeared, place on top of it ½ to 1 inch of colored concrete, made as described above. This method requires a little more labor, but there may be a considerable saving in the cost of materials.

The dry shake method is the least expensive, but it is the most difficult to carry out satisfactorily. If you want to risk it, you'd better buy your dry-shake mix of mineral oxide, white portland cement, and special fine aggregate, ready made. The manufacturer will specify the area a given amount should cover.

After the concrete has been placed and screeded, and the surface water has evaporated, work over the surface with a magnesium or aluminum float. This will remove any ridges or depressions that might cause variations in color intensity, and also bring to the surface sufficient moisture to combine with the dry coloring material. Then immediately shake about two-thirds of the mixture as evenly as you can over the surface.

In a few minutes the powder will appear moist. It should then be worked into the surface with the float. Immediately this floating is finished, distribute the remainder of the dry-shake material evenly over the surface. Work this also in with the float. If you want the surface to be smoother, now go over it with a trowel.

Colored concrete must be cured as thoroughly as ordinary concrete. During drying and curing take care to avoid any staining by dirt or foot traffic. After curing, give interior surfaces at least two coats of concrete floor wax containing the same mineral oxide pigment used in or on the concrete.

HOW TO CLEAN CONCRETE

If concrete floors, walls, or walks become discolored beyond the capabilities of ordinary methods to clean them, here are several more drastic ones that should do the job:

Cleaning with mortar. Repair all defects in the surface, and let the repair material set. Then make a cleaning mortar of 1 part portland cement and 1¼ parts fine sand, mixed with enough water to make a thick paste. If a light-colored surface is desired, use white portland cement. Apply the mortar to the surface with a brush, and immediately after scour the surface with a wood float such as is used in making concrete. After an hour or two, remove excess mortar from the surface with a trowel, leaving that which sticks in the pores. After the surface has dried, rub it with dry burlap to remove all visible remaining mortar. Complete each section without stopping. Mortar left on the surface overnight is very difficult to remove.

Another mortar cleaning method consists in rubbing the mortar over the surface with clean burlap. The mortar in this case should have the consistency of thick cream, and the surface should appear almost dry. Wait long enough to prevent smearing, but not long enough for the mortar to harden, and then wipe off the excess with clean burlap. Let the remainder set for 2 hours, after which keep it damp to cure it for the next 2 days. Then let it dry and sand it vigorously with No. 2 sandpaper. This removes all excess mortar not removed by the sand rubbing and leaves a surface of uniform appearance. For best results, mortar cleaning should be done in the shade on a cool, damp day.

Acid cleaning. You can wash a concrete surface with acid if the staining is not too severe. First wet the surface and, while it is still damp, scrub it thoroughly with a 10-percent solution of hydrochloric acid (the "muriatic" acid sold in paint and hardware stores is generally a 20-percent solution of hydrochloric acid. If you use this, just dilute it with an equal amount of water). Then rinse off the acid with plain water. (*Caution*: Wear rubber gloves, a rubber or plastic apron or jacket, and protective goggles when scrubbing with hydrochloric acid. It is harmful to skin and clothing.)

PREPARING CONCRETE FLOORS FOR PAINTING

Because most concrete floors are below ground level, moisture may creep to the surface from the underside in sufficient quantity to cause the paint film to peel. Unless they have aged at least 6 months, there also may be free alkali on the surface which will attack the paint.

To neutralize the alkalinity and also to provide a slightly rougher surface for better adhesion, all concrete floors should be acid etched before painting.

To do this, scrub the surface with a solution of 1 part concentrated muriatic acid in 3 parts of water, using a stiff fiber brush. (*Caution*: Muriatic acid is corrosive. Mix in a glass or polyethylene container, wear rubber gloves when applying it, and don't spatter on clothes or furniture.)

Allow about 1 gallon of solution to each 100 square feet of surface. Let it remain until all bubbling stops and then flush it off thoroughly with plain water. If the surface has not dried uniformly within a few hours, some of the acid still remains, so flush it again.

Depending upon the porosity of the surface, the floor will dry in several hours or it may take a day or more. As soon as it is completely dry, it may be painted.

If the finish on an old floor is poor, it should be removed before etching. Rubber-base paints require special solvents, but most other paints may be removed with a solution of 1 pound of lye in 5 pints of water (or 1 13-ounce can to 2 quarts). (*Caution*: Handle lye with care, as it is poisonous and caustic.

Never mix it in hot water or in an aluminum container. Wear rubber gloves while handling it.)

After the paint has softened, remove it with steel wool or a scraper. Flush the surface with plain water to remove remaining paint and lye. Then etch with the muriatic solution mentioned above, applied at a rate of about 75 square feet to the gallon.

HARDENERS FOR CONCRETE FLOORS

Concrete floors that are not to be painted can be hardened, and so given longer life and freedom from "dusting," by treating with a diluted solution of sodium silicate prepared as follows:

Sodium silicate solution (commercial grade, 40° Baumé)	1 gallon
Water	3 gallons

Mix thoroughly and apply three coats, letting each dry a day or more before putting on the next. Succeeding coats will penetrate better if you scrub preceding coat with a stiff fiber brush and water.

Another hardener for concrete floors is a solution of zinc sulfate. This darkens the concrete somewhat, but produces a hard, uniform surface. Here is a formula recommended by the Portland Cement Association:

Zinc sulfate	3 pounds
Sulfuric acid, concentrated	¼ ounce
Water	2 gallons

Stir the sulfuric acid (*Careful*: extremely corrosive! If you spatter any on yourself or surroundings, flush off immediately with plenty of plain cold water) into the water and then stir in the zinc sulfate until thoroughly dissolved. Apply two coats—the second, 4 hours after the first. Before applying the second coat, scrub the surface with hot water and mop it dry.

REINFORCING CONCRETE

Here is a trick that makes reinforcing rods or mesh do the best possible job of internal bracing. Remember that concrete has great compressive strength, but much weaker tensile strength. Therefore place the rods where the concrete has the most tendency to pull apart under the load. In other words, if a slab is to be supported under its middle, with its ends unsupported, place the reinforcing rods near the top of the slab. On the other hand, if the slab is to be supported at its ends, embed the rods near the bottom. In either case, however, be sure that the rods are far enough from any surface so they are strongly keyed in the concrete.

REPAIRING CRACKS IN CONCRETE

For this purpose, use regular cement mortar, made by mixing 1 part portland cement with 3 parts of fine sand and adding enough water to make a putty-like consistency. Before packing in the mortar, widen the crack, dust it out, and wet it with water.

PATCHING A CONCRETE FLOOR OR SIDEWALK

A sidewalk that has settled, a crack in the basement floor, or other damaged concrete can often be restored by timely patching. Here are the steps that insure a good job:

1. Thoroughly clean the areas to be patched and roughen them with a chisel. Then go over the surface with a wire brush and wash away all dust and loose particles with clean water.

2. Dampen the surface that is to be patched, but leave no excess water on the surface.

3. Make a thick, creamy mixture of portland cement and water and brush it on the prepared surface. The patch should be applied before this creamy mixture dries.

4. Make a stiff mix of 1 part portland cement, 2 parts sand, and 2 parts pea gravel. Tamp this mixture firmly into the cavity and smooth off lightly with a wood float. After the concrete begins to stiffen, finish with a steel trowel or wood float. For narrow cracks where pea gravel cannot be used, use mortar made of 1 part portland cement and 3 parts sand.

5. Keep the freshly patched place damp for a minimum of 5 days.

WORKING WITH MORTAR

Mortar for Concrete Masonry

Good mortar for bonding together concrete blocks must have sufficient strength, good workability, and a property called *water retentivity* which resists rapid loss of water to blocks that may be highly absorptive. The latter is highly important, because concrete blocks, unlike some types of brick, should never be wetted to control suction before the application of mortar. The accompanying table shows formulas for mixes to be used under ordinary and under unusually severe conditions.

MORTAR MIXES FOR CONCRETE BLOCKS
(Proportions by volume)

Type of service	Portland cement	Hydrated lime	Mortar sand, in damp, loose condition
For ordinary service	1	½ to 1¼	4½ to 6
To withstand unusually heavy loads, violent winds, or severe frost conditions	1	0 to ¼	2¼ to 3

Use clean sharp sand of a type suitable for making concrete, but with all grits and pebbles larger than ¼ inch screened out. Mix the dry ingredients first with a hoe or a shovel until no variations in color are visible. Then form in a ring, add a little water at a time to the center of this ring, and hoe the mixture into the water until the combination forms a smooth and plastic paste. If the paste is too stiff, add water sparingly.

Mortar for Brick Masonry

Unless properly mixed and applied, mortar will be the weakest part of brick masonry. Both the strength and the watertightness of brick walls depend largely on the strength of the mortar bond.

The general instructions described earlier for mixing mortar for cementing concrete blocks apply also to mixing mortar for bricks. There is one exception, however, in the application. Porous or high-suction brick, if laid dry, will absorb enough water from the mortar to prevent the cement from properly setting. Therefore, such brick must be drenched with a hose and then allowed to surface dry before they are laid. A rough way to tell if a brick should be wet before laying is to sprinkle a few drops of water on one of its sides. If these drops sink in completely in less than 1 minute, the brick should be wet before laying it.

One of the types of mortar on the adjacent table should suit almost any kind of brick construction job.

Retempering Mortar

Mortar that has become too stiff on the mortar board to work with properly because of evaporation may be restored to workability by thorough remixing and the addition of sufficient water. Mortar that has stiffened because it has started to set, however, can-

MORTAR MIXES FOR BRICK MASONRY
(Proportions by volume)

Type of service	Portland cement	Hydrated lime	Mortar sand, in damp, loose condition
For general use in work below ground level and in contact with earth, such as walks, foundations, and retaining walls	1	¼	3
For general use, especially where high lateral strength is needed	1	½	4½
This is the commonest and most economical mortar for general use, and is suitable for most exterior walls above ground	1	1	6
Still less expensive, this mortar will do for solid load-bearing walls where compressive forces do not exceed 100 lb per sq inch and which will not be exposed to freezing and thawing in the presence of great moisture	1	2	9

not be thus retempered and should be discarded. If you can't determine the cause of stiffening, make it a rule to discard mortar that is more than 2½ hours old when the air temperature is 80 degrees F or higher, or more than 3½ hours old at lower temperatures.

Speeding the Setting of Mortar

By adding up to 2 percent of calcium chloride to

the weight of the cement, you can hasten the setting of mortar and cause it to gain full strength earlier. Dissolve the calcium chloride in a small amount of water and add this solution with the mixing water. A trial mix will give you an idea of the proper amount of the chemical to produce the desired rate of hardening.

Antifreeze Chemicals

The use of calcium chloride or other chemicals to lower the freezing point of mortars during winter construction should be avoided. The amount of such chemicals required for any appreciable effect would ruin the strength and other desirable qualities of the mortar.

SIZES AND TYPES OF BRICKS

Standard bricks made in the United States are 2¼ by 3¾ by 8 inches. English bricks are 3 by 4½ by 9 inches. Roman bricks are 1½ by 4 by 12 inches. The actual dimensions of brick may vary a little because of shrinkage during burning. Here are some common types of brick you have occasion to deal with:

1. *Building brick* was formerly called common brick, and is made of ordinary clays or shales and burned in kilns in the usual manner. It is used generally where it can't be seen, as in the backing courses in solid or cavity brick walls.

2. *Face brick* has better durability and is better looking than backup or building brick, and so is used in the exposed face of a wall. It is produced in various shades of brown, red, gray, yellow, and white.

3. *Pressed brick* is made by a dry press process and has regular smooth faces, sharp edges, and perfectly square corners. Ordinarily it is used entirely as face brick.

4. *Glazed brick* has one surface of each brick glazed in white or some color. This glass-like coating makes such brick particularly suited for walls in hospitals, dairies, laboratories or other buildings where cleanliness and ease of cleaning are necessary.

5. *Cored brick* is made with two rows of holes extending through its beds to reduce weight. It is just about as strong and as moisture-resistant as solid brick, and may be used to replace the solid type wherever it is available and the lighter weight is desired.

6. *Fire brick* is made of a special type of fire clay that will stand the heat of fireplaces, furnaces, and other locations of intense heat without cracking or otherwise deteriorating. It is usually larger than regular brick and is often molded by hand.

PLASTERING

Plastering whole walls and ceilings is not a job for the novice do-it-yourselfer. To produce finished plaster work over large surfaces is an art that requires long experience. In case you would like to experiment on a modest scale, however, here is the general procedure:

A professional plaster job usually consists of three coats: A rough or "scratch" coat is applied directly to the wood or metal lath; a "brown" coat is applied over this; and a thin smooth finishing coat is finally skimmed over the brown coat, which has been roughened to make it hold. The first two coats are made of gypsum or hydrated lime plaster mixed with sand and with cattle or goat hair (or in cheaper jobs, jute, wood fiber, or asbestos) to give the plaster greater strength. The finishing coat usually consists of plaster of Paris mixed with hydrated lime.

A typical formula for the scratch coat might be: 25 pounds of hydrated lime; 100 pounds of dry plastering sand, and ¼ pound of hair or fiber. These ingredients are mixed with water to produce a workable paste stiff enough to cling to the lath and not drop off. The plaster is applied with enough force to cause it to penetrate the openings between the lath and so anchor it firmly. The batch mentioned should cover about 2¼ square yards on wood lath to a thickness of ⅜ inch.

The scratch coat is roughened with a comb before it sets hard, to give tooth to hold firmly the brown coat, which is applied after the scratch coat has dried. The brown coat usually has a smaller proportion of lime and hair than the scratch coat—say, 12 pounds of hydrated lime, 60 pounds of sand, and 1 ounce of hair, for a batch that would cover the same area to the same thickness. This coat should be applied as straight and as evenly as possible, and within about ⅛ inch of the final finished surface desired.

For a white smooth finish, mix 10 pounds of hydrated lime with 2½ pounds of plaster of Paris. This mixture is then mixed with water to form a thick paste, which is applied to the brown coat in two or three very thin layers, one after the other. The brown coat should be thoroughly dry. To make the surface still smoother, go over it as soon as it has initially set with a brush wet with plain water, followed by a steel trowel. Dampen the surface only enough to soften it slightly, then buff it with the trowel.

REPAIRING PLASTER

Cracks, holes, and other surface imperfections on plaster walls can be repaired easily. If the ingredients are at hand, you can make up your own patching plaster or crack filler from one of the following formulas. If they are not, you can buy excellent and inexpensive ready-made preparations at your local paint or hardware store. If a hole is deep, the filling should be built up in two or three layers, letting one set before applying the next. For repairing very thin surface imperfections better use a ready-made *spackling* compound, a combination that contains a glue as well as plaster for better adhesion.

Filling Cracks in Plaster Walls

Cracked plaster walls can be repaired with plaster of Paris combined with a small amount of slaked lime and mixed with thin glue size. Mix only enough for about 15 minutes' work at a time, as this crack filler hardens quickly.

If plaster walls are to be painted with oil paints, the cracks may be filled with thick white lead paste to which either whiting or plaster of Paris has been added. If the walls have already been painted, the crack filler may be colored with oil pigment to match.

Patching Plaster or Crack Filler

An inexpensive patching plaster or crack filler can be made as follows:

Plaster of Paris	1 lb
Casein glue or yellow dextrin	2 oz
Whiting	2 oz

Dental plaster of Paris, if available, is better than the ordinary grade because it does not shrink so much. Mix thoroughly. Stir the mixture into water to make a thick paste, mixing only as much as you can use immediately. Apply to dents or bruises with a flexible putty knife, let dry hard, and sand clean. Apply more after drying, if not puttied up to level the first time.

To prepare a crack filler or cold water putty, the following may also be used:

Dental plaster of Paris	12 oz
Yellow dextrin	3 oz
French ochre or other dry color	1 oz

Mix thoroughly, then work up only enough with water for immediate use.

Corrective for Soft Plaster

The final coat of plaster sometimes develops soft, chalky areas in dry weather due to too rapid drying. These may be hardened by moistening with this solution:

Zinc sulfate	¼ oz
Alum	¼ oz
Water	32 fl oz

Plaster Stipple Coat

A stipple coat for use on interior walls or craft-work projects to which you wish to give a stippled and glazed finish can be mixed as follows:

Soft white lead paste	5 lb
Plaster of Paris	10 lb

Use flatting oil to make as thin or heavy a consistency as required. For most wall work, thin to a very soft paste that can be brushed on from 1/16 to ⅛ inch thick. Then stipple the coating with a floor-scrubbing brush dipped in water, a wad of crumpled paper, or the cut face of a sponge, according to the texture desired. Do not coat too much wall surface before stippling, and avoid any regular pattern effects. Let dry overnight before painting or other finishing.

5

Adhesives and Sealing Compounds

HOW TO CHOOSE A WOODWORKING GLUE

Do the many types and tradename brands of glues on the market make selection of the proper glue seem difficult? A few suggestions may help make it easier to choose. In general, glues fall into two main groups: (a) Glues from materials of natural origin, and (b) synthetic-resin glues.

Glues of Natural Origin

These include the animal, vegetable, casein, soybean, and blood glues. Only the animal and casein glues are of use to the home worker, the others requiring high temperatures and special equipment for their proper application.

Animal glues, also called hide glues or hot glues, are probably the oldest type of wood glue; they are prepared from the hides, bones, sinews, and hide fleshings of cattle. Most animal glues come in dry form and are prepared for use by soaking in water and then melting, and are applied hot. Liquid animal glues, ready to use at room temperature, are also available. Animal glues come in different grades, the higher grades being preferable for joint work, and the lower grades for veneering. Hot animal glues develop strength first by cooling and gelling and later by drying, and are often preferred for spreading on irregularly shaped joints and for furniture. The chief disadvantages of these glues are their relatively high cost, the importance of temperature control in their use, and the low moisture resistance of the joints.

Casein glues are made from casein curd precipitated from skim milk either by natural souring or by the addition of acids or enzymes. Lime and other chemical ingredients are added to the casein to prepare the glue for use.

Casein glues have sufficient strength for either veneer or joint work. They are used cold and when properly mixed can be spread with a brush. The moisture-resistant casein glues are intermediate in moisture resistance; they are superior to animal glues but poorer than synthetic-resin glues. Disadvantages of casein glues are their tendency to stain veneers, the relatively short working life of some types, and the dulling effect of the gluelines on tools.

Liquid glues include those glues of natural origin offered in ready-to-use form. Originally they were made from heads, skins, bones, and swimming bladders of fish, and so were called fish glues, but more recently they are also prepared from animal-glue bases by special treatments. These liquid glues tend to vary considerably in quality from sample to sample, but the better glues produce joints comparable to those of hot animal glue. Liquid glues are more expensive than other nonresin glues and find their greatest use for small-scale operations, such as assembly or hobby work. They are also used in place of hot animal glue when convenience is more important than cost.

Synthetic-Resin Glues

The synthetic-resin glues, or simply resin glues, were introduced as woodworking glues about 1935, but their development and acceptance on a large scale began during World War II and is still increasing. These resin glues are products of the chemical industry and originate from raw materials derived from coal, air, petroleum or natural gas, and water. Although the intermediate raw materials are available, the complex production methods required for the resins and the fact that some are covered by current patents make the small-scale manufacture of resin glues by the user not ordinarily practical.

The first two resin glues to be described are *thermosetting* types; they undergo irreversible chemical curing reactions to produce insoluble, infusible glue films in the joint. The polyvinyl-resin emulsion glues are *thermoplastic* resins, that is they do not undergo chemical curing during the gluing process but remain in a reversible state and soften on subsequent heating.

Urea-resin glues are available in powder and liquid forms to be used with or without catalysts, fillers, and extenders. Those suitable for the home worker are formulated for curing at room temperature, or about 70 degrees F. The gluelines are colorless to light tan and have only a moderate dulling effect on tools. Several types are available in small retail packages for small-scale shop work, and require only the addition of water to prepare them for use.

Pure urea-resin glues have high water and moisture resistance at normal room temperature, but tend to break down at temperatures of 150 degrees F or higher, particularly under conditions of high humidity. They are generally not recommended for exterior service.

Resorcinol- and phenol-resorcinol resin glues are dark-reddish and are generally supplied as liquids to which a liquid or powdered curing agent is added before use. These glues have high durability, and they cure sufficiently for many applications at temperatures as low as 70 degrees F. They are, however, the most expensive of the current woodworking glues.

Recent formulations of phenol-resorcinol resin glues are appreciably cheaper than straight resorcinol-resin glues and appear to retain most of the desirable characteristics of the resorcinol resins. Both types are used for laminating or assembly of articles where a high degree of durability to exterior or other severe service is required. Several brands of resorcinol-resin glue are available in small retail packages for home shops and are of particular interest to the amateur boat builder.

Polyvinyl-resin emulsion glues are the newest type of wood glue and are available in a ready-to-use liquid form that sets at room temperature to a colorless glueline. Unlike the other resin glues described, these glues do not cure by a chemical reaction, but set by losing water to the wood. They remain somewhat elastic and thermoplastic, which makes their use in highly stressed joints inadvisable. The polyvinyl-resin emulsion glues may be useful, however, for certain types of assembly joints where greater elasticity is an advantage.

Other adhesives. A number of new types of adhesives, developed originally for bonding other materials than wood, are finding some use in wood gluing. Among these are the epoxy resins and the rubber-base contact cements. Such glues, however, are generally reserved for small and specialized applications.

MAKING YOUR OWN ADHESIVES AND SEALERS
Hide Glue

Although the ready convenience of liquid, casein, and synthetic resin glues have caused these newer products to largely replace hot hide glue in the home workshop, this versatile and time-tested adhesive is still widely used in commercial wood fabrication and by the meticulous cabinetmaker. It combines quali-

GENERAL PROPERTIES
OF WOODWORKING GLUE

Property	NATURAL ORIGIN GLUES			SYNTHETIC-RESIN GLUES		
	Animal	Casein	Liquid	Urea-resin	Resorcinol-resin	Poly-vinyl-resin
Ready to use as received			X			X
Requires mixing for use	X	X		X	X	
Applied hot to wood	X					
Applied cold to wood		X	X	X	X	X
Colorless or nearly colorless glueline	X	X	X	X		X
Dark-colored glueline					X	
Tends to stain certain woods		X				
Working life of 1 to 8 hours at 75°F		X		X	X	
Working life of over 8 hours at 75°F			X	X		X
Low moisture resistance	X		X			X
Medium moisture resistance		X				
Good to high moisture resistance				X	X	
Limited resistance to elevated temperatures	X		X	X		X
Good to high resistance to elevated temperatures		X			X	
Can usually be purchased in retail stores	X	X	X	X	X	X
Relatively low cost				X		
Intermediate cost	X	X	X			X
High cost					X	

ties obtainable in no other type of adhesive at comparable cost.

Hide or animal glue can be bought by the pound in flake or ground form. If protected from moisture, this dry glue will keep indefinitely. The proper proportion of glue to water must be determined by experiment, if it is not stated on the glue you buy, as this may vary somewhat with a particular glue and job.

As a test, try 1 part glue to 2 parts water, measured by weight. Add the glue to the cold water and stir until the glue is thoroughly wet. Let soak for an hour, or until the glue is thoroughly swollen. Then melt the glue by heating the combination to 145 degrees F, either in a regular glue pot or in a Pyrex or stainless steel container heated by hot water. (It will lose strength if overheated.) After stirring into a smooth solution it is ready to use at 140–145 degrees F.

Don't make the glue too thin under the common misconception that it must thoroughly penetrate the wood in order to produce tendrils or hooks that will mechanically attach the glue to the pores of the wood. This can only result in weak and glue-starved joints. Hide glue does not work by hooking on. It apparently bonds a substance to itself because of a true electro-chemical attraction between its own molecules and those of the substance. (For example, hide glue will grip smooth, nonporous glass with a bond stronger than the glass!) For maximum strength of adhesion, make the glue just thick enough so it will form a thin but continuous film between the wood surfaces.

Here are the basic rules for making a perfect bond:

1. Apply the glue with a brush in a thin continuous film to one surface only of the matching parts to be joined.

2. Permit the glue film to thicken slightly to a tacky condition before applying pressure.

3. Apply enough pressure to squeeze out the excess glue and to bring perfect contact over the entire assembled area.

4. Maintain this pressure until the initial set of the glue is strong enough to keep the parts from separating.

When held at the recommended temperature of 140–145 degrees F, and covered to prevent evaporation, hot animal glue will keep in usable condition for at least 8 hours.

If further mechanical operations are to be done on a glued piece, it is best to wait at least overnight to allow the glue to develop its maximum strength.

If you use this type of glue in small quantities, it may be more convenient to buy it in combined powder form, ready to mix with water. For large-scale gluing, however, you may want to mix your own at the place where it is to be used. In this case, do not mix more than you need, or mix it too soon, for it will remain usable in wet form for only about 6 or 7 hours.

	Parts by weight
Casein	100
Water	150
Sodium hydroxide	11
Water	50
Hydrated lime	20
Water	50

Mix in glass, enameled, or stainless-steel vessels. Soak the casein in the proportion of water indicated for about 15 to 30 minutes. Add the solution of sodium hydroxide in water (*Caution*: Be careful with sodium hydroxide; it is caustic to skin and surroundings!) and stir thoroughly until the casein is completely dissolved. Then add the lime suspended in its proportion of water and stir until smooth.

A casein glue with better water resistance can be made by omitting the sodium hydroxide and adding sodium silicate and a salt of copper. Here is a formula of this type developed by the Forest Products Laboratory:

	Parts by weight
Casein	100
Water	200
Hydrated lime	25
Water	100
Sodium silicate solution	
40° Baumé	70

Cupric chloride or	
cuprice sulfate	2 to 3
Water	30 to 50

Stir the casein in the water, and let soak as in the previous formula. Stir into it the dissolved copper salt. Mix the hydrated lime and water in another container and, while stirring constantly, add it to the casein-water-copper mixture. In about 1 minute after the lime and casein have been united, the glue will thicken a little. Immediately pour in the sodium silicate and continue stirring until the glue is free from lumps.

How to Make Your Own Paste

The word "paste" come from the late Latin word "pasta," which means roughly a thick mixture of flour and water. Down through the ages this useful adhesive, used largely for sticking paper, has been made either from this combination, from water and a derivative of flour such as starch or gluten, or from some admixture of ingredients that looks and acts like its ancestor. Here are a few sample formulas:

FLOUR PASTE

This simple and inexpensive paste is excellent for children's paper work and as a general household paste for emergencies.

Wheat flour	4 tablespoons
Cold water	6 tablespoons
Boiling water	1½ cups

Blend the flour into the cold water to make a smooth paste. Stir this into the boiling water in a saucepan. Boil over very low heat for about 5 minutes, stirring and smoothing constantly to remove lumps. Use when cold.

STARCH PASTE

Here is a thinner paste that is just as easy to make:

Corn starch	3 tablespoons
Cold water	4 tablespoons
Boiling water	2 cups

Blend the starch into the cold water to make a smooth paste. Stir this into the boiling water. Stir until the opaque white liquid becomes translucent. Use when cold.

HOUSEHOLD PASTE

This paste may be used for making scrapbooks, mounting photographs, preparing paper decorations, and so on:

White dextrin	9 oz
Sugar	½ oz
Glycerin	½ fl oz
Alum	¼ fl oz
Water	15 fl oz

Stir the dextrin (which should be the *white* and not the yellow variety) in 13 ounces of the water and heat to 140 degrees F, with continued stirring, until completely dissolved. Dissolve the alum, sugar, and glycerin in the rest of the water. Add this solution to the first one and heat to about 176 degrees F until the combined solution becomes clear.

LIBRARY PASTE

For mounting valuable pictures and clippings on paper, here is the formula for a paste used by a number of important museums and libraries:

Wheat flour	18 oz
Alum	¼ oz
Water	4¾ pints
Formaldehyde	¼ fl oz

Blend the flour with part of the water to form a thin paste. Heat the rest of the water to a boil and dissolve the alum in it. Then stir the flour paste into the boiling water. Continue to heat, with constant stirring, for another 5 minutes over a very low flame or in the top of a double boiler. The formaldehyde in this formula will preserve the paste for some time.

WALLPAPER PASTES

Wheat flour	8 oz
Powdered rosin	⅓ oz
Water	1 quart

Blend the flour into 8 ounces of the water to make a smooth paste. Bring the rest of the water to a boil in a saucepan or the top part of a double boiler. Then stir in the flour paste, bring nearly to a boil again, and sprinkle in the rosin. Hold at this temperature for about 5 minutes while stirring and smoothing constantly to remove lumps. If the paste is too thick when cool, stir in a little more hot water.

Here is another wheat flour paste that uses alum in place of rosin:

Wheat flour	1 lb
Cold water	1 pint
Alum	½ oz
Hot water	2 oz
Boiling water	3 pints

Blend the flour into the cold water to make a smooth paste. Stir this into the boiling water, and continue stirring and boiling very gently until the liquid thickens. Dissolve the alum in the small amount of hot water and then stir this into the paste.

Some paperhangers prefer a paste made from rye flour, which depends more on gluten than on starch for its adhesiveness. Here is a typical formula for rye flour paste:

Rye flour	1 lb
Cold water	1 pint
Boiling water	1½ qt
Powdered rosin	½ oz

Blend the rye flour with the cold water to make a smooth paste. Stir this into the boiling water and sprinkle in the rosin. Reheat nearly to boiling and stir for several minutes until the paste is smooth. If the paste is too thick when cool, it may be thinned with a little hot water.

FLEXIBLE PASTE

The glycerin in this paste helps keep it pliant. It is useful for cloth or paper where the joints must be flexed.

Corn starch	2 oz
White dextrin	1 oz
Cold water	4 fl oz
Borax	½ oz
Glycerin	2 fl oz
Boiling water	1 qt

Mix the dextrin and starch in the cold water to make a smooth paste. Dissolve the borax in the boiling water, add the glycerin, and then stir the dextrin-starch mixture into this solution. Reheat nearly to the boiling point, and stir for several minutes longer until the paste is smooth.

HOBBY AND CRAFT PASTE

Made from household ingredients, this paste is good for fastening together paper toys and decorations, mounting photos, and so on:

Corn starch	¼ cup
Water	¾ cup
Corn syrup (Karo), light	2 tablespoons
White vinegar	1 teaspoon

Combine these ingredients in a medium size saucepan. Cook, stirring constantly, over medium heat until mixture is thick. Remove from heat.

In another vessel, stir together the following until smooth:

| Corn starch | ¼ cup |
| Water | ¾ cup |

Immediately stir, a little at a time, into the thickened mixture. Stir smooth after each addition. Finally, to act as a preservative, stir in:

| Oil of wintergreen | ¼ teaspoon |

The resulting paste may be used immediately, but will set up to thicker consistency in 24 hours. Stored in a covered container, it will keep about 2 months.

Mucilage

Gum acacia	2 oz
Corn starch	2 oz
Sugar	8 oz
Benzoic acid	50 grains
Water	20 fl oz

Use powdered gum acacia. Soak it in part of the water until it becomes jellylike. Mix the starch and sugar with enough water to make a smooth paste. Combine these mixtures, add the rest of the water in which you have dissolved the benzoic acid, and boil gently until the solution becomes clear.

Another mucilage substitutes glycerin for the starch and sugar:

Gum acacia	2 oz
Glycerin	2 fl oz
Benzoic acid	50 grains
Water	30 fl oz

Prepare the gum acacia as in the previous formula. Stir the resulting jelly into the water in which has been dissolved the glycerin and benzoic acid. Boil gently, with stirring, until smooth and clear.

Cement for Porcelain and Earthenware

Porcelain and earthenware articles that are not heated in use can be repaired or cemented together securely with ordinary sealing wax or stick shellac. The trick is to first heat the parts sufficiently so they will melt the shellac or wax. A little of either of these materials is then smeared on the edges to be joined and the parts are then held or clamped tightly together until cool. If melted wax or shellac is applied to cold edges, the joint will break apart at the slightest strain.

China Cement

Stir plaster of Paris into a thick solution of gum arabic until it becomes a viscous paste. Apply to broken edges of china and clamp the parts tightly together until the cement has hardened.

Marble Cement

This is a good cement for mending marble or any other kind of stone:

Litharge	20 parts
Quicklime	1 part
Boiled linseed oil	enough

Mix the lime and litharge thoroughly. Then work the linseed oil into this mixture to form a thick paste. It sets in a few hours, having the appearance of light stone.

Another marble cement can be made of the following:

Portland cement	12 parts
Hydrated lime	6 parts
Fine sand	6 parts
Kiselguhr	1 part
Sodium silicate solution	enough

Mix the dry ingredients thoroughly and then mix into a thick paste with the sodium silicate. The object to be cemented need not be warmed. The cement will set within 24 hours and be as hard as the original stone.

Aquarium Cement

This term is applied to various waterproof cements used in making tanks constructed of glass panels fitted in metal frames. One of the most reliable aquarium cements is litharge-glycerin cement, described in a separate item below. Here is another:

Litharge	3 parts
Plaster of Paris	3 parts
Fine white sand	3 parts
Powdered rosin	1 part
Boiled linseed oil	enough

Mix the dry ingredients well, and then work in enough of the boiled linseed oil to make a thick putty. Let it stand 4 or 5 hours before using it, kneading it occasionally during this time. Apply it by working it well into all the joints of the tank. Then let it set for several days. Finally test for leaks by filling the tank with water. Before putting fish in the tank, wash the tank out several times.

Cement for Roof Flashings

Where sheet metal meets chimneys, or where it is desired to repair open seams in a metal roof without soldering, use white lead and washed and dried sand mixed into a thick paste with boiled linseed oil and a few drops of a drier. If white lead paste is used, only a very small amount of linseed oil will be needed. The sand acts as a filler which keeps the joint from opening up.

Skylight Cement

Red lead, powder	8 oz
Litharge	16 oz
White lead, dry	24 oz
Linseed oil	8 fl oz
Varnish	8 fl oz

If white lead paste is used instead of the dry form, decrease the amount of linseed oil, adding just enough oil to give the desired consistency.

Oil-Proof Cements

A stopper for small leaks in water- and oil-containing vessels, which can be easily removed when a permanent repair is to be made, can be made of the following:

Gelatin powder	2 parts
Glycerin	1 part
Water	7 parts

Put the water in the top part of a double boiler, add the gelatin and let it soak for about an hour. Then heat the water to about 140 degrees F. As soon as the gelatin melts, stir until it is uniformly distributed throughout the water. Finally stir in the glycerin. Apply it warm to the leaks. It will stiffen rapidly.

An emergency stopper for small leaks in oil-containing pipe lines and containers can be made by mixing up a stiff paste of flour and molasses. Work it well into holes or cracks.

Where you can temporarily shut off pressure, a tight seal can be made with a stiff paste of sodium silicate or water glass with whiting or precipitated chalk.

For a permanent seal against oil leaks, as well as water and acid, try litharge-glycerin cement, described below.

The following cement will produce a leakproof barrier between joints on gasoline, water, or oil lines:

Powdered iron	1 part
Portland cement	1 part
Litharge	1 part

Mix these powders thoroughly and then stir in enough sodium silicate solution to make a paste of the desired consistency. The cement will harden in about 20 minutes.

Litharge-Glycerin Acid-Resisting Cement

Here is a cement useful for a number of applications for which ordinary cements would be neither practical nor desirable. It will withstand an unusual degree of combined heat and moisture. Its most conspicuous feature, however, is its resistance to practically all acids, provided they are not of full strength. Among other uses, it may be used for making watertight connections between iron pipes and porcelain fittings. It also makes an excellent aquarium cement.

Make it by mixing thoroughly—preferably by grinding in a mortar—enough litharge with 95-percent glycerin to form a paste of the desired consistency.

This combination remains soft for only about 10 minutes, then sets in the form of a chemical compound of incredible hardness. The addition of about 10 percent of inert matter such as silex, Fuller's earth or asbestos flock will delay the setting time considerably and also help prevent cracking.

Other Acid-Resisting Cements

Mix asbestos powder in sodium silicate solution to the consistency of thin paste. If allowed to dry for 24 hours, the resulting cement will resist the strongest acids.

Kaolin or China-clay mixed to a thick paste with boiled linseed oil also makes an acid-resisting cement.

Quicklime mixed to a thick paste with boiled linseed oil is a time-tested formula for a cement that will resist both heat and acids.

Iron Cement

Here is a cement that can be used to fill holes and cracks in cast-iron parts, make steam-tight joints, or cement iron parts into stone or cement:

Fine iron filings	40 parts
Flowers of sulfur	10 parts
Sal ammoniac	1 part
Portland cement	20 parts
Water	enough to make thick paste

First mix the dry ingredients thoroughly together. Then blend in the water, after adding a few drops of a wetting agent or a household liquid detergent to help the water wet the sulfur. Mix just before using, as this cement sets quickly.

It works by chemical reaction. Mixed with sulfur in the presence of an electrically conducting solution of sal ammoniac, the iron first rusts and then reverts to iron sulfide. In doing so, the iron expands, cementing the mass solidly together.

Sodium Silicate Cements

When mixed into a thick paste with certain white or colored dry pigments, sodium silicate solution or water glass will harden overnight into a strong and waterproof cement which can be used for mending and filling cracks in ceramics and other materials. Here are some of the colors you can make and the pigments to use to make them:

White: Whiting or precipitated chalk.

Gray: Zinc dust. This combination will make an exceedingly hard cement, which, on buffing, will exhibit the white and brilliant appearance of metallic zinc. It may be used to mend and fill ornaments and objects of zinc. It will also stick well to metals, stone, and wood.

Bright green: Powdered copper carbonate.
Dark green: Chromium oxide green pigment.
Blue: Cobalt blue.
Orange-red: Dry red lead.
Bright red: Vermilion.

Common or Glazier's Putty

This is an inexpensive and good putty for general use:

| Whiting | 16 oz |
| Boiled linseed oil | 9 fl oz |

Mix the whiting into the oil until it becomes of the usual putty consistency. Because of the differences in the fineness of the whiting, the proportions may vary somewhat. If you have time, let the putty stand in a tightly closed glass or plastic container for a week; if it has then become too soft, work some more whiting into it.

White Lead Putty

Professional painters often consider white-lead putty to be the best for all-round use. You can make this by mixing white-lead paste (white lead ground in linseed oil) with whiting. Work in enough of the whiting to make the putty stiff, but still tacky.

Colored Putty

Colored putty to match paint or to lend a touch of contrast can be made by mixing oil paint with the regular putty. Use colors-in-oil or the thick pigment from the bottom of the paint can. To prevent a streaky appearance, work it well into the putty.

For Removing Hardened Putty

Soap flakes	4 oz
Washing soda	10 oz
Hydrated lime	12 oz
Water	16 oz

Dissolve the washing soda in the water and then stir in the lime and the soap flakes. Apply this solution to the putty. After several hours the putty should be soft enough to be easily removed.

House-Joint Caulking Compounds

Whiting	10 oz
Asbestos fiber	4 oz
Boiled linseed oil	10 oz

Mix about three-quarters of the whiting thoroughly into the oil and then stir the asbestos into this mixture. If the compound is not thick enough, then blend in more of the whiting.

A more up-to-date, but more complex, caulking compound can be made as follows:

Asbestos fiber	10 oz
Asbestine	10 oz
Powdered talc	5 oz
Boiled linseed oil	18 fl oz
Drier	2 oz
Kerosene	4 oz

Because they become finally so thick, mixing this and the preceding compound is quite strenuous work and is best done by a heavy mixing machine.

Mix the drier with the linseed oil. Mix thoroughly together the dry ingredients. Then combine the latter into the oil by rigorous stirring. A heavy mixing machine would help here, but the job can be done by a little strenuous effort and a strong wooden paddle. After the dry materials are blended with the oil, work in the kerosene.

Pipe Joint Sealers

White-lead or red-lead paste, just as it comes from the can, is excellent for making threaded pipe joints gas-tight, water-tight, and air-tight. Apply it to the threads before screwing the parts together.

Commercial pipe-joint compounds may consist of the following:

White lead ground in oil	8 oz
Red lead ground in oil	8 oz
Linseed oil	4 fl oz

Mix the ingredients thoroughly and keep any that is not to be used immediately in an air-tight container.

For air and gas pipe connections. Several coats of shellac make an easy and effective seal for joints in gas and air lines. Just paint it on with a brush. Because a shellac film is brittle, the pipes can be easily taken apart at any time.

For steam-pipe joints. To permanently stop leaks in steam pipes where plugging or caulking is not practicable mix enough powdered manganese dioxide with raw linseed oil to make a thick paste. Apply this

to the joint or leak. Take off steam pressure, but keep
the pipe warm enough to cause absorption of the oil.
This cement should be very hard within 24 hours.

For resistance to heat, acids, and oil. Use the
litharge-glycerin cement described above, mixing the
litharge with about 10 percent of asbestos flock.

Gasket Compounds

Many cements may be used with rings of asbestos
and other materials to form gaskets. Asphalt, tar, and
pitch are simple ones. Mixtures that will stand heat,
steam, and acids can be made by mixing sodium silicate solution with asbestos, with asbestos and slaked
lime, with fine sand, or with fireclay, to form a thick
liquid. Paint this liquid on the rings, or let them
soak in it until they are thoroughly impregnated.

THE MANY USES OF EPOXY CEMENT

Epoxy cement or glue is one of the newer won-
ders of the chemical laboratory. You can't make it
yourself and it is too expensive for routine gluing,
but with it you can make money-saving repairs and
fasten together objects and materials that otherwise
would be ungluable. Besides wood, you can use it to
join iron, steel, aluminum, brass, concrete, porcelain,
china, glass, leather, and most hard plastics. Epoxy
glue sets to a hard waterproof substance that in most
cases is far stronger than the materials it joins.

Unlike most adhesives, the setting of epoxy glue
does not depend on the evaporation of a solvent but
on the reaction between two chemical components.

Epoxy glue comes in two separate tubes or cans. To activate it, blend thoroughly equal parts of the material in each. Apply to both faces of the joint immediately after mixing. Areas to be joined must be clean and, if nonporous, roughened with sandpaper. Parts should be pressed together and any glue that squeezes out wiped away. It is not necessary to apply pressure during setting, but the parts should be held so they don't shift.

At ordinary room temperatures of 60–72 degrees F, epoxy sets in about 2 hours and cures overnight. To speed up setting time to 20 minutes, and cut curing time proportionately, place a 250-watt infrared heat lamp about 16 inches from the joint. Or, if the work is movable and small enough, place it in a kitchen oven heated to 150 degrees for about 90 minutes.

If properly mixed and cured, a joint of epoxy glue will last indefinitely. It will withstand boiling water, can be repeatedly frozen and thawed, and is resistant to most dilute acids and alkalis. If resistance to heat is more important than maximum strength and flexibility (as in the case of chinaware and glass exposed to scalding water and steam) compound the glue using 2 parts resin to 1 part hardener.

Uses for Epoxy-Metal Compound

Epoxy-metal compounds consist of epoxy cement or glue blended with minute particles of metallic aluminum. The result is a full-bodied compound with which you can stop leaks in your auto radiator or house plumbing, caulk metal window frames set in masonry, fill dents in a car fender, replace threads in a bolt hole, or perform scores of other difficult and off-beat jobs around the home and shop.

Here you deal with two putty-like chemicals, packed in identical cans. Mix equal parts of each in a disposable container and apply right away with a putty knife or other spreading tool. Immediately after use, clean the tools with denatured alcohol, acetone, or lacquer thinner.

For bonding, use epoxy-metal compound in the same way you use the regular epoxy glue. Apply compound on both surfaces of the joint, press together, and wipe off the squeeze-out unless you want some compound outside the joint for extra strength. Pressure need not be maintained during setting, but the parts should be kept from moving.

For caulking to make permanent seals between metal windows or door frames and masonry walls, apply the compound as you would putty, pressing it to final form with the end of a dowel or other shaping tool. Epoxy-metal compound should *not* be used on exterior joints between wood and wood, wood and metal, or wood and masonry. It is too rigid to compensate for the unequal expansion and contraction of these combinations.

To fill a dent in sheet metal, apply only enough compound to make the surface sufficiently high for dress-up filing or sanding after the substance cures. There is almost no shrinkage. If dents on vertical surfaces are deep, apply several coats, letting one set before applying the next.

To seal a small hole in a car radiator or pipe joint, first drain out the water to remove dampness and pressure. Only a dab of epoxy is then needed to make a permanent seal. For a rust-out in a metal gutter, apply a patch of the same metal, imbedding the edges in compound and feathering them smooth.

To surface epoxy-metal compound, let it harden thoroughly, and then bring it to shape and smooth it with ordinary woodworking or metalworking tools and abrasives. Almost any kind of paint or lacquer can then be applied without special priming.

To renew stripped threads in a bolt hole, bore the hole to a larger diameter and fill with epoxy. After the compound has cured, drill an undersize hole through the center of the plug, and then tap it. Latheing, milling, and other machining operations can be done on epoxy-metal compound just as on conventional metals.

6

Household Cleaning
and Polishing

Many of the most popular proprietary soap and scouring powders, wall cleaners, wax and paint removers, paint-brush cleaners, and even denture baths are composed largely, if not entirely, of one or both of two cheap and time-tested household chemicals—sodium carbonate (sal soda or washing soda, or its dry form soda ash) and trisodium phosphate (TSP).

You will therefore find these old faithfuls included frequently among the following formulas. For further information on ways in which they may be used by themselves, turn to Chapter 8, Common Products with Many Uses.

CLEANING HOUSEHOLD METALS

Although today you can buy a special ready-made cleaner for every type of metal in your home, for many years and even centuries housewives kept their metalware shining by the use of common sense backed by kitchen chemicals. Here are a few suggestions of how this can be done:

Aluminum. Never leave food in aluminum utensils any longer than necessary. Leaving food in the pan, soaking the pan for a long time, or boiling an alkali in it will cause the metal to become pitted or darkened. Aluminum can be brightened by boiling in it a solution of a weak acid such as one containing cream of tartar or vinegar, or by cooking rhubarb, tomatoes, tart apples, sour milk, or buttermilk in the utensil.

Brass. Unlacquered brass can be kept in condition by daily dusting with a soft cloth. Spots on brass should be rubbed with hot vinegar and salt, hot buttermilk, hot sour milk, tomato juice or rhubarb juice.

Bronze. Clean with weak soapsuds, hot vinegar, or hot buttermilk. Rinse thoroughly and dry thoroughly.

Chromium plate. If soap and water won't clean it, use a soft abrasive paste such as whiting mixed with water.

Copper. Keep copper absolutely clean if you use it for food, otherwise it is dangerous. Follow recommendations for brass.

Iron. Wash in hot sudsy water or in hot water containing washing soda. When not in use always keep it thoroughly dry, because even slight moisture may cause it to rust. Remove rust with steel wool or scouring powder. If you want to store an iron pan for long, coat it with a saltless fat or oil, wrap it in paper or plastic tissue, and put it in a dry place.

Stainless steel. Clean off hard-to-remove spots or burned-on food on the inside of the pot with steel wool or a gritless cleaning powder. Clean the polished outside with just soap or detergent in hot water.

Tinware. Don't try to keep tin shiny. If you do, you will take off the very thin coating of tin and leave the metal underneath open to rust. Remove burnt foods by boiling washing soda and water in the pan for less than 5 minutes.

POLISHES AND CLEANERS FOR METAL

Metal polishes generally consist of a powdered abrasive suspended in a liquid or semiliquid which lubricates the abrasive and also helps remove soil. To be acceptable, the abrasive must be hard enough to remove oxide and other surface coatings, yet fine enough and soft enough so that it polishes without scratching. The vehicle must not contain any mineral acid or other material that might eat or discolor the metal.

Mild abrasives for tableware and other highly polished surfaces include jewelers' rouge (oxide of iron), powdered talc, and precipitated chalk or whiting (calcium carbonate). Harder ones for kitchenware and similar relatively dull surfaces include silica dust, kieselguhr (diatomaceous or infusorial earth), and tripoli (rottenstone). Vehicles may include thin petroleum products, soap solutions, and emulsions for liquid polishes, and heavier oils, soaps, and waxes for paste polishes.

As a rule, liquid polishes are more efficient where a great deal of tarnish has to be removed.

Equal parts by weight of the heavy, pleasant-smelling solvent, orthodichlorobenzene (technical grade) and whiting make a safe and effective cleaner-polish for highly polished kitchen appliances and auto trim. Apply with a soft cloth, and rinse off thoroughly after application. Orthodichlorobenzene is not considered flammable, though it will burn if deliberately ignited.

COPPER CLEANER

Oxalic acid	1 oz
Rottenstone	6 oz
Gum acacia	½ oz
Cooking oil	1 oz

Mix these ingredients thoroughly and add enough water to make a paste. Apply to a small surface at a time, with rubbing, and then rub dry with a clean soft cloth. (*Caution*: Wash your hands carefully after using oxalic acid. It is poison if swallowed.)

COPPER CLEANER AND POLISH

A non-poisonous but a little more complicated copper cleaner and polish is composed as follows:

Shaved soap or soap flakes	16 oz
Precipitated chalk	2 oz
Jewelers' rouge	1 oz
Cream of tartar	1 oz
Magnesium carbonate	1 oz
Water	

Heat the soap in the top of a double boiler with just enough water to bring it into solution. Add the other ingredients to the solution, with constant stirring, while it is still hot. The mixture will form a paste, which should be put up in wide-mouthed shallow containers before it is completely cold.

ALUMINUM CLEANER AND POLISH

Trisodium phosphate	1 oz
Finest tripoli	8 oz
Water glass	4 fl oz
Water	48 fl oz

Dissolve the trisodium phosphate in the water, stir in the water glass, and sift in the tripoli. As the tripoli does not dissolve, you must agitate the liquid when bottling it to make sure you distribute the tripoli equally.

Shake the bottle before use. Apply with a soft cloth and only in one direction. Polish with a clean soft cloth.

PEWTER CLEANERS

For brilliantly polished pewter use polishing rouge rubbed on with a soft cloth. Then wash with detergent or soap and water and dry thoroughly.

For dull finish pewter use finest pumice powder and water, rubbed on with a soft cloth.

CHROMIUM CLEANER

Orthodichlorobenzene
Whiting

Make a paste by mixing equal parts of these by weight. Apply with a soft cloth or soft paper towel, and rub off with a clean cloth or towel.

SILVER POLISH

An excellent and nonscratching silver polish that is also cheap can be made on the spot simply by moistening precipitated chalk or finely powdered whiting with household ammonia. Apply with a soft rinse dry. The tarnish should be gone.

LIQUID SILVER POLISH

If you prefer a liquid polish you can keep on hand, here is a simple one that also includes whiting and ammonia:

Whiting	8 oz
Soap flakes	4 oz
Ammonia	½ oz
Water	32 oz

Heat the water and dissolve the soap flakes in it. Then stir in the whiting. As soon as the mixture is cool, add the ammonia. Keep in tightly stoppered bottles and shake before using.

CLEAN SILVER ELECTRICALLY

Solutions and "magic" plates of aluminum or magnesium that are sold to clean silverware without scouring depend upon the principle of exchange of metals discussed in the chapter on household chemistry. A solution of ordinary baking soda (sodium bicarbonate) or of trisodium phosphate, plus an old aluminum pan, will enable you to work the same magic.

A rectangular cake pan is excellent. Place the silver so that each piece touches the pan. Cover with an almost-boiling solution of 1 teaspoon of trisodium phosphate or of 1 tablespoon of soda in each quart of water. After several minutes, take out the silver, rinse dry. The tarnish should be gone.

Touching the aluminum and surrounded by the electrolyte, the silver forms one plate of an electric cell. By action of this cell, the tarnish of silver sulfide is dissolved. Then the sulfur is separated and the silver is redeposited. Actually this method removes less silver than does ordinary polishing. The finish is slightly duller, however, a matter which may be remedied by giving the pieces a light buffing occasionally with regular polish.

Do not use this method on cemented pieces, as the hot solution might loosen the cement. Don't use it on oxidized or "French finish" silver, either, as it may alter the finish.

SILVER DIP FOR SILVER CLEANING

Instant silver cleaners are old. In the past, however, they were based on the very poisonous chemicals sodium and potassium cyanide. More recently, silver dips have appeared which use materials that are quite safe when in the concentrations required for the product. Here is a typical formula:

Thiourea	8 parts
Hydrochloric acid, 38%	5 parts
Liquid dishwashing detergent	½ part
Water-soluble perfume	⅛ part
Water	86 parts

To use, merely dip the silverware into the undiluted compound. The chemicals dissolve away the tarnish, leaving a surface of clean silver.

Despite its general convenience, the dip method has several limitations. Like the electrolytic method just described, it should not be used on oxidized or "French finish" silver, and it leaves a slightly dull or hazy surface which must be buffed occasionally to bring back a high shine. It may also stain "stainless" steel knifeblades if left in it too long.

To Prevent Tarnish on Silver

Good-grade furniture or floor waxes will give lasting protection against tarnish on ornamental objects of silver. They should not be applied to tableware or other items that come in contact with food. Apply two coats, letting the first coat dry and harden 2 hours before putting on the second. The "no-rubbing" liquid waxes go on easiest. If, after some months, they begin to yellow, they may be removed with soap or detergent in hot water, and new coatings applied.

NONTARNISH STORAGE FOR SILVER

Polyethylene bags, used for wrapping foods for storage in home freezers, make excellent nontarnish containers for storing silverware between use. They may be bought from the large general mail-order houses or from any store selling home-freezer supplies.

NONTARNISH CLOTH FOR SILVER

Soak cotton flannel in a solution made by dissolving 1 ounce of zinc acetate to each pint of water. Squeeze out excess solution and dry the cloth. Make cloth into a bag, or simply wrap silverware in it. Silver completely surrounded by the cloth won't tarnish. After removing the stored silver, wash it before using.

CLEANERS AND POLISHES
FOR SPECIAL PROBLEMS

To remove scorch from glass or enamelware

Make a solution of 1 part household liquid chlorine bleach to 4 parts water. Cover burned areas with it and bring solution slowly to a boil, or soak overnight. Rinse. (Do not use this bleach on *chipped* enamelware. It will react with the bare metal.)

Removing ink spots from wood

Ink spots can usually be removed from woodwork with a strong solution of oxalic acid. Prepare the solution by dissolving oxalic acid crystals in a small amount of water until no more will dissolve. If several applications do not cause the spots to disappear, apply the acid once more and immediately flush with sodium hypochlorite laundry bleach. Be sure to remove all traces of the chemicals from the surface with water and allow the wood to dry thoroughly before attempting to refinish it. (*Caution*: Oxalic acid is poison. Wash your hands thoroughly after using it.)

Rust remover powder

Rust remover in powder form can be made by mixing thoroughly 2 ounces of potassium bitartrate (cream of tartar) with 1 ounce of oxalic acid.

To use this, moisten the spot and place some of the powder on it for about 10 minutes. Then wash thoroughly in plain water.

Porcelain cleaner

Toilet bowls and the smooth, glazed finish in sinks, bathtubs, and wash bowls are made of porcelain, which is a type of glass. Care must therefore be taken to avoid scratching and chipping. Although harsh scouring powders effectively remove soil, they also damage the surface, making it harder to clean thereafter.

To clean these surfaces, wash them with detergent and water, and then rinse and dry them. If an abrasive is needed, use the finest powdered whiting. Or, if preferred, a paste of soap and whiting made as follows:

Soapflakes	¼ cup
Boiling water	1 cup
Fine whiting	1 cup

Dissolve the soapflakes in the water and pour into a wide-mouth glass jar. When cool and jelled, add the whiting and mix thoroughly. To use, apply with a soft cloth and rub lightly.

To CLEAN WINDOWS

For normally soiled windows, any synthetic dishwashing detergent in warm water will do a good job. Ordinary soap is apt to streak.

For very soiled windows, wipe off some of the loose dirt with a damp cloth or crumpled paper. Then wash with a mixture of 1 quart warm water with one of the following:

1. 1 tablespoon household ammonia, or
2. ½ tablespoon kerosene, or
3. 3 tablespoons denatured alcohol

Use a soft cloth, a clean damp chamois, or a squeegee to polish. Do not work in direct sunlight since the liquids may dry too quickly and so show streaks.

WINDOW CLEANING PREPARATIONS

A paste of powdered whiting and water can also be used to clean windows. Apply paste to glass, let it dry slightly, then remove with a soft lintless cloth or paper towel.

The following may do a better job, but is a little more complicated to prepare:

Powdered whiting	1 oz
Denatured alcohol	1 fl oz
Household ammonia	1 fl oz
Water	1 pint

Mix, shake before using, and apply to the window with a soft cloth or a spray bottle. After the surface has dried, wipe off any remaining film with another soft cloth.

Here is a somewhat similar formula that does not contain water:

Denatured alcohol	8 fl oz
Household ammonia	8 fl oz
Powdered talc	1 oz

Mix and apply as with the previous formula.

WALLPAPER CLEANERS

The basic ingredient of many wallpaper cleaners is gluten, which may be supplied satisfactorily by the use of rye or wheat flour. The flour is made up into a dough with plain water or with water containing about 25 percent of common salt. Preservatives may be added, such as sodium salicylate, sodium benzoate, or borax.

Here is a good cleaner if the paper is extremely soiled:

Water	1 qt
Salt	1¼ lb
Aluminum sulfate	1 oz
Kerosene	1 fl oz
Flour	2½ lb

Dissolve the salt and aluminum sulfate in the water, and heat the solution to a temperature of 180 degrees F. Remove from the source of heat and stir in the kerosene. Then slowly sift in the flour, stirring constantly to prevent lumps. Finally knead into a dough with which you can rub off the soil.

DISHWASHING POWDER

This can be used for washing dishes and for cleaning porcelain and glass. Mix thoroughly by shaking together in a box or bag for several minutes.

Trisodium phosphate	24 oz
Borax	2½ oz
Powdered soap	1 oz

To use, just add a little of the powder to the dishwater.

DUSTLESS DUST CLOTHS

Cloths that will pick up dust without scattering it can be made by saturating clean rags or cotton flannel with kerosene, hanging them up to allow the

more volatile parts to evaporate, and then rubbing
the oiled cloth on a wooden surface until it no longer
streaks.

Other dustless cloths can be made by saturating
similar materials with a mixture of 1 part mineral
spirits or benzine with 2 parts mineral oil, linseed
oil, cottonseed oil, or corn oil. Wring out the cloths
and dry them at room temperature. (If one of the
vegetable oils is used, be sure to dry the cloths in a
cool place with a good circulation of air to avoid the
danger of spontaneous combustion.) For a typical
cleaning odor, add a little cedar oil or lemon oil to
any of the above preparations.

A solution for coating a dusting cloth more heavily can be made without using a solvent. The following mixture is a sample:

Light mineral oil	12 oz
Corn oil	4 oz
Cedar or lemon oil	½ teaspoon

Saturate cloths with this, wring them out, and
hang them to dry in a well-ventilated place.

DUSTLESS MOP OIL

The preparations just mentioned for dustless
cloths can also be used for making or retreating dustless mops. Here is the formula for an effective mop
oil that has even the expected aroma:

Mineral oil	2 parts
Turpentine	1 part
Cedar oil	as desired

Abrasives for Cleaning and Scouring Powders

For general use, such an abrasive should be of 200-mesh or finer. It should be hard enough to do its job efficiently, but not so hard it will scratch the surface to be cleaned. Porcelain enamel, wall tile, and painted woodwork require the softest abrasives, such as talc, whiting, or diatomaceous earth. (Coarser abrasives used in some proprietary cleaners may take off the dirt faster at first, but they also roughen polished or soft surfaces, making subsequent cleaning more difficult.) Concrete or stone floors, bare wood, unpolished metalware, and other rougher or tougher surfaces may be cleaned safely and more efficiently with the harder abrasives.

Here is a list of the common abrasives used in cleaning powders—the softest ones first:

Talc: A natural hydrous magnesium silicate. Very soft, and so suited for scouring powders for porcelain enamel and tile, but not for a general household powder.

Diatomaceous earth (also called tripolite, kieselguhr, infusorial earth, etc.): A soft earthy material made up of the siliceous skeletons of small aquatic plants called diatoms. Although safe for all surfaces, it is too expensive for general household cleaning.

Whiting: A special finely powdered form of calcium carbonate. Originally powdered crude chalk such as came from the chalk cliffs of England, Belgium, and France, it is now also produced chemically. Cheap, and good for tile cleaners, but also too soft for general cleaning.

Volcanic ash: Material made up of volcanic dust, ash, and cinders. Cheap and of medium hardness, and good for general household cleaners.

Pumice: A relative of volcanic ash, but slightly harder. May be used for the same purposes.

Feldspar: A mixture of various aluminum silicates. About as hard as volcanic ash but usually whiter. This is a favorite when it can be obtained.

Quartz: Natural, crystallized silicon dioxide. Quite hard and apt to scratch softer metals such as copper and aluminum, though sometimes useful for very rough scouring.

Sand: Grains of disintegrated siliceous rock. It is mostly quartz, and just about as hard.

GENERAL PURPOSE SCOURING POWDER

Soda ash	12 parts
Powdered soap	7 parts
Abrasive powder	81 parts

Soda ash is a crude and dry form of sodium carbonate. Be sure to use powdered soap and not soap powder; the latter is a combination of soap with fillers and other ingredients. For the abrasive, use feldspar, pumice, or volcanic ash. Mix thoroughly by stirring and passing through a sieve several times.

SCOURING POWDER FOR TILE OR TERRAZZO FLOORS

Soda ash	5 parts
Powdered soap	8 parts
Abrasive powder	87 parts

Use same ingredients and mix as in previous formula.

SCOURING POWDER FOR FINE MARBLE FLOORS

Soda ash	4 parts
Powered soap	3 parts
Feldspar, pumice, or volcanic ash	93 parts

Mix as in last two formulas. So that it does not scratch the marble, 95 percent of the abrasive should be able to go through a 200-mesh sieve, and all must go through a 100-mesh sieve.

SCOURING PCWDER FOR KITCHEN UTENSILS

Powdered soap	20 parts
Powdered borax	5 parts
Soda ash	5 parts
Fine pumice	35 parts

Mix thoroughly by stirring and sieving as in the other formulas. To clean with it, shake this powder onto dampened utensils. Rub with a damp cloth and then rinse. Do not use on highly polished ware.

NONSCRATCHING SCOURING POWDER

Measure out 9 parts of whiting or precipitated chalk and 1 part of trisodium phosphate. Mix thoroughly by shaking together in a box or bag for several minutes. The combination makes an inexpensive, nonscratching, and effective compound for cleaning porcelain, brass, copper, nickel, and stainless steel. To use, just dampen with water, and rub with a cloth.

SOAP-TYPE ABRASIVE CLEANING COMPOUND

This is suitable for porcelain enamel, tile, painted surfaces, and other surfaces that might be scratched by harsher compounds.

Transparent soft soap	100 parts
Fine talc or whiting	30 parts
Soda ash	1½ parts

Mix these ingredients thoroughly in a solution of 2 parts of sodium silicate of 38 degrees Baumé dissolved in 25 parts of water. When thoroughly mixed, stir into combination 20 parts of a 5-percent solution of starch in water. Apply the resulting paste with a soft damp cloth.

How to Clean Marble

For routine cleaning of polished marble use only plain warm water applied with a soft clean cloth. If the marble has become soiled by ordinary use or exposure, try a solution of general household detergent (such as Tide, Fab, or All) in warm water. Ingrained dirt on unpolished marble may generally be removed by scrubbing with a fiber brush. In either case, rinse with plenty of plain water and immediately wipe dry with a cloth or chamois to prevent streaks or water spots.

Stains are easiest to remove if you can wipe them up as soon as they occur, thus preventing penetration into the pores of the stone. If this is impossible, you will get best results if you can first determine the general type of stain and treat it accordingly.

If you have trouble in getting marble cleaning and polishing materials, or prefer prepackaged kits for marble care, try "Marble dealers" listed in the "Yellow Pages" of your phone directory, or write to the Marble Institute of America or the Vermont Marble Company, listed among Sources of Supply at the back of this book.

Poultice method. If the marble is really grimy, the application of a detergent poultice may be better than scrubbing. Make a thick paste of household detergent and water. Apply with your hand, a putty knife, or a trowel in a layer at least ¼ inch thick over the whole area to be cleaned. Then cover with plastic sheeting or a damp cloth (which should be kept damp) for 24 hours. After that, let the poultice dry in place for another 24 hours. Finally remove the poultice, flush the marble with clean water and dry with a cloth or chamois.

Oil and grease stains are generally more or less circular spots, darkest toward the center. If you wet the area with water, the spot will repel the water and so appear lighter than its surroundings. Such spots are often the most difficult to remove. The poultice method, however, will generally do the trick. In this case make your poultice by mixing powdered talc or whiting (for small jobs, ordinary talcum powder or precipitated chalk will do just as well) with V.M.&P. naphtha, or a combination of equal parts of acetone and amyl acetate, to make a thick paste. As all three of these solvents are highly flammable, use

them only outdoors or in a well-ventilated room and
away from all fire. Apply the poultice over the spot
in a thick layer and leave in place until dry. If the
spot is not then completely gone, try again. Any remaining greaseless stain may usually be removed by
bleaching, as described below. When stain is gone,
wash the spot with detergent solution, rinse, and dry.

Tea, coffee, soft drink, wine, tobacco, and many
stains produced by inks and dyes usually respond
readily to bleaching. First wash the area with warm
water, and dry. If the piece is horizontal then pour
on a little household liquid chlorine bleach (Clorox,
Rose-X, Purex, etc.) or a 6-percent (hair-bleach concentration) solution of hydrogen peroxide. If you
use the latter, after pouring activate it with a few drops
of household ammonia. If the stained area is vertical, apply a heavy poultice made up of a thick paste
of whiting or talc mixed with either bleach. Let dry.
Remove, rinse marble, and dry.

Iron and rust stains that are fresh can usually
be wiped off or washed off with household detergent
solution. More stubborn fresh stains may be removed
with fine pumice powder or mild scouring powder
and water. If the stain has gone deeper, sprinkle
with sodium hydrosulfite powder (the dye-remover
chemical sold with some packaged household dyes),
dampen the powder, and leave for not more than
half an hour. Follow right away with a solution of
sodium citrate. Repeat the sequence, if necessary. Finally wash with water and dry. This treatment works

by changing colored insoluble salts into colorless soluble ones that can be washed away. It may, however, dull polished surfaces somewhat, possibly necessitating repolishing.

Copper and bronze stains from oxidized fitting or plaques are usually muddy brown or green. They can often be removed by applying a poultice of 1 part ammonium chloride (sal ammoniac) and 4 parts whiting made into a paste with household ammonia. Apply over stain and leave to dry. Repeat if necessary. Finally rinse and dry.

Superficial smoke stains can usually be removed by thoroughly washing and scrubbing with an abrasive cleaner. On fire stains from creosote that have penetrated deeply, try alternately the bleach and the oil stain removing methods.

Paint should be removed as soon as possible from marble to eliminate the absorption and spreading of the oil. First carefully scrape off the surface paint with a razor blade or knife. Then apply liquid or paste varnish and paint remover over the stained area. Remove with cloths after a short time and scrub with a fiber brush and a solution of household detergent. Bleach any color that remains with a poultice of hydrogen peroxide or liquid chlorine bleach as described above under tea and coffee stains.

Stains that are not stains. What is often mistaken for a stain may be just a dull spot in the polish of the marble caused by the etching action of acid-containing liquids or foods. You can determine this by comparing the gloss on the spot with that of the surrounding area. To repolish large dull spots, or pitted or scratched areas, requires the equipment and experience of the professional marble worker. Faint rings and small spots slightly rough to the touch, however, can be restored to a fine finish with a little patience and elbow grease. The polishing material universally used is tin dioxide, known in the stone trade as "putty powder" or "polishing powder." Buy the smallest amount you can from a marble dealer, monument maker, or chemical supply house.

To polish away dull spots, just sprinkle the powder lightly on the surface of the marble and buff steadily and persistently with a pad made of medium-hard felt (such as a piece cut from an old hat), short-nap wool carpeting, or chamois, dampened with water. Add a few drops of water whenever additional lubricant seems necessary. Also add powder occasionally, so that a thin, dry slurry remains on the marble surface. Rub straight back and forth, not in circles. After long rubbing, for a time depending on the depth of the etch, the surface will take on the characteristic shine of polished marble. Continue rubbing until this shine is uniform. Then rinse the surface and dry thoroughly with a soft cloth.

Toilet Bowl Cleaners

Chemicals for toilet bowl cleaning consist usually of sodium hydroxide (lye), sodium carbonate (washing soda) combined with sodium hydroxide, or sodium bisulfate, a by-product in the manufacture of nitric and hydrochloric acids.

Lye. The oldest and cheapest cleaner, lye alone works as well as any. To use it, flush the bowl and as soon as it fills again slowly shake about 2 table-spoons of lye into the bowl. Allow it to dissolve; then stir, and rub the lye solution over the entire interior with a long-handled brush or swab. Flush again. (*Caution*: Because lye is a very caustic poison, be careful in handling it. If you spill any on your skin or surrounding objects, wash immediately with plenty of cold water.)

Washing soda and lye. This is milder than plain lye and so takes longer to work, but is just as effective. Make it by shaking together in a covered and partly filled glass jar or tin can (don't use aluminum, as lye attacks this metal) 1 pound of washing soda with 3 tablespoons of lye (careful with the lye!). Flush the bowl and let it fill again. Then sprinkle into it about 4 tablespoons of the mixture, letting some coat the porcelain above the water line. Stir with a stick to mix, let stand about 15 minutes. Then rub the whole interior with a long-handled brush or swab, as above, and flush again.

Sodium bisulfate. This is the chief or sole ingredient of many proprietary bowl cleaners. It depends for its action on the formation of sulfuric acid on contact with water. For this reason, sodium bisulfate cleaners should be used only on solid porcelain bowls. They should not be used on bathtubs, washstands, sinks, or other metal or enameled fixtures. They are harmless, however, to plumbing and septic tanks.

Only the crude grade is needed for toilet cleaning. You should be able to get this considerably cheaper under its own name, or simply as "toilet bowl cleaner," from a supplier of institutional or industrial cleaning materials than under a brand name at the supermarket. Use it according to the directions for the cleaner above. (*Caution*: Handle sodium bisulfate as carefully as you would lye. If you spill any, flood the spot immediately with cold water.)

Drainpipe Cleaners

The basic ingredient of most drainpipe cleaners is again sodium hydroxide in the form of lye. This is used either alone or mixed with aluminum turnings or chips which are sometimes zinc coated. In the latter case the lye reacts with the aluminum to produce bubbles of hydrogen gas, which helps the cleaning action by producing a physical turbulence.

Drain sluggishness is usually caused by a build-up of hardened grease, hair, and lint. Lye does its job by combining with the grease to form a soluble soap, and by dissolving the hair and lint.

The best way to prevent the clogging of drains is to give them a mild treatment with either lye or washing soda every week or so. If you use washing soda, pour 3 tablespoonfuls into the drain or drain basket and run very hot water slowly through the drain until the granules are completely dissolved. If you use lye, put 1 tablespoonful in the drain sieve and flush into the pipe with 1 cup of hot water. Allow to remain 5 minutes, then flush with more water. (Be sure to rinse spoon thoroughly!)

To open a badly-clogged drain, remove all the water possible from the inlet of drain. Then slowly dissolve 1 13-ounce can of lye in 2 quarts of cold water. Use only a pyrex, enameled, iron, or stainless steel utensil—never aluminum. Stir with a stick or a plastic or stainless steel spoon. Then pour the solution (which will have been heated by the lye) slowly and carefully down the drain. In 10 minutes flush with water. (*Caution*: Lye is caustic poison. If you spill any on your skin or surrounding objects, wash immediately with cold water.)

Car Cooling System Cleaners

For many years nearly all automobile radiator cleaners were alkaline cleaners, consisting usually of washing soda, trisodium phosphate, a silicate of sodium, or of combinations of these chemicals. Sometimes a corrosion inhibitor such as sodium, potassium, or zinc chromate was added.

Although alkaline cleaners have no ability to dissolve rust or remove hard caked-on scale, they do cut through grease and flush out loose rust and dirt. As they are cheap, easy to obtain and use, and are satisfactory for most ordinary cleaning jobs, they are still widely used.

The general procedure in using them follows the pattern for most types of radiator cleaners. Drain the cooling system, add the cleaner, and fill the system with water. Then run the engine at fast idling speed for about 20 to 30 minutes. Cover the radiator, if necessary, to build up and maintain a temperature of between 180 and 200 degrees F, so that the thermostat valve remains open and the flow of cleaning solution is continuous.

At the end of this period, stop the engine and drain out the cleaning solution along with the dissolved and loosened scale, grease, and dirt. Then thoroughly flush the system with clean water.

The simplest and cheapest alkaline cleaner can be made by dissolving about 1 pound of washing soda or 10 ounces of trisodium phosphate in 3½ quarts of water in a 1-gallon bottle. Washing soda will dissolve more easily if you use warm water. In pouring, be careful not to spill any of either of these solutions on any of the car's aluminum, decorative metal, or paint. If you should do so accidentally, wash it off immediately with plain water.

An alkaline cleaner that will inhibit further corrosion in the cooling system can be made by dissolving about ⅛ ounce of sodium chromate in the trisodium phosphate solution just mentioned.

Saddle Soap

Once used chiefly for cleaning saddles and harness, saddle soap is now used for cleaning all kinds of leather equipment. Any neutral soap may be used for cleaning leather, though preparations most used generally contain oils and waxes to lubricate the leather and to leave a preservative film. Here are two sample formulas:

Soap powder	7½ oz
Water	36 oz
Neatsfoot oil	2½ oz
Beeswax	4 oz

Dissolve the soap in hot water. Heat the neatsfoot oil and wax together until the wax is melted.

Then pour the hot mixture into the hot soap solution. Stir until thickening begins and pour into containers.

Palm oil	3¾ oz
Coconut oil	3¾ oz
Glycerin	1½ oz
Powdered rosin	½ oz
Flake lye	1½ oz
Powdered whiting	½ oz
Water	17½ oz

Put first four items in the top of a double boiler and heat to 167 degrees F, stirring until the rosin is melted and thoroughly mixed in. Dissolve lye in water and heat the solution also to 167 degrees F. Then add slowly to first mixture, stirring until the two are completely emulsified. Finally stir in the whiting. (*Caution*: Do not spill lye on skin or surroundings; it is extremely caustic.)

Leather Polish

Montan wax	8 oz
Paraffin wax	6½ oz
Stearic acid	1 oz
Oil-soluble dye	⅛ oz
Turpentine	24 fl oz

Melt the montan wax, the paraffin wax, and the stearic acid over low heat in separate containers. Remove the montan wax from the heat, and stir in slowly the paraffin wax, then, also slowly, the melted stearic acid. Next stir in dye of desired color, or leave the polish colorless if preferred. When the mixture cools enough it begins to solidify. At this point add it slowly to the turpentine, stirring constantly. (*Caution*: Keep the turpentine away from all open flames.)

To Preserve Leather

The commonest cause for the cracking and peeling of the leather in luggage, upholstery, straps, and bookbindings is the gradual destruction of the oil in the leather. Prevention should start when the articles are new and should then be repeated every year or two.

For leather in good condition, the simplest dressing is neatsfoot oil, or neatsfoot oil mixed with an equal quantity of castor oil. These, or any other dressing, will darken leather slightly, but will greatly prolong its life.

Apply either the plain oil or the combination with a small swab of soft cloth. With a firm, rapid stroke spread the dressing in a thin film uniformly over as much of the leather at one time as is feasible. Rub the dressing into the leather until it is completely absorbed. After several hours, repeat the application.

To preserve the leather on new books and to restore that on old ones, one large library uses the following formula:

Neatsfoot oil	25 parts
Lanolin, anhydrous	17½ parts
Japan wax	10 parts
Sodium stearate, powdered	2½ parts
Distilled water	45 parts

In a double boiler melt together the first three ingredients. In another pan mix the sodium stearate and water. Cover this pan and heat gently until the stearate is dissolved. Pour the resulting solution in a thin stream into the melted grease, stirring vigorously as you pour. Allow to cool. Stir the cold mixture until it becomes a smooth ointmentlike emulsion. Then transfer it to screwcap jars.

The library applies this dressing with a flat varnish brush and the book is then set aside for a few hours. The binding is finally polished with a soft cloth. The same method may be used on other leather goods.

A large law library has preserved its sheepskin-bound books for more than 40 years merely by the similar application of medicinal grade white petroleum jelly.

Do not apply any dressing directly on gold lettering or decorations. This might loosen or remove the gold.

Bleaching Ivory Objects

Discolored ivory may be restored to its original condition by several methods. In one, immerse the ivory objects in a solution of 1 part household hydrogen peroxide in 2 parts of water for from ½ to 1 hour, or until the ivory is sufficiently bleached. Then polish them by rubbing briskly with a woolen cloth.

If the ivory has become yellow through handling or contact with dishwater, it is advisable to first immerse it in denatured alcohol or paint store naphtha. After drying, rub vigorously with a cloth dipped in household hydrogen peroxide or a 10-percent solution of citric acid in water. After bleaching, rinse the ivory with clean water and wipe it dry.

If the ivory forms the handles of tableware, care should be taken to protect the metal parts by first coating them with petroleum jelly and then wrapping them with paper to prevent the grease from spreading. If necessary, the process may be repeated.

Cleaning Concrete Floors

To clean an unpainted concrete floor, first wet the surface with clear water, and then apply a solution of about 2 to 2½ ounces of washing soda to a gallon of hot water. Sprinkle a good scouring powder uniformly over this. Brush the surface, and then rinse with clear water. Do not use straight soap on unpainted concrete because this often forms a scum of lime soap.

To clean painted concrete floors, wash or mop with plain water. Water containing a small amount of soap or detergent may be used on very dirty floors. Rinse with clear water.

How to Care for Asphalt Tile

1. Don't wash it more than two or three times a year.

2. Never use strong soaps or detergents.

3. Sweep or dry mop for cleaning.

4. Most soil spots, including those from cement, can be removed by rubbing carefully with a moistened, soap-impregnated steel-wool pad of the type sold for cleaning pots and pans.

5. Wax frequently for long wear. Use a self-polishing wax and apply in a thin coat. Fit all furniture legs with flat furniture rests that distribute the

weight. This is important. Roller-type casters and dome rests will dent and disfigure asphalt tile. Use large flat cup rests under pianos and other heavy pieces. Never slide a heavy piece of furniture over an asphalt tile floor; carry it.

Maintenance of a Shellac Finish

Shellac coatings may be cleaned with a damp rag or, where stubborn stains are involved, mild soap and water. Wood floors should never be flooded. Water gets in between cracks and causes the floor to swell or buckle.

Like lacquer, shellac will spot when exposed to standing water. Ordinarily this can be cured by rubbing with an alcohol-dampened rag. Where the damage is too severe for this remedy, or where a spot has been damaged by a burning cigarette or is otherwise marred, remove the old film, in the damaged area only, by sanding. Then apply 2 or more thin coats of 2-pound shellac to the area. Allow to dry. Finally buff with 2/0 steel wool until the new finish blends with the old.

Maintaining Wood Floors

Unwaxed varnished and shellacked floors. Dust these with a soft brush or dry mop. Rub the floor with an oiled mop or a cloth lightly moistened with turpentine, floor oil, or furniture polish. In general, avoid using water, but if surfaces are badly soiled, wipe with a mop or cloth dampened with warm slightly soapy water, and then with a cloth moistened with clear water. Wipe the surface dry at once and polish with an oiled mop or cloth. Apply wax to worn varnish surfaces.

Oiled and painted floors. Use a soft brush to sweep oiled and painted wood floors, and then rub them with an oiled mop or cloth. Occasionally they may be washed with slightly soapy water and rinsed with a wet cloth or mop, then wiped dry and polished with an oiled cloth or mop.

To re-oil a wood floor, apply one coat of oil made by mixing equal volumes of boiled linseed oil and mineral spirits. Mop the oil on the floor and rub it in across the grain with a stiff brush. Remove excess with a clean dry cloth or mop and allow 24 hours for the oil to penetrate and dry.

Waxed floors. Clean these with a soft brush or mop. Do not use oil, since oil softens wax. To remove dirt-and-wax film that darkens the surface, use a cloth moistened with warm soapy water. Turpentine works better, but if you use it have plenty of ventilation and be sure there are no open flames in the room. If water-cleaning has whitened a waxed floor, restore its luster and color by rubbing with a woolen cloth or a weighted brush, applying a little wax if needed. Remove spots by rubbing with a little turpentine and refinishing with a thin coat of wax.

Polishes

Car cleaner and polish

This liquid combination cleaner and polish contains a mild abrasive to help remove surface dirt, an oil which leaves a slight surface sheen, and a gum to emulsify the water and oil and to help keep the abrasive suspended.

Light mineral oil	22 parts
Kieselguhr	26 parts
Gum acacia	1 part
Glycerin	6 parts
Water	145 parts

The gum acacia should be in powdered form. To dissolve it readily, put it in a bowl and add a considerable part of the water all at once, then stir well until combined. Add the rest of the water and the other ingredients, stir well or shake together to produce an emulsion and put in bottles. Shake well before each use.

INSTANT FURNITURE POLISH

Many commercial furniture polishes of the straight oil type consist of light mineral oil alone, or mineral oil scented with a small amount of pine or cedar oil. To save money and get the same results, use any light medicinal or mineral lubricating oil, scenting it similarly if you desire. Apply with a soft cloth, and polish with another clean one.

FURNITURE WAX FOR OLD FURNITURE

This old-time and easy-to-make wax works well on any furniture, but is especially good for old furniture. Just melt 1 pound of pure beeswax in a vessel placed in hot water. (Do not heat over an open flame!) Then add 1 pint of gum turpentine, remove from the hot water, and stir constantly while the mixture cools. Package in a wide-mouth container before it really hardens.

Apply with a soft cloth. Let stand until solvent evaporates, and then polish with a clean cloth.

EMULSION-TYPE FURNITURE POLISH

This is an easy-to-make emulsion-type furniture polish that will give a smooth, soft sheen:

Beeswax	4 oz
Soap flakes	1 oz
Potassium carbonate	½ oz
Water	1 qt

Dissolve the soap and potassium carbonate in hot water. Add the beeswax and continue to heat gently until the beeswax is melted. Then remove from heat and stir thoroughly to produce an emulsion. Bottle, and shake before using.

WATER-FREE FLOOR POLISH

Carnauba wax	6 parts
Paraffin (melting point 48-50°C)	12 parts
Beeswax	12 parts
Gum turpentine	70 parts

Melt together waxes in double boiler (never over an open fire!) at about 90 degrees C. Remove from all fire and add turpentine in a thin stream with constant stirring. Pour into wide-mouth containers when cooled to about 40–45 degrees C.

WAX AUTOMOBILE POLISH

Paste polishes are applied to a car finish after it has been thoroughly washed or cleaned by other means. They require more labor in application than do liquid polishes, but the tough, durable film they produce is worth the extra effort. This relatively simple paste wax is a basic type:

Carnauba wax	2 parts
Ceresin	2 parts
Turpentine	3 parts
Mineral spirits or V.M.&P. naphtha	3 parts

Melt the waxes in a vessel placed in hot water (never over an open fire!). Add the turpentine and mineral spirits or naphtha rapidly in a thin stream, with constant stirring. Then cool the mixture as rapidly as possible, while stirring vigorously to produce a smooth creamy consistency.

This formula may be modified, as determined by experiment, by mixing other waxes with the carnauba wax base. Candelilla or montan waxes are suggested. By increasing the amounts of turpentine and mineral spirits or naphtha a liquid wax may be made.

7

Laundering, Stain Removing, and Dyeing

DETERGENTS FOR LAUNDERING

To clean a fabric, the essential steps are these: To wet the material and the dirt, to remove the dirt from the fabric, and, finally, to hold the removed dirt in suspension—that is, to keep it from redepositing or settling back on the fabric before it is rinsed away.

Water alone has little cleaning ability. The addition of a soap or other detergent to water increases enormously both its wetting and its suspending ability. When soiled fabric is agitated during the washing process, oily dirt is broken up into small particles, each of which is surrounded by a film of the detergent solution. As the dirt is lifted off the fabric, the detergent suspends it in the solution so that it does not settle back to coat the cloth with a gray film.

Soaps

The oldest and most familiar laundry detergent is soap, made since ancient times from fat and lye. For removing dirt from heavily soiled fabrics, a combination of soap and alkali is still probably the most effective. Although the newer synthetic detergents wet fabrics more thoroughly, they are not the match for soap and alkali in prying loose and suspending the dirt.

Laundry soap comes in two general types—"built" and "unbuilt." Unbuilt soap products consist generally of from 93 to 97 percent pure soap, with the remaining fraction made up usually of water, sodium chloride, and perhaps a colorless fluorescent dye. The latter becomes fixed on the fabrics during washing and glows with a pale blue fluorescence under daylight to make the fabrics appear a brighter and bluer white.

Unbuilt soaps are intended for laundering fine fabrics and lightly soiled garments. They are recommended for cotton, linen, and manmade fibers. They are relatively safe for most dyes and are mild on hands. Examples of unbuilt soaps are Chiffon Flakes, Ivory Flakes, Ivory Snow, Kirkman Flakes, Lux Flakes.

Built soaps contain at least 50 percent soap and varying amounts of alkaline chemicals. The chemicals, or "builders," increase sudsing, improve the cleaning action of the soap, and help to soften hard water so that less soap scum forms. Builders include sodium carbonate (washing soda), borax, sodium silicate, trisodium phosphate, and various other phosphates.

Common brands of built soap contain from 55 to 80 percent soap, from 10 to 30 percent builder, about 5 percent moisture, and usually a fluorescent-dye brightener.

Built soaps are general-purpose soaps for the family wash and for laundering heavily soiled cloth—rugs, grimy play clothes, and greasy overalls. They are harder on hands and on some dyes than the unbuilt soaps, and because of their increased alkalinity they are not recommended for silk or wool.

Examples of built soaps are American Family Flakes, Duz, Fels Naphtha, Instant Fels, Rinso, and White King.

Soap powders, or washing powders, contain only 10 to 15 percent soap, with the rest builders or inert fillers. These should not be confused with powdered soaps, which are true soaps in powdered form instead of bar, chip, flake, or bead. Soap powders are sometimes used for laundering but more often for dishwashing.

Synthetic Detergents

Synthetic detergents began their meteoric rise during the war years of 1939–1945 when fats became scarce. Since then their use in laundering has overtaken and passed that of soap. They are complex compounds having as their base ingredient a chemically synthesized by-product of petroleum or other nonfatty-based raw material. This base ingredient, known technically as a surface active agent, gives the synthetic detergent its principal cleaning power. The synthetic detergents are neutral in solution, and they do not depend on alkalinity for their cleaning ability.

Synthetic detergents dissolve readily, do not form scum in hard water, and have a pronounced ability to emulsify oil and grease. In hand laundering, however, the latter ability may be a disadvantage as it tends to remove oil from the skin and so may be drying or even irritating to the hands.

Some synthetic detergents form suds readily, like soap, whereas others clean with little or no suds. Like soaps, they come in two types—unbuilt (light-duty) and built (heavy-duty) and in liquid, powder, and tablet forms.

Unbuilt synthetic detergent products may contain only 30 to 40 percent detergent. The remainder in powdered products may be from 50 to 60 percent neutral salts, such as sodium chloride (common salt) or sodium sulfate (Glauber's salt); in liquids, 50 percent may be water. Both contain a fluorescent brightener. The neutral diluents contribute little or no cleaning power but are added chiefly to give greater bulk. This enables a detergent to be measured in amounts comparable with a less powerful product and to be competitive in price.

Unbuilt synthetic detergents may be used for the same purposes as unbuilt soap. Because they are non-alkaline in solution they are safe for dyed fabrics and for wool and silk which an alkali might harm.

Examples of unbuilt synthetic detergents:

GRANULAR		LIQUID
Dreft	Chiffon	Octagon Liquid
Gentle Fels	Fels	Swan
Swerl	Ivory Liquid	Thrill
Trend	Joy	Trend
Vel	Lux Liquid	Vel

Built synthetic detergents, like built soaps contain alkaline salts that increase their cleaning ability. These salts make the products alkaline in solution. In addition, they may contain any or all of the following: fluorescent dyes; carboxymethylcellulose (CMC) to help prevent loosened soil from redepositing on clothes; silicates to prevent corrosion in the washing machine; bleach to aid in stain removal; water softener to help combat hardness; bacteriostatic agents to help retard bacteria growth.

Manufacturers recommend built synthetics as general-purpose detergents for washing heavily soiled clothes. Both high-sudsing and low-sudsing products are available. The latter are made for use in certain types of automatic washing machines where high suds interfere with mechanical action. Examples:

HIGH SUDSING

GRANULAR

Breeze	Felso	Super Suds
Cheer	Oxydol	Surf
Duz Detergent	Rinso Blue	Tide
Fab	Silver Dust	White King Detergent

LIQUID

Dynamo	Fels—All Purpose	Wisk

LOW SUDSING

GRANULAR	LIQUID	TABLETS
Ad	All	Salvo
All	Cold Power	Vim
Spin	Cold Water All	

Suiting the Detergent to the Water

The type of detergent to use depends in part on whether the water for washing is soft or hard. In soft or softened water, soap is economical to use and does an excellent job of cleaning. Hard water, however, is an extravagant waster of soap. The soap combines with the minerals in it to form an insoluble scum that sticks to tub and washer parts and settles on clothes as gray specks that are almost impossible to remove. Hard water wastes synthetic detergents, too. These do not form a scum, but more of them are required to do a good job.

If hard water causes a laundering problem, you may either choose a synthetic detergent, or soften the water and use soap. In the latter case, it pays to soften both the wash water and the water for the first rinse. A water-softening system installed in the water-supply line is a great convenience. Or you can use a water-softening chemical, as described later in this section under Hard and Soft Water.

Suiting the Detergent to the Fabric

What the cloth is made of and the type of dye used also influence the choice of a detergent.

Wool and silk are damaged by alkali. To prolong the life of these fabrics, wash them therefore with a mild neutral soap or an unbuilt synthetic detergent. The shrinkage of wool fabrics from laundering depends more on the agitation during the washing process than on the type of detergent used. Agitation, squeezing, or other manipulation of wool should be kept to a minimum.

Cotton, linen, and synthetic fibers (acetate, Acrilan, Dacron, Dynel, nylon, Orlon, and rayon) resist alkalies better than wool and silk. So for these, the amount of soil and the type of dye are more important in choosing a detergent than the fabric itself.

For white cloth, be governed by the amount of soil. If light, use unbuilt detergent. For the regular wash and for heavy soil, use built products.

Fabrics with colorfast dyes may be treated the same way. If you are not sure about the dye, however, it is safest to use an unbuilt synthetic detergent.

In tests made by textile chemists of the U.S. Department of Agriculture, it was found that cottons washed in soft-water solutions of both unbuilt and built soaps came slightly cleaner than those washed in similar solutions of unbuilt synthetic detergents. Some of the high-sudsing built synthetics, however, removed as much soil as the soaps. In hard water, both unbuilt and built synthetics were more effective than the soaps.

Similar tests with manmade fibers came out about the same. All the detergents removed more soil from the acetate and nylon samples than from the others. Laundering fabrics of all the manmade fibers 75 times caused only slight loss in strength and little change in whiteness.

Suiting the Detergent to the Washer

.   In machine washing, the kind of detergent to use depends somewhat on the kind of washer. Because of their washing action, some machines work better with low-sudsing than with high-sudsing detergent. If this is so, the instructions should say so.

Soaps depend on suds for keeping removed dirt suspended, therefore enough should be used to maintain good suds. The cooler the water and the dirtier the clothes, the more soap will be needed.

Synthetic detergents suspend dirt in a different way, so the volume of suds is not necessarily an indication of the amount of detergent to use. Some detergents clean with little or no suds, while others produce a great volume of suds even when used in quantities too small to clean well. Follow the directions on the package.

Tips on Using Detergents

For laundering lightly soiled fine fabrics—
Use unbuilt soaps or unbuilt synthetic detergents.
For general laundering and for heavily soiled fabrics—
Use built soaps or built synthetic detergents.
For fabrics of cotton, linen, and manmade fibers—
If white or colorfast, use either soaps or synthetic detergents—unbuilt for lightly soiled materials, built for those more heavily soiled.

If not colorfast, use unbuilt synthetic detergents.
For wool and silk, and for blends of these with other fibers—

Use unbuilt synthetic detergents.
In soft water—

Both soaps and synthetic detergents, built or unbuilt, are suitable.
In hard water—

Built synthetics are the most efficient. Or soften the water and use soap.
If fabrics and color will stand it—

Wash in hot water instead of warm, since detergents are generally more efficient at high temperatures. Remove stains first, however, for some are set by hot water.
When using soaps—

Maintain a good suds.
When using synthetic detergents—

Use the amount recommended by the manufacturer. Some synthetics are high-sudsing; others clean with little suds. The low-sudsing types are especially suited to certain designs of washing machines.

Bleaching Agents

Bleaching does not remove ordinary dirt and is not a substitute for good washing methods. It is helpful, however, in removing problem stains, in reducing the natural yellowing of age in fabrics, and in some cases as a sanitizing agent.

Most bleaching agents are chemicals that oxidize the colored compounds in stains to colorless ones. If bleaching is necessary, you should choose a type of bleach to suit the fabric. For household use, there are two general types, chlorine and peroxygen. Following are suggestions for the use of these bleaches in general laundering; for their use in removing specific stains, see the article on stain removal that appears later in this chapter.

Chlorine bleach, the more powerful of the two, is the most effective in removing difficult stains and the yellow of old age from the bulk of the family wash. In its liquid form it comes as a 5- to 6-percent solution of sodium hypochlorite (Clorox, Rose-X, Purex, etc.) and must be used carefully and sparingly to prevent fabric damage. The usual dilution is 1 tablespoon per gallon of water (about 1 cup for top-loading washers, and ½ cup for the front-loading type). Either mix it thoroughly with the wash water before adding the clothes, or blend dosage with at least 1 quart of warm water before adding to the wash cycle. *Never pour it directly over the clothes.* Except for a variation of less than 1 percent in strength, there is no essential difference between brands of liquid chlorine bleach. It pays, therefore, to buy the least expensive.

Granular chlorine bleach (Action, Linco, Stardust, etc.) is initially safer to handle than the liquid, because its chlorine is not released until the granules begin to dissolve. It is better, however, to dissolve it completely before adding the clothes, as partially dissolved particles trapped in the folds of the fabric might cause damage.

Chlorine bleach should never be used on fabrics containing silk, wool, or spandex fibers, or on "wash-and-wear" materials with a chlorine-retentive resin finish. Such fabrics are usually marked "Do not use a chlorine bleach" either on the label or on attached washing instructions. The use of chlorine bleach on these fabrics usually results in yellowing rather than bleaching and may seriously damage them.

Do not use too much chlorine bleach or use it too often. Rinse it out thoroughly after use. Bleach carry-over will damage fabrics.

Peroxygen bleaches come in powder form and may contain either sodium perborate (Dexol, Lestare, Snowy) or potassium monopersulfate (Beads O' Bleach, Dri Brite, Glo). Though less effective than the chlorine type, the peroxygen bleaches are safe on all washable fabrics—natural and synthetic—and for resin-finished cottons. The sodium perborate bleach is totally effective, however, only in water of about 160°F, a temperature seldom reached in home washing machines. According to the manufacturer, the monopersulfate type is effective in water of all temperatures.

Bleaching by sunlight. An age-old method of bleaching is to spread wet fabrics in the sun. Some fibers, however, are weakened by sunlight, so keep such treatment brief and infrequent.

Hard and Soft Water

The water you use for drinking, cooking, and washing may contain the dissolved salts of calcium, magnesium, and other elements. If it reaches you with less than 5.8 grains per gallon or 100 parts per million (ppm) of such salts, water is said to be "soft." If it contains more, it is called "hard."

Hard water can be expensive in two ways: it wastes soap and synthetic detergent, and it forms scale inside pipes and boilers which may cause them to corrode, crack, or get stopped up.

Temporary hard water. Water containing dissolved calcium bicarbonate and occasionally smaller amounts of the bicarbonates of magnesium and iron is sometimes called "temporary" hard water. When such hard water is boiled, the bicarbonates are decomposed into insoluble compounds which settle out and leave the water soft.

Permanent hard water usually contains the sulfates, nitrates, or chlorides of calcium or magnesium, which must be removed by treatment with other chemicals or by distillation.

How to soften water. If you don't have a water-softening system, you can easily soften water for washing by adding one or another of common household chemicals. Washing soda and trisodium phosphate are the least expensive. These will settle or precipitate the water-hardness minerals. Sodium hexametaphosphate, sold under the trade name of Calgon, costs a little more and works in a different way. Instead of precipitating the minerals, it holds them in suspension in such form that they cannot produce soap scum. In either case it is best to add the water softener to the warm or hot water at least 1 minute before you add the soap or detergent.

Amount of softener to use. To find out how much of a particular softener is needed with your own hard water and a particular kind of powdered or flake soap, make the following test:

1. Dissolve ½ teaspoon of softener in 1 gallon of water at about 140°F.

2. Half fill a quart jar with this water. Add ½ teaspoon of soap, cap the jar, and shake vigorously for 10 seconds. If good suds form and hold for 5 minutes, the water is softened. Try again, using less softener, to find out if a smaller amount would do to make good suds.

3. If the ½ teaspoon of softener does not make good suds with the soap, repeat the test with fresh water, using 1 teaspoon of softener to 1 gallon of water.

4. Continue until the minimum amount is found that will make and sustain good suds.

Repeat this test, and make a record of your findings, for each combination of softener and soap that you use.

If you know the hardness of your local water in terms of grains per gallon or parts per million, you can soften it with washing soda according to the following table. Amounts needed are based on concentrated or partially-dehydrated soda such as Con-Sal or Arm & Hammer. If you use the ordinary crystalline kind, use twice as much.

To be fully effective as a water softener, the washing soda should be put in the water and given time to dissolve before adding soap or detergent.

Water hardness		Washing soda needed to soften 10 gallons
Parts per million	Grains per gallon	
50	2.9	.1 oz
100	5.8	.2 oz
150	8.7	.3 oz
200	11.7	.4 oz
300	17.5	.6 oz
400	23.3	.8 oz
600	35.0	1.2 oz

Washing Soda and Soap

One of the most commonly used "builders" in "built" or heavy-duty soap and synthetic detergent products is sodium carbonate. It is included to help cut grease and to make the soap or synthetic more effective by softening the water. Because sodium carbonate (in the form of "sal soda" or "washing soda") is considerably cheaper than the combination product, you can get the same results more economically by buying it separately and adding it together with unbuilt soap or detergent to each wash. For fabrics with average soil, just add 4 heaping tablespoons of sal soda to your washer or tub and less soap or detergent than you normally would. Use more if the wash is heavily soiled. To prevent the sal soda from caking, be sure the water is warm. Dissolve the granules thoroughly by stirring the water, and let the solution stand at least 1 minute before adding the soap or detergent. Do not use sodium carbonate for washing silk or wool, materials with which you should not use *any* built soap or detergent.

Trisodium Phosphate in Laundering

Trisodium phosphate (TSP) may be used in laundering in the same manner as washing soda. Because it is stronger, however, use only about half as much. For very dirty fabrics of cotton or linen, presoaking loosens the dirt so it can more readily be washed out. Soak for half an hour or more in a solution of 1 tablespoon of TSP to about 10 gallons of lukewarm water. Don't use hot water for soaking. Hot water coagulates starch and albuminous matter, making them stick more tenaciously to the clothes.

For washing cotton curtains, lingerie, and other delicate fabrics without soap, use 1 tablespoon of TSP to 3 gallons of water. Let soak for an hour, wash gently by hand, rinse thoroughly and dry.

For further uses of TSP, see Chapter 8, Common Products with Many Uses.

Uses for Sodium Hexametaphosphate

Don't let the name of this chemical frighten you. It is a common product obtainable in any supermarket under the name of Calgon. The great usefulness of Calgon in laundering is twofold: It can prevent hard water from forming on fabrics a dingy and insoluble scum, and it can remove this scum once it has formed. Either results in a brighter wash. Unlike other water-softening chemicals, Calgon is nearly neutral rather than alkaline in reaction and so can be used safely on all fabrics.

You can find out if Calgon will benefit your regular washing procedure by making this simple test:

1. Fill washing machine with warm or hot water of the temperature you would normally use.

2. Add 1 cup of Calgon and a load of soiled clothes. Do not add soap, synthetic detergent, or any other washing ingredient.

3. Run clothes through wash and rinse cycles.

If suds appear during any of this operation, they are from soap or synthetic detergent that has been trapped in the fabric from previous washings and just released by Calgon. (Calgon itself does not form suds.) This means you have not been using enough soap, synthetic detergent, or water softener to prevent hard-water scum. If no suds appear, your normal washing procedure is adequate.

Sodium hexametaphosphate, alias Calgon, can be used to correct the first condition in either, or both, of two ways. First, you can use it in the wash water in place of a more conventional water softener. In this case, instead of precipitating the hardness minerals, it holds them to itself so they can't join with the soap or synthetic detergent to coat the fabric with a gray film. Second, you can use it in the rinse water to detach any film that may have formed. Or, for more complete guarantee against film formation, you can do both.

Dissolve the Calgon completely before adding soap or synthetic detergent. For more information about the nature and uses of this chemical, see Chapter 8, Common Products with Many Uses.

Here are suggested amounts of the compound to use for different degrees of water hardness and washers of different capacity:

Washer tank capacity Gallons	Soft water (up to 5 grains per gallon)	Medium water (5 to 10 grains per gallon)	Hard water (10 to 15 grains per gallon)	Very hard water (over 15 grains per gallon)
5	1/8 cup	1/4 cup	1/3 cup	1/2 cup
10	1/4 cup	1/2 cup	2/3 cup	1 cup
15	1/3 cup	2/3 cup	1 cup	1-1/2 cups
20	1/2 cup	1 cup	1-1/2 cups	2 cups

SANITATION IN HOME LAUNDERING

In the days when housewives boiled their clothes in laundering them, there was little chance for bacteria to survive. With today's relatively low washwater temperatures, however, bacteria usually thrive. In tests made in the Clothing and Textiles Laboratory of the U.S. Department of Agriculture, the wash of nine families was laundered regularly for several months. An automatic household washer and typical home laundry methods were used. Examination of the laundry at the end of the test showed that 30 kinds of bacteria were still alive.

According to the experts' findings, neither the water temperatures nor the detergents ordinarily used in today's automatic washers can be relied on to reduce the number of bacteria in fabrics to a safe level. Even at the "hot" water setting, 12 gallons of wash water may contain as many as 1,536,000,000 bacteria!

Home equipment specialists, for instance, recommend a temperature of 140°F for hot water laundering. At that temperature, it takes 20 minutes to kill *Staphylococcus aureus*, a type of bacterium that can cause boils and carbuncles, as well as skin respiratory, kidney, and other types of infections. However, the average hot water temperature in home washers is not 140° but 125° to 130°, while the average washing cycle is only from 5 to 10 minutes. Besides, in an attempt to spare fabrics, much laundry is now washed in cold or lukewarm water.

Most bacteria, luckily, are harmless. Occasionally, however, a dangerous strain will spread stubborn infections from one member of a family to another through contact in the home washer, or from one family to another family through a public washing machine.

Can These Bacteria Be Controlled?

USDA experts say they can be through the use of suitable disinfectants. The following were chosen as being lethal to most bacteria, harmless to fabrics and dyes, harmless to humans at the end of the wash cycle, compatible with detergents, readily available, and reasonable in cost. In using any of them, be sure to read the label and follow all directions and precautions carefully.

Liquid chlorine bleach, containing 5 to 6 percent sodium hypochlorite (Clorox, Rose-X, Purex, etc.), is probably the most familiar. This household chemical turns out to be an effective and inexpensive bacteria killer as well as a fabric whitener when used in quantities recommended on the bottle for regular bleaching. Usually 1 cup should be added to a top-loading machine or ½ cup to a front-loading machine. It should not, of course, be used on wool, silk or spandex, or on dyes or other finishes where chlorine bleach would not normally be used.

Quaternary disinfectants, sometimes known as "quats," work well when added to the wash water at the beginning of the rinse cycle. One brand, Co-op Sanitizer, is available in certain supermarkets; another, Roccal, is available from janitors', dairy, and poultry supply houses. Use the amount recommended on the label. Or else add ½ cup to rinse water in a top-loading machine or 8 tablespoons to rinse water in a front-loading machine.

Pine oil disinfectants, available in grocery stores under such names as Fyne Pyne, Fyne Tex, King Pine, Pine-o-Pine, White Cap, should contain at least 80 percent of pine oil. Add them at the beginning of the wash cycle—if possible, mixing them with the water before placing clothes in the machine. Use ¾ cup for a top-loading machine and ½ cup for a front-loading machine.

Phenolic disinfectants may be added either to wash or rinse water. Examples are Pine-Sol and Al Pine, containing approximately 3 percent of active ingredient and available at grocery stores. When obtained at this concentration, use 1 cup for a top-loading machine or 10 tablespoons (5 fluid ounces) for a front-loading machine.

Besides sanitizing the clothes, sanitize the washing machine occasionally to kill bacteria that may abide on its inner surfaces. Pour a disinfectant into the empty machine and then complete a 15-minute cycle at the hot-water setting.

How Hot Should the Wash Water Be?

This depends on the amount of soil, the type of fabric, and whether you depend on the temperature of the water to provide sanitizing. The hotter the water, the better it penetrates fabrics and liquifies grease so that it may be more easily removed. If the temperature is above 140°F, it also kills germs. On the other hand, water that is too hot can damage silk, cause wool to shrink, make colors run, and weaken and wrinkle modern synthetic materials.

To help you get the cleanest wash with the least damage to materials, here are some general suggestions:

Hot. This includes temperatures from 140° to 160°F, provided only from the "hot" line of the water heater and with temperature control on washer set for "hot." Although higher temperatures may get out more dirt, it is better not to set the thermostat of the water heater much above 140°. This is to prevent shortening the life of pipes and heater and also accidental scalding. If you want the water very hot, and have an ample supply, you can preheat the washer with hot water, then empty the washer and refill it.

Water in this temperature range provides the most soil removal and sanitizing. It is ideal for white cottons and linens, and for heavily soiled articles of these materials in washfast colors. It softens and so reduces the resilience of synthetic and resin-treated fibers, causing wrinkles and preventing them from returning to their original shape. It also may cause some colors to run.

Medium. By mixing cold water with the hot, water of about 120°F is produced by automatic washers on the "medium" setting. This is good for lightly soiled clothes, also for washing many bright or dark colors that do not actually run in the wash but may fade in time from washing in hot water. Provides no sanitizing, but is somewhat superior to warm water in removing dirt.

Warm. The "warm" setting of an automatic washer usually regulates temperature at about 100°F. This is suitable for silk and washable woolens, and comfortable for hand washing. Protects colors from running and wrinkles synthetic fibers less than hot water. Most automatic washers rinse at this temperature.

Cold. Water of 80°F or less from unheated supply is recommended only for lightly soiled laundry or laundry pretreated by working concentrated detergent thoroughly into the heavily soiled areas. Use in it plenty of liquid detergent, a cold-water detergent, or a granular detergent that has been dissolved in hot water before adding. Cold water adds the fewest new wrinkles to synthetic or coated "wash-and-wear" fabrics, but on the other hand it may not remove those that are already there.

Tips on Hanging Wash

• Always start with a clean clothesline. Fold a soapy cloth so that it encircles the line as you draw it along. Follow this with a cloth wrung out in clear water.

• Sheets, slipcovers, and other large pieces dry faster when you hang them over parallel lines.

• To prevent plastic tablecloths and shower curtains from sticking together, weight the hems with spring clothes pins.

• Hang chenille spreads and shag rugs wrong side out so that the tufted surfaces blow against each other. This will raise the pile.

• Hang towels and linens one-third over the line. This prevents "dog-ears" at the corners and along the edge.

• Be sure your "drip-dries" are dripping wet. Remember, it's the water that erases wrinkles.

• After hanging clothes in freezing whether, let them thaw before folding. The fibers may crack if frozen clothes are folded.

• When drying clothes indoors, place an electric fan on a small table 2 to 3 feet from the garments. Direct flow of air between the lines. Operate at high speed. Tests show that this will have from 2 to 4 hours' drying time.

REMOVING STAINS FROM TEXTILES

Complicated by the endless variety of dyes, synthetic textiles, blends, and surface finishes in use today, successful stain removal has become an art that requires a combination of considerable skill with a fair knowledge of chemistry.

Before you begin you must select a method best suited to stain, dye, and fabric. To make sure that it does not cause fading or running of the dye, change of surface of the textile, or the removal of a non-permanent finish, first test the treatment on some hidden part of the article.

If you are in doubt, or an article is of great value, don't attempt to remove the stain yourself but take the article to a professional cleaner. But remember that even he may not be able to remove it. There are some types of stain on some materials that cannot be removed by *any* treatment without damaging the material!

Following is a description of materials used in stain removal, methods for removing stains of general types, and finally methods for removing specific stains.

Solvents for Nongreasy Stains

Water or water with a detergent will remove many nongreasy stains.

Acetone will dissolve such stains as fingernail polish, lacquer, and ballpoint ink. It should not be used on acetate, Arnel, Dynel, or Verel. Flammable. Poison if swallowed.

Amyl acetate can be used for some stains as acetone on fabrics that would be damaged by acetone. Use the chemically pure grade. Flammable. Poison if swallowed.

Alcohol (denatured ethyl alcohol, or ethyl or isopropyl rubbing alcohol) may be used for a number of stains if it is safe for the dye on the fabric. Flammable. Poison if swallowed.

Solvents for Greasy Stains

Use these with care. Some are flammable, and all can cause serious illness or death from swallowing the liquids or from breathing too much of the vapors. If used away from flame, with good ventilation, and only in the small quantities needed for spot removal, however, they can be safe and effective.

Nonflammable. Carbon tetrachloride, perchloroethylene, trichloroethane, and trichloroethylene are nonflammable grease solvents. They are sold under these names and under various trade names. Carbon tetrachloride was once very popular as a household cleaning solvent, but has in late years fallen into disfavor because of the high toxicity of its vapors. The others are less toxic.

Flammable. These are less expensive than the nonflammable solvents and are usually distillation products of petroleum. Two suitable types are Stoddard solvent, a petroleum naphtha of high flash point made especially for dry cleaning (and sold also under various other trade names), and V.M. & P. (Varnish Makers' and Painters') naphtha, available in grocery, drug, hardware, and paint stores.

Never use these near an open flame. Don't put them in a washing machine or put articles that have been cleaned with them in a dryer.

Mixtures. Many spot removers sold in grocery and drug stores under various brand names are mixtures of flammable solvents with enough of the nonflammable type to keep them from burning.

Bleaches for Removing Stains

Bleaches are the most widely used of the chemical stain removers and the ones most likely to damage fibers and fade dyes if directions are not carefully followed.

Three kinds of bleaches are recommended for home use—chlorine bleaches, peroxygen bleaches, and color removers. The first two may generally be used interchangeably. Color removers are used where the bleaches are not effective.

Chlorine bleaches. Never use these on fabrics that contain silk, wool, or spandex fibers, polyurethane foams, or on fabric with a special finish unless the manufacturer states on the label that chlorine bleach is safe.

The commonest bleach of this type is a solution of sodium hypochlorite, sold under such names as Clorox, Purex, Rose-X, and so on. For treatment on washable articles mix 2 tablespoons of liquid bleach with 1 quart of cool water. Apply to small stains with a medicine dropper; soak large stains in the solution. Leave for 5 to 15 minutes. Rinse well with water. Repeat if necessary.

For stubborn stains mix equal parts of bleach with water. Apply as above, but rinse immediately. Repeat if necessary. Ᵽe sure all bleach is finally rinsed out.

On nonwashable articles use solution of 1 teaspoon liquid bleach with 1 cup of cool water. Apply with medicine dropper and leave for 5 to 15 minutes. Rinse well and repeat if necessary.

Peroxygen bleaches. These consist of sodium perborate and of potassium monopersulfate, which are powders also sold under various trade names.

For washable articles mix 1 to 2 tablespoons of either chemical with 1 pint lukewarm water for wool, silk, or Dynel, or 1 pint hot water for other fabrics. (Hot water shrinks Dynel and is not safe for silk and wool.) Mix just before using, as the solution loses strength on standing.

Cover stained area with solution or soak entire article. Soak until stain is removed. This may take several hours or overnight. Rinse well.

If wool or silk is yellowed by the solution, sponge with 10-percent acetic acid or vinegar. Then rinse.

For a stronger treatment, sprinkle sodium perborate or potassium monopersulfate powder directly on stain. Dip stain into very hot or boiling water (do not use this treatment on wool, silk, or Dynel). Stains should vanish in a few minutes. Rinse well. Repeat if necessary.

For nonwashable articles sprinkle either powder on stain. Cover with a pad of cotton, dampened with lukewarm water for wool, silk, and Dynel, and hot water for other fabrics. Keep damp until stain is removed, which may take hours. Rinse well. To remove yellowing caused by bleach, treat with acetic acid or vinegar as mentioned above.

For strong treatment, dampen stain with cool water. Sprinkle on powdered bleach. With spoon or medicine dropper apply small amount of boiling water to stain. Use a sponge or other absorbent pad under stain to absorb the water. Repeat if necessary.

General Stain-Removal Directions

If you can't identify the exact nature of the stain, try at least to determine whether it is a greasy stain, a nongreasy stain, or a combination of both. Then proceed as follows:

Greasy stains on washable articles. Some may be removed merely by regular washing; others by rubbing liquid detergent into the stain, then rinsing with hot water. If this doesn't work, dry the article and apply grease solvent, repeating, if necessary.

If yellow stain remains after solvent treatment, use chlorine or peroxygen bleach.

Greasy stains on nonwashable articles. Sponge stain well with grease solvent. Dry. Repeat if necessary. Remove any remaining yellow stain as above.

Nongreasy stains on washable articles. Some nongreasy stains are removed by regular laundry methods; others are set by them. Sponge stain with cool water; or soak in cool water from 30 minutes to overnight. If stain remains, work a detergent into it, then rinse. If still there try chlorine or peroxygen bleach.

Nongreasy stains on nonwashable articles. Sponge stain with cool water. Or force cool water through stain with a small syringe, using sponge under stain to absorb water. If stain remains, rub detergent in it and work into fabric. Rinse. A final sponging with alcohol helps to remove detergent and to dry fabric. Test alcohol first on fabric. If stain remains, use chlorine or peroxygen bleach.

Combination stains on washable articles. Sponge stain with cool water. Or soak in cool water for 30 minutes or longer. If stain remains, work detergent into stain. Then rinse and allow to dry. If a greasy stain remains, sponge with grease solvent. Dry. Repeat if necessary. If colored stain remains, use chlorine or peroxygen bleach.

Combination stains on nonwashable articles. Sponge stain with cool water. Or force cool water through stain with small syringe, using sponge under stain. If stain remains, rub detergent on stain and work it into fabric. Rinse spot well with water. Dry. If greasy stain remains, sponge with grease solvent. Dry. Repeat if necessary. If colored stain remains, use chlorine or peroxygen bleach.

Removing Individual Stains

Acids. Rinse with water immediately. Apply household ammonia and rinse again.

Adhesive tape. Scrape off gummy matter carefully with dull knife. Sponge with grease solvent.

Airplane glue, household cement. Follow directions for mimeograph fluid.

Alcoholic beverages. Follow directions above for nongreasy stains. Or sponge the stain with alcohol, if alcohol does not affect the color. Dilute alcohol with 2 parts of water before using on acetate. If a stain remains, use a chlorine or peroxygen bleach.

Alkalis. Rinse with water immediately. Then apply vinegar and rinse again.

Antiperspirants, deodorants. Wash or sponge stain thoroughly with detergent and warm water. Rinse. If stain remains, use chlorine or peroxygen bleach. Antiperspirants that contain such substances as aluminum chloride are acidic and may cause fabric damage and change the color of some dyes. You may be able to restore color of fabric by sponging it with ammonia. Rinse thoroughly. Dilute ammonia with an equal amount of water for use on wool or silk.

Blood. Follow directions for nongreasy stains. If detergent does not remove stain put a few drops of ammonia on the stain and repeat with detergent. Rinse. Follow with bleach treatment if necessary.

Butter, margarine. Follow directions for greasy stains.

Candle wax, paraffin. Remove excess wax carefully with a dull knife. Then place the stained area between clean white blotters or several layers of facial tissues and press with warm iron. Remove remaining wax with grease solvent.

Candy, syrup. If chocolate, follow directions for combination stains. For other candy and syrup follow directions for nongreasy stains.

Carbon paper. For regular carbon paper, work detergent into stain. If not removed put a few drops of ammonia on stain and repeat. Rinse well.

For duplicating carbon paper, sponge stain with alcohol. Dilute alcohol with 2 parts water for use on acetate. If stain remains rub detergent into it. Wash and rinse well. Repeat if necessary.

Chewing gum. Scrape off as much as you can with dull knife, a job made easier if you first harden the gum by rubbing it with ice. If stain remains, sponge thoroughly with a grease solvent.

Chocolate and cocoa. Follow directions for combination stains.

Coffee, tea. With cream, follow directions for combination stains; without cream, for nongreasy stains.

Cosmetics. On washable articles apply liquid detergent to stain. Or dampen stain and rub in detergent to form thick suds. Work in until outline of stain is gone. Rinse. Repeat if necessary.

On nonwashable articles sponge with a grease solvent as long as any color is removed. If not removed, use method for washable articles.

Crayon. Follow directions for cosmetics.

Dyes. Follow directions for nongreasy stains. If bleach is needed, use chlorine bleach or color remover. A long soak in sudsy water is often effective on fresh dye stains.

Egg. Scrape off as much as possible. Follow directions for nongreasy stains.

Fingernail polish. Follow directions for lacquer.
Nail polish removers can also be used to remove stains. Do not use on acetate, Arnel, Dynel, or Verel without testing to be sure it won't damage the fabric.

Food coloring. Follow directions for nongreasy stains.

Fruit. Follow directions for nongreasy stains. Sponge fresh stains immediately with cool water. Some fruit stains, including citrus, are invisible on fabric right after they dry, but turn yellow on aging or heating. This stain may be difficult to remove.

Glue, mucilage, adhesive. Casein glue. Follow directions for nongreasy stains.

Plastic glue. Wash stain with detergent and water before glue hardens; some types cannot be removed afterward.

Rubber cement. Let dry and rub off as much as you can with cloth. Remove remainder with grease solvent.

Other types of glue and mucilage. Follow directions for nongreasy stains, except use hot water instead of cool.

Grass, foliage, flowers. Washable articles: Work detergent into stain, then rinse. If safe for dye, sponge stain with alcohol. Dilute alcohol with 2 parts of water for acetate. If stain remains use bleach. Nonwashable articles: Use same methods, but try alcohol first if it is safe for dye.

Gravy, meat juice. Follow directions for combination stains.

Grease, car grease, lard. Follow directions for greasy stains.

Ice cream. Follow directions for combination stains.

Ink, ballpoint. Washing removes some types of ballpoint ink stains, but sets others. To see if stain will wash out, mark a similar piece of fabric with the ink and wash it. If stain remains, treat as follows: For fresh stains sponge repeatedly with acetone or amyl acetate. Use amyl acetate on acetate, Arnel, Dynel, and Verel. Use acetone on other fabrics. Old stains may also require bleaching.

Ink, drawing. Black (India ink): Treat as soon as possible. On washable articles force water through stain until all loose pigment is removed. Wash with detergent, several times if necessary. Then soak in warm suds containing 1 to 4 tablespoons of ammonia to a quart of water. Dried stains may need overnight soak.

On nonwashable articles force water through stain to remove loose pigment. Sponge stain with solution of 1 tablespoon of ammonia per cup of water. Rinse. If stain remains, moisten with ammonia, then work in detergent. Rinse. Repeat if necessary. If ammonia changes color of fabric, sponge first with water, then moisten with vinegar. Rinse well.

Colors other than black: Follow directions for nongreasy stains. If bleach is needed, use a color remover if it is safe for dye of fabric. If it is not safe, try other bleaches.

Ink, mimeograph and printing. For fresh stains follow directions for greasy stains, or sponge with turpentine. For stubborn stains follow directions for paint stains.

Ink, writing. Follow directions for nongreasy stains. Because writing inks vary in composition it may be necessary to try more than one kind of bleach. Try chlorine bleach on all fabrics for which it is safe. For other fabrics try peroxygen bleach. A few types of ink may require color removers. If a yellow stain remains after bleaching, treat as a rust stain.

Iodine. Long soaking in cool water may remove it. The quickest way is to wet the stain with a solution containing 1 tablespoon of sodium thiosulfate (photographers' "hypo") in a pint of warm water, or to sprinkle the crystals on the dampened stain. Rinse well.

Lacquer. Sponge stain with acetone or amyl acetate. Use amyl acetate on acetate, Arnel, Dynel, and Verel—acetone on other fabrics.

Mayonnaise, salad dressing. Follow directions for combination stains.

Medicines. (See also Iodine, Mercurochrome, Silver nitrate.) Medicines with an oily base, gummy and tarry medicines: Follow directions for greasy stains.

Medicines in sugar syrup or in water: Wash out with water.

Medicines dissolved in alcohol (tinctures): Sponge stain with alcohol. Dilute with 2 parts of water for use on acetate.

Medicines that contain iron: Follow directions for rust.

Medicines that contain dyes: Follow directions for dyes.

Mercurochrome, merthiolate, metaphen. If washable, soak article overnight in warm detergent solution containing 4 tablespoons of ammonia to each quart of water.

If not washable, and alcohol is safe for the dye, sponge with alcohol as long as any stain comes out. Dilute alcohol with 2 parts of water for acetate. If alcohol is not safe, wet stain with liquid detergent. Add a drop of ammonia with a medicine dropper. Rinse.

Mildew. Wash mildewed article thoroughly. Dry in the sun. If stain remains treat with bleach. If article cannot be washed, send to a good dry cleaner.

Milk. Follow directions for combination stains.

Mimeograph correction fluid. Sponge stain with acetone or amyl acetate. Use amyl acetate on acetate, Arnel, Dynel, and Verel—acetone on other fabrics. (*Caution*: Both of these liquids are flammable and are poisonous if swallowed.)

Mud. Let mud dry, then brush well. If spot remains, follow directions for nongreasy stains. Stains from iron-rich clays not removed by this method should be treated as rust stains.

Mustard. Washable articles: Rub detergent into dampened stain. Rinse. If stain is not removed, soak article in hot detergent solution for several hours, or overnight. If stain remains, use bleach.

Nonwashable articles: If safe for dye, sponge stain with alcohol. Dilute alcohol with 2 parts of water for use on acetate. If alcohol cannot be used follow treatment for washable articles, omitting soaking.

Oil—fish-liver, linseed, machine, mineral, vegetable. Follow directions for greasy stains.

Paint, varnish. Treat stains quickly before paint dries. Read the label on the paint container. If a certain solvent is recommended as a thinner, use this in preference to others.

Washable articles: For fresh stains rub detergent into stain and wash. If stain is dry or is only partially removed by washing, sponge with turpentine. For aluminum paint, trichloroethylene may be more effective. Do not use this solvent on Arnel or Kodel.

While spot is still wet with solvent, work in detergent, soak in hot water overnight. Launder.

Nonwashable articles: Sponge fresh stains with turpentine; or for aluminum paint with trichloroethylene. Do not use the latter on Arnel or Kodel.

If necessary, loosen more of paint by covering stain for 30 minutes or longer with a pad of cotton dampened with the solvent. Repeat sponging.

If stain remains, put a drop of liquid detergent on stain and work it into the fabric with the edge of the bowl of a spoon.

Alternate sponging with turpentine and treatment with detergent as many times as necessary.

Pencil marks. A soft eraser will remove lead pencil and colored pencil marks from some fabrics. If mark cannot be erased follow directions for regular carbon paper.

For indelible pencil follow directions for duplicating carbon paper.

Perfume. Follow directions for alcoholic beverages.

Perspiration. Wash or sponge stain thoroughly with detergent and warm water. If perspiration has changed the color of fabric, try to restore it by treating with ammonia or vinegar. Apply ammonia to fresh stains; rinse with water. Apply vinegar to old stains; rinse with water. If oily stain remains, follow directions for greasy stains.

Remove any yellow discoloration with bleach.

Rust. Moisten stain with solution of 1 tablespoon of oxalic acid (*Caution:* poison if swallowed!) in 1 cup warm water. If stain is not removed, heat the solution and repeat. If stain is stubborn, place oxalic acid crystals directly on stain. Moisten with water as hot as is safe for fabric and let stand for a few minutes. Repeat if necessary. Do not use this method on nylon.

Rinse article thoroughly. If allowed to remain, oxalic acid will damage fabric.

Color removers for dyes can be used to remove rust stains from white fabrics.

For mild rust stains, spread the stained portion over a pan of boiling water and squeeze lemon juice on it. Or sprinkle salt on the stain, squeeze lemon juice on it, and spread in the sun to dry. Rinse thoroughly. Repeat if necessary.

Sauces, soup. Follow directions for combination stains.

Scorch. If article is washable follow directions for nongreasy stains. To remove light scorch on non-washable articles use hydrogen peroxide.

On heavy fabrics you may be able to remove surface scorch with very fine sandpaper.

Severe scirch damages the fabric.

Shellac. Sponge the stain with alcohol, or soak the stain in alcohol. Dilute alcohol with 2 parts water for use on acetate. If alcohol bleeds the dye, try turpentine.

Shoe polish. Because there are so many kinds of shoe polish no one method will remove all stains. It may be necessary to try more than one of the following methods:

1. Follow directions for cosmetics.
2. Sponge stain with alcohol, if safe for dye in fabric. Dilute alcohol with 2 parts water for use on acetate.
3. Sponge stain with grease solvent or turpentine. If turpentine is used, remove by sponging with a warm detergent solution.

If none of these work, use a bleach.

Silver nitrate. Dampen stain with water, then put a few drops of tincture of iodine on it. After several minutes, treat as an iodine stain.

Unless stain on silk or wool is treated when fresh a brown discoloration will remain.

Soft drinks. Follow directions for nongreasy stains.

Soot, smoke. Follow directions for cosmetics.

Tar. Follow directions for greasy stains.

Tea. (See coffee)

Tobacco. Follow directions for grass.

Urine. Follow directions for nongreasy stains.

If color of fabric has been changed, sponge stain with ammonia. If this does not restore color, sponging with acetic acid or vinegar may help.

If none of these methods work, see directions for medicines and yellowing.

Vegetables. Follow directions for nongreasy stains.

Yellowing, brown stains. If these are caused by the use of chlorine bleaches on fabrics with some types of Wash-and-Wear finishes, use one of the following treatments:

For any fabric: Rinse thoroughly with water, then soak for at least 30 minutes in a solution of 1 teaspoon of sodium thiosulfate to each quart of warm water. Rinse thoroughly. To intensify treatment make solution as hot as is safe for the material.

Treatment for white or fast-color fabrics: Rinse thoroughly with water, then use a color remover according to instructions on package.

To remove stains of unknown origin, try as many of the following treatments as necessary, in the order given:

1. Wash.
2. Use a mild treatment of bleach.
3. Use oxalic acid method for rust.
4. Use a strong treatment of bleach.

8

Common Products
with Many Uses

TRISODIUM PHOSPHATE—TSP

Need a wall cleaner, a floor-wax remover, a water softener, a detergent for grimy clothes, a cleaner for silverware, your car radiator, or your grandpa's dentures? Just mix trisodium phosphate with the proper amounts of water and you can make them all! Under one or another of hundreds of brand-names and use-names, you have probably been using this versatile chemical right along. By buying it under its own name, or as TSP, however, and learning how to mix it for its various uses, you can not only save money but need store only one product that will do jobs that previously required a dozen.

TSP comes as a white crystalline powder that dissolves completely in hot or cold water and differs from soap in that it makes no suds and leaves no scum. It cleans by emulsifying oil and grease-bound dirt, breaking them down into particles which plain water can wash away.

Although TSP is now harder to get by its own name than it used to be, it is still plentiful at dealers in institutional and janitors' supplies, some paint and hardware stores, and from big mail-order firms such as Sears and Montgomery Ward. A single pound costs from 16 to 20 cents, while in 100-pound bags the price may drop below 10 cents a pound. Get the same thing by such names as "wax remover" or "denture cleaner," and you pay to $1.50 a pound!

Here are a few of the many ways you can use it:

Woodwork. 1 to 2 teaspoons in a pail of luke-warm water cleans paint. Rinse with a wet cloth and wipe off. Never sprinkle dry TSP on the cloth or on the painted surface to be cleaned. A little stronger or hotter solution will remove high gloss. Don't make it too strong or too hot, however, as real strong and hot TSP is a paint *remover*!

Floors. TSP will not injure marble, tile, linoleum, or rubber. Use 1 tablespoon in a pail of water, and clean in usual manner. Will not turn marble yellow or leave floors slippery. For thoroughly cleaning unpainted cement or concrete floors, use 2 to 4 tablespoons of TSP in a pail of water, scrubbing the surface with a mop or a long-handled scrubbing brush. Rinse with clear water and let dry.

Tile and tubs. Scum on wash bowls, sinks, and bathtubs is undissolved grease or soap deposits made insoluble by the minerals in hard water. Scouring with TSP on a wet cloth will remove it. The powdered chemical will not harm porcelain or ceramic tile, but do not use it to scour other finishes.

Ranges and refrigerators. Clean these and other equipment having a finish of baked-on enamel with TSP at a strength of 1 teaspoon to a pail of lukewarm water. Wash your refrigerator inside and out with a cloth wet with the solution. Rinse and wipe dry. Clean your gas or electric range, washing machine, and enameled steel cabinets the same way.

Dishwashing. One teaspoon in warm water brings out dishes clean and sparkling without soap. Greasy pans and cooking utensils caked with burned food can be cleaned by boiling in them a solution of about 2 tablespoons of TSP per gallon of water. Do not, however, boil TSP or any other alkaline solution in aluminum pans, as aluminum is corroded and darkened by alkalis. Give this metal a quick wash with warm TSP solution, but do not soak or boil.

Cleaning silverware. A solution of TSP and an aluminum pan is all you need for a popular no-rub method of cleaning silver tableware. For full directions, see article "Clean silver electrically" in Chapter 6, Household Cleaning and Polishing.

Laundry. Soaking clothes for half an hour or overnight in a bath of TSP helps loosen heavy soil and makes subsequent washing easier. TSP in the wash water permits the use of less detergent. It may be used alone to wash delicate fabrics. For further information, see Chapter 7, Laundering, Stain Removing, and Dyeing.

Car cooling systems. For many years TSP was one of the principal cleaners for car radiators and cooling systems. It is still widely used. For details, see article "Car cooling-system cleaners" in Chapter 6, Household Cleaning and Polishing.

Grease from machines. TSP is excellent for removing grease from motors, engines, and other mechanical parts. Use about an ounce in a pail of hot water, and apply with a rough rag or a stiff brush. Rinse with plain water and wipe dry. For cleaning metals before electroplating, use 4 ounces to a gallon of hot water.

Paint and varnish remover. One of the cheapest and best. See next entry.

Paintbrush cleaner. Especially good for brushes on which the paint has dried hard. To find out how to clean brushes and to remove paint with TSP, see Chapter 2, Paints and Paint Removers.

Denture cleaner. The Council on Dental Therapeutics of the American Dental Association considers TSP one of the best cleansers for artificial dentures, and many proprietary denture cleaning preparations consist of TSP alone or with color, flavor, or scent added. For formulas, see Chapter 11, Soaps, Cosmetics and Medicinal Preparations.

SODIUM HEXAMETAPHOSPHATE—CALGON

Did you know you could use a popular laundry and dishwashing chemical to soak beans faster, remove scale from inside your steam iron, keep spots off your photo prints and negatives, make your eyeglasses sparkle, tint Easter eggs more evenly, wash your dog?

This chemical-of-many-uses had been a laboratory curiosity for more than a hundred years. Then, in 1929, it was put to its first commercial use as a conditioner of boiler water. Whenever hard water is used in producing steam in heat and power plants, a thick coating of calcium and magnesium salts gradually builds up inside the boilers, drastically reducing their thermal efficiency. Ordinary water softeners precipitate the harmful salts, but leave them as a sludge that has to be removed from time to time.

After long investigation, Dr. R. E. Hall, a Bureau of Mines researcher retained by a chemical company in Pittsburgh, found that the rare chemical, sodium hexametaphosphate, could change all this. Instead of precipitating the offending salts, sodium hexametaphosphate "sequestered" them. That is, it seized them and so tied them in a complex compound with itself that they completely lost their identity and, along with that, all their harmful effects. Hall invented the trade name Calgon from "calcium gone," a description of one of the chemical's abilities in softening water.

From conditioning boiler water, it was just a short step to softening water for all kinds of cleaning purposes. Grayness commonly seen on laundered linens, the traditional "bathtub ring," a cloudy film on washed glassware and dishes, are all due to insoluble calcium soap that cannot be washed away by ordinary means. Calgon was put to work on all such jobs.

During World War II, almost the entire production of Calgon was used by the United States armed forces to help speed ships and for military dishwashing and laundry. Since then, it has found a thousand new jobs in industry and has also come to the grocery store and supermarket as a water conditioner for home laundering (see Chapter 7) and for hand dishwashing. (Calgon*ite*, designed specifically for *automatic dishwashers*, is a separate product that contains several strong detergents as well as Calgon.)

Besides these two everyday applications, the unique properties of Calgon enable it to do many other things around the house that are not so well known. Here are just a few:

In the bath. Put about 4 tablespoons of Calgon in the bathtub and let it dissolve under the faucet as the tub is filling. Use less soap than usual and get full lather. When finished, there will be no greasy soap film on your skin and no ring around the tub.

Bathroom sinks, showers, toilet bowls. Soap scum and stains in these facilities may be eliminated by rinsing them regularly with a solution of about 1 teaspoon of Calgon to a gallon of water. It disperses and washes away these accumulations and other substances that clog drains.

Bathing your dog. By using Calgon with soap in the bath and Calgon alone in the first rinse, you can keep your dog's hair softer and glossier. The water conditioner removes dulling film and helps prevent skin irritation. Rinse finally with plain water.

Shampooing your hair. What's good for your dog's hair is good for yours, too! Add about 1 teaspoon of Calgon to a gallon of warm water. Thor-

oughly wet your hair with this solution, then wash
it with a mild soap or shampoo preparation. Rinse
with what's left of the Calgon solution, and then
with plain water.

Shaving. This will be cleaner and faster if you
first wash with conditioned water and soap. After
shaving, rinse with conditioned water to remove remaining soap.

Hand dishwashing. Conditioned water prevents
the formation of a film that dulls and spots dishes.
Grease and dirt stay suspended, to finally go down
the drain. No ring will form in the dishpan, and
dishes, glasses, and silverware will dry spot-free, after
rinsing, without wiping. Follow this procedure:

1. Dissolve 2 teaspoons of Calgon in dishpan of
hot water—more, if water is very hard.

2. Add about ½ the usual amount of soap or
detergent.

3. Wash glasses first, then silver, and finally
dishes.

4. Rinse with hot water.

5. Merely stack to dry—do not towel dry.

Note: Do not use Calgon*ite* for hand dishwashing; this different product contains an alkali effective for machine washing but irritating to the hands.

Discoloration on aluminum utensils. To remove
dark discoloration from inside of aluminum pans,
fill with water and add ½ to 1 teaspoon of Calgon.
Bring water to boil and simmer for 3 minutes. Be-

cause Calgon solution is practically neutral, it will not injure aluminum as solutions of alkaline water softeners or detergents will.

Coffee pots can be kept free from film and odor by washing them regularly in conditioned water.

Electric appliances that can't be completely immersed in dishwater respond also to Calgon treatment. To clean electric skillets, deep-fat friers, and electric cookers, follow this method:

1. Scrape the appliance clean or wipe with a paper towel.

2. Fill with water, stir in a tablespoon of Calgon, and add your regular soap or detergent. Boil for 5 minutes.

3. Pour off the soapy water and refill with warm water to rinse. The Calgon will hold any remaining grease in suspension so it can be poured safely down the drain.

Cleaning fruits and vegetables. Unlike any other cleaning aid, Calgon is tasteless and nontoxic. For this reason you can use it to soak and clean fruits and vegetables, with results superior to the use of water alone. Cleaning berries, for instance, is easier with this method. Soak them for 5 minutes in water containing 1 tablespoon of Calgon per gallon, then rinse them in plain water. Soil and most spray residues will rinse away. To remove fine sand and grit from leafy vegetables, separate the leaves and soak and rinse them the same way. Likewise with fresh mushrooms.

Quick soaking for navy beans. These need not be soaked overnight before cooking. Just soak them for several hours in the conditioner bath mentioned for berries and vegetables.

Steam irons. Just as Calgon can remove scale from the boilers of steamships and power plants, it can do so from the inside of your steam iron. At least once a month use a solution of Calgon to remove mineral incrustations from the water reservoir of the iron and to open the steam holes. Pour a solution of 1 teaspoon of Calgon to a cup of water into the iron and set the heat control on cotton. When steam starts coming out, hold the iron at arm's length over the sink and shake gently to circulate the water in the reservoir. Be careful, for the water in the iron is boiling hot! Keep the solution in the iron for about 15 minutes, shaking it several more times. Drain it and fill with tap water. Repeat the above procedure with water alone. Drain and rinse several times. Be sure all the water is out before storing.

Eyeglasses can be kept spotlessly clean by washing them frequently with conditioned water and then rinsing them.

Coloring Easter eggs can be done with less streaking and spotting if you add a pinch of Calgon to the dye solution. This will help spread the dye more evenly.

Spots on prints and negatives can be reduced if you add about ¼ teaspoon of Calgon to each quart of developing solution. By reacting with the developer, water hardness minerals can cause "sludge" or "scum" that produces spots or streaks on paper or film. Conditioned water ties up these minerals, pre- venting the reaction.

WASHING SODA

Sodium carbonate, in the form of sal soda or washing soda—another old standby of the housewife --is a more alkaline relative of the bicarbonate. By cutting through oil and grease, sal soda helps in heavy-duty cleaning. As a softener for hard water, it lets you use less of the more expensive soap or de- tergent to get the same cleaning results with clothes or dishes.

Laundry. For soiled play clothes and greasy work clothes add ¼ cup of washing soda to your tub or washer and less soap or detergent than usual. The combination will get rid of stubborn dirt better than soap or detergent alone. To clean tub or washer af- ter use, fill with warm water and add ¼ cup of wash- ing soda. Let stand 15 minutes, then drain and rinse.

Dishes, glassware, pots and pans. For dishes and glassware add 1 heaping tablespoon of washing soda to the water in your dishpan. Use less soap or de- tergent. Double the amount of soda for pots and pans. For scouring, apply the granules with a moist cloth or sponge. Do not, however, boil or soak *alu- minum* ware in soda or any other alkaline solution.

Ranges. Clean broilers and clogged-up gas burn- ers by soaking them for a few minutes in hot water to which 2 heaping tablespoons of washing soda have been added. Boiling (not in an *aluminum* pan, however!) hastens the action.

Drains and traps. Washing soda will help keep drains and traps open without endangering a septic tank or corroding plumbing. Pour 3 tablespoons down the drain at least once a week and run *very hot* water slowly until the granules dissolve.

Barbecue grill. To remove hardened accumulations of grease, apply washing soda dry with a moist, stiff-bristled brush. Rinse and dry.

Garbage pails stay sanitary if washed regularly with a solution of ¼ pound of washing soda to a pail of water.

Garage floors. Scatter washing soda generously over grease spots, sprinkle with water and let stand overnight. Next day scrub with water and hose off.

Car radiators. See Chapter 6, under "Car cooling-system cleaners."

BAKING SODA

Bicarbonate of soda or baking soda has been a household standby for more than a century. Your great-grandmother used it to raise her bread and cake, to clean pots and clothes, relieve insect bites and sore feet, settle an upset stomach, clean teeth, and to gargle throats. On occasion she also used it to smother a fire. Although much more expensive products to perform the same jobs have been evolved during the years since, cheap, easily-obtain-able "bicarb" can still hold its own with the best of them.

Bicarbonate of soda owes its cleaning and sweet-ening action to the fact that it breaks down slowly into carbon-dioxide gas and alkaline sodium carbon-ate when it is dissolved in water. Heating the solu-tion hastens this decomposition. The evolution of carbon-dioxide gas from sodium bicarbonate enables it to raise bread and to put out fires.

Bicarbonate for Cleaning

Laundry. The gentlest of the household cleaning alkalis, baking soda is easy on delicate fabrics as well as on your hands. As a natural deodorizer, it is es-pecially effective for soaking and washing diapers. Add ½ cup of soda to an ordinary washing-machine load.

Refrigerators and freezers. For inside surfaces sprinkle baking soda on a damp cloth and wipe all surfaces including shelves and racks. Rinse with clear hot water and dry. It cuts film and removes stains without scratching. Wash ice trays, crisper boxes, and food containers in a solution of 3 tablespoons of baking soda in a quart of warm water. Rinse in clear hot water and dry. By chemical action the soda re-moves unpleasant ordors.

Coffee pots. Wash glass or stainless steel (not *aluminum,* for any hot alkaline substance will dark-en or pit this metal) coffeepots in a solution of 3 tablespoons of soda in 1 quart of warm water. Or, if you prefer, run the coffee maker (with aluminum coffee basket removed) through its regular cycle with a solution of the same strength in place of coffee. Rinse in clear hot water and dry well. This will remove film of coffee oils that soap and detergents can't reach.

Food and drink containers. Vacuum bottles, picnic jugs, ice buckets, lunch boxes, and bread boxes can all be purged of stale odors that might be absorbed by subsequent food by simple soda treatment. Wash containers first in hot soapy water. Sprinkle 2 tablespoons baking soda in each. Partly fill with warm water and wash. Shake bottles well. Rinse in clear hot water. Dry containers but let bottles air dry.

Silverware. Baking soda sprinkled on a damp cloth can pinch-hit for regular silver polish. Rub until tarnish has gone. Rinse well and dry.

Porcelain, glass, and plastic. Baking soda cuts soil and grease from all these surfaces without scratching. To clean porcelain or enameled bathtubs and sinks, tiled surfaces, shower curtains, mirrors, glass or plastic dinnerware, sprinkle soda on damp cloth and rub. Rinse with clear hot water and dry.

Marble-topped furniture. Wash in a solution of 3 tablespoons of soda in 1 quart of warm water. Let stand a few minutes then rinse with warm water. For stubborn stains, scour with a paste of soda, then rinse and dry.

Combs and brushes. Soak a few minutes in the soda solution mentioned above. This will loosen the dirt particles and oily film for easier cleaning.

Burned food from frying pans. Moisten the pans, if too dry, and sprinkle generously with baking soda. Food then rubs off more easily.

Onion and fish scent from hands. Dampen hands and sprinkle baking soda over them. Rub hard. Rinse and dry.

Ash trays. Sweeten and clean with 1 tablespoon soda dissolved in 1 quart of water. Wipe or scrub trays, rinse, and dry. A sprinkling of dry soda in the bottom of trays will prevent smoldering and reduce odor of ashes.

Bicarbonate in Baking

Bicarbonate of soda was the first chemical leavening agent used. It works by reacting with a mild acid to release carbon dioxide gas. This gas forms in the batter or dough and expands during the baking causing the product to raise. Today most cakes, cookies, and hot breads are still leavened by it.

Baking powder is merely a combination of baking soda with an acid in powder form, plus an inert powder to keep the other ingredients dry.

Here is one you can put together in a jiffy:

Cream of tartar	2 parts
Baking soda	1 part
Cornstarch	1 part

Stir these ingredients well and sift them together several times to make sure they are thoroughly mixed. The purpose of the cornstarch is to prevent the other two substances from reacting with each other before use because of moisture from the air. If you intend to use the entire batch immediately, you may omit the starch.

Buttermilk and vinegar. Before the invention of baking powder, carbon dioxide was released from baking soda by mixing it with sour milk. Today other acid ingredients such as molasses, fruit, buttermilk, or vinegar are combined with baking soda for the same purpose. For most uniform action, the soda is first mixed and sifted with the flour. The acidic substance is added with the liquid ingredients.

As the acid content of vinegar is constant, a fixed proportion of soda to vinegar assures uniform results. This proportion is 1 level teaspoon of soda to 2 tablespoons of vinegar. The acidic content of other acid ingredients is apt to vary, therefore the final product may not always be the same. To produce full leavening from 1 teaspoon of baking soda with buttermilk, for instance, may require anywhere from 1 to 1½ cups of the latter. Specific recipes using baking soda may be found in regular cook books and also may often be obtained free from soda manufacturers.

Bicarbonate in the Bathroom

Upset stomach. Wherever effervescing tablets or powders will relieve acid indigestion or heartburn, baking soda will usually do just as well because it is the active ingredient in these products. Take ½ teaspoon in ½ glass of water.

Gargle. Use a solution of the same strength to gargle your mouth and throat. It cleans and sweetens as well as many more costly preparations.

Dentifrice. Natural teeth and dentures can be cleaned effectively with baking soda. Just sprinkle a goodly amount on a wet toothbrush and clean as usual.

Insect bites. Apply directly as a paste made with a little water. Keep the soda moist by applying a wet cloth. Soothes the stinging and itching.

Rashes and poison ivy. For local rashes apply as for insect bites. When the skin irritation is more general take a soda bath, using a cup of soda to a tub of warm water.

Bicarbonate Fire Extinguisher

Most dry-powder fire extinguishers owe their effectiveness to carbon dioxide, derived by the action of heat on bicarbonate of soda. On being heated, the bicarbonate decomposes to form sodium carbonate and carbon dioxide. This reaction extracts a large amount of heat from the fire. In addition, the carbon dioxide acts as a smothering agent.

In the kitchen. Wherever you have a box of baking soda, you therefore have an emergency fire extinguisher. For grease and oil fires around the kitchen range—where water would only spread the blaze—bicarbonate is especially effective. Just break open the box and scatter the powder loosely by the handful. Since soda is itself a cooking ingredient, it cannot harm food and it can be rinsed away once the fire is out.

In the car and garage, a box of bicarbonate of soda may also be a lifesaver. It could end a fire in seat cushions, floor mat, engine, or an oil fire on the garage floor, in seconds—without damaging anything it touches. Again, the best way to apply it is to scatter it by the handful, separating the particles as much as possible to form a cloud of powder.

COMMON SALT

Everybody knows that without sodium chloride or common salt food is tasteless. Not many know, however, that there are many other uses for salt around the kitchen and home. Here are a few:

Around the Home

Wooden clothespins will last longer and will not freeze onto your clothes line in cool weather if you first boil them in a strong solution of salt.

Cracked eggs can be boiled without their contents oozing out if a teaspoon of salt is added to each pint of water. The salt in the water increases its density so the osmotic pressure between the fluids inside and outside the egg shell is balanced. This prevents additional fluid from making its way inside the egg and forcing the contents out.

Nut meats will come out whole from their shells if you soak the nuts overnight in salt water before cracking them. The water expands the shells, while the salt prevents the loss of flavor from the meats.

Brass, copper, and pewter respond brilliantly to a paste made of salt and vinegar, thickened with flour. Apply the paste, allow to remain for an hour, then rub it off. Wash and polish with a soft cloth. Do not, of course, use this or any other metal cleaner on lacquered objects. Use it only on bare metal.

Cut flowers will keep longer if you add a little salt to the water in which they stand. The salt resists the growth of decay bacteria.

To remove a new stain or ink spot from the carpet, pour a mound of table salt immediately on the wet spot. After a few moments brush up the salt and apply more, repeating until the stain has been soaked up and as much as possible of what remains has been bleached. Old spots may be lightened and made less conspicuous by wetting with water and applying a thick coating of salt.

Cream whips more rapidly if a pinch of salt is added to the cream before you begin. The salt strengthens the fat cells.

Flatirons that have become rusty, rough, or sticky from caked starch can be smoothed to a glasslike finish by rubbing with slightly dampened salt applied with a piece of rumpled paper.

Slippery fish can be made skidproof during cleaning if you dip your fingers in a dish of salt before starting.

Food will cook faster in a double boiler if you add salt to the water in the outer part. The salt raises the boiling point of the water.

Ivory-handled knives and piano keys can be cleaned with a mixture of lemon juice and salt. In cleaning the latter make sure none of the liquid runs down between the keys.

Patching plaster to fill a hole left in a plaster wall by a nail can be made in a jiffy from equal parts of salt and starch, with just enough water to make a stiff putty. You can paint over it immediately with water or emulsion paints, but must wait for it to dry before applying oil-solvent paints.

In the Bathroom

Eyewash, mouthwash, and gargle can be made by dissolving a scant teaspoon of table salt in a pint of warm water. Because salt water at this concentration has approximately the same density as the body fluids, its action is more soothing than higher or lower concentrations.

Tooth powder. Dry salt, sprinkled on a wet toothbrush, makes a cheap and excellent dentifrice.

Hot water bottle substitute can be made from a bag of hot salt. Pour the salt into a pan and heat it in the oven until it is quite hot. Then pour it into a cotton bag. It will hold its heat for a long time.

Chimney Sweep

When the fireplace is blazing hotly, throw a handful of salt into it. The flame will turn a weird yellow and the combination of flame and salt will act as a "chimney sweep," helping to clean out soot that otherwise might lead to a fire or a burned-out flue.

Salt for Killing Weeds

Rock salt is one of the oldest and most economical weed killers. Apply it generously where weeds come up in the cracks of sidewalks and beside driveways or any place where unwanted weeds can grow. Spread the dry salt liberally. The first rain will dissolve it completely and the resulting brine will attack the roots and kill the plant.

Use rock salt to prevent the growth of weeds on tennis courts and parking areas. To reduce fire hazards, use it also to remove vegetation from fire lanes, around oil tanks, piles of lumber, and so on. Less is needed to kill tender grass than is needed for more stubborn weeds. Under average conditions, about 2 pounds should be used for each square yard. To kill poison ivy, use 4 pounds to the square yard.

Cut high and thick vegetation immediately before or after application. A second application may be needed for the complete eradication of all growth.

Caution: Since salt is so effective in making ground sterile, do not use it near grass plots, trees, flower gardens, or vegetable gardens—with one exception, asparagus beds.

EXTRA USES FOR SOAP

From creating realistic artificial snow for your Christmas tree to detecting gas leaks, from stopping runs in silk stockings to lubricating stubborn windows and drawers, ordinary household soap may be put to dozens of uses besides the fundamental one of washing with it. Here are a few suggestions:

Patterns for casting small metal parts for ship and other models can be carved in soap. Having no grain, it is much easier to carve into small objects than soft wood, the material commonly used for this purpose. Because of its greasy nature, it will not stick to a plaster mold.

Plaster castings will not stick to rubber or plaster molds that have been lubricated with soap. All you need to do is to brush strong soapy water or liquid soap over the inside of the mold before pouring the plaster.

Greasing screws by rubbing them on a bar of soap makes it easier to drive them into hard wood. Nails take less pounding, too, when given this treatment. Soaping not only saves work, but also lessens the danger of splitting.

Before tackling a dirty job, rub wet soap into your hands and scratch some under your fingernails. Let it dry there. When your work is done, the grime will wash off much more easily —and your nails will be perfectly clean!

Leaks in gas-pipe joints are located easily and safely by painting around the suspected joint with soapsuds. Gas flowing through the suds will produce bubbles that will reveal the point of the leak.

How much softener does your tap water need? Put a measured amount of distilled water in a bottle and, drop by drop, add a strong solution of soap in rubbing alcohol until an even layer of suds is formed when the bottle is shaken. Now empty the bottle, fill it with tap water and see how much softener must be added to this tap water to give the same result with the same number of drops of the solution.

Sticking drawers slide easily after their runners have been rubbed with a moistened cake of soap. The same treatment is effective for doors that stick, the soap being rubbed on the places that scrape. For loosening stubborn windows, rub soap in the jambs and stop strips—if you can move the window enough to get at them.

Suction cups stick better and stay put longer on walls, tile, or woodwork, if their edges are rubbed on a wet piece of soap or a soapy cloth before they are applied. If this is done, the cup will also have less tendency to leave an indelible ring on the wall when it is removed.

Retouching photographs is simplified by mixing a little soap in the water used for moistening the spotting colors. It makes the colors spread more easily on a glossy or oily surface.

Runs in nylon stockings can be stopped temporarily with soap. Just moisten the corner of a cake of soap and rub it on the top of the run. This treatment will keep the run from spreading until there is an opportunity to change stockings and make permanent repairs.

As a pincushion, a bar of soap makes a handy place to stick needles and pins. What's more, it lubricates them so they will go through stiff fabrics with less effort. In sewing, an occasional jab of the needle into soap helps.

Artificial snow for your Christmas tree can be made by beating up a thick suds of powered soap or flakes with an egg beater and applying it to the branches with a spatula or a cake icer. To give it more sparkle, some of the mica or plastic flakes sold as artificial snow may be mixed with the suds, or sprinkled on the branches while the foam is still wet.

LINSEED OIL HAS MANY USES

Besides serving as a smooth-flowing and durable vehicle for paint, varnish, and stain, linseed oil can perform many other useful jobs around the home and shop. It can beautify and protect wood surfaces and keep them from drying out, it can protect metal from moisture and give longer life to rope.

Raw linseed oil may be used where drying time is not important. *Boiled* linseed oil—raw oil containing drying chemicals—should be used where quick drying is desirable.

Caution: When practical, burn rags that have been used to apply linseed oil immediately after use; otherwise store them temporarily in covered metal cans or spread them out to dry in a well-ventilated place. The heat produced by the oxidation of the oil may cause exposed piles of rags to catch fire spontaneously.

Remove excess oil from surfaces that must be handled. Rub to a finger-touch dry to eliminate any stickiness. If they stay sticky, remove the excess with turpentine or mineral spirits.

Do not use linseed oil and turpentine mixture on lacquered finishes, since turpentine may dissolve the lacquer.

Never *boil* a mixture of linseed oil and turpentine; it will catch fire!

Here are some things you can do with it:

Bread boards will clean easily if you treat their surfaces. First scrub the board and let it dry thoroughly, then sand the surface smooth. Apply boiled linseed oil with a soft cloth. After 30 minutes rub oil into the wood and wipe off excess. Sand very lightly after it is dry, and let stand at least 24 hours before using.

To prevent chopping blocks from staining and getting water soaked give the wood two or three coats of raw linseed. Apply each coat liberally and wipe off excess after 2 hours standing. Then rub well with coarse cloth. Let dry about 48 hours between coats. After long use, another coat may be necessary.

Handles of hand tools will last longer and keep looking like new if you treat them with a thin coat of linseed oil, and repeat whenever the finish begins to show signs of wear.

Ladders. To maintain the flexibility and the strength of your ladder and to prevent splintering, coat it at least once a year with boiled linseed oil.

Wooden hammer handles shrink and dry out, causing heads to loosen. To prevent this, tighten the head onto the hammer with a wedge. Then stand the hammer on its head in linseed oil. This treatment will keep the hammer head securely in place.

Nails and screws will drive easier if you first dip them in linseed oil. The thin tough coating that the oil forms around them will also help prevent wood rot.

Before glazing a window, give the wood where the glass is to rest a coat of boiled linseed. This will seal the wood and keep it from absorbing oil from the putty. Then spread a thin coat of putty in the sash to form a bed. Lay in the pane, and press gently in place. Drive in glazier's points and apply remainder of putty. If putty is too stiff, add a few drops of linseed oil and knead thoroughly.

Bird houses. For a bird house with a long-lasting natural-wood finish, here is a suggestion: First cut all pieces to size, then soak them for 24 hours in boiled linseed oil. Let pieces dry before assembling.

Flag pole ropes will last longer if you treat them with linseed oil. Wipe new rope with the oil before stringing. If rope is already in place, put a little oil in a pan and draw the rope through it.

To remove tar from your car or other metal surface, soak spots with raw linseed oil. Allow to stand until soft. Then wipe clean with a soft cloth dampened with the oil.

Screens and windows. Before installing them, touch up unpainted edges with boiled linseed oil to seal the wood and prevent swelling from moisture. Wiping the screen mesh with a mixture of 2 parts boiled linseed oil and 1 of turpentine, applied with a piece of short-nap carpet, will help prevent rust. Remove excess oil and let screen dry before hanging.

Sticking doors, drawers, and windows usually get in that condition because moisture enters through the raw edges, causing them to warp or swell. To prevent this, apply with a cloth a thin mixture of the 2 to 1 oil-turpentine mixture mentioned in the last paragraph to the window grooves and to the unpainted edges of the sash, window frame, door, or drawers runners. All should be dry before treatment.

9

Arts and Crafts

ETCHING ON METAL

In etching, a metal plate is first covered with a ground or resist, which is an acid-resisting coating of wax, pitch, or asphaltum. The desired design is scratched through this and the plate is then treated with the etching fluid.

Of the waxes, paraffin is widely used, being cheap and always available. A thin, even coat is produced by pouring the melted paraffin over the plate which has itself been warmed. Waxes, however, sometimes cause trouble during scribing. If the coating is too cold and hard, it will chip; if too warm, it will pull.

Ready-made asphaltum varnish may prove more satisfactory for most decorative work. When it is allowed to dry hard, it will cut well and leave clear, sharp lines. If asphaltum varnish gets too cold it may become too stiff to apply. If, at 70°F, it is still too thick to spread well, thin with a little turpentine.

After etching, the varnish may be removed with naphtha or turpentine.

Etching Solutions

Solutions for etching metal should always be mixed and applied in glass containers or containers heavily coated with asphaltum. Glass photographic trays or baking pans are excellent for flat work. Rectangular, one-piece fish tanks will serve for large work.

Nitric acid is used in etching most metals. For fast etching, this may be used full strength. For slower action carefully stir 1 part of acid in 1 part of water. When the process is carried out with a diluted solution, it is well to stir occasionally or to rock the tray to remove bubbles and scale that may interfere with even biting. Store the acid and solution in Teflon bottles or in glass bottles with acid-proof caps.

(*Caution:* Handle nitric acid with great care; it is extremely corrosive. Wear rubber gloves when mixing or using it; always add the acid to the water, and not vice versa; don't spill or spatter it. If you spill any on your skin, flush immediately with plenty of cold water.)

Etching Copper and Brass

First clean the metal with any available soft abrasive powder, such as whiting or talc, and then wipe the surface with a soft cloth, being careful to remove all fingerprints. Paint all portions not to be etched with an even coat of asphaltum varnish. If a design is to be etched in, coat the entire surface. When the coating is dry, draw or trace the design on the asphaltum with a soft lead pencil. With a sharp scratch awl or other needle-pointed tool then cut the lines through to the metal.

When ready, lower the piece carefully into the etching bath with plastic tongs. Full-strength, technical-grade nitric acid will etch copper and brass to a depth of about 0.002 inch in a minute; for all ordinary purposes the etching will be deep enough in from a minute to a minute and a half. A half-and-half solution will require considerably longer, but should be used where a deep etch is wanted.

Etching Aluminum and Steel

Aluminum is etched in the same way as copper and brass, except that muriatic (hydrochloric) acid is used instead of nitric. Full-strength muriatic acid will etch to a depth of about 0.003 inch per minute. The etching will be slower, but can be kept under better control, if the acid is diluted 1 part acid to 2½ to 3 parts water.

An easy way to etch aluminum is to first heat the metal enough to melt paraffin, lay it flat on half a dozen thicknesses of newspaper, and flow on a thin coat of the wax. When the coated metal is cold, scratch on the design or lettering, cutting right through the wax film to the metal. Apply the solution to the scratched areas with a small wad of absorbent cotton fastened to the end of a short stick with a rubber band. When the metal has been etched deeply enough, wash thoroughly with water and then remove the wax with boiling water. (*Caution:* Although muriatic acid is not quite as corrosive as nitric acid, it should be handled with the same care. See "*Caution*" under "Etching Solutions".)

Steel may be etched quickly and satisfactorily with a solution made by mixing 1 part muriatic acid with 1 part technical nitric acid (*Caution:* Be especially careful with this combination, as it is more corrosive than either of the separate acids! If you store it in a bottle, leave the cap loose for the first 15 hours, as during that time it gives off gas).

Among other applications, you may use this solution for etching names and designs on tools. Clean the metal thoroughly with whiting or other mild abrasive powder and wipe with a cloth. Outline the name or design with asphaltum varnish, or coat the tool all over with asphaltum and scratch the figure in this after it is hard and dry. Then apply a few drops of the solution to the part to be etched and let remain until the etching is deep enough. Rinse with water. After removing the asphaltum with solvent, dry the tool and coat it with oil or other rust preventive.

Etching Pewter

Old-style pewter is difficult to etch because the metal is soft and porous. The new type of pewter so commonly used today for decorative metal working contains a large proportion of tin and may be successfully etched with nitric acid. Follow instructions for etching on copper and brass. With pewter, all the parts that have been etched are left black. In most cases this adds to the effectiveness. If desired, the black can be removed by polishing or buffing.

Cut-outs and Silhouettes

To etch cut-outs, letters, and silhouettes in copper and brass, use thin metal and clean it with a dry abrasive. Paint all parts that are to be left untouched by the acid with an even coat of asphaltum, including the back and the edges. In designs that are to be etched out to form a picture or a word, a section of one part should join the next part so that the design will not finally fall apart. Irregular lines may be corrected by scraping away the asphaltum after it is thoroughly dry.

Slow etching is advisable in this case, as in all etching where more than 0.002 or 0.003-inch depth is required. Make a bath of 1 part nitric acid to 1 part water (see Etching solutions item above). After immersing the prepared plate, watch closely and remove promptly as soon as the acid has eaten through the metal.

Another method is to coat the entire surface of the metal on both sides with the asphaltum and let dry hard. Outline the letters or design with a soft lead pencil. Then scratch only the outline through the coating. In this case only the outline will be attacked. If clean sharp lines have been scratched, the parts will separate when the acid has eaten through.

SILVER JEWELRY FROM DENTAL AMALGAM

Dental amalgam, an alloy of silver and mercury used by dentists for filling teeth, is also an excellent material for making jewelry in the home workshop. With it you can duplicate admired pieces, or you can make ring settings, brooches, watch charms, pendants, earrings, and other pieces of your own design.

Besides an ounce or two of amalgam, which you should be able to get at your dentist's or a dental supply house, you will need an ounce of mercury to mix with it and increase its workability. You will also need a little plaster of Paris and powdered pumice. With this you can make a number of pieces of jewelry at a cost of no more than a dollar each.

The simplest way to make a cast is to press the amalgam in a mold made of the plaster.

For an original piece, mix some of the plaster with water and allow it to set until firm and only slightly damp. Then cut the design in its face with an etching tool, knife, or motor-driven hand grinder. For a reproduction of an existing piece, simply grease the piece lightly with petroleum jelly and press it into the damp plaster, leaving it there until the plaster sets.

As soon as the mold has set, mix a very little mercury with the silver amalgam to make it pliable. Squeeze out excess mercury through twisted cheese-cloth, and then, with the amalgam the consistency of stiff putty, press a little at a time into the plaster mold. Use a wooden clay-modelling tool or any other blunt instrument and pack the amalgam into every corner. Let it set overnight and then carefully pull it from the mold.

When the silver is first taken from the mold, it will be light in color and lusterless. Brisk polishing, however, with pumice and a stiff brush will soon bring out its silver sheen. The amount of polishing controls the degree of luster. Like all silver, amalgam is subject to tarnish, but a little silver polish will restore its shine. Or, if you wish, you can apply a coat of clear lacquer to protect its finish.

Copper Amalgam

A similar amalgam of mercury with copper can also be used to make small pieces of jewelry. In addition, it can be used to fill holes in copper work, to take accurate impressions of small pieces in art and modelmaking, or to serve as an electrical conducting cement to join connecting wires to carbon brushes.

Although metallic mercury will combine with copper sheet to produce a bright silvery surface, this method cannot be used to produce amalgam in bulk form because the alloying action stops with this surface. You can make a pliable amalgam, however, by combining mercury with finely divided copper obtained by precipitation.

To make copper in this form, suspend several strips of iron or zinc in a solution of either copper sulfate or copper nitrate. The iron or zinc will dissolve, and copper from the solution will precipitate on the strips in the form of a fine powder. Scrape off and collect the powder, and keep adding iron or zinc as long as the solution remains blue.

Place the precipitated copper in a porcelain mortar and wash it well with running water. Then drain it and pour over the copper a solution of mercuric nitrate (*Caution:* Poison!). Allow this solution to act for about 10 minutes, or until the color of the copper has changed somewhat, and then pour it off. Finally, add to the copper several times its weight of metallic mercury, fill the mortar nearly full of hot water, and knead the mass under the hot water with a pestle.

The kneading will cause the mercury to unite with the copper to form a putty-like amalgam. This can be pressed into a mold, used to fill a hole, or used as a cement. It will form a solid mass of metal as soon as it cools and sets.

TO METALLIZE BABY SHOES
WITHOUT ELECTROPLATING

It is impossible to preserve baby shoes merely by coating them with varnish or enamel. Natural flexibility of the material, changes in temperature and humidity, and possibly mildew will eventually cause the leather or cloth to deteriorate and the coating to crack or chip. For permanent preservation, the shoe material must first be stiffened and sealed against the weather and then given a decorative coat—usually metallic.

For those who do not have facilities for electroplating, the following procedure, using both clear and metallic lacquer, provides a similar appearance in a coating that is just as long lasting.

First remove all wax and polish from the shoes with lacquer thinner. To stiffen the shoes, submerge them for 12 hours in lacquer diluted with an equal amount of lacquer thinner. Cover the container in which this is done to prevent evaporation. Then remove the shoes, let them dry for 1 hour, shape them and let them dry for another 36 hours. Next dip them for just a few seconds (to prevent softening the sealer coat) in lacquer of full strength and let them dry another 36 hours. Finally spray or brush on metallic lacquer of the desired color.

MODELING AND CASTING ORNAMENTS

Nonhardening Modeling Clay

Kaolin	67 parts
Sulfur	33 parts
Lanolin	60 parts
Glycerine	40 parts

Extra kaolin may be substituted for the sulfur, which acts only as a preservative. Knead all the ingredients together thoroughly. Dry pigments may be worked in to give desired color.

Plastic Molding Materials

A puttylike material that can be used in taking impressions, duplicating rosettes or other raised designs, or for filling cracks in wood can be made of a mixture of plaster of Paris and fine sawdust made into a paste with water containing a little glue.

Another plastic material that is unusually adhesive, dries hard, and can be carved, sandpapered, or colored can be made by mixing:

Whiting	1¼ cup
Linseed oil	2 tsp
Clear varnish	3 tsp
Thick liquid glue	4 fl oz

Mix thoroughly with a spatula or thin-bladed knife. The material can be applied with a brush if a bit more linseed oil is added, or with modeling tools if used stiff. A cookie or cake-icing gun is useful in applying the composition.

This material has many uses. Picture frames, lamp stands, shades, turned vases, shade pulls, and other craft objects can be coated with it to form ropes, scrolls, beads, spatter effects, and so on. It is also useful in filling cracks and in building up small pieces of wood work which would otherwise require hand carving or delicate fitting.

When dry, the material becomes hard and can be colored with lacquer or colored varnishes. Gold or aluminum bronze powder can be mixed with the plastic material to create metallic colored effects, or it may be dusted on after the material has been applied to an object, thus decreasing the amount of powder needed.

A third plastic material can be made from:

Plaster of Paris	20 parts
White lead	16 parts
Litharge	6 parts
Fine sawdust	4 parts
Liquid glue, sufficient	

Mix the powders thoroughly and add enough glue to make a paste or slurry which should be rather thin if it is to be applied with a brush, or stiff if it is to be molded or applied with bladed tools.

Cornstarch "Ceramics"

A claylike material that can be used to model toys, knick-knacks, and costume jewelry can be mixed in a few minutes from ingredients found around the kitchen. Here they are:

Corn starch	1 cup
Bicarbonate of soda (baking soda)	1 lb
Cold water	1¼ cups

Blend corn starch and baking soda together thoroughly in a saucepan. Mix in the water and place over medium heat for about 4 minutes, stirring constantly until mixture thickens to mashed potato consistency. Turn out on a plate and cover with a damp cloth until cool.

When easy to handle, knead like dough. Work with one portion at a time, wrapping rest in plastic to prevent drying. Knead a few drops of white glue into pieces of clay for added strength. Roll out and cut figures with cookie cutters or a knife, or shape by hand. When joining pieces, lightly moisten facing parts and press together.

Dry objects on waxed paper for about 36 hours, or until hard. Paint with tempera colors. Spray with clear plastic or coat with shellac for shiny, protective finish.

Wax Molds for Plaster Casts

Formula 1

Beeswax	4 oz
Olive oil	1 oz
Corn starch	4 oz

Melt the beeswax over low heat and stir in the olive oil. Sift the starch and then stir in the oil and beeswax until the mixture is as thick as biscuit dough.

The resulting substance will be hard when cold. For use it must be slightly softened by warming it. When soft enough, dust the object to be copied with talcum powder (French chalk) and press this object carefully into the wax. After cooling again, the object may be removed by tapping the wax. The resulting mold may then be filled with the usual plaster of Paris mixture.

FORMULA 2

Beeswax	4 oz
Lard	4 oz
Raw linseed oil	4 fl oz
Four	8 oz

Melt the beeswax and lard together in a container placed in a pan of hot water. Stir in the linseed oil and then the flour, continuing to stir until all are thoroughly mixed.

FORMULA 3

Paraffin wax	4 oz
Olive oil	4 fl oz
Whiting	8 oz

Melt the wax as in the previous two formulas (never over an open flame, as it might catch fire!) and stir in the whiting. When it has cooled slightly but before it has started to set, dump the mixture on a flat board and knead like dough until the consistency is uniform and pliable.

Parting Medium for Plaster Mold

Tincture of green soap is often the medium applied to a plaster mold to permit the subsequent removal of the cast made in it. Lacking green soap, here is a good substitute:

Place 4 cubic inches of ordinary white soap and 1 tablespoon of olive oil in 1 pint of boiling water. Stir constantly and keep boiling until the soap is completely dissolved. Solution will be hastened if you first shave the soap or cut it into small pieces.

To Hasten or Retard the Setting of Plaster of Paris

To hasten the setting, add ½ teaspoon of salt to each pint of water used in mixing the plaster.

To retard the setting, add 1½ ounces of a saturated solution of borax to each pint of water. This will delay the setting from 15 to 30 minutes, and will make impressions in the plaster harder and sharper.

Coloring Plaster of Paris

Plaster of Paris for ornamental objects may be colored before casting by mixing with water containing household dyes. Royal Blue, Jade Green, Scarlet, Yellow, Purple, and Coral, of the Rit brand, all color the plaster in subdued pastels. Use 1 package of dye to each quart of hot tap water. Approximately 4 ounces of this concentrated solution should be mixed with each pound of plaster.

Hardening Plaster Casts

Casts made of plaster of Paris can be hardened by soaking them in a solution made by dissolving 1 part of alum in 6 parts of hot water. A very small cast should be immersed in the alum water for at least an hour, while larger casts should remain for several days or a week.

If you want to harden just the surface of plaster casts, they may be soaked in melted paraffin or brushed over thoroughly with melted stearin. (*Caution:* Melt either of these in a double boiler; never over an open fire!) When cool and dry, the surface may be given a high polish. If large figures of plaster are to be placed outdoors, you can protect them from the weather by brushing them inside and outside with two or three coats of linseed oil, letting one coat dry before applying the next. Let the last coat of oil dry for 24 hours and then give the plaster a coat of waterproof paint. Then the cast may be painted to simulate metal or stone. If properly done, this treatment should be able to withstand the weather for at least two years.

Color Finishes for Plaster Casts

Ivory. Dissolve yellow beeswax (in an amount best judged by experience) in turpentine or mineral spirits. Add a little dry yellow ochre. Apply to the cast with a stiff brush, working quickly as the mixture is rapidly absorbed. Before completely dry, rub the color from high parts of the cast with cheese cloth. Leave color in depressions to give an effect of natural ivory.

Antique. Apply the same mixture as for ivory, but with the addition of a little dry umber and Paris green. To increase the appearance of age, give the cast a second coat.

Pompeian bronze. To prevent too much penetration, prime the cast with a thin coat of shellac. Make a thick mixture of lampblack with varnish, add a little copper bronze, then thin to easy brushing consistency with turpentine. The combination should dry without gloss. Using a stiff brush, apply a streaky, uneven coat to the cast. Wipe partly off with cheesecloth. When dry, apply a coating of turpentine in which has been dissolved a little white beeswax and Paris green. When this is dry, polish the highlights very lightly with cheesecloth.

Ebony. Prime with a coat of thin shellac. Make a thick mixture of ivory black with varnish, thin to easy brushing consistency with turpentine, and apply two coats to insure complete coverage. When dry, apply a coating of white beeswax to the high parts. When this is dry, polish only lightly.

To Clean Plaster Casts

Add enough cornstarch to hot water to make a thick paste. Apply a thick layer of this paste, while still hot, to the cast. Leave overnight to dry. Most of the starch can then be easily broken off, taking the surface dirt with it. The little that remains can be removed with hot water.

Cast Imitation Stone

Anything that can be cast in plaster can be cast in imitation stone, which is really a special mixture of cement. Cast stone is more durable than plaster and can be reproduced just as many times from a given mold. It can be colored with earth pigments to imitate many kinds of real stone.

Here is one common formula:

Portland cement	1 part
Sand	3 parts
Marble dust	
Dry earth colors	
Water	

Another popular formula contains Keene's cement, a harder relative of plaster of Paris made from more thoroughly heated gypsum to which alum or aluminum sulfate has been added:

Portland cement	1 part
White Keene's cement	1 part
Sand	4 parts
Marble dust or chips	
Dry earth colors	
Water	

Both formulas are mixed the same way. First combine the dry ingredients thoroughly on a board of sufficient size. The amount of marble dust or chips to be used depends on the amount of sparkle you want; about 1 part would be an average. The amount of pigment depends on the stone you are trying to imitate and must be determined by making trial batches. Use only earth colors or those sold particularly for coloring cement. Among your choices are red and brown iron oxides, yellow and brown umbers and ochres, and green chromium oxide. For gray or black, you can use lampblack, carbon black, black manganese oxide, or black iron oxide.

Sprinkle one or a combination of these colors into the other dry ingredients as you mix them. When the color appears to be about right, take a little of the mix, stir into it enough water to make a thick paste, and spread it out on an old piece of glass to set. Though it will still be several shades darker than its final color, you should be able to judge in four or five days if the color is satisfactory. If it is not, make what corrections you believe to be needed and test again. In the meantime, keep the main batch of material covered and dry.

When you are sure you have the right combination, mix only enough to meet your requirements for the day. Any excess mixture will set overnight and so be useless. Lay the mixture into a greased mold with a trowel and tamp it down gently with a stick padded on the end with a wad of cloth.

CRAYONS AND PAINTS

How to Make High-Grade Pastel Crayons

Pastel crayons or sticks of higher quality than the average sold in art stores can be made easily and cheaply at home from artists' dry colors held together by a simple gum binder. The famous German chemist, Ostwald, described the method of making them at the beginning of this century. With slight modifications, his method is followed widely by artists today.

The materials you need are dry pigments of desired colors, precipitated chalk for white and to make tints, and a small amount of gum tragacanth and beta-naphthol which you can get from a drugstore or chemical supply house. Any permanent pigments may be used except poisonous ones that contain lead and arsenic (chiefly lead whites, chrome yellows and greens, Naples yellow, emerald green, cobalt violet). The latter would be especially dangerous with pastel, as you get pastel pigments on your hands and breathe their dust.

To make the binder, put about $\frac{1}{3}$ ounce of gum tragacanth in a bottle, pour on it a pint of water and set the bottle overnight in a warm place. The next day, shake the bottle until the gelatin-like mass that has formed in it is dispersed uniformly through the water, then add about $\frac{1}{4}$ teaspoon of the beta-naphthol as a preservative. Label the bottle Solution A.

Dilute part of this solution with an equal amount of water and put the diluted solution in another bottle labeled Solution B. Dilute another part of Solution A with three parts of water and bottle it as Solution C. Gum solutions of different strengths are required to compensate for differences in the binding ability of different pigments.

Do your mixing on a slab of glass or marble or plastic tile, using a moderately flexible spatula as a mixing tool. Begin with white pastels to get an easy introduction to the general procedure. Take about 2 ounces of precipitated chalk and work into this a little more than $\frac{1}{2}$ fluid ounce of Solution C. Rub up the mass with the spatula until it has the consistency of putty. If the mass is so thin it runs, add more chalk; if too thick, add a little more solution. When you can roll it into a ball between your hands without finding it either too sticky or too crumbly, the mass is ready to form into sticks. Do this by rolling out portions into sausage-like sticks on a sheet of news-paper or paper towel, using either your hand or a small flat stick as a roller. The sticks are then left in a warm place until they are dry and hard.

Sticks can be made similarly with the colored pigments. With these, however, you will have to find by experiment the best combination of binder and pigment. For full-strength colors, use the pigment as it comes. For tints, combine colored pigment with varying amount of chalk. So you will be able to make predictable changes or to reproduce past satisfactory results, keep careful records of quantities used and of combinations of pigment and binder.

In mixing pigments for pastels, remember that the color produced in the final picture will be the same as that of the original *dry* powders. This color will darken when wet with the solution, but will return to its original value when the pastel stick dries.

Permanent Pigments for Oil Painting

Do you want to be sure you are getting what you think you are when you buy oil colors—long-lasting pigments of precise hue? Time was when certainty was almost impossible. Composition of pigments varied from one manufacturer to another, and identical names were often applied to entirely different products. Since 1942, however, the National Bureau of Standards has published standards of name and composition for the most used and most permanent of artists' oil paints. These were chosen by a committee of leading American artists and manufacturers, and are now adhered to voluntarily by most makers of such colors.

Following are some of the standard pigments that are commonly used. In several cases a color may also be known by a second name, but the use of a standard name for another pigment of similar color but different composition is not permitted.

COLOR	PAINT NAME	PIGMENT COMPOSITION
White	Zinc white	Zinc oxide
	Flake white	Basic lead carbonate
	Titanium white	Titanium dioxide combined with barium sulfate or zinc oxide
Black	Ivory black	Carbon from charred animal bones
	Lamp black	Carbon from condensed smoke
	Mars black	Ferro-ferric oxide
Blue	Ultramarine blue	Silicate of sodium and aluminum with sulfur
	Cobalt blue	Combined oxides of cobalt and aluminum
	Cerulean blue	Combined oxides of cobalt and tin
	Phthalocyanine blue	Copper phthalocyanine, made from synthetic organic dyestuff
Brown	Raw umber	Natural earth that consists chiefly of hydrous oxides and silicates of iron and manganese
	Burnt umber	Pigment prepared by heating raw umber

COLOR	PAINT NAME	PIGMENT COMPOSITION
	Burnt sienna	Prepared by heating raw sienna
	Burnt green earth	Prepared by heating green earth
Green	Viridian	Hydrous chromic oxide
	Green earth	Natural earth consisting chiefly of hydrous silicates of iron, aluminum, magnesium, and potassium
	Chromium oxide	Anhydrous chromic oxide
	Phthalocyanine green	Chlorinated copper, made from synthetic organic dyestuff
Red	Cadmium red	Pure cadmium sulfoselenide
	Light red	Nearly pure iron oxide
	Indian red	Nearly pure iron oxide
	Mars red	Artificial ochre, consisting chiefly of iron and aluminum oxides
	Alizarin crimson	Made from 1-2-dihydroxy anthraquinone and aluminum hydroxide
Yellow	Cadmium yellow	Pure cadmium sulfide
	Cobalt yellow	Potassium cobaltinitrite
	Mars yellow	Artificial ochre, consisting chiefly of hydrous oxide of iron and aluminum

COLOR	PAINT NAME	PIGMENT COMPOSITION
	Raw sienna	Natural earth consisting chiefly of hydrous oxides and silicates of iron and aluminum
	Naples yellow	Lead antimoniate
Violet	Cobalt violet	Anhydrous cobalt phosphate or arsenate
	Manganese violet	Manganese ammonium phosphate
	Mars violet	Artificial iron oxide

Cottage Cheese Casein Paint

For centuries before purified casein became available, artists and others made casein paint from curd cheese—plain cottage cheese made from skim milk without the addition of salt or cream. Some artists still do, getting their uncreamed and unsalted cottage cheese from the delicatessen or supermarket. Here's all you need:

	Parts by volume
Plain cottage cheese	5
Lime putty	1

For directions for making lime putty, see Chapter 2, Paints and Paint Removers. Stir the lime putty with the cheese and leave for several hours, until the cheese lumps have dissolved completely.

Use lime-proof pigments (also listed in Paint chapter) and work up into paste with water. Add to casein solution and dilute with water as necessary.

Paint for Craftwork or Finger Painting

This paint, made easily from kitchen products and household dyes, can be used by the craft worker for finger painting, block printing, screen painting, stenciling, and brayer printing. It can also serve as the binder in making a sawdust molding material or papier mâché.

Corn starch	½ cup
Cold water	1 cup
Unflavored gelatin (1 envelope)	¼ oz
Hot water	2 cups
Mild soap flakes or synthetic detergent	½ cup

Combine corn starch and ¾ cup of the cold water in a medium-size saucepan. Soak gelatin in remaining cup of cold water. Add hot water to starch mixture and cook over medium heat until mixture comes to a boil and is clear, stirring constantly. Remove from heat; blend in softened gelatin. Add soap or detergent and stir until mixture thickens and soap or detergent is thoroughly dissolved. Makes about 3 cups.

In place of the gelatin, you may use 1 tablespoon of glycerin. If used, combine the full cup of cold water with the corn starch before cooking. Stir in the glycerin when the mixture is removed from the heat.

To each cup of this base thoroughly stir in 1 teaspoon of household dye. Store in covered jars.

Scarlet, yellow, and royal blue, plus black and brown are suggested for a basic set of colors. Orange, Kelly green, and fuchsia may be added for larger sets. Precipitated chalk or whiting may be used for white.

Save Money on Turpentine

You can save money in buying turpentine for thinning artists' oil colors by buying sealed cans of "pure gum turpentine" in paint, hardware, and food stores. If it bears the seal of the Turpentine Farmers' Association, it is identical with that sold in small bottles at a higher price by artists' supply stores. It is also apt to be fresher. Although still cheaper "wood turpentine" will also serve as a thinner, it has a less agreeable odor.

Transparent Paper for Tracing

Canada balsam	1 oz
Gum turpentine	1 oz

Mix these ingredients and apply the resulting liquid to one surface of white, unsized paper, using a small flat brush. If the paper is still too opaque after the coating has dried, apply another coat.

TRANSFERRING NEWSPAPER PRINTS

Transferring pictures and comic strips from newspapers and magazines to plain white paper may provide hours of fun for the youngsters. Here is a simple preparation with which they may do this:

Water	4 oz
Liquid dishwashing detergent	1 squirt
Turpentine	2 oz

Put the water into a bottle or jar, add the detergent and turpentine and shake thoroughly to emulsify the mixture. Brush this liquid uniformly over the picture to be transferred, blot up the surface drops gently with a paper towel. Place the paper on which the picture is to be transferred on a plate, lay the moist picture face down on this and rub firmly and evenly over the back of it with the bowl of a spoon or with a wallpaper seam roller. On removing the original, a copy of it, in reverse, will be found on the paper beneath. Colored pictures may be transferred, as well as black-and-white.

HECTOGRAPH DUPLICATING DEVICE

More than half a century before the invention of most of the present office copying machines, small runs of menus, circular letters, club and church notices, and so on were made on a device called the *hectograph*, a word which means literally "hundred writing." Because the device—often homemade—is so simple and effective it still has considerable use for the same purposes.

The operation of the hectograph is based on absorption. The original writing is done on a sheet of bond paper with a water-soluble ink. This sheet is placed face down in contact with the moist surface of a clay, glue, or gelatin composition. The writing is absorbed from the paper and appears in reversed form on the surface. If then a sheet of blank paper is pressed in contact with the surface, the impression is transferred to the paper. When done properly, allowing a little more time of contact for each sheet, at least two dozen good copies may be made.

Here is the simplest formula for the pad:

Powdered whiting	16 oz
Glycerin	4 oz

Mix 8 oz of the whiting with the glycerin and beat the mixture thoroughly. Let it stand 12 hours, then mix in rest of the whiting and knead like dough. When it kneads stiff, set it aside for the glycerin to work through. Again knead well and then put in a shallow rectangular pan and flatten out roughly with your fingers. Finally make a perfect surface on it by scraping with the edge of a straight stick.

If, on standing, glycerin appears on the surface, sprinkle on some dry whiting and re-knead the mixture. Don't wipe off the glycerin. The mixture should be just moist to work best. Add either glycerin or whiting to secure this consistency.

Write or draw what you wish on glazed paper or hard bond paper with readymade hectograph ink bought at an office stationery supply store (you can also buy there special duplicating paper from which you can make the best possible originals and copies) or with homemade ink described below. When the writing is just dry lay the paper face down on the pad and smooth it flat with a photographic roller or with your hand. Let it remain 3 or 4 minutes, then care-

fully peel it off. Put on a sheet of blank paper of
the same type and smooth it down similarly. Let the
first sheet remain just an instant, the next a little
longer, and so on until you have either finished your
run or the copy is too weak to be satisfactory. Wash
off the surface of the pad with a slightly damp cloth
to remove the writing and prepare it for fresh copy.

Here is a formula for a glue or gelatin pad, a
type more expensive and a little more difficult to
make but preferred by many:

"A-Extra" grade glue, or
  unflavored food gelatin   3 oz
Water   6½ oz
Glycerin   18 oz
Sodium bicarbonate   ⅓ oz

To prepare the composition, follow this procedure:

1. Put cold water in top part of double boiler.
2. Add bicarbonate of soda and stir until dissolved.
3. Add glue or gelatin and let soak 1½ hours.
4. Heat water in lower part of double boiler until
mixture in top part has reached 140°F and the glue or
gelatin has melted. Don't stir until free foam has all
been released; then stir slowly until the gel is uniformly dissolved in the water.
5. Slowly add the glycerin and stir into solution
when the combination has again reached 140°F.
6. Let stand at 140°F until solution clears and
cools to 120°F.
7. Pour into 9-by-12-inch pan.

HECTOGRAPH INK

Acetone	2 oz
Glycerin	5 oz
Acetic acid (28%)	2½ oz
Water	12 oz
Dextrin	½ oz
Dye	2½ oz

Use water-soluble dyes: methyl violet, Victoria blue, emerald green, or, for red, rhodamine B. First dissolve the dextrin by stirring in hot water. When cool, stir in the other ingredients. (*Caution*: Keep the acetone away from all fire, as it and its vapor are very flammable.)

FROSTING OR ETCHING GLASS

Solution 1

Sodium fluoride	1 oz
Potassium sulfate	90 grains
Water to make	8 fl oz

Solution 2

Zinch chloride	100 grains
Hydrochloric acid (36%)	1 fl oz
Water to make	8 fl oz

Mix the two solutions separately and store them in polystyrene or Teflon bottles (the first one will eat glass). When needed, mix equal amounts of each in a plastic or hard-rubber container. Apply with a pointed stick or a brush, depending on the area to be covered. Rinse after about 30 minutes. A fine mat surface should have been produced. (*Caution:* Wear rubber gloves while handling the solutions and do not breathe the vapors of the mixed solution.)

Here is another formula for producing a finely-etched surface on a glass plate:

Sodium fluoride	60 grains
Powdered gelatin	60 grains
Water	32 oz

Soak the gelatin in 6 ounces of cold water until it is soft. Dissolve the sodium fluoride (*Caution*: Poison!) in the remainder of the water, heated to 125°F and transferred to a plastic or hard-rubber container, and then add the gelatin solution, stirring until the gelatin is completely dissolved. Coat the resulting liquid uniformly on the glass to be frosted and let it dry thoroughly.

Then dip the dry coated glass in a solution made by diluting 1 part of concentrated (36%) hydrochloric acid with 30 parts of water for 1 minute, and permit to dry without rinsing. After the acid has dried, the coating may be washed off with hot water, leaving a finely etched surface on the glass. (*Caution:* Wear rubber gloves while handling the solutions.)

Imitation Frosted Glass

For uniform frosting: Dissolve ½ ounce of gum arabic in 1 pint of water. Then, with stirring, add Rochelle salts until the water will hold no more. Let stand in a cool place for 12 hours and then filter. Clean the glass thoroughly, lay it flat, and flow on the solution. When dry, coat with thin varnish or lacquer.

For a pattern resembling frost crystals: Dissolve a little dextrin in a strong Epsom salt solution. Apply to the glass as above. As the water slowly evaporates, beautiful crystal patterns develop which cling securely to the glass. When fully developed, they may be protected with a thin coating of varnish or lacquer.

Coloring Glassware

Vases, bottles, bulbs, test tubes, and other glassware intended for decorative or novelty purposes can be frosted with the aid of sodium silicate silution. At the same time, they may be tinted any color by adding a water-soluble dye to the sodium silicate.

This viscid liquid which sticks so firmly to glass may be painted on or a sufficient quantity may be used to allow the glassware to be dipped bodily. If desired, just one part of the glassware may be treated. After being coated and dried, the glass should be immersed for a moment in a boiling hot concentrated solution of Epsom salt or of sal ammoniac and then dried again.

FLOWERS

Dyeing Cut Flowers

Packaged dyes used for dyeing cloth are also suitable for dyeing flowers. Just cut the flower stems on a slant and immerse the stems in a solution of the dye in water.

Only white flowers can be colored the original color of the dye, but many combinations can be made. Yellow flowers can be changed to orange, saffron, green, and other colors. Pink can be changed to lilac, red to purple, and so on through the list of colors and shades.

Changing the Color of Flowers

The colors of many flowers may be changed chemically. Red roses can be bleached white by exposing them to the fumes from burning sulfur. Because sulfur fumes are irritating, do this outdoors or in a well-ventilated room. Make a little mound of sulfur on a disposable metal pie plate or can cover and place this on a surface that will not burn. After dampening them thoroughly, support the flowers several inches above the sulfur. Then light the top of the sulfur pile and place a carton over everything to act as a fume chamber. The petals often become variegated, making the effect more interesting. The sulfur dioxide produced by the burning reacts with the red coloring matter and changes it to a compound that is colorless or white.

Another way to produce sulfur dioxide is to add a dilute solution of sulfuric acid to sodium sulfite in a glass dish.

Some flowers placed over ammonia fumes also change color. Just support them over a dish of household ammonia, and place a box over everything as before. Many purple flowers turn green when exposed to this gas.

Sun Pictures on Leaves or Fruit

If a monogram, word, or design cut from aluminum foil is coated with varnish and then applied to a mature leaf, or to a fruit that is almost ripe but which has not yet developed color, the parts covered will not be exposed to the sun's rays and so will not develop as fully as the uncovered area. When you later remove the foil, you will find a clear image of itself—a photograph made by nature—on the leaf or fruit. It is important to use a waterproof adhesive such as varnish. Otherwise the cut-out may be washed away by rain.

LEATHER FOR CRAFT WORK

Leather in many colors may be purchased from handicraft stores or leather companies by whole or half skins, or by the square foot or square inch. Dealers will also cut leather from your pattern, and many of them will furnish project kits of their own design. If much leather is used, it is cheaper to buy whole or half skins.

The best tooling leather is calfskin, but tooling steerhide also works well. Considering economy rather than durability, tooling sheepskin may be used. Calfskin makes excellent billfolds, ladies' purses, coin purses, cigarette and comb cases. Tooling steerhide makes durable billfolds, key and card cases, book ends, notebooks. Tooling sheepskin is used for bookcovers, bookmarks, card-table covers. Pigskin may be tooled in staight lines for letter cases, key cases, coin purses.

Embossed leathers have designs impressed upon them. Embossed steerhide and cowhide are used for briefcases, notebooks, camera cases. Sheepskin is sold with fancy embossed designs or imitation grains of expensive leathers, such as ostrich, and is used for coin purses, book covers, billfolds. Suedes are used for

linings, handbags, belts. Reptile leathers are used for
billfolds, coin purses, handbags. Ostrich is used for
billfolds, coin purses, book covers. Heavy steerhide,
cowhide, and elkhide are used for belts, knife sheaths,
moccasins. "Skiver" is thin leather used only for
linings.

Dyeing Leather

Dyes for leather may be water stains, oil stains,
acids and oxides, spirit stains, and waterproof drawing
inks. The amateur must be very careful if acids and
oxides are used since they will burn the leather and
cause it to crack if used in too strong solution. Best
results will be obtained if commercial dyes are purchased from leather-supply companies.

Before dyeing natural leather, first clean the surface thoroughly. A commercial cleaning solution may
be purchased, or a very weak solution of hydrochloric
acid may be made by adding 1 part of the acid to 20
parts water. Rub the surface of the leather lightly
with a soft cloth dampened with either cleaning solution. Allow the leather to dry slightly before starting
to dye it.

Always test the dye on a piece of scrap leather.
Flow on the dye with a soft brush. After it has dried,
a second coat may be applied if a darker effect is desired. Use a small camel's-hair brush to apply dye to
all cut edges of leather, being careful not to get dye
on the finished surface. Two-tone effects may be obtained by applying spirit dyes to leather that is already colored. Allow ample time for the dye to dry,
and polish the surface with a clean, soft cloth.

Finishing Leather Articles

Finish laced edges of leather articles by placing the laced edge on a smooth surface. Tap the lacing lightly with a smooth hammer. Clean and polish natural and dyed leather with saddle soap. Apply a thin coat with a soft, damp cloth and rub the surface lightly. Let it dry a few minutes; then polish with clean, soft cloth or use the palm of the hand. Work all new leather well between the hands to make it soft and pliable. To produce a high luster, a commercial polishing solution may be applied and the article polished according to directions. Too much wax, however, will cause the leather to become hard and crack.

Recondition used leather articles by cleaning them several times a year or as often as needed. Clean them with saddle soap or some mild white soap. White shoes, if made from a good grade of leather, may be cleaned with saddle soap and then treated with a high grade of white shoe polish, applied according to directions. Slide fasteners on leather articles may be made to move easier if a drop of light oil is applied to the slide. Too much oil will cause the tape to deteriorate. Worn lacing should be replaced immediately with new to prevent excessive wear to the edges.

DECORATIVE CANDLES FROM PARAFFIN

Beautiful decorative candles for holidays and anniversaries can be made easily and inexpensively from household paraffin wax and other items found around the home or obtainable from the local supermarket.

For molds you can use cardboard milk and ice-cream containers, plastic containers, cookie cutters, cups, gelatin molds, etc. So you can get the hardened wax out in one piece, just make sure that the opening of the mold is the largest part. Grease all molds with cooking oil and chill before pouring wax into them.

Paraffin is flammable! So melt it in a double boiler, with plenty of water in the outer part; never over direct heat.

One way to color the wax is to stir into it shavings from wax crayons. As the color will lighten as the candle solidifies, add crayon until the wax looks darker than desired.

Another way to color it is to stir into the melted wax 2 teaspoons of powdered Rit household dye for each 1 pound of wax. For brightest results, use lighter shades of dye.

Candle wick can be bought in hobby shops. Or you can make a good wick from carpenters' chalkline, a braided cotton cord that burns well. To slow its burning rate, soak it overnight in a solution of 1 tablespoon of salt and 2 tablespoons of borax in 1 cup of water, and then hang it to dry. To stiffen it, dip it in melted paraffin.

One way to fasten the wick is to tie one end to the middle of a pencil and the other to a small weight. Then lay the pencil across the top of the mold so the weight hangs down in the center and pour the wax around it.

Another way is to insert the wick in a hole melted in the center of the solidified candle by means of a heated wire or icepick. Then fill around the wick with melted wax.

Whipped wax, or "wax snow," is one form of decoration for your candles. Melt wax in a double boiler. Let cool until a thin film forms on top, and then whip with a fork or an egg beater until it becomes fluffy like a meringue. Apply this to the candle with a fork while it is still soft. If the candle is colored, leave open spaces for the color to show through. Holiday glitter will stick if sprinkled on the whipped wax while it is still warm and soft.

Floating candles. Flat candles molded of whipped wax in gelatin or cookie molds will float in a bowl of water, making a novel centerpiece.

Scented candles can be made by adding a few drops of perfume, pine oil, or other scent to the melted wax.

To clean pans and utensils, reheat them until wax melts. Pour off excess. Wipe off all the wax you can with a paper towel and then wash with hot soapy water.

10

Photography

HOW TO MAKE LIFETIME PRINTS

Contact prints and enlargements made by routine methods will probably remain brilliant and unstained for at least a few years. To make prints that will last as long as the paper on which they are printed requires, however, that you pay exacting attention to the drab jobs of fixing and washing.

When you watch a print in the fixing bath, nothing seems to happen except a slight whitening of the emulsion after the first few seconds of immersion. But don't let that fool you. The hypo must convert all undeveloped silver salts to a form that can be dissolved by water. In turn, thorough washing is required to carry away both the converted salts and the hypo itself. Any remaining salts will cause eventual overall darkening; any remaining hypo will react with the silver image, causing yellowing and fading.

If agitated constantly in a bath of fresh hypo, a single print should fix in about 1 minute. But under ordinary conditions, it's best to leave prints in the fixer, with frequent agitation, for from 5 to 10 minutes.

Better still, divide the fixing bath into two parts, and fix the prints in each in succession. After developing and before fixing, immerse the prints for 5 to 10 seconds in an acid stop bath. Then fix them for 3 to 5 minutes in the first fixing bath, drain for 5 seconds, and fix for another 3 to 5 minutes in the second bath.

After fifty 8-by-10-inch prints, or their equivalent in area, per quart of first bath have been fixed, discard the first bath. Replace the first bath with the second, and prepare a new second bath. After five such changes (for a total of 250 8-by-10 prints), discard both baths and replace with new ones.

A rapid flow of water doesn't greatly speed up the washing time of prints. But be sure a supply of fresh water constantly circulates around them. Wash single-weight prints at least 30 minutes, double-weight at least an hour.

Hypo test. One of several chemical tests will tell you when a print has been safely washed. The iodine-starch test, for instance, detects 1 part hypo in 2,500 parts of water. It consists of three solutions that are mixed just before using. The separate solutions will keep indefinitely in well-stoppered bottles. An amber bottle will preserve the mixture briefly.

Make solution A by dissolving ¼ ounce potassium iodide and 50 grains iodine crystals in ¼ ounce water; add water to make 4 ounces. Make solution B by dissolving 10 grains soluble starch in 4 ounces water; heat to boiling and cool. Solution C consists of ¼ ounce concentrated hydrochloric acid diluted with 3¾ ounces water. To make the test solution, add 18 drops of solution A and an equal amount of solution C to ½ ounce of solution B; add water to make 4 ounces.

Use by letting water drip from a print into a test tube and adding an equal amount of test solution. If the blue test solution loses its color, hypo remains in the print.

Hypo eliminator. Ordinarily you need not worry about the minute amount of hypo that clings to a print even after prolonged washing. For valued prints, you can remove this last trace with a solution that changes the hypo to a compound that washes out more readily.

Make this by mixing 4 fluid ounces of hydrogen peroxide (3-percent solution) and 3¼ fluid ounces of 3-percent ammonium hydroxide with 25 ounces of water. After washing the prints for the usual time, immerse for 6 minutes in this solution. Wash 10 minutes longer.

Gold protective solution. Even when prints are well fixed and washed, hydrogen sulfide and other contaminants in the air can cause the solver image to yellow and fade. This can be prevented by treating the print in a solution that coats the silver with gold.

Make the solution by adding 2½ fluid drams (about ⅓ fluid ounce) of 1-percent gold chloride stock solution (made by dissolving a 15-grain tube of gold chloride in 3½ ounces water) to 24 ounces water. Dissolve 145 grains of sodium thiocyanate in 4 ounces water. Add this slowly to the gold chloride solution while stirring rapidly. Add water to make 32 ounces.

Immerse the well-washed print in this solution for 10 minutes at 68°F, or until a faint change in image tone (toward bluish-black) takes place. Wash 10 minutes and dry as usual.

For best results, the gold protective solution should be mixed immediately before use. About eight 8-by-10 prints may be treated with 32 ounces.

HOW TO MAKE PRINTS IN A HURRY

Ever take a shot with your sheet-film camera that could mean extra fun or money to you if you could produce a finished blow-up from it in, say, 15 minutes? Perhaps a news scoop for a newspaper; a dinner, party, or club shot you would like to deliver before the gathering breaks up?

Such photo-finishing demands shortcuts. It will also help to have all your equipment arranged and your solutions mixed, ready for work the instant you hit the darkroom. Sheet film is specified because it is the most practical for rapid finishing. The system can be adapted for larger roll-film sizes if you are adept at handling such film in a tray.

Film developers for rapid work can be either the single or two-solution variety. In a two-solution developer, the developing agents and preservative are in the first tray, the alkali in the second. Such developers have longer life and make it easier to control development. The first solution may be stored and reused repeatedly. The second should be renewed after becoming badly discolored.

Solution 1. In 24 ounces water at 125°F, dissolve 75 grains metol, 1 ounce sodium sulfite, anhydrous, and ¼ ounce, 35 grains hydroquinine; then add water to make 32 ounces.

Solution 2. In 24 ounces water at 125°F, dissolve 3½ ounces sodium carbonate, monohydrated; add water to make 32 ounces.

To use, pour each solution into a separate tray without diluting.

Submerge the film quickly and evenly, and agitate the film constantly. At 70°F, immerse the negative 1 minute in the first solution and an equal time in the second, without rinsing in between. At 75°F immerse in each solution 45 seconds.

If you prefer a single solution, Kodak Dektol or D-72 is excellent. Use a stock solution without dilution. At 70°F develop for 1 minute, 40 seconds; at 75°, 1 minute, 20 seconds.

After development, swish the film for 5 seconds in a short-stop bath made by diluting 1½ ounces of 28-percent acetic acid with water to make 32 ounces. If the temperature of the solutions is above 70° dilute the stop bath with an equal amount of water to prevent blisters.

To speed up fixing, add 4 ounces plain hypo to each 32 ounces of the regular acid hardening fixing solution. After the film has been submerged for half

a minute in this fixer, it's safe to turn on the light.
Continue fixing until the negative has completely
cleared. This should take about 1½ minutes.

Next wash for 2 minutes in a tray through which
water is running rapidly. Then place the negative on
a clean ferrotype plate or sheet of glass and wipe the
surface with a soft plastic sponge.

You now have the choice of printing from a wet
negative or of drying it by rapid methods. The wet
technique is faster.

For enlarging, place the wet negative in a glass-
less carrier or squeegee it lightly, emulsion side down,
on a glass plate. For contact printing, wipe off the
surface moisture and sandwich the negative between
two sheets of film from which the emulsion has been
cleared. Squeegee lightly to remove air bubbles. Handle all wet negatives carefully, since the emulsion is
soft and easily damaged. Keep exposure time to a
minimum.

If you prefer a dry negative, you can dehydrate
it chemically by immersing it in a saturated solution
of potassium carbonate for 4 or 5 minutes. Make this
solution by dissolving about 8 ounces potassium carbonate (salts of tartar) in 7 ounces warm water and
allowing to cool.

After immersion, place the negative on a ferrotype plate and wipe the surface moisture from both
sides. It will now be dry enough for printing. Wash it
thoroughly later.

Two 250-watt reflector-spot infrared bulbs also
provide a quick method of drying. Wipe off surface
moisture from the negative, suspend it from one edge,

and set the bulbs, facing each other, about 10 inches on either side. Direct a fan breeze between the lights and across both sides of the negative to carry away moisture and to prevent overheating. Always start the fan before turning on the bulbs, and leave it on until after the bulbs are out. Before trusting a valuable negative to this drying method, better try it first with an old one to determine the best distances.

Hardening negatives. Negatives to be dried by artificial heat should be chemically hardened between developing and fixing. You can make a good hardener by dissolving ½ ounce potassium chrome alum in 16 ounces water, adding ¾ ounce of 28-percent acetic acid, and then adding water to make 32 ounces. Place the negative in this instead of in the ordinary stop bath and agitate for 3 minutes.

Develop the prints for 1 minute in a Dektol or D-72 type of developer diluted 1 to 1. Rinse for 5 seconds in running water and five for 1 minute in a separate batch of fixer with added hypo.

Wash for 2 minutes in running water, blot off the surface water, and dry on an electric dryer or put between blotters and dry by pressing with an electric iron. In using an electric drier, put blotters between the print and the drier apron to keep hypo from contaminating the apron. Prints that you want to keep for any length of time should be fixed an additional several minutes and washed at least half an hour.

Stabilized prints. Quick prints that will last still longer without fading or discoloring can be made by eliminating the fixing step and replacing it with the stabilizing process described later in this chapter under Standard Darkroom Formulas. If you choose this method, bathe the prints for a few seconds in a bath of 5 percent acetic acid after development and before placing them in the stabilizing solution.

HOW TO DOCTOR PRINTS
WITH FARMER'S REDUCER

Farmer's reducer (described under Standard Darkroom Formulas) may sound like a slimming agent for stout agricultural workers. Experienced photographers, however, know it as a versatile darkroom aid developed by Howard Farmer back in the 1880's. Besides its use in saving overexposed and fogged negatives, it can perform a number of jobs in altering and improving prints.

After using reducer on prints, always fix prints again in regular hypo solution and wash them thoroughly to prevent stains. Don't mix more reducer at a time than will keep you going for 5 minutes.

To remove black spots on prints, apply reducer sparingly with a fine brush. Take up any excess with a clean blotter before applying more. In portraits you can lighten skin blemishes the same way.

Pep up clouds, add highlights, and lighten any dark areas by swabbing on Farmer's reducer, diluted with extra water. Always stop a little before you have reached desired reduction, for it may continue slightly after you have removed the solution.

Overexposed prints can be saved by placing them in a tray of weak reducer. Agitate the tray continuously until print has been reduced sufficiently.

Pick a person or other desired object from a photo by eliminating the background. First outline the subject with a fine brush charged with reducer. Then apply solution to broad areas with a cotton swab.

TO REVIVE FADED PHOTOGRAPHS

Most prints or negatives that have faded can be easily restored by bleaching and redeveloping. Fading results from the reaction of the silver image with hydrogen sulfide in the air or sulfur compounds in the emulsion.

First immerse the print in a formaldehyde hardening bath (see Standard Darkroom Formulas) for 3 minutes.

After rinsing the print for 5 minutes, put it into a bleach made of two stock solutions. The first consists of 37 grains of potassium permanganate in 16 ounces water. The second is made by adding ¼ fluid ounce concentrated sulfuric acid (*Caution:* caustic poison. Always add acid to water, and not vice versa) and 1¾ ounces table salt to 16 ounces cold water. Do not combine these solutions until ready to use. After use discard, as the bath does not keep in combination.

For negatives mix equal parts of the solutions. Do likewise for prints, but dilute with 2 parts of water. Immerse print until the image has almost disappeared.

Remove the brown stain by immersing the print in a 1-percent solution of sodium bisulfite. Then rinse thoroughly and redevelop in any standard developer.

Do this under a strong light. Then wash for 10 minutes and dry. No hypo is necessary.

If a negative or print is irreplaceable, it may be best to make a copy negative first.

COPYING WITHOUT A CAMERA

Reflex printing is a handy photographic process to know even though you have no interest in photography as a hobby. With it, you can make quick copies of such things as letters, drawings, or text matter and diagrams in books and magazines.

No camera is required. For copying material, a special thin high-contrast paper such as Kodagraph Contact Paper, obtainable from dealers in professional photographic supplies, is best, but any single-weight contact paper in grade 4 or 5 should do. For apparatus, all you need is a sheet of plywood covered with black felt or paper, a little larger than the matter to be copied, a sheet of plate glass about the same size, plus ordinary developer, short stop, and fixing solution.

The job must be done under darkroom conditions. A yellow-green safelight may be used. You can probably get by with a dim red or orange bulb.

If what you want to copy is on thick or opaque paper, or has printing on the reverse side, you must first make a negative by the reflex method. For this, the original is placed face up with a sheet of reflex paper on it emulsion side down. They are held in contact by placing the sheet of glass on top of them. Light thrown on the back of the reflex paper passes through and bounces back in proportion to the relative lightness of each area in the original.

For sharp definition, the original must be held firmly and evenly in contact with the paper by pressing down on the margins of the glass. If there is any printing on the reverse of the original, it must be backed by black.

Make the exposure with a 100-watt bulb suspended above the paper. Exposure varies according to the bulb-to-paper distance and the nature of the original. After exposure, develop the paper for about 30 seconds at 68°F in a standard developer such as D-72 or Dektol, diluted 1 part water to 1 part stock developer. Rinse, fix, wash, and dry. The result is a negative, and is reversed left to right. To make a positive, use this as you would a film negative; place it face down on another sheet of printing paper and print through the back.

If a white on black copy will serve, and the original is printed on one side only of thin paper, you can use the original as a negative. In this case, both the original and the photographic paper must face the light.

PRINTS WITHOUT NEGATIVES

Want a quick and inexpensive way to make black-and-white enlargements of your color slides? Want to check lighting and exposure for expensive large-size color film before you shoot the actual film? Want to make quick portraits of your friends with your sheet-film camera without the need for making an intermediate negative?

Then why not try the process used in the coin-operated strip-picture machines, while-you-wait booths, and identification picture cameras—direct positive photography? Although little known to the amateur photographer, the process is simple and useful. All you need is a special direct positive paper and several solutions you can make up from regular photographic chemicals. With the solutions in readiness in the darkroom, you should be able to turn out a finished print in 4 or 5 minutes.

There are two limitations to the process. One is that the paper is *ortho*chromatic rather than *pan*-chromatic, which means that reds will appear darker than normal. The other is that pictures made with it in an ordinary camera will be reversed from left to right; identification cameras correct this by using a prism in the lens system that turns the image around. Slides, however, can be printed correctly by proper placement in the enlarger.

The processing directions that follow are for Kodak Super Speed Direct Positive Paper, which you can get from a dealer in professional photographic supplies. It comes in 200-foot rolls from 1½ to 5 inches wide and in standard cut sizes from 2½ by 3½ to 8 by 10 inches to fit regular sheet-film holders. It is made on a water-resistant paper base that permits rapid processing and drying, and has an exposure speed comparable with Kodachrome II.

Correct exposure is essential to making good-quality direct-positive prints. As is true with reversal color films, overexposure will result in a light print and underexposure in a dark print. In judging exposure, you must do so in relation to a fixed developing time, preferably the recommended one of 45 seconds at 68°F. There is a difference, too, in effective speed with different methods of redevelopment. If you use the original developer, D-88, as the redeveloper, the Exposure Index is 20 for daylight and 10 for tungsten light; if, instead, you use the Sulfide Redeveloper T-19, the speed is boosted slightly to 25 for daylight and 12 for tungsten. For optimum results, however, it would be best to establish your own rating from tests of the paper made with your own lens and shutter, or with your enlarger with typical slides projected at desired degrees of enlargement.

Processing procedure. The processing of direct positive paper is both rapid and simple. After exposure, the paper is first developed to form a regular negative image. This image is then bleached out, leaving a colorless positive, or reversed, image that contains silver salts in inverse proportion to those in the negative. The print is next exposed to light (if you use redeveloper T-19, this step is not necessary) and finally redeveloped to make the positive image visible. If the redevelopment is carried to completion, fixing is not necessary, and final washing can be done in half a minute.

Development and bleaching must be done in a darkroom lit only by a safelight fitted with a 15-watt bulb and a Wratten Series 2 (dark red) filter, kept at least 4 feet from the material. The remaining steps may be carried out in ordinary room light. Here is the detailed procedure:

Development. Develop the exposed prints in the following Developer D-88 for 45 seconds at 68°F. For uniform results, keep the solution at an even temperature. Do not use exhausted developer; replace it as soon as printing time has noticeably slowed down. Throughout the entire process, be sure that one solution does not contaminate another. Otherwise the prints will be streaked and stained.

DEVELOPER D-88

Water, about 125°F	96 oz
Sodium sulfite, desiccated	6 oz
Hydroquinone	3 oz
Boric acid, crystals	¾ oz
Potassium bromide	145 grains
Sodium hydroxide	3 oz
Water to make	1 gallon

Dissolve the chemicals in the order named. *Caution*: Be careful not to spill the sodium hydroxide on yourself or your surroundings as it is very caustic. Dissolve it in a small amount of cold water in a separate container of enameled ware, stainless steel, or heat-resisting glass (never aluminum!). Stir constantly while dissolving, to hasten the process and to distribute the heat involved. When dissolved, add it to the solution of the remaining ingredients, and dilute the whole to 1 gallon.

Note: D-88 has a short life after exposure to air. You can store it longer after mixing by dividing the solution and putting it into a number of small bottles filled to the neck and tightly stoppered.

After development, rinse the prints for at least 15 seconds in running water, or, lacking this, use a separate container of water to rinse the prints after each solution. Thorough rinsing is important to prevent one solution from contaminating the next.

Bleaching. Bleach the prints in the following Bleaching Bath R-9 for about 30 seconds, or until the image has completely disappeared. Follow this with a 15-second rinse in running water, or in a container of water separate from the first rinse.

BLEACHING BATH R-9

Water	1 gallon
Potassium bichromate	1¼ oz
Sulfuric acid, concentrated	1½ fl oz

Caution: Always add the acid to the solution, and not vice versa, with continuous stirring.

Clearing. The purpose of Clearing Bath CB-1 is to remove the yellow or brownish stain left by the bleach. Leave them in this bath for about 30 seconds at 65° to 70°F. Then rinse them again for 15 seconds as you did before. As soon as the prints are in the clearing bath, the ordinary white light of the room can be turned on and left on.

CLEARING BATH CB-1

Sodium, sulfite, desiccated	12 oz
Water	1 gallon

Redevelopment. If you redevelop the cleared prints in the following Sulfide Redeveloper T-19, no re-exposure to light is required. Just redevelop the prints for about 60 seconds; then rinse for 30 seconds and dry them.

SULFIDE REDEVELOPER T-19

> Sodium sulfide (not sulfite)   290 grains
> Water   32 oz

As an alternative you can redevelop the prints in the original developer, D-88. If you do this, re-exposure to light is necessary before redevelopment. Re-exposure automatically takes place if you turn on the room white light when the prints are first put in the clearing bath. If you don't turn on the white light then, expose the prints for about 2 or 3 seconds to a 40- or 60-watt bulb placed 6 to 8 inches from the paper.

If prints are redeveloped with D-88, they can be made slightly more brilliant by rinsing them and then fixing them for about 30 seconds in a regular hypo fixing bath. Then they should be washed for 5 or 10 minutes to remove the hypo. The fixing process is not, however, necessary to make the prints permanent.

Prints from slides. Direct positive prints can be made from either black-and-white or color slides in a regular enlarger. Color slides should be placed in the negative carrier with the emulsion side toward the paper. On the other hand, black-and-white slides that have been printed from camera negatives should be placed in the carrier with the emulsion side toward the light source. In this way the prints will not be reversed from left to right. For good-quality prints from slides, not only should the exposure be correct, but the density and contrast of the slide should be normal. Too thin or too dense a slide gives prints that lack contrast.

To find the best exposure for prints from slides of normal density, make this test: Set the enlarger to a magnification of 5X, stop the lens down to f/22 and make a series of exposures at ½, 1, 1½, and 2 seconds. One of these exposures will probably provide a base from which the final adjustment can be made.

A check for color film exposure. Make test shots to find best exposure for direct positive paper. When this is obtained, you can easily calculate the exposure for the color film from the relative speed of the two emulsions.

MAKING PEN DRAWINGS FROM PHOTOS

To make a pen drawing from a photo, first make a rather light print on smooth matte enlarging paper. Trace out the drawing directly on the print with waterproof India ink. After the ink is thoroughly dry, bleach away the photograph in permanganate reducer R-2.

After the photo image is completely gone, fix in plain hypo solution or acid fixing bath to remove yellow stain. Then wash thoroughly. Be careful, however, not to smear the ink lines, as they are delicate while wet.

STAY-FLAT EASEL ADHESIVE

A temporary easel that will hold large pieces of paper flat for big blowups, or hold large pictures flat before a copying camera, can be made by coating a piece of plywood with the following pressure-sensitive adhesive:

Powdered gelatin	1 oz
Corn syrup	1 oz
Glycerin	1 oz
Potassium chrome alum	8 grains
Add water to make	16 oz

Stir the glycerin and syrup in 12 ounces of water and let the gelatin soak in this mixture for 30 minutes, heating it to 120°F. Dissolve the alum in 1 ounce of water. Pour this into the mixture and add water to bring the total to 16 ounces. Coat the plywood with this liquid, allowing about 1 ounce to each 100 square inches, and let set for 24 hours.

Paper will adhere firmly to this surface merely by pressing it on lightly. It can also be readily peeled off. When not in use, the surface can be preserved by covering it with a sheet of plastic wrap. Any mixture remaining in the container must be discarded. Once set, it cannot be liquified again.

STANDARD DARKROOM FORMULAS

Note: Unless otherwise mentioned, all the numbered formulas that follow are formulas that have been developed and proved at the Eastman Kodak Laboratories—the pioneer research organization in this field. For all practical purposes, these formulas are identical with those recommended for the same uses by other makers of photographic materials.

Developer for Large-Camera Film, DK-50

This clean-working and moderately fast developer is suitable for sheet film, film packs, and all kinds of roll film larger than 35 millimeter. It is recommended particularly for portrait negatives.

Water, about 125°F	16 oz
Elon (metol)	36 grains
Sodium sulfite, desiccated	1 oz
Hydroquinone	36 grains
Kodalk	145 grains
Potassium bromide	8 grains
Water to make	32 oz

For tank development of portrait negatives, dilute 1:1 with water, and develop about 10 minutes at 68°F. For tray development, use without dilution and develop about 6 minutes at 68°F.

For general snapshots and commercial work, use without dilution. Develop about 6 minutes in a tank or 4½ minutes in a tray at 68°F. The literature in individual film packages may give specific instructions.

Replenisher, DK-50R

To maintain constant time of development with DK-50, add 1 ounce of the following replenisher for each 80 square inches of film processed. If the developer is diluted 1:1, dilute the replenisher in the same proportion.

Water, about 125°F	24 oz
Elon (metol)	73 grains
Sodium sulfite	1 oz
Hydroquinone	145 grains
Kodalk	1 oz 136 grains
Water to make	32 oz

Borax Fine-Grain Developer, D-76

If you could have a choice of only one developer to use with all types of film, this should probably be it. A pioneer among "fine grain" developers, Kodak D-76 (DuPont 6-D, Ilford ID-11, and Gevaert G.206 are either identical or practically so) remains unsurpassed for its ability to give full emulsion speed and maximum shadow detail with normal contrast. It gives excellent results with most sheet and larger size roll film, and is also used in preference to ultra-fine-grain developers for 35-millimeter film by many professionals and advanced amateurs.

Water, about 125°F	24 oz
Elon (metol)	30 grains
Sodium sulfite, desiccated	3 oz 145 grains
Hydroquinone	75 grains
Borax, granular	30 grains
Water to make	32 oz

Use without dilution. Average development time is about 9 minutes in a tray or 11 minutes in a tank at 68°F. Follow instructions that accompany particular film you use.

Replenisher, D-76R

To keep development time of D-76 developer uniform, add 1 ounce of the following replenisher for each 80 square inches of film processed:

Water, about 125°F	24	oz
Elon (metol)	45	grains
Sodium sulfite, desiccated	3 oz 145	grains
Hydroquinone	¼	oz
Borax, granular	290	grains
Water to make	32	oz

Additive to Boost D-76

According to experienced photographers, D-76 and similar developers can be given an even wider range of performance by the simple addition of a proprietary chemical concentrate called "Crone Additive C." Boosted by this supplement, a developer is said not only to produce greater effective speed in a film, but to give better shadow detail in negatives exposed under dim light and better balanced negatives exposed under extremely contrasty light. One ounce of the concentrate must be added to each quart of developer.

Fine-Grain Developer, D-25

The grain produced by this developer is comparable to that of the once-popular paraphenylenediamine type of developer. D-25 has the advantage, however, of being nontoxic and nonstaining.

Water, about 125°F	24 oz
Elon (metol)	¼ oz
Sodium sulfite, desiccated	3 oz 145 grains
Sodium bisulfite	½ oz
Cold water to make	32 oz

Average development time for roll films about 20 minutes in a tank at 68°F.

Replenisher, DK-25R

To maintain constant time of development with D-25, add the following replenisher at the rate of 1¼ ounces per roll of film for the first 12 rolls per 32 ounces of developer, and at ¾ ounces per roll for the next 12 rolls per 32 ounces. The developer should then be replaced.

Water	24 oz
Elon (metol)	145 grains
Sodium sulfite, desiccated	3 oz 145 grains
Kodalk	290 grains
Cold water to make	32 oz

High Contrast Copy Developer, D-19

To make satisfactory copies of book pages, manuscripts, drawings, letters, and so on, on 35-mm film, you must use a film of high contrast with extremely fine grain and resolving power, and also a special developer to bring out these qualities in the film.

One film made especially for this purpose is Kodak High Contrast Copy Film, which is available in 35-mm magazines and also in long rolls. The recommended developer is Kodak D-19, given here:

Water, about 125°F	16 oz
Elon (metol)	30 grains
Sodium sulfite, desiccated	3 oz
Hydroquinone	115 grains
Sodium carbonate, monohydrated	1¾ oz
Potassium bromide	75 grains
Cold water to make	32 oz

Develop in a tank for 6 minutes at 68°F, agitating the film at 30-second intervals.

This combination of film and developer produces images of such high sharpness and resolving power that the degree of enlargement possible will usually be limited by the camera and the subject conditions rather than by the film.

Universal Paper and Film Developer, D-72

Probably the best known and most versatile of all photographic developers is a metol-hydroquinone developer represented by Kodak D-72, the formula for which is given below.

With proper dilution and the possible addition of potassium bromide, it can be used to develop not only all kinds of printing and enlarging papers, but negatives for large cameras where speed is more necessary than fine grain.

DuPont developer 53-D and Ilford ID-36 are essentially the same, and Kodak Dektol is a packaged

developer of similar type but with extended capacity
and shelf life.

STOCK SOLUTION

Water, about 125°F	16	oz
Elon (metol)	45	grains
Sodium sulfite, desiccated	1½	oz
Hydroquinone	175	grains
Sodium carbonate, monohydrated	2 oz 290	grains
Potassium bromide	30	grains
Water to make	32	oz

To use with contact printing papers, dilute 1
part stock solution with 1 part of water, and develop
about 1 minute at 68°F. With enlarging papers, dilute 1:2. For warmer tones on these papers, dilute
1:3 or 1:4, and add ¼ ounce of 10-percent potassium
bromide solution for each 32 ounces of working solution. Develop 1½ minutes.

For press and other large negatives, follow time
and temperature instructions that come with the particular film. Typically, dilute developer 1:1. Develop
about 5 minutes without agitation or 4 minutes with
agitation at 68°F for average contrast. For less contrast dilute 1:2. For greater contrast use full strength.

If well stoppered, a full bottle of stock solution
will keep for 6 months; a half-full bottle for 2 months.
In a tray, a 1:1 working solution will keep about 24
hours.

Warm-Tone Paper Developer, DuPont 55-D

This developer will produce warmer tones than DuPont 53-D or Kodak D-72 on most enlarging papers:

STOCK SOLUTION

Water, at about 125°F	24	oz
Metol	36	grains
Sodium sulfite, desiccated	1¼	oz
Hydroquinone	146	grains
Sodium carbonate, monohydrated	1 oz 205	grains
Potassium bromide	73	grains
Cold water to make	32	oz

To use, dilute 1 part of stock solution with 2 parts of water. For still warmer tones, up to ½ ounce of potassium bromide may be added to each 32 ounces of stock solution. If this is done, expose the print more than the usual time and develop for 1½ minutes.

Soft-Working Paper Developer, Ansco 120

If you desire prints from ½ to 1 or even 1½ grades softer than those given with D-72 or Dektol and the paper you are using, here is a developer that will enable you to produce them. This formula is of the same general type as D-72, but with the contrast-producing chemical, hydroquinone, left out. Because it is compatible, you can either use it alone, mix it with D-72, or use it for 2-tray development, to produce the contrast you want.

Stock Solution

Water, 125°F	24 oz
Metol (Elon, Pictol)	¼ oz 70 grains
Sodium sulfite, desiccated	1 oz 88 grains
Sodium carbonate, monohydrated	1 oz 88 grains
Potassium bromide	27 grains
Cold water to make	32 oz

For use, dilute 1 part stock solution with 2 parts water. Develop 1½ to 3 minutes at 68°F.

An Easy Method for Adding Potassium Bromide

Developer formulas often require the addition of a definite small amount of potassium bromide. The easiest way to do this is to make a 10-percent solution of the chemical in water—say, ½ ounce of bromide in enough water to make a total of 5 ounces. Ten drops of this solution will equal 1 grain of potassium bromide.

Stop Bath for Films, SB-5

To stop development and make fixing solution last longer, treat the films in this for about 30 seconds, with agitation, between development and fixing:

Water	16 oz
Acetic acid, 28%	1 oz
Sodium sulfate, desiccated	1½ oz
Water to make	32 oz

Hardening Stop Bath, SB-4

Recommended for use with film developers containing sodium sulfate, when working at temperatures above 75°F.

Water	32 oz
Potassium chrome alum	1 oz
Sodium sulfate, desiccated	2 oz

Agitate the film for 45 seconds after immersion to prevent streakiness. Leave in bath for at least 3 minutes. If the temperature is below 85°F, rinse for 2 seconds in water before immersing in this bath.

When freshly mixed, the bath is a violet-blue color, but it ultimately turns to a yellow-green with use. It is then worn out and should be replaced. Don't overwork it. An unused bath will keep indefinitely, but the hardening power of a partially used bath decreases rapidly on standing for a few days.

Stop Bath for Paper, SB-1

Water	32 oz
Acetic acid, 28%	1½ oz

After developing, rinse prints in this for about 5 seconds before placing in fixing bath. This will prevent developer stain and increase the life of the fixer. Capacity: about twenty 8-by-10-inch prints per quart.

How to Dilute Acetic Acid

Most photographic formulas call for 28-percent acetic acid. You can get the acid already in this dilution, but you can save more than half if you buy glacial acetic acid and dilute it yourself. Just mix 3 parts of the glacial acid with 8 parts of water. (*Caution:* Both the glacial and 28-percent acetic acids are poison, and can cause burns. If you spill any of either on your skin, flush it off immediately with plenty of plain water.)

Acid Hardener for Fixing Bath, F-5a

To convert plain hypo solution to an excellent acid fixing bath, add 1 part of the following stock hardener slowly to 4 parts of cool 30-percent hypo solution, with rapid stirring:

Water, about 125°F	20 oz
Sodium sulfite, desiccated	2½ oz
Acetic acid, 28%	7½ oz
Boric acid, crystals	1¼ oz
Potassium alum	2½ oz
Cold water to make	32 oz

Universal Fixing Bath

This acid hardening fixing bath may be used for films, plates, and papers. It has the advantage over baths that do not contain boric acid in that it gives better hardening and has less tendency to precipitate a sludge of aluminum sulfite.

Water, about 125°F	20 oz
Sodium thiosulfate (hypo)	8 oz
Sodium sulfite, desiccated	½ oz
Acetic acid, 28%	1½ oz
Boric acid, crystals	¼ oz
Potassium alum	½ oz
Cold water to make	32 oz

Be sure to use crystalline boric acid, as mentioned. The powdered form is extremely difficult to dissolve.

A freshly prepared bath should properly fix films or plates in from 5 to 10 minutes. The bath will remain clear and need not be discarded until negatives take over 10 minutes to clear. Fix prints 5 to 10 minutes.

Plain Hypo Fixing Bath

When prints are to be toned, it is sometimes better to first fix the print in a plain hypo solution. In making acid fixing baths, many photographers also prefer separate solutions of plain hypo and acid hardener—mixing the two just before use. This method is quick, and allows longer storage without deterioration.

To make a plain hypo solution, just dissolve 2½ pounds of sodium thiosulfate (hypo) in 1 gallon of water at about 125°F. This makes a 30-percent solution—the optimum for fixing both films and papers.

Test for Exhausted Fixing Bath

Add 3 or 4 drops of a 10-percent solution of potassium iodide to 1 ounce of the fixing bath in a small glass or bottle. Stir. If, on standing, a yellow precipitate forms, for all practical purposes the bath may be regarded as exhausted and should be discarded.

Silver Test for Fixing Bath

An overworked fixing bath also contains insoluble silver thiosulfate compounds which it deposits on negatives and prints and which cannot be removed by continued washing. These salts may produce stains months or years later. A bath which leaves such salts should be discarded.

To test for residual silver salts, make up a solution of 18 grains of sodium sulfide (not *sulfite*) in 2 ounces of water. This will keep in a small stoppered bottle for not more than 3 months. To use: Dilute 1 part with 9 parts of water. (The diluted solution will not keep longer than a week.)

Place a drop of the diluted solution on the margin of a squeegeed film or print. Remove with a clean white blotter after 3 minutes. Any color more than a just-visible cream tint indicates the presence of unwanted silver compounds.

Stabilizers to Replace Fixing and Washing

When you need prints in a hurry and they are not required to be absolutely permanent, you can eliminate fixing and washing by a process called *stabilization.* This is used extensively in photo-copying devices and in the popular new print processing machines that turn out a finished print in less than a minute. Stabilization is a sort of incomplete fixing process in which undeveloped silver salts are converted into reasonably stable colorless compounds.

Under favorable storage conditions, stabilized prints should keep for many months without fading or discoloring. After their original temporary use they can, if desired, be made permanent by fixing for about 10 minutes in a normal fixing bath and then washed and dried in the ordinary way.

You can make a simple stabilizing bath by dissolving 1 ounce of thiourea (sometimes called thiocarbamide) and a few drops of 28 percent acetic acid in 32 ounces of water. A print left in this solution for 3 minutes will be fully stabilized. Put your print in this bath instead of in the usual fixer.

A still commoner stabilizer is a solution of ordinary hypo combined with sodium sulfide and bisulfite, as in this typical formula:

Sodium sulfite, anhydrous	200 grains
Sodium bisulfite	1½ oz
Hypo	10 oz
Water to make	32 oz

After development, and before putting a print in this bath, dip it for a few seconds in a tray containing a 5 percent solution of acetic acid in water. Then leave it for about 30 seconds in the stabilizer, after which wash it for 10 seconds in running water. This short wash will increase the stability of the print; a longer one, short of complete washing, however, will decrease it.

Dry the prints on unheated ferrotype plates or between blotters. If you use blotters, don't use them thereafter for drying ordinarily fixed and washed prints, as the chemicals picked up by the blotters will contaminate regularly processed prints.

Because stabilized prints are impregnated with active chemicals, they should not be filed or stored next to negatives or to valuable regular prints that might be affected by them.

Caution: If you use thiourea, be careful to keep it away from the immediate area of other processing chemicals, and of film and paper in other stages of being processed. Thiourea is a powerful fogging agent and if it comes in contact with light-sensitive materials it may cause black spots on them or gray them. It is hard, also, to get the last traces of this chemical off your hands and utensils simply by washing them with water. To remove it fully, rinse your hands and other objects that have come in contact with it with a solution of 1 ounce of household liquid chlorine bleach (Clorox, Purex, Rose-X, etc.) in 1 quart of water. Then wash them thoroughly with warm water.

Processing at Higher Temperatures

When possible, the temperature of photographic processing solutions should be kept at between 65° and 75°F. At lower temperatures, the action of the chemicals slows down and becomes erratic. At higher temperatures, the emulsion tends to fog and also to swell and soften to the point of melting.

By using a special prehardener that contains an anti-fogging agent, however, film may be processed successfully at temperatures as high as 110°F. Here is the formula:

PREHARDENER SH-5

Solution A

Formaldehyde, about 37% solution by weight	1¼ fl drams

Solution B

Water	28 oz
0.5% solution of Kodak Anti-Fog No. 2 (6-nitrobenzimidazole nitrate)	1¼ oz

Sodium sulfate, desiccated 1 oz 290 grains
Sodium carbonate,
   monohydrated   175 grains
Water to make   32 oz

To prepare the 0.5-percent solution of the anti-fog chemical, dissolve 18 grains of it in 8 ounces of distilled water.

The working solution of the prehardener should be prepared just before using by adding Solution A to Solution B and mixing thoroughly. One quart of solution will process at least forty 4-by-5-inch films or their equivalent.

To use the prehardener, bathe the exposed film in it for 10 minutes with moderate agitation. Then drain for a few seconds, immerse in water for half a a minute, drain thoroughly, and immerse in the developer. Up to about 90°F, conventional developers such as D-76, D-19, etc., may be used without modification.

Development times should be approximately as follows:

At 75°F, use same time recommended at 68°F without prehardening.

At 80°F, 85 percent of normal time.

At 85°F, 70 percent of normal time.

At 90°F, 60 percent of normal time.

At 95°F, 50 percent of normal time.

After developing, rinse the film, fix it in an acid hardening fixing bath, and then wash and dry it in the usual way.

At temperatures above 95°F add up to twice the amount of the anti-fog agent to the prehardener. The average development time at 110°F, after prehardening, is only about 25 percent of the normal time at 68°F. To avoid an excessively short development time, use a slower-working developer such as D-76, or slow down another developer by adding sodium sulfate.

High-temperature processing without prehardener. If the prehardener is not available, film may be processed at temperatures up to about 95°F by adding sodium sulfate and observing several physical precautions:

1. All solutions—developer, stop bath, fixer, and wash water—must be kept to within about 5°F of the same temperature.

2. After developing, the film should be immersed in a hardening stop bath, such as SB-4. Agitate at first and then leave for 3 minutes.

3. The film should be fixed in a fresh acid hardening fixing bath.

4. The film must not be washed too long. Wash it no more than 10 to 15 minutes in running water or in several changes of water.

The amount of sodium sulfate to be added to different developers at different temperatures is indicated in the following table. At temperatures up to 90°F, use normal developing time for the particular developer without the sulfate. If necessary to develop at 90 to 95°F, decrease this time about one-third.

Developers	Range of temperatures	Sodium sulfate, desiccated per quart
D-76	75 to 80°F	1 ounce 290 grains
D-19	80 to 85°F	2½ ounces
	85 to 90°F	3 ounces 145 grains
DK-50	75 to 80°F	3 ounces 145 grains
D-72 (1:1)	80 to 85°F	4 ounces 75 grains
Dektol (1:1)	85 to 90°F	5 ounces

Intensifiers and Reducers

With the quality and range of modern films and papers, and modern control techniques, it is seldom necessary to intensify or reduce a negative. Occasionally, however, these processes can save a picture that it is not possible to retake.

There are two ways to intensify a negative image. You can treat the image to change it from silver to a silver compound that is more opaque, or use chemical action to deposit additional opaque material in proportion to the amount of silver originally present.

Caution: Intensification or reduction always involves the risk of ruining a negative. It is best, therefore, to make the best possible print that you can from it before treatment. To reduce the possibility of chemical or physical damage to the negative, harden it before treatment in the special formaldehyde hardener that follows:

FORMALDEHYDE FILM HARDENER, SH-1

Water	16 oz
Formaldehyde, about 37% solution	2½ drams
Sodium, carbonate, monohydrated	90 grains
Water to make	32 oz

After immersion for 3 minutes, film should be rinsed and immersed for 5 minutes in a fresh acid fixing bath. Then they should be washed thoroughly before giving any further chemical treatment.

CHROMIUM INTENSIFIER, IN-4

Water	32 oz
Potassium bichromate	3 oz
Hydrochloric acid, concentrated	2 oz

To use, take 1 part of stock solution to 10 parts of water. After hardening in formaldehyde hardener, bleach thoroughly in this diluted solution at 65° to 70°F, and then redevelop in artificial light or daylight (but not direct sunlight) in a quick-acting, nonstaining developer, such as Kodak D-72 or DuPont 53-D, diluted 1 to 3. (Slow-working developers, containing an excess of sodium sulfite, tend to dissolve the bleached image before the developing agent can act on it.) Rinse, fix for 5 minutes, and wash. Greater intensification can be secured by repeating the process.

SILVER INTENSIFIER

This may be used on either negative or positive film, and will not change the color of the image when

projected. It gives proportional intensification, controlled by varying the time of treatment. It acts more
rapidly on fine-grain materials, and also gives greater
intensification, than on coarse-grain materials.

Solution A
(Store in a brown bottle)

Silver nitrate, crystals	2 oz
Distilled water to make	32 oz

Solution B

Sodium sulfite, desiccated	2 oz
Water to make	32 oz

Solution C

Sodium thiosulfate (hypo)	3½ oz
Water to make	32 oz

Solution D

Sodium sulfite, desiccated	½ oz
Metol (or Elon)	365 grains
Water to make	96 oz

To prepare intensifier solution: Add 1 part of
Solution B to 1 part of Solution A, while stirring constantly. Dissolve the white precipitate which appears
by adding 1 part of Solution C. Allow the resulting
solution to stand until it is clear. Then, with stirring,
add 3 parts of Solution D. The intensifier is now
ready for use, and must be used within 30 minutes of
mixing. The degree of intensification is proportional
to the time of treatment, which should not be more
than 25 minutes. After treatment, immerse the film in

a plain 30-percent hypo solution for 2 minutes and then wash thoroughly.

Use this intensifier under artificial light, as direct sunlight causes the solution to deteriorate rapidly.

QUINONE-THIOSULFATE INTENSIFIER, IN-6

This type of intensifier produces the greatest degree of intensification of any known single-solution formula when used with high-speed negative materials. The intensified image is brownish and is not indefinitely permanent, but under ordinary storage conditions will remain usable for several years. The intensified image is destroyed by acid hypo, so negatives thus treated should *never* be placed in a fixing bath or in water contaminated with fixer.

This intensifier is not suitable for fine-grain materials or for use when only moderate intensification is desired.

Solution A

Water (about 70°F)	24 oz
Sulfuric acid, concentrated	1 oz
Potassium dichromate	¾ oz
Water to make	32 oz

Solution B

Water	24 oz
Sodium bisulfite	52 grains
Hydroquinone	½ oz
Wetting agent (Kodak Foto-Flo solution)	1 dram
Water to make	32 oz

Solution C

Water	24 oz
Sodium thiosulfate (hypo)	¾ oz
Water to make	32 oz

The water used should not have a chloride content greater than about 15 parts per million. If in doubt as to chloride content, use distilled water.

(*Caution:* Always add the sulfuric acid to the water, with constant stirring, and not vice versa. Do not spill the concentrated acid on anything, as it is extremely corrosive.)

For use: To 1 part of Solution A add 2 parts of Solution B, with stirring, then 2 parts of Solution C. Continue stirring and finally add 1 more part of Solution A. It is important to follow this order of mixing.

The separate solutions will keep in stoppered bottles for several months, and the mixed intensifier is stable for 2 or 3 hours without use. The bath should be used only once and then discarded, because a used bath may produce a silvery scum on the surface of the image.

Wash the negatives 5 to 10 minutes, harden in formaldehyde film hardener mentioned above for 5 minutes, and wash again for 5 minutes before intensification.

For greatest intensification, treat for about 10 minutes at 68°F, then wash 10 to 20 minutes, and dry as usual. For a lower degree of intensification treat for shorter times. Agitate frequently to prevent streaking. Treat only 1 negative at a time when processing in a tray.

TYPES OF REDUCERS

Reducers may be grouped into three general types:

Subtractive or cutting reducers remove an equal amount of silver from all parts of the image. In effect this increases the contrast at the same time it decreases the overall density. If the action is continued long enough, the lower densities will be completely removed. They are useful in treating fogged or overexposed negatives.

Proportional reducers remove silver in direct proportion to the amount present in any given area of the image. This action lowers the contrast and compensates for overdevelopment.

Super-proportional reducers remove more silver from high-density areas than from those of low density. They are used to correct extreme contrast such as is found in overdeveloped negatives.

Caution: To prevent physical damage to the film during reduction, first harden it in formaldehyde hardener. If you do not reduce the film immediately after the wash, soak it in plain water at 68°F for at least an hour before reduction.

PERMANGANATE REDUCER, R-2 (SUBTRACTIVE)

Stock Solution A

Water	32 oz
Potassium permanganate	1¾ oz

Completely dissolve the permanganate crystals in a small volume of water at about 180°F. Then dilute to volume with cold water.

Stock Solution B

Water	32 oz
Sulfuric acid concentrated	1 oz

Caution: Always add the acid to the water, stirring constantly, never vice versa. Do not spill the concentrated acid on anything; it is extremely caustic.

To use, take one part of A, 2 parts of B, and dilute with 64 parts of water. When the film has been reduced sufficiently, place it in a fresh fixing bath for a few minutes to remove brownish stains, then wash thoroughly.

If reduction is too rapid, dilute the solution before use with a larger volume of water. Do not combine the solutions until immediately before use, as they will not keep well in combination.

FARMER'S REDUCER (SUBTRACTIVE)

Stock Solution A

Potassium ferricyanide	1¼ oz
Water to make	16 oz

Stock Solution B

Sodium thiosulfate (hypo)	16 oz
Water to make	64 oz

To use, mix 1 ounce of A with 4 ounces of B, and add water to make 32 ounces. Pour the mixed solution immediately over the negative to be reduced, which, for better seeing, should be in a white tray. Watch the action closely, rocking the tray continuously during the process. Use the mixed solution no longer than 5 minutes. For additional reduction,

repeat the process with a freshly mixed working solution. When reduction is sufficient, stop the action by
flooding the negative with water. Then wash the
negative thoroughly.

FARMER'S REDUCER (PROPORTIONAL)

Farmer's reducer may also be used as a two-solution formula that gives an almost proportional development suitable for correcting overdevelopment.

Solution A

Potassium ferricyanide	¼ oz
Water to make	32 oz

Solution B

Sodium thiosulfate (hypo)	6¾ oz
Water to make	32 oz

Treat the negative in solution A with uniform
agitation for 1 to 4 minutes at 65° to 70°F depending
on the degree of reduction desired. Then immerse it
in solution B for 5 minutes and wash thoroughly.
The process may be repeated if more reduction is desired.

PROPORTIONAL REDUCER, R-5

Solution A

Water	32 oz
Potassium permanganate	4 grains
Sulfuric acid, 10%	½ oz

Solution B

| Water | 96 oz |
| Potassium persulfate | 3 oz |

To use, mix 1 part of A with 3 parts of B. When sufficiently reduced, clear the negative in a 1-percent solution of sodium bisulfite. Wash thoroughly before drying.

SUPER-PROPORTIONAL REDUCER, R-15

Solution A

| Water | 32 oz |
| Potassium persulfate | 1 oz |

Solution B

| Water | 15½ oz |
| Sulfuric acid, 10% | ½ oz |

To use, mix 2 parts of A with 1 part of B and pour into a glass, plastic, or unchipped enamelware tray. After hardening with formaldehyde hardener, and then washing thoroughly, immerse the negative in the reducer. Agitate frequently and watch closely. When required reduction is almost obtained, remove from the solution, immerse in an acid fixing bath for a few minutes, then wash thoroughly before drying. Used solutions don't keep and should be discarded.

Solution A will keep best in storage if it is kept away from excessive heat and light. At 75°F it should keep about 2 months.

Toners

SEPIA TONER

This toner is recommended for warm-brown sepia tones.

Solution A (bleach)

Water, 125°F	24 oz	
Potassium ferricyanide	1½ oz	80 grains
Potassium bromide	¼ oz	35 grains
Sodium carbonate, monohydrated	½ oz	70 grains
Cold water to make	32 oz	

Solution B (redeveloper)

Sodium sulfide, desiccated	1½ oz
Cold water to make	16 oz

For use, dilute 1 part solution B with 8 parts water.

Important: Be sure to use sodium sulfide and not sodium sulfite in the redeveloper. Be sure your trays have no exposed iron spots. Otherwise blue marks may form on prints.

Prints should be washed thoroughly and then bleached in solution A until the black image is changed to a very light brown. Prints should then be washed for 15 minutes and redeveloped in solution B.

Redevelopment should be complete in about 1 minute. Wash the prints for about 30 minutes and then dry them. If the toner leaves a sediment in the form of streaks or fingermarks, immerse the print for a few seconds in a 3-percent solution of acetic acid, wash for 10 minutes.

HYPO ALUM TONER

This toner will produce beautiful reddish-brown tones.

Solution A

| Water | 80 oz |
| Sodium thiosulfate (hypo) | 15 oz |

Solution B

| Water | 1 oz |
| Silver nitrate | 20 grains |

Solution C

| Water | 1 oz |
| Potassium iodide | 40 grains |

Add solution B to solution A. Then add solution C to the mixture. Finally add 3½ ounces potassium alum to the combined solution, and heat the entire bath to the boiling point or until it becomes milky.

Tone prints (after treating with the formaldehyde hardener) 20 to 60 minutes in this bath at 110° to 125°F, agitating them occasionally.

Be sure that the blacks are fully converted before removing the prints from the toning bath.

POLYSULFIDE SEPIA TONER, T-8

This single-solution toner has the advantage over hypo-alum toners in that it will tone in a much shorter time and does not require heating. Raising the temperature to 100°F, from 68°, will, however, decrease the toning time from 15 to 3 minutes. It may be used on most, but not all, papers.

Water	24 oz
Polysulfide (liver of sulfur)	¼ oz
Sodium carbonate, monohydrated	36 grains
Water to make	32 oz

Immerse the well-washed print for 15 to 20 minutes at 68°F or for 3 or 4 minutes at 100°F, with occasional agitation.

After toning, rinse the print for a few seconds in running water and place for 1 minute in a solution of 1 ounce of sodium bisulfite in 32 ounces of water. If sediment appears on print, wipe with a soft sponge. Wash for at least half an hour before drying.

BLUE TONER

This toner will produce brilliant blue tones on many contact and enlarging papers:

Water, 125°F	16 oz
Ferric ammonium citrate	¼ oz
Potassium ferricyanide	¼ oz
Acetic acid, 28%	9 oz
Cold water to make	32 oz

Use distilled water, if available, as tap water may contain impurities that will affect the color. If enameled iron trays are used, be sure they are not chipped or cracked.

Prints to be toned blue should be fixed in a plain, nonhardening hypo bath, which should be kept at a temperature of 68°F or below to prevent undue swelling of the emulsion. When fully toned, prints will at first appear greenish, but will become a clear blue during the washing process.

The depth of blue will vary somewhat with the character of the print, light-toned prints generally toning to a lighter blue. Prints should be slightly lighter than the density desired in the final print, as toning intensifies the print somewhat.

Because the blue tone is quite soluble in alkaline solutions, it is best to acidify the wash water slightly with acetic acid.

GREEN TONER

This formula produces rich green tones by combining the effects of blue toning and sepia toning. It must be applied, however, strictly according to directions, and with great care to cleanliness in handling the prints throughout the operation. It is not adaptable to all types of papers, so you must do a little personal experimenting.

Solution A

Potassium		
ferricyanide	1¼ oz	35 grains
Water	32 oz	
Ammonia water, 28%		3 drams

Solution B

Ferric ammonium		
citrate (green)	1¼ oz 30	grains
Water	32	oz
Hydrochloric acid,		
concentrated	1¼	oz

Solution C

Sodium sulfide	30	grains
Water	32	oz
Hydrochloric acid,		
concentrated	2½	drams

Important: Do not add hydrochloric acid to solution C until immediately before use. Be sure to use sodium sulfide and not sulfite.

Prints to be toned should be darker and softer than normal. They should be thoroughly washed and completely dried before toning.

Soak prints in cold water until limp and then place them in solution A until bleached. Bleaching should be completed in 60 seconds or less. Then transfer immediately to running water where prints should be washed at least 30 minutes.

After washing, place bleached prints in solution B for 45 seconds to 1 minute. Let toning continue until deepest shadows are completely toned. Then wash prints for 4 to 6 minutes in water slightly acidulated with acetic acid.

Next immerse prints in solution C for about 30 seconds, or until the previously blue tone becomes sufficiently green. Give the toned prints a final washing in neutral or slightly acidulated water for 30 minutes. Dry at room temperature.

Prepare all solutions within 24 hours before use. Take great care to avoid contamination of solutions A and B. Use solution C in a well-ventilated room, preferably near an open window or exhaust fan, for the hydrogen sulfide gas evolved from it is bad-smelling and irritating to the lungs.

Tray Cleaner

This solution will remove stains produced by oxidation products of developers, also most silver and dye stains. Do not spill it on your skin, clothing, or surroundings, as it is corrosive.

Water	32 oz
Potassium dichromate	3 oz
Sulfuric acid, concentrated	3 oz

Dissolve the dichromate in water and then add the acid slowly with stirring (never add water to the acid!).

To use, pour a little of the solution into the tray to be cleaned and rinse it around until it has touched all stained portions. Then pour it out, and rinse the tray with plain water until all evidence of the solution has disappeared. (*Caution*: If you pour this solution down an ordinary sink, first dilute it with plenty of water and flush it down with plenty more. Better still, flush it down the toilet.)

Two-Solution Tray Cleaner and Hand Stain Remover

Although this tray cleaner is a little more complicated to prepare and use, it is highly effective and is mild enough to use for cleaning developer stains from your hands.

Solution A

Water	32 oz
Potassium permanganate	29 grains
Sulfuric acid, concentrated	1 dram

Dissolve the permanganate in the water, and then stir in the acid (not vice versa!). Store the solution in a Teflon, polyethylene, or dark glass bottle away from the light.

Solution B

Water	32 oz
Sodium bisulfite	1 oz
Sodium sulfite, desiccated	1 oz

(Note: In place of Solution B, you may use an ordinary acid fixing bath. If you do, be sure to wash thoroughly with plain water after cleaning to remove all hypo from the tray and your hands.)

To clean trays, pour a little of Solution A into the tray, rinse it around until it has touched all stained portions, and allow to remain for several minutes. Rinse well with water and then replace with a similar volume of Solution B. Swish this around so as to clear the brown stain completely, then wash thoroughly.

The solutions may be used to clean several vessels in immediate succession, but should then be discarded.

To clean stains from skin or fingernails, remove rings from fingers and immerse the hands from 1 to 3 minutes in Solution A, contained in a glass, plastic, or porcelain-enameled vessel. Rub the stained areas gently. Rinse for a moment in running water and immerse for a few minutes in Solution B. Then wash your hands thoroughly in warm water.

Stain Removers for Cloth

You can remove developer and fixer stains from white or uncolored cotton, nylon, or linen by rinsing the cloth in plain water immediately after it has been stained. If the chemicals have dried out, or have remained longer, however, soak them in the following solution for 5 to 10 minutes:

Sodium Hypochlorite Bleach

Clorox, Purex, etc.	½ oz
White vinegar	½ oz
Lukewarm water	1 gal

Then soak the stained portion in fresh fixer, and rinse in plain water and dry.

The following is a still more powerful formula for removing brownish fixer stains from cloth or clothing:

Water	24 oz
Thiourea	2½ oz
Citric acid	2½ oz
Water to make	32 oz

Keep the stain wet with this solution until the stain disappears. New stains may vanish in a moment, old ones may take several minutes. The garment or cloth should be thoroughly washed after the stains have been removed, and the recommended amount of liquid chlorine bleach should be used in the first rinse. If the material is other than white cotton, nylon, or linen, test a little of the stain remover on a hidden portion to determine whether bleaching or other damage may occur. The material must also be able to withstand the subsequent chlorine bleach.

Caution: To avoid contamination of photographic materials by thiourea, read caution under stabilizing item.

Longer Life for Tray Solutions

Developing and fixing solutions left in trays may be given a longer life by protecting them against dust, evaporation, and oxidation. A simple way to do this is to float on the solution a piece of polyethylene sheeting cut to the size of the surface. To prevent contamination of one solution by another, always use the same piece for a given solution and rinse it after use.

PHOTOGRAPHIC WEIGHTS AND MEASURES— CONVERSION TABLES

In the United States solids are weighed by either the avoirdupois or the metric system and liquids are measured by the U.S. liquid or metric measure. The following tables give the equivalent values required for converting photographic formulas from one system to the other.

AVOIRDUPOIS TO METRIC WEIGHT

Pounds	Ounces	Grains	Grams	Kilograms
1	16	7000	453.6	0.4536
0.0625	1	437.5	28.35	0.02835
		1	0.0648	
	0.03527	15.43	1	0.001
2.205	35.27	15430	1000	1

U. S. LIQUID TO METRIC MEASURE

Gallons	Quarts	Ounces (Fluid)	Drams (Fluid)	C.C. or Milliliters	Liters
1	4	128	1024	3785	3.785
0.25	1	32	256	946.3	0.9463
		1	8	29.57	0.02597
0.000975	0.0039	0.125	1 (60 mins.)	3.697	0.003697
		0.03381	0.2705	1	0.001
0.2642	1.057	33.81	270.5	1000	1

SOLID-IN-LIQUID CONVERSION TABLE

Grains per 32 fluid oz x 0.06847 = grams per liter
Grams per liter x 14.60 = grains per 32 fl oz
Ounces per 32 fluid oz x 29.96 = grams per liter
Grams per liter x 0.03338 = ounces per 32 fl oz
Pounds per 32 fluid oz x 497.3 = grams per liter
Grams per liter x 0.002086 = pounds per 32 fl oz

CONVERSION OF SODIUM CARBONATE

1 part of monohydrated sodium carbonate is equal to 0.85 part desiccated

1 part of monohydrated sodium carbonate is equal to 1.76 parts crystal

FILM-SPEED CONVERSION TABLE

This table will help you to relate foreign film ratings to American exposure meters and cameras, and vice versa. Although still widely used, the familiar "ASA" rating was officially changed to the "USA Standard" rating when the name of the originating organization was changed from the American Standards Association to the United States of America Standards Institute. BSA, an identical rating, is sponsored by the British Standards Association. The table should be used only as a guide, however, as the ratings of the different systems are arrived at by somewhat different methods.

USA Standard (ASA) and BSA	DIN (German system)	European Scheiner	GOST (Russian system)	Weston (for older meters)
1	1/10	....	....	0.75
1.2	2/10	....	....	1
1.6	3/10	....	....	1.3
2	4/10	....	....	1.5
2.5	5/10	....	....	2
3	6/10	....	....	2.5
4	7/10	18	....	3
5	8/10	19	10	4
6	9/10	20	12	5
8	10/10	21	16	6
10	11/10	22	20	8
12	12/10	23	25	10
16	13/10	24	32	12
20	14/10	25	40	16
25	15/10	26	50	20
32	16/10	27	65	24
40	17/10	28	80	32
50	18/10	29	100	40
64	19/10	30	125	50
80	20/10	31	160	64
100	21/10	32	200	80
125	22/10	33	230	100
160	23/10	34	320	125
200	24/10	35	400	160
250	25/10	36	500	200
320	26/10	37	650	250
400	27/10	38	800	320
500	28/10	39	1000	400
650	29/10	40	1250	500
800	30/10	41	1600	650
1000	31/10	42	....	800

11

Soaps, Cosmetics, and Medicinal Preparations

SOAPMAKING

Pure homemade soap that is superior to many commercial soaps can be made easily from nothing but household lye and leftover fat and grease that ordinarily would be wasted. It is a good cleanser, contains natural glycerin which is soothing to the skin, and is completely lacking in weight-making fillers.

Six pounds of waste cooking grease and fat from meat scraps, a 13-ounce can of lye, and a few minutes' time will make 9 pounds of fine all-purpose soap at a cost of little more than one cent for a large bar. By varying the basic formula slightly, you can make a special soap to suit every purpose in the home.

As with cooking, the quality of the product will depend on the quality of the ingredients used and the care taken in preparation. Avoid using rancid fat or grease and strain any that is dirty. Measure accurately and watch your temperatures. Use pure flake lye of a reputable brand (Dixie, Babbit, etc.). Flake lye makes no dust and dissolves easier than powdered lye.

Preparing fat. Good soap requires fats that are free from dirt, rancidity, lean meat, salt, and other impurities. Fat rendered from tallows, meat trimmings, and rinds is ready for soap without further treatment. Meat fryings and other refuse fats should be washed as follows: Add an equal amount of water and bring the combination to the boiling point. Remove from fire, stir, and then add 1 quart of cold water to 1 gallon of the hot liquid. The cold water precipitates foreign substances, and the clean fat rises to the top. Remove the fat when firm.

Basic soap formula. To make 9 pounds of pure, hard, smooth soap suitable for toilet, laundry, or soap flakes, follow this simple recipe:

Cold water	2½ pints
Pure flake lye	1 13 oz can
Clean fat (tallow or lard, or combination)	6 lb
(6 lbs of fat is about 6¾ pints of liquid fat)	

Slowly pour the lye into the water in a Pyrex, iron, or enamel vessel (*Caution*: Don't spill lye solution on your skin, clothing, or furnishings, as it is extremely caustic). Stir until the lye is completely dissolved. Then let cool to the correct temperature as shown in the table to follow.

Melt fat to clear liquid and let cool to correct temperature as shown in table, or until the fat offers resistance to the spoon. Stir occasionally to prevent crystals from forming. Pour the lye solution into the fat in a *thin, steady stream with slow, even stirring.* (Rapid addition of lye solution or hard stirring is apt to cause a separation.) A honey-like consistency is formed which becomes thick in from 10 to 20 minutes.

Pour the thickened mixture into a wooden box that has been soaked in water and lined with clean cotton cloth wet in water and wrung nearly dry. Place in a protecting pan. Cover with a board or cardboard, then with an old rug or blanket to retain the heat while it is texturing out. Leave it alone for 24 hours.

To remove the soap from the mold, lift it by the ends of the overhanging cotton lining. Cut into bars by wrapping the soap with a fine wire and pulling the wire through. Place so air can reach it, but avoid drafts and cold. Aging improves soap. In 10 to 14 days it is ready for use.

Temperature table. Follow these temperatures closely:

Type of fat	Temp. of fat	Temp. of lye sol.
Sweet lard or other soft fat	98°F	77°F
Half lard and tallow	105°F	83°F
All tallow	125°F	93°F

To save soap that separates. If soap mixture becomes too hot or too cold, is stirred too hard or not thoroughly mixed, or it contains salt, a greasy soap may form at the top while liquid separates out at the bottom.

So save the batch, cut or shave the soap into a pot, add the lye solution that has separated and about 5 pints of water. Melt with gentle heat and occasional stirring. Then raise heat and boil gently until it becomes ropy when dropped from the spoon. Pour into mold as mentioned above. Don't worry about too much water: it can be boiled off.

Variations in Soapmaking

Besides all-purpose soap, many other kinds can be made at home. Here are a few:

Floating soap. Almost any type of soap can be made to float. When the soap mixture becomes thick enough, just fold air into it as egg white would be folded into a cake mixture.

Perfumed soaps. You can, of course, scent your soap with small amounts of oils of sassafras, lavender, lemon, almond, rose geranium, or some perfume of your choice. If you do, select one that does not contain alcohol.

A tea made with leaves of rose geranium gives a delightful perfume, and may be colored, if you wish, by adding the extract of blossoms of pink roses or tulips. You can color soap green by adding to the original water a few drops of juice pounded from beet tops.

Because all soap absorbs odors, it can be inexpensively perfumed by placing with it the leaves of a favorite flower, or a perfume.

Soap flakes and powder. For flakes, rub three-day-old soap over a vegetable shredder. Stir occasionally while drying. To make powder, first flake the soap and dry in a 150° oven. When thoroughly dry, pulverize it.

Rosin soap. A laundry soap that is darker and softer, but which has greater lathering power, can be made by adding rosin. Add 8 ounces of powdered rosin to 5½ pounds clean fat and heat until the rosin is melted or dissolved in the fat. Cool to 100°F, add the lye solution mentioned above for the basic soap and cool to 90°F.

Saddle soap. All-tallow soap is often referred to as "saddle soap" because it is an excellent cleaner and preserver of leather. Use 6 pounds mutton or beef tallow, 2¾ pints of water. Have lye solution 90°F and fat 130°F. This soap will lather better if you substitute 1 pound of lard, coconut oil, or olive oil for that weight of tallow.

Glycerin soap. Just add about 6 ounces of glycerin to any soap shortly after lye solution has been added.

Imitation castile soap. A high grade soap that is in many respects superior to real castile soap can be made as follows:

Olive oil	24 oz
Good grade tallow	38 oz
Coconut oil	24 oz
Water	32 oz
Pure flake lye	13 oz

Use procedure for basic soap. Pour lye solution into fat when both are 90°F.

Linseed oil soap. This is a soft soap recommended for washing automobiles and furniture:

Water	2 qt
Pure flake lye	1 can
Linseed oil	5¾ lb

Cool lye solution to 90°F and oil to 100°F. Add lye solution a little at a time and combine it well before adding more.

Abrasive soap. Good for cleaning your hands after any dirty, greasy job. When basic soap mixture thickens add, gradually, 5 to 6 pounds of powdered pumice, emery dust, or Tripoli powder and stir until the mixture is thoroughly blended. Mold and cover. Yield: 14 to 15 pounds.

Abrasive soap paste. Another good product for household scouring and mechanics' hands. Shave 3 pounds basic soap and melt in 3 pints of water. Add 3 ounces light mineral oil. When thoroughly blended, cool to thick consistency and work in 5 pounds of powdered pumice or Tripoli. Keep tightly covered to prevent drying out. Yield: 11 pounds.

Jelly soap. This is a convenient and economical soap for use in washing machines and for washing dishes. It melts immediately in hot water and makes thick suds. Cut 1 pound of hard soap into fine shavings and add 1 gallon of water. Boil for about 10 minutes, then transfer to a suitable vessel to cool. Keep covered to prevent drying out.

Mechanic's hand soaps. Here is a good cleaner for greasy and grimy hands after work in garage or shop:

Powdered pumice	7 oz
Powdered soap	5 oz
Borax	1¼ oz
Washing soda	1 oz
Glycerin	½ oz
Water	13 oz

Dissolve the washing soda, borax, and glycerin in 3 ounces of the water, and dissolve the powdered soap in the rest of the water. Stir the solutions together. Then stir in the pumice until thoroughly blended.

In the following formula, extra sodium carbonate or washing soda acts as a water-softening agent and takes over the cleaning action of part of the soap:

Washing soda	2 oz
Borax	½ oz
Powdered soap	2½ oz
Glycerin	½ oz
Powdered pumice	10 oz
Water	20 oz

Heat the water and dissolve the washing soda, borax, and soap flakes in it. Then add the glycerin with constant stirring. When thickening begins, add the powdered pumice slowly as you continue to stir. Keep stirring until the mixture is smooth enough and thick enough so the pumice will not settle. Then pack it in glass or plastic containers.

Hand-Cleaning Powders

A mild hand cleaner that leaves the hands smooth and soft uses corn meal as an abrasive and includes sodium perborate as a gentle bleach:

Fine corn meal	8 oz
Powdered soap	16 oz
Powdered borax	12 oz
Sodium perborate	1½ oz

Mix thoroughly by stirring and then shaking in a box or passing through a flour sifter several times. For more heavily soiled hands substitute 4 ounces of fine pumice powder for the corn meal. Use from a flour shaker. Sprinkle on moistened hands, rub, wash, and rinse.

Note: In this and in similar formulas that call for it, be sure to use powdered soap and not soap powder. Powdered soap is pure soap in powdered form, while soap powder is powdered soap combined with powdered alkalies, abrasives, and other builders.

A more powerful cleaner can be made by substituting wood flour (fine sawdust) for the corn meal and adding a little trisodium phosphate to help cut grease:

Wood flour	10 oz
Powdered soap	8 oz
Trisodium phosphate	1 oz
Borax	1 oz

Mix and use as described in the previous formula.

Liquid Soap

This can be used from a regular liquid soap dispenser or from a bottle.

Potassium hydroxide	1 oz
Water	11 oz
Oleic acid	4 oz
Glycerin	4 oz

Dissolve the potassium hydroxide in the water in a stainless steel or heat-resisting glass vessel. (*Caution:* Keep this chemical off your hands and clothing, as it is extremely caustic.) Then mix the glycerin with the oleic acid and add to the solution. Heat to about 172°F, and stir until completely emulsified.

Improvised Liquid Soap

Dissolve any good soap, soap flakes, or powdered soap in hot water, making a thick paste. To each quart of this add a mixture of 1 pint of warm water and ½ pint of ethyl rubbing alcohol. When stirred in, this acts as a clarifying agent. Besides serving as a good liquid soap for general purposes, this preparation also makes a simple and inexpensive shampoo.

Liquid Shampoo

A shampoo comparable to many proprietary brands may be made as follows:

Potassium hydroxide	2¼ oz
Water	22 oz
Coconut oil	8 oz
Ethyl rubbing alcohol compound (70% alcohol)	6 oz
Perfume	if and as desired

Dissolve completely the potassium hydroxide in 6 ounces of the water in a stainless steel or heat-resisting glass vessel. (*Caution:* Keep this chemical off your hands and clothing, as it is extremely caustic.) Mix the oils in the top of a double boiler also made of glass or stainless steel, heat them to 158°F and, with constant stirring, add the potassium hydroxide solution. Keep this temperature for about 1 hour, stirring occasionally. Then heat the rest of the water to 158°F and stir into the mixture. Let cool, add the alcohol and, if you want, the perfume.

COSMETICS

Protective Hand Creams

A mixture of lanolin and castor oil is frequently used on the hands and arms of machinists susceptible to skin trouble caused by constant contact with lubricating oil. This type of "extra skin," however, is not so suitable for those doing general work about the shop, garage, or home.

A good protective cream for all-around use can be made from 1 part by volume of gum acacia (in the form of small globules, or "tears") and 2 parts of powdered soap. Put the gum acacia in a wide-mouth jar and add only enough water to cover the drops. Cover the jar, and allow to stand overnight. Then stir in the soap to form a thick cream.

Rub this cream well into your hands before starting work. When you have finished, you can easily wash it off along with the dirt.

Glycerin Hand Lotion

Boric acid	2 oz
Gum tragacanth	½ oz
Glycerin	8 oz
Witch hazel	16 oz
Water	16 oz
Perfume	as desired

Add the gum tragacanth and boric acid to the water and let soak for 12 hours, with occasional stirring. Then add the witch hazel and glycerin and stir or shake well. Strain through clean muslin. If you would like the lotion scented, add perfume to suit.

Hand Lotion

Soft soap	1 oz
Glycerin	4 fl oz
Ethyl rubbing alcohol compound (alcohol 70%)	15 fl oz
Water	15 fl oz
Perfume	as desired

Mix the rubbing alcohol with the water (use distilled water if your tap water is hard) and dissolve the soft soap in the mixture. Then stir in the glycerin. Add perfume if you want.

Lanolin Skin Lotion

White powdered soap	½ oz
Lanolin	5 oz
Borax	¼ oz
Water	44 oz
Perfume	as desired

Dissolve the borax and soap in the water, heated to about 110°F. Melt the lanolin separately and then pour into the water solution with vigorous stirring. Finally add perfume, if desired. Shake before using.

Cold Cream

Heavy mineral oil	200 parts
White beeswax	50 parts
Borax	30 parts
Water	80 parts

Put the oil in the top of a double boiler, add the wax, and heat gently until the wax is melted. Dissolve the borax in the water. Heat both liquids to not more than 150°F. Pour the borax solution into the wax solution steadily with gentle stirring. At this point, blend in a little perfume, if desired. Remove from heat and pour it into glass or plastic containers when it has cooled to 120°F.

A second formula for cold cream substitutes paraffin for part of the beeswax:

Heavy mineral oil	21 fl oz
White beeswax	6½ oz
Paraffin wax	2¼ oz
Borax	½ oz
Water	17 fl oz
Perfume	as desired

Dissolve the borax in water and heat to about 168°F. Mix wax and oil in top of double boiler, raise temperature to 158°F, and stir until wax is melted and combined. Then stir vigorously into the hot borax solution. Keep stirring until mixture cools to about 125°F. Perfume, if desired, may then be mixed in.

Petrolatum Cold Cream

Heavy mineral oil	48 fl oz
White petrolatum	12 oz
White beeswax	8 oz
White ceresin wax	8 oz
Borax	¼ oz
Water	12 fl oz
Perfume	as desired

Place the petrolatum, waxes, and mineral oil in the top of a double boiler and heat to about 160°F. Stir until the solids have completely melted and combined. Dissolve the borax in the water, heated to the same temperature. Then pour the borax solution into the wax mixture and stir well. Remove from the heat and keep stirring until mixture begins to thicken. Then mix in the perfume.

Vanishing Cream

Vanishing creams are greaseless creams that are essentially stearic acid soaps having excess stearic acid suspended in water. The usual pearly appearance is caused by crystallization of the acid. To bring this about, the cream should be allowed to stand a few days after making, stirring it slowly for several minutes each day.

Stearic acid	12½ oz
Anhydrous lanolin	4½ oz
Water	30 fl oz
White mineral oil	9½ fl oz
Potassium carbonate	1 oz
Perfume	as desired

Melt the stearic acid and the lanolin, mixed with 20 ounces of the water, in the top of a double boiler. Raise the heat to 170°F. Dissolve the potassium carbonate in the remainder of the water, heated also to 170°. Add this solution to the first mixture. Stir until foaming caused by the reaction of the stearic acid with the carbonate subsides. Then remove from the heat and keep stirring until the mixture thickens. Add perfume at this time, and pour into containers before the cream completely solidifies.

Brushless Shaving Cream

Heavy mineral oil	8 oz
Diglycol stearate	8 oz
Water	40 oz
Perfume	as desired

Heat the mineral oil and diglycol stearate (also called glycostearin) to 150°F in the top of a double boiler. Heat the water separately to the same temperature and stir slowly into the mixture. Let cool to lukewarm and stir in perfume. Keep stirring until at room temperature. Store in jars or tubes.

After-Shave Lotion

This is a cooling and astringent solution for use after shaving. Use crystalline boric acid, as supplied for photographic formulas, as the powdered form is more difficult to dissolve.

Boric acid	½ oz
Ethyl rubbing alcohol compound (70% alcohol)	20 fl oz
Water	15 fl oz

Nail Polish Remover

This inexpensive nail polish remover is as effective as any:

Ethyl acetate	1 fl oz
Acetone	3 fl oz
Cooking oil (corn, soybean, cottonseed, olive)	30 drops

Just stir the ingredients until thoroughly blended, and store in a tightly-stopped bottle. The oil is included to prevent the solvents from drying out the nails.

Anti-Perspirant Solution

A simple and effective preparation for the control of perspiration is a solution of aluminum chloride in water. Your druggist may have it already prepared as "aluminum chloride solution, N.F.," or he may make it up for you. Here is the formula, if you want to make it yourself:

Aluminum chloride	2 oz
Water to make	8 fl oz

Just dissolve the chemical by stirring it in about 6 ounces of water, and then adding enough more water to make 8 ounces. If the solution is cloudy, filter until it becomes clear.

Pat lightly on unbroken skin with a swab of cotton. Repeat two times more, on successive nights. If necessary, repeat again in a week.

This chemical may irritate some skin and may stain clothes if they come in contact with it when wet.

Therefore do not rub it in or use it more than necessary. Also let the skin dry thoroughly before letting clothing touch it.

How Hexachlorophene Cuts B.O.

Unpleasant body odor is often the result of byproducts of bacteria that live on the skin. It has been found that such bacteria—and hence the odors that they produce—can be almost entirely eliminated by bathing regularly with a soap containing the bacteriostat, or bacteria inhibitor, hexachlorophene. Discovered in the 1940's, this remarkable chemical was the first powerful bacteriostat that was odorless, nonpoisonous, and nonirritating to the skin that could be combined with soap and other cleaning materials without losing its own effectiveness.

Dial soap was the first to introduce hexachlorophene to the general public. Now many other soaps and cleaning agents—as well as deodorants, such as *Arrid, Man-Power, Secret,* and *Mum*—contain it, as you can find out from their labels.

A single scrubbing with hexachlorophene soap will have little effect, but daily use for a week should reduce the bacteria on your skin to as little as 5 percent of normal.

Bargains in Talcum Powder

The finest talcum powder is so inexpensive, it wouldn't pay to try to mix your own. Essentially talcum is a native magnesium silicate that has been mechanically milled, ground, sifted, and mixed for many hours to reduce it to an impalpable dust. It owes its usefulness and popularity to its softness, slight greasiness, and its ability to cling to the skin.

If you pay a lot for talcum, you are paying for a brand name or for a drop or two of perfume. To get quality talcum at a bargain price, buy the largest containers of unscented or faintly scented "baby talcum" of any reputable maker. These are often sold as "come-ons" in drugstores and supermarkets.

MOUTHWASHES

Any mouthwash you can buy without a doctor's or dentist's prescription is essentially a liquid with a pleasant taste and odor that is useful for rinsing loose food and debris from your mouth. According to authoritative medical opinion, claims for significant germicidal or antibacterial action by such solutions are baseless. Although it may occasionally be necessary to use medicated solutions containing astringents, germicides, and other special agents, these should be used only under medical supervision to treat definite ailments of the mouth. The normal mouth does not need them, and if used indiscriminately they may do more harm than good.

Most proprietary mouthwashes are slightly alkaline, because alkalies are more effective in removing mucus and saliva. If too strong, however, alkalis will damage mouth and throat tissues. If, on the other hand, a mouthwash is acid, it may damage your teeth.

The simplest mouth wash is plain warm water. This wash will be slightly kinder to your mouth and a little more effective in removing debris if you make it approximately isotonic, or the density of your body fluids, by adding a teaspoon of table salt to each pint.

A slightly alkaline mouthwash can be made by dissolving 2 teaspoons of bicarbonate of soda in each pint of water. Or you can use half a teaspoon, each, of bicarbonate and salt in a pint of water.

If you prefer a flavored mouthwash, try this:

Sodium chloride	1 teaspoon
Sodium bicarbonate	½ teaspoon
Amaranth solution, U.S.P.	40 drops
Peppermint water to make	1 pint

Peppermint Water

The peppermint water included in the formula above is one of a number of pleasingly flavored waters that have been included in medical preparations down through the centuries chiefly to make them acceptable in aroma and taste. Technically peppermint water is a saturated solution of peppermint oil in distilled water. Because peppermint oil is almost insoluble in water, however, a tiny amount of oil flavors an amazing amount of solution.

To make peppermint water, add about ½ teaspoon of peppermint oil to 1 quart of water in a 2-quart bottle. Shake the mixture at half a dozen intervals during a period of 15 minutes. Stopper the bottle, and set the mixture aside for half a day or longer. Then filter through a filter paper that has first been wetted with water to prevent the excess of oil from going through. Although most of the oil remains behind, you will discover that the water will be saturated with its odor and taste.

TEETH CLEANING PREPARATIONS

Powders and pastes for cleaning teeth are generally composed of precipitated chalk, salt, bicarbonate of soda, soap, borax, magnesia, glycerin, saccharin for sweetening, flavors and essential oils for taste, water, and color. Some may taste and smell better than others, others contain bleaches that lighten stains faster, and harsher abrasives that remove soil with less brushing. None, however, has value in treating mouth or gum disease, and almost none in helping to preserve teeth. If the abrasive in a paste or powder is too hard or too coarse, it cleans teeth faster but also wears down their surface. Recent tests indicate that fluorides in some preparations may be useful in reducing decay, but this is a matter of tooth medication and not of cleaning.

According to the Council on Dental Therapeutics of the American Dental Association, at least 25 percent of all persons could keep their teeth satisfactorily clean by brushing them regularly with plain water. Most of the remainder could do a good job with nothing more than common salt or bicarbonate of soda—or a combination of the two—sprinkled on a wet brush.

If stain still builds up under these simple means, an occasional brushing with a proprietary paste or powder of your choice may help, or you could use one of the following very mildly abrasive and inexpensive products you can make yourself.

Inexpensive Tooth Powder

A cheap toothpowder as effective as the most expensive, yet one that won't damage the enamel on your teeth, is simply precipitated chalk you can buy at any drugstore. Plain chalk or flavored chalk was indeed the sole or main ingredient of almost all tooth powders until recent years, and it still holds top place. If you'd prefer it flavored, mix thoroughly into it a little oil of wintergreen, spearmint, or peppermint, according to your taste.

Foamy Tooth Powders

For those who like foamy or sudsy toothpowders, here is a simple formula of this type:

Precipitated chalk	5 oz
Sodium bicarbonate	1 oz
Powdered soap	¾ oz
Flavor, as desired	

Be sure to use powdered soap in this and the next formula, and not soap powder, which is a cleaning preparation made of soap mixed with various "builders."

Mix the powders thoroughly and sift them together. If desired, stir in one of the flavors mentioned in the previous formula.

The following foamy powder, a little more complex, is similar to one recommended by the National Formulary:

Powdered soap	1 oz
Precipitated chalk	19 oz
Soluble saccharin	18 grains
Oil of peppermint	½ tsp
Oil of cinnamon	¼ tsp
Methyl salicylate	1 tsp

Grind and mix thoroughly together the saccharin, oils, and methyl salicylate with about half of the precipitated chalk, and mix the soap with the other half. Then mix the two powders together and sift through a fine sieve.

Denture Cleaners

Dental plates and bridges may be cleaned by brushing them with any of the proprietary tooth powders or pastes, or with the powders just described.

To remove the stains from dentures and to sweeten and disinfect them, they may be soaked in a solution of one or another of common household chemicals. These are the same chemicals you would pay a great deal more for if bought under their proprietary names as denture cleaners.

First brush the denture to remove obvious particles and then let it stand for 15 minutes or overnight in one of the following solutions:

| 1. Clear household ammonia | 4 tsp |
| Water | ½ glass |

| 2. Trisodium phosphate | ¼ tsp |
| Warm water | ½ glass |

3. 5% sodium hypochlorite solution	
(Clorox, Rose-X, Purex, etc.)	½ tsp
Water	½ glass

All these preparations are safe for the usual acrylic plastic dentures. Those made of chromium-cobalt alloys should not, however, be left in the sodium hypochlorite solution for more than a few minutes as they may corrode. After soaking, dentures should be rinsed in plain water before using.

A denture cleaner that includes a mild bleaching agent can be made by thoroughly mixing together the following:

Trisodium phosphate	10 oz
Sodium perborate	5 oz
Salt	5 oz

Here is another that does not require soaking, but is used immediately with a brush:

Trisodium phosphate	5 oz
Cinnamon oil	7 drops

Put the trisodium phosphate in a dry wide-mouth bottle. Drop the oil on it, cover the bottle, and shake until the oil is thoroughly mixed with the powder. To use, dissolve a scant ¼ teaspoonful in half a glass of water and brush the appliance with the solution. Rinse with plain water.

DENTURE ADHESIVES

Although not recommended by dental authorities for routine use, denture adhesives are often useful in helping a person get used to new dentures, in easing a transitory sore spot, or in preventing dentures from popping out while making a proposition or a speech.

Most of the proprietary adhesives consist of just one or two common gums, or a combination of them, with the addition of a trace of flavor. The simplest and probably the most widely used is powdered gum tragacanth. Powdered karaya gum may also be used alone, but a few people are sensitive to it. A combination powder, with flavor, may be made as follows:

Powdered gum tragacanth	3 oz
Powdered karaya gum	1 oz
Sassafras oil	35 drops

Shake the two powdered gums together in a dry wide-mouth bottle until thoroughly mixed. Add the oil and shake again until the oil has blended with the powders. Sprinkle sparingly on the denture, and place in the mouth.

BASIC OINTMENTS

White Ointment

This is a bland and basic ointment that may be used either alone or with medication incorporated in it.

Lanolin (wool fat)	1 oz
White beeswax	1 oz
White petroleum jelly	20 oz

Melt the beeswax in the top of a double boiler. Add the lanolin and petroleum jelly and continue to heat until they are also melted. Then remove from heat and stir the mixture until it begins to harden. Pour into wide-mouth jars.

Boric Acid Ointment

Finely powdered boric acid	2 oz
Lanolin	1 oz
White ointment	17 oz

Work the boric acid into the lanolin with a spatula until you form a uniform paste. Then similarly work into this the white ointment.

Zinc Oxide Ointment

Finely powdered zinc oxide	3 oz
Lanolin	1 oz
White ointment	11 oz

Preparation is the same as for the formula above.

Sulfur Ointment

Precipitated sulfur	2 oz
Lanolin	1 oz
White ointment	11 oz

With a spatula, work the sulfur into the lanolin and about 1½ ounces of the white ointment. Then blend the mixture with rest of white ointment.

FOOT POWDER

This preparation is mildly fungicidal and also acts as a drying and soothing agent.

Salicylic acid	½ oz
Zinc stearate	½ oz
Boric acid	½ oz
Powdered talcum	7½ oz
Corn starch	10 oz

Put all these ingredients into a large, dry wide-mouth bottle and shake together until thoroughly mixed. Sprinkle between the toes and in the socks. *Caution:* Some people are sensitive to all preparations containing salicylic acid. If redness and a slight swelling appear within a day, do not continue the use of this powder.

ALCOHOL FOR MEDICINES AND COSMETICS

Because it is practically impossible for an ordinary individual to get straight ethyl alcohol that is safe for internal use, no formulas requiring it are included in this book. Manufacturers of medical products may obtain pure or specially denatured alcohol by permission, and under the strict control, of the Internal Revenue Service.

The specially and completely denatured alcohols that are sold for fuel, cleaning, and as a solvent for surface coatings contain extremely poisonous wood alcohol, gasoline, and other denaturants that make them completely unfit for any preparation either to be taken internally or to be applied to the skin.

Vodka as alcohol. If you so desperately want to prepare a medical product that requires undenatured ethyl alcohol that you are willing to pay a premium price for it, you can, of course, use vodka. That is, provided your formula does not require alcohol of more than 55 percent strength by volume. For present-day American vodka is simply ethyl or grain alcohol ("neutral spirits") diluted with from

45 to 60 percent water. To find the percentage by volume of alcohol in a given vodka, just divide the "proof" number by 2. For percentage by weight, see the following table:

ALCOHOL IN VODKA

PROOF	PERCENT ALCOHOL BY VOLUME	PERCENT ALCOHOL BY WEIGHT
80	40	33.36
100	50	42.49
110	55	47.24

MEDICINAL DOSES FOR CHILDREN

One long-used and still popular rule for calculating the fraction of an adult dose of medicine that may safely and effectively be given to a child is called *Young's rule*, after the physician who devised it. Usually it is stated simply as "age over age-plus-12." For example, here is how to calculate the dose for a child of 4:

$$\frac{4}{4+12} = \frac{1}{4} \text{ part of an adult dose.}$$

Many physicians, however, disregard age and base a child's dose simply on the proportion of the child's weight to that of an adult, which is set arbitrarily at 150 pounds.

HOW TO READ PRESCRIPTION LATIN

The familiar prescription (from Latin *prae*, before; and *scribere*, to write) is simply an order from a physician, dentist, or other licensed practitioner instructing a pharmacist to compound and dispense certain medication for his patient.

For a number of reasons, a prescription is often written in Latin. Three of these are still valid: Because Latin is a dead language, terms in it do not change; Latin is the world-wide language of medicine; and the Latin names of drugs are more definite than the popular terms of the local country. A fourth reason—to conceal from the patient the nature of the ingredients and the instructions for administration—has become dubious with the discovery of amazing new drugs and the vastly increased knowledge of the general public about disease and medicine.

The following glossary of common terms used in prescription Latin is therefore included not only to dispel some of the unwarranted mystery surrounding prescriptions, but to help patients apply them more intelligently.

THE LATIN ON YOUR PRESCRIPTION

ABBREVIATION OR SHORT FORM	EXPANDED FORM	MEANING
a.	auris	ear
aa.	ana	of each
a.c.	ante cibos	before meals
ad	ad	to, up to
add	adde	add
ad lib.	ad libitum	at pleasure
agit.	agita	shake
alb.	albus	white
aq.	aqua	water
b.	bis	twice
bene.	bene	well
b.i.d.	bis in die	twice a day
c.	cum	with
cap.	capiat	let the patient take
caps.	capsula	capsule
caps. amyl.	capsulae amylaceae	wafer-type capsule
chart.	charta	paper, a powder in paper
chart. cerat.	charta cerata	waxed paper
chartul.	chartula	small paper
coch. amp.	cochleare amplum	tablespoonful
or coch. mag.	cochleare magnum	tablespoonful
coch. parv.	cochleare parvum	teaspoonful
collyr.	collyrium	eyewash
d.	dies	a day

THE LATIN ON YOUR PRESCRIPTION

ABBREVIATION OR SHORT FORM	EXPANDED FORM	MEANING
d.	dosis	a dose
da	da	give
d.t.d.	dentur tales doses	give such doses
dieb. alt.	diebus alternis	every other day
disp.	dispensa, dispensetur	dispense
div.	divide	divide
dos.	dosis	a dose
ejusd.	ejusdem	of the same
et	et	and
ex aq.	ex aqua	with water
e.m.p.	ex modo praescripto	as directed
flav.	flavus	yellow
ft.	fiat, fiant	make
gtt.	gutta, guttae	a drop, drops
hor.	hora	an hour
h.s.	hora somni	at bedtime
m.	misce	mix
mitt.	mitte	send
no.	numero	in number
non	non	not
non rep.	non repetatur	do not repeat
O.	Octarius	a pint
ocul.	oculus	the eye
o.d.	oculo dextro	in right eye
o.l.	oculo laevo	in left eye
o.s.	oculo sinistro	in left eye

THE LATIN ON YOUR PRESCRIPTION

ABBREVIATION OR SHORT FORM	EXPANDED FORM	MEANING
o.u.	oculo utroque	in each eye
p.c.	post cibos	after meals
p. ae.	partes aequales	equal parts
per	per	by means of
p.o.	per os	by mouth
placebo	placebo	to please or satisfy
p.r.n.	pro re nata	as needed
pro tus.	pro tussi	for the cough
q.i.d.	quater in die	four times a day
qq. hr.	quaqua hora	every hour
q.q.h.	quaqua quarta hora	every four hours
q.r.	quantitas recta	quantity is correct
q.s.	quantum sufficit	a sufficient quantity
R_X	recipe	take
sig.	signa, signetur	label, let it be labeled
s.	sine	without
s.a.	secundem artem	according to the art
s.c., sub cut.	sub cutem	under the skin
s.o.s.	si opus sit	if needed
ss.	semis	half
stat.	statim	immediately
s.v.r.	spiritus vini rectificatus	alcohol
tal.	tales	such
t.i.d.	ter in die	three times a day
ut dict.	ut dictum	as directed
v.	vel	or
virid.	viridis	green

12

Bugs, Fungi,
and Bacteria

SAFETY WITH PESTICIDES

Poisons for troublesome insects, fungi, and other pests are usually also poisonous to man and pet animals. They can therefore be dangerous if used carelessly. They are safe, however, if you observe a few simple rules:

Use pesticides only when and where needed, and in recommended amounts.

Follow the directions and heed all precautions on the labels. What may be safe with one type may be dangerous with another.

Keep pesticides in closed, well-labeled containers in a dry place, where they will not contaminate food and where children and animals cannot reach them.

While applying a pesticide, be careful not to contaminate water supply, food, dishes, or utensils.

Do not apply oil sprays where they could be ignited by a flame, such as that of a pilot light, or by electric sparks.

Avoid prolonged contact of insecticide with your skin. Some insecticides, such as chlordane, lindane, and dieldrin can be absorbed directly through the skin in harmful quantities.

Do not treat an entire room with insecticides that are meant only for local surface spraying.

High dosages of aerosol mists may be irritating to eyes and lungs. Keep people and pets out of a treated room for at least an hour after the aerosol has been applied.

Wash all exposed parts of the body with soap and water after applying a pesticide.

Dispose of empty pesticide containers at a sanitary land-fill dump, or bury them at least 18 inches deep in a level, isolated place where they will not contaminate water supplies. If you have trash collection service, thoroughly wrap small containers in several layers of newspaper and place them in the trash can.

HOW TO USE INSECTICIDES

There are at least 120,000 different kinds of insects in the United States and Canada, but only a few kinds are in any way injurious to man. In fact, many kinds are beneficial. Some of these feed on injurious insects. Without others, plants could not be pollinated and so would have no fruit. Unnecessary use of insecticide often kills beneficial insects which, if allowed to live, would have kept the injurious insects under control.

Do not, therefore, apply an insecticide unless it is necessary to prevent actual damage to flowers or vegetables, or to cure an unhealthful or unpleasant condition in the home.

Very few of the insect pests in your garden will cause appreciable damage unless you have already killed off their parasites and predators with insecticide. If, however, you do have a pest that usually causes serious damage unless an insecticide is used, apply the insecticide when the infestation first appears.

Watch out especially for spider mites, aphids, Japanese weevils and other weevils, lacebugs and thrips in the flower garden; spider mites, cabbage caterpillars, the Colorado potato beetle, and the Mexican bean beetle in the vegetable garden. These are some of the insects likely to need prompt treatment with insecticides. Repeat the treatment in a week or 10 days if infestation continues. Do not treat for soil insects unless you find numbers of cutworms, white grubs, or wireworms when preparing the soil for planting.

You can apply most garden insecticides as a dust or as a spray. Either will give satisfactory control if properly used. Ready-to-use dusts cost more than sprays, but this added cost may be offset by their convenience. In windy weather, however, sprays are easier to handle than dusts in preventing drift of insecticide to other plants.

No matter which you use, be sure the material contains the correct percentage of active ingredient. Refer to the formulations mentioned here, and also follow the directions on container labels.

Using dusts. You can buy ready-to-use dusts at insecticide dealers. If desired, you can get one that contains a fungicide as well as one or more insecticides. Such a "general purpose" dust is preferred by many gardeners because it kills a larger variety of pests. Or you may wish to obtain two or more dusters and fill each with an insecticide suited for a particular purpose.

For most uses, purchase dusts that contain the following percentages of active ingredients:

	Percent
Carbaryl	4
Chlordane	6
DDT	5
Diazinon	2
Dicofol (Kelthane)	2
Lindane	1 or 2
Malathion	4
Methoxychlor	5
Naled (Dibrom)	4
Rotenone	¾
TDE	5
Tetradifon	3
Toxaphene	10

Determine from a gardening book or from the insecticide label which material is best suited for a particular insect and plant.

On vegetables, apply an even, light coating of dust at the rate of 1 ounce per 50 feet of row or 125 square feet. On flowers, apply it at the rate of 1 ounce to each 30 feet of row or each 75 square feet of border area. Force dust through the foliage so it reaches both sides of each leaf. Apply dust when the air is still—preferably at dusk or early in the morning.

Mixing and using sprays. Few sprays can be purchased ready to use. It is generally necessary to make the spray by mixing water with a wettable powder (WP) or with an emulsifiable concentrate (EC). Before you buy a powder or concentrate, read the container label to make sure it is prepared for use on plants.

Spray materials are sold in different strengths. The accompanying table shows the dilution recommended for general use. If you buy a product in which the percentage of active ingredient differs from that mentioned in the table, mix proportionately more or less of it with water.

When mixing a spray, first break up lumps in the powder or shake concentrate vigorously before measuring. If you use an emulsifiable concentrate, add an equal amount of water to it, and shake or stir thoroughly to make a stable emulsion. Then add this emulsion to the full amount of water and stir until completely mixed.

Do not mix wettable powders and emulsifiable concentrates in the same batch of spray.

Mix a fresh batch of spray for each application. Many spray mixtures deteriorate or otherwise change after standing for only a few hours in a spray tank. Some mixtures may lose their effectiveness against pests; others may cause serious plant injury.

On vegetables, apply 1 quart of spray to each 50 feet of row or 125 square feet. On flowers apply 2 quarts of spray to each 50 feet of row or to each 75 to 100 square feet of border area. Usually, spraying should be stopped just before the spray starts to run off the foliage. Shake applicator frequently to prevent powder from settling to bottom of the spray tank.

GUIDE FOR MIXING SPRAYS

(WP means wettable powder and EC means emulsifiable concentrate.)

INSECTICIDE	FORMULATION AS BOUGHT	AMOUNT TO MIX WITH 1 GALLON OF WATER
Carbaryl (Sevin)	50-percent WP	2 level tablespoons
Chlordane	40-percent WP, or	4 level teaspoons
	45-percent EC	2 teaspoons
DDT	50-percent WP, or	2 level tablespoons
	25-percent EC	1 tablespoon
Diazinon	50-percent WP, or	2 level teaspoons
	50-percent EC	1 teaspoon
Dicofol (Kelthane)	18.5-percent WP, or	1 level tablespoon
	18.5-percent EC	1 teaspoon
Dimethoate*	23.4-percent EC	1 teaspoon
Lindane	25-percent WP, or	1 level tablespoon
	20-percent EC	1 teaspoon
Malathion	57-percent EC	2 teaspoons
Methoxychlor	50-percent WP	2 level tablespoons
Naled (Dibrom)	8-pounds-per-gallon EC	1 teaspoon
Pyrethrum	Ready-prepared spray	Mix with water as directed on container label
Rotenone	Derris or cube root powder (5-percent rotenone content)	4 level tablespoons (first mix powder with small quantity of water, then add remaining water)
Sulfur	Wettable sulfur	3 level tablespoons
Summer-oil emulsion	100-percent EC	5 tablespoons
TDE	50-percent WP	4 level tablespoons
Tetradifon	25-percent WP	1 level tablespoon
Toxaphene	40-percent WP	3 level tablespoons

*Do not apply dimethoate to chrysanthemum, Chinese holly, Easter lily, flowering almond, flowering plum, flowering peach, flowering cherry, cherry laurel, or to any plant not specified on the label.

Formula for General-Purpose Spray

DDT or methoxychlor, 50-percent WP	2 level tablespoons
Malathion, 57-percent EC, or dimethoate, 23.4-percent EC	2 teaspoons
Wettable sulfur	2 level teaspoons
Zineb, 65-percent WP	1 level tablespoon
Water	1 gallon

"Weighing" Insecticide Powders with a Spoon

In preparing small quantities of insecticide, the weight of powders may be determined closely enough by measuring the powders with a tablespoon. Here are the approximate quantities of common powdered insecticides required to weigh 1 ounce:

Carbaryl wettable powder	6 level tablespoons
Chlordane wettable powder	5 level tablespoons
DDT wettable powder	6 level tablespoons
Diazinon wettable powder	5 level tablespoons
Dicofol wettable powder	5 level tablespoons
Malathion wettable powder	4 level tablespoons
Methoxychlor wettable powder	4 level tablespoons
Sulfur wettable powder	3 level tablespoons
Toxaphene wettable powder	3 level tablespoons

Compatibility of Pesticides

Some types of pesticides—insecticides and fungicides—should not be mixed. The following are compatible and may be used together in spray mixtures. Any pesticide on the list can be used with any one or several of the others:

Chlordane	Ferbam	Rotenone
Diazinon	Malathion	Thiram
Dicofol	Maneb	Toxaphene
Dieldrin	Naled	Zineb
Dimethoate	Pyrethrum	

Most other pesticides recommended for use on green foliage of plants are also compatible except as follows:

Emulsifiable concentrates of DDT, methoxychlor, or TDE may cause injury to foliage if mixed with sulfur, ferbam, maneb, thiram, zineb, or ziram. DDT, methoxychlor, or TDE wettable powders are compatible with these fungicides. Mixtures of the fixed coppers (such as basic copper sulfate, copper oyxchloride sulfate, and cuprous oxide) with diazinon, ferbam, ziram, maneb, thiram, or zineb may decompose upon standing.

Mixtures of captan with emulsifiable concentrates of DDT, methoxychlor, TDE, dieldrin, chlordane, dicofol, or malathion may cause injury to the foliage. Captan is compatible with wettable powders of these insecticides.

General Contact Insecticide

Compounded of only kerosene, laundry soap, and water, the following formula makes a cheap and effective insecticide for general garden use. Prepare it as a stock emulsion to be diluted as needed.

Kerosene	2 gal
Laundry soap powder or chips	½ lb
Water	1 gal

Heat the water quite hot and dissolve the soap in it. Remove from flame, but while still hot, add the kerosene very slowly with constant stirring. Continue to stir vigorously until a creamy emulsion is formed.

Diluted with water to a 5 percent emulsion, this formula is effective against red spiders, immature scales, mealybugs, and rose midge larvae in the soil. Diluted to 1 percent, it is effective against thrips, aphids, and ants in the soil. Soil swarming with ants may be rid of these pests without harming plants by soaking with this 1 percent emulsion. Kerosene emulsion should be applied late in the afternoon and the plants thoroughly sprayed with water the next morning before sunrise.

Stoddard Solvent as Weed Killer

Ordinary Stoddard solvent (see more about it in Chapter 7) makes an excellent herbicide for controlling crabgrass, chickweed, lambsquarters, pigweed, and many other broad-leaved weeds and weed grasses in patios and along the margins of walks, roads, and flowerbeds.

Use full strength in a hand sprayer adjusted to give a coarse spray. Thoroughly wet the foliage with the solvent, being careful not to get it on wanted plants. In hot weather, the weeds die the day of treatment. The solvent evaporates quickly and leaves no chemical residue. Repeat the treatment as new weeds appear. Three or four treatments usually control the weeds for the growing season.

Against weeds in woody ornamental and tree plantings, use Stoddard solvent as a carefully directed spray. Keep it away from the bark and foliage of valuable plants.

For the use of common salt as a weed killer, see unit on salt in Chapter 8, Common Products with Many Uses.

Bordeaux Mixture

One of the oldest fungicides, this mixture is still used to control leaf spot on iris, gray mold on peonies and lilies, dogwood blight, twig blight on yews and junipers, and anthranose and leaf spot on maples and sycamores. It is also useful on potatoes for blight, apples for bitter rot, and on strawberries for leaf spot.

To make a 3-gallon batch:

1. Dissolve 3 tablespoons of copper sulfate fine crystals in 1 gallon of water in a plastic or enameled container large enough to hold the entire mix.

2. Mix 5 tablespoons of spray lime in 1 gallon of water in another container.

3. Pour the lime mixture into the copper sulfate solution, stir well, and then stir in another gallon of water.

4. Pour the combination into the spray tank.

Bordeaux mixture does not keep well after the lime and copper sulfate solutions are mixed, so mix them just before use and stir occasionally while using. The solutions will keep for a long time, however, as separate solutions.

SOIL TREATMENT FOR TERMITE CONTROL

Subterranean or ground-nesting termites occur throughout the United States, but most abundantly in the South Atlantic and Gulf Coast states and California. Their chief food is cellulose from wood, and by eating the woodwork of buildings they cause many millions of dollars' damage every year.

The best way to thwart this damage is to construct buildings so termites can't get into the woodwork. Another way is to treat the soil near the foundations and under concrete slabs with suitable chemicals.

Risks of Infestation

The risk of infestation is greatest beneath buildings having a concrete slab on the ground, a crawl space with inadequate clearance, ventilation, and drainage, or a basement with enclosed porches and terraces where filled earth comes close to the building timbers.

How to Detect Infestations

Telltale signs of subterranean termites are the earthen tunnels built by them over the surfaces of foundation walls to reach the wood above. When feeding in wood, the pearly-white worker termites make galleries that follow the grain. You can seldom see these on the wood surface, but they may be found by removing weatherboarding or trim boards or by probing with a knife or other tool the places where you suspect the insects are at work. Unlike powderpost beetles, termites do not push out sawdustlike material from their galleries.

Another evidence of termites is the swarming of winged adults early in the spring or fall. Each adult has four silvery wings, which are of equal length and twice as long as the body. Large numbers of detached wings may be found where swarming has taken place, even after the swarm has gone. Winged reproductive termites may be distinguished from winged reproductive ants by their wings and their waistlines. Ants also have two pairs of wings, but of unequal size. Termites have thick waistlines while ants have thin ones.

Principle of Control

The main objective in termite control is to break contact between the termite colony in the ground and the woodwork in the building. You can do this by removing all wood supports, formboards, debris, and so on from around and beneath the house, and making any necessary changes in the structure of the house to block the passage of termites from soil to wood; by chemically treating the soil; or, better still, by combining these methods.

The suggestions that follow relate chiefly to some of the simpler soil treatments. If properly applied, protection should last several years. Each case of termite trouble, however, requires individual consideration. Some of them may require special equipment and be otherwise too complicated for an average homeowner to handle. For such jobs, it may be best to get help from a reliable pest-control man.

Preparation for Treatment

Houses without basements. To control infestations along interior walls or around supporting piers of basementless houses, dig a trench 6 to 8 inches wide and a few inches deep, next to the walls or piers, taking care not to go below the top of the footing. If the land slopes or the footing is more than 12 inches deep, use a crowbar, pipe, or rod to make holes about an inch in diameter and a foot apart from the bottom of the trench to the footing. Dig another trench the same width, but about 12 inches deep, around the outside foundation walls. If necessary, make holes in the trench bottom as described for the inside walls.

Basement houses. Where termites are coming from beneath the concrete floor in the basement, remove any wood that may extend from the foundation into the ground, treat the soil with poison, and then seal all cracks or holes through which termites might enter. Fill large holes with a dense cement mortar, and small ones with a roofing-grade coal-tar pitch. Where the infestation is located in an expansion joint between the floor and the wall, or around a furnace, make a series of 1-inch holes, about a foot apart, through which a chemical can be poured. Holes along a wall should be made about 6 to 8 inches from it, so as to clear the footing and reach the soil beneath.

Where infestation occurs along exterior foundation walls in houses with full basements, it is necessary to treat the soil to greater depth. Prepare the trench in the same way, but extend the pipe or rod holes right down to the top of the footing. This is especially important in foundations of brick or concrete block where imperfect mortar joints may make termite entry easy.

Concrete slab on ground. Infestations in houses built with a concrete slab on the ground are the hardest to control, because it is hard to place chemicals in the soil under such floors where they will be effective.

One way to do it is to drill holes about ½ inch in diameter through the concrete slab close to the point where the termites are or where they may be entering. Space the holes about 6 inches from the wall and about 12 inches apart. Be careful, however, not to drill into electrical conduits or plumbing. Apply the chemical through the holes by any means available, although it would be distributed best if applied under considerable pressure.

Dig a trench around the outside foundation walls as described for basementless houses.

Poisons for Termites and How to Prepare Them

The chemicals recommended are all water emulsions. Unlike oil solutions, they will not injure plants when used along exterior foundation walls. Neither will they creep up walls and damage floors, as oil may, when applied along the interior of foundations. The concentrations recommended allow a margin of safety and provide protection for several years.

Caution: Like most pesticides, the chemicals to be mentioned are poisonous to man and other warm-blooded animals and must be handled with care. Do not permit them to come in contact with your skin. Wear rubber or rubberized gloves to protect your hands. If the poison is being applied with pressure through holes in walls or piers, use a plastic face guard so the chemical cannot splash back on your face. If contact with the soap poison occurs, wash the skin immediately with warm soapy water. When the chemical is being applied in an enclosed area, provide a free circulation of air. Never apply these chemicals in places where they might be leached from the soil and enter wells that supply drinking water. Keep children and pets away from areas where the poisons are being prepared and used.

CHLORDANE, 1-percent emulsion

Chlordane is available as 46–48, or 72–74 percent water emulsion concentrates. Prepare the 1-percent emulsion by adding 48 gallons of water to 1 gallon of the 46-percent concentrate, or 99 gallons of water to 1 gallon of the 72-percent concentrate. The ratio is 1 to 48, and 1 to 99, respectively, whether the measure is in gallons or in cupfuls.

DIELDRIN, 0.5-percent emulsion

This chemical is available in an 18-percent emulsion concentrate, containing 1.5 pounds of technical dieldrin per gallon. To prepare an 0.5-percent strength, add 36 gallons of water to each gallon of concentrate.

BENZENE HEXACHLORIDE (BHC), 0.8-percent emulsion

BHC is frequently sold as a liquid concentrate containing 12-percent gamma isomer, the part toxic to insects. To make the 0.8-percent emulsion, dilute 1 gallon of the concentrate with 15 gallons of water.

ALDRIN, 0.5-percent emulsion

The concentrate contains either 2 or 4 pounds of technical aldrin per gallon. For an 0.5-percent emulsion, add 1 gallon of the 2-pound concentrate to 47 gallons of water, or 1 gallon of the 4-pound concentrate to 95 gallons of water.

HEPTACHLOR, 0.5-percent emulsion

The concentrate contains either 2 or 3 pounds of the actual chemical per gallon. For a 0.5-percent emulsion add 1 gallon of the 2-pound concentrate to 48 gallons of water, or 1 gallon of the 3-pound concentrate to 72 gallons of water.

Rate of Application

Slab-on-ground houses. Apply at least 2 gallons of the diluted emulsion for each 5 linear feet of wall, through holes made in the floor or foundation, so it will reach the infested soil. It is advisable to treat around the entire slab and around other openings left for plumbing, and so on. Apply the emulsion at the same rate in the trench made along the exterior foundation walls, if the footing is not more than 15 inches deep. If deeper in some places, apply as directed below for basementless, or crawl-space houses.

Basementless houses. Apply 2 gallons of the diluted emulsion for each 5 linear feet of trench made along the interior of the foundation walls, or around piers or other materials connecting the ground with wood above. Along the exterior foundation walls, including those adjacent to entrance platforms, porches, etc., apply the chemical at the same rate for each foot of depth from the surface to the footing. If the footing is 2 feet deep, for example, increase the dosage to 4 gallons for each 5 linear feet of trench, or if it is 5 feet deep, use 10 gallons for each similar unit. Entrance platforms, sunparlors, and other enclosed areas adjacent to the foundation wall should also be trenched and treated, or have holes bored through the slabs and the chemical applied through them.

Basement houses. Where necessary to treat through the basement floor, apply the chemical in the same manner and at the same rate as recommended for treating the slab-on-ground house. Treat the exterior of the foundation wall the same as mentioned for the basementless house.

Applying Chemicals in Trenches

Pour or sprinkle some of the chemical at the bottom of the trench. Cover with a layer of soil about 6 inches thick. Pour or sprinkle more of the chemical on top of this soil layer. Mix the chemical thoroughly with this layer, and tamp well. Continue to add layers of soil, mixing each with the chemical and tamping as before, until the trench is filled. Do not apply chemicals to frozen or water-soaked soils.

HOW TO GET RID OF POISON IVY

Poison ivy can readily be destroyed by herbicides, special poisons for plants. The most satisfactory ones for poison ivy, poison oak, and poison sumac are amitrole, ammonium sulfamate, 2,4,5-T, and a mixture of 2,4-D and 2,4,5-T called brush killer. These herbicides are sold under their common names and under various trade names. Workable but less satisfactory herbicides include borax, carbon disulfide, fuel oil, sodium arsenite, kerosene, ammonium sulfate, and common salt.

Any field or garden sprayer, or even a sprinkling can, can be used for applying the spray liquid, but a common compressed air sprayer holding 2 to 3 gallons is convenient and does not waste the spray.

Use moderate pressure giving relatively large spray droplets, rather than high pressure giving a driving mist, because the object is to wet the leaves of the poison ivy, and to avoid wetting the leaves of desirable plants.

Apply when leaves are fully expanded, and wet the foliage to the point of runoff. Drench the stems as high as possible when the plants are growing on a wall, and allow the excess spray to run down to the roots. Plants growing in the shade require more amitrole or brush mixture than those growing in the sun.

Amitrole. Use 2 to 4 pounds of active ingredient per 100 gallons of water. Be careful not to spray on nearby plants. If ivy is growing on a desirable tree, cut ivy stem at ground level in winter (see section on the safe handling of poison ivy in Chapter 14,) and treat the sprouts after leaves come out in the spring. If ivy is intertwined with desirable plants, paint the ivy leaves with a long-handled brush. Mix 2 tablespoons of the 50-percent product in 1 quart of water for the paint. Cover at least one-half of the leaves. Amitrole can also be applied dry.

Where brush is to be killed along with the ivy, oak, or sumac, brush killer is more effective than amitrole.

(*Caution:* Amitrole kills most lawn grasses. It is slow in action; effects may not show up for 2 or 3 weeks.)

Ammonium sulfamate. Use 2 to 2½ pounds of the 95-percent product in 3 gallons of water and add a "spreader-sticker," a surface-active chemical that helps the spray to stick, spread, and cover. Lacking the latter, a tablespoon of liquid dishwashing detergent will help do the same things. Keep spray off nearby desirable plants.

(*Caution:* Ammonium sulfamate sterilizes the soil for several months. To prevent corrosion, do not use near metal pipes and tanks. Whenever possible, use copper, stainless steel, bronze, or aluminum, but not brass, for sprayer parts. Coat other exposed metal parts with acid-resisting paint or rubberized undercoating used on cars.)

Brush killer mixture and 2,4,5-T. These two herbicides are used more by large-scale operators with professional spraying equipment. Use 2 to 3 pounds acid equivalent (the strength term by which these chemicals are rated) per 90 gallons of water and 10 gallons of diesel oil. The combination is mixed thoroughly to form an emulsion. If any regrowth occurs, repeat the treatment.

(*Caution:* Prevent drift by applying on calm days and at least 100 feet from sensitive plants. Treat in winter if sensitive plants are to be grown nearby.)

CONTROL OF HOUSEHOLD INSECTS

Insects that invade your home may endanger your health, damage household goods, or become a general nuisance. You can control these pests, however, by means of a combination of modern insecticides and proper sanitation.

An accompanying table will help you choose the proper kind and concentration of insecticide to use against the common pests discussed below.

Ants may steal into a house unnoticed until their trails become heavily populated. The best way to get rid of them is to follow their trail to their nests, which may be either indoors or outdoors. Then treat the nest with an insecticide such as chlordane, diazinon, dieldrin, lindane, or malathion.

You might hasten their eradication by applying a surface or residual spray over the area of their trail. But they may make a new trail which you will also have to spray.

Bedbugs, thanks to the newer insecticides, are not as common in the United States as they once were. But they still may be carried home from theaters, hotels, or public conveyances. They feed largely on human blood, and they usually dine at night.

If bedbugs have recently moved in, they may usually be found along the tufts, seams, and folds of mattresses and sofas. Gradually they spread to crevices in the bedsteads, then they establish themselves in other furniture and cracks or crevices of each room.

Household sprays containing DDT, or pyrethrins plus a synergist (a chemical that increases their efficiency) are generally effective against bedbugs. In some localities, however, the bugs may have developed resistance to DDT.

Spray the slats, springs, and frames of beds until they are thoroughly wet. Spray mattresses lightly, paying particular attention to seams and tufts. Allow to dry for about 2 hours before you use the bed.

HOUSEHOLD PEST CONTROL CHART

INSECTS OR PESTS	SURFACE SPRAYS*										AEROSOLS OR SPACE SPRAYS						DUSTS*					
	Chlordane, 2-3%	DDT, 5%	Diazinon, 0.5%	Dieldrin, 0.5%	Fenthion, 3%	Lindane, 0.5%	Malathion, 2-3%	Methoxychlor, 5%	Pyrethrins, 0.2% plus synergist	Ronnel, 2%	DDT, 3-5%	Dichlorvos, 0.5%	Malathion, 2-3%	Methoxychlor, 3%	Pyrethrins, 0.1-0.25% plus synergist	Ronnel, 0.4%	Chlordane, 5-6%	DDT, 5-10%	Dieldrin, 1%	Lindane, 1%	Malathion, 4-5%	Methoxychlor, 10%
Ants	×	×	×	×		×	×										×		×	×	×	
Bed bugs		×							×													
Cockroaches	×	×	×	×		×	×			×							×	×	×	×	×	
Crickets	×	×		×		×	×										×	×	×	×	×	
Earwigs	×	×		×		×	×										×	×	×	×		
Firebrats	×																×	×				
Fleas			×			×	×			×											×	
House flies		×	×				×	×	×	×	×	×	×	×	×	×					×	×
Millipedes												×	×		×							
Mites		×																				
Mosquitoes		×		×	×		×				×	×	×	×	×							
Pantry pests							×															
Scorpions	×					×											×		×			
Silverfish	×	×	×	×		×											×	×				
Spiders	×			×		×	×										×		×	×	×	
Ticks	×	×	×			×	×										×			×	×	
Wasps	×	×		×			×					×						×	×		×	

*Limited areas, such as baseboards, except DDT, methoxychlor, or pyrethrins plus synergist.

If necessary, spray other furniture, baseboards, and cracks and crevices in walls and floorboards. Apply spray again in 2 weeks if any bugs remain.

Cockroaches are among the hardiest and cleverest of household insects. They should not be pampered, however, as they destroy food, damage fabrics and bookbindings, and may spread disease by carrying filth on their bodies and legs.

Among about 55 kinds of cockroaches in the United States only 5 kinds can cause trouble in buildings. The rest are outdoor types that cannot develop indoors. If brought in accidentally, they either leave or die.

Cockroaches develop best where there is warmth, moisture, and generally unclean conditions; they grow slowly when this combination of conditions is not present. Thorough cleaning reduces greatly the likelihood of infestation.

Even in a clean house, however, roaches may enter from outdoors, in infested containers from other buildings, or from adjoining homes or apartments. To keep them out, fill all cracks passing through floors or walls, and cracks leading to spaces behind baseboards and door frames, with plaster, caulking compound, or plastic wood. Pay special attention to spaces around water and steam pipes. When you bring laundry or containers of food into the house, look for hidden roaches and kill any you may find.

Attack whatever cockroaches that remain with an effective insecticide. The most common kind of household cockroach, the German cockroach (also called croton bug and water bug), is not very responsive to DDT, and in some areas has developed resistance to such insecticides as chlordane, dieldrin, and lindane. Diazinon, malathion, or ronnel should therefore be used against this variety. Any of the insecticides checked on the chart will do for the other four kinds.

Use the insecticide of your choice either as a surface spray or a dust. A combination of spray and dust is effective for severe infestations.

If you use the combination treatment, apply the surface spray first. Allow it to dry. Then apply the dust into cracks and openings difficult to reach with a spray and areas where the dust will not be unsightly. Surface sprays or dusts may be applied with an ordinary household spray gun or dust gun.

A space spray or aerosol mist containing pyrethrum may be used to penetrate deep cracks and crevices and so drive the cockroaches onto surfaces treated with surface spray or dust.

For best results, apply the spray or dust where the roaches hide. You may be able to discover the hiding places by entering a dark room quietly, turning on the light, and watching where they run. Some favorite places are under the kitchen sink and drainboard; inside, around, and under cupboards and cabinets; near pipes and conduits that pass along or through walls; behind window or door frames; behind loose baseboards or molding strips; behind and under refrigerators and ranges; and on closet and bookcase shelves.

When treating cupboards and pantries, take everything from shelves and remove drawers so that food and utensils will not become contaminated.

If the roaches have not disappeared after 3 or 4 weeks, apply the insecticides again, especially if the house is reinfested from outside.

Crickets sometimes invade a house, though they do not normally do so as their breeding sites are outdoors. They may chew and otherwise damage clothing.

To keep crickets out, make sure all windows, screens, and doors close tightly. A surface spray containing DDT, lindane, chlordane, dieldrin, or malathion may be applied along baseboards, in cracks, in closets, and other places where crickets may hide. Dusts also may be used in places where they will not be unsightly.

Earwigs usually live outdoors, but they sometimes crawl into houses or are brought in with flowers, vegetables, or fruit. They are reddish brown, about ¾ inch long, and have a pair of strong forceps on the rear part of the body. They can bite and pinch, and they emit a foul odor when crushed.

Control them by using surface sprays of chlordane or DDT along baseboards and across the thresholds of outside doorways. The application of emulsion sprays or dusts to the soil near outside steps also helps keep them out.

Firebrats and silverfish are slender, gray, wingless insects about ½ inch long. They have three slender "tails."

For food, they prefer sugar and starch, and so love the paste on wallpaper, the glue on bookbindings, and starch in cloth.

Control them with chlordane, DDT, diazinon, dieldrin, or malathion.

Fleas can be expected if a dog or a cat shares the house with you. If you don't inspect and treat the pet regularly, fleas may become so numerous they may attack you as well as the animal.

The female flea lays her eggs on the pet. They fall off and hatch in chairs, sofas, rugs, carpets, and the pet's bed. The baby fleas grow up and a new horde of adult fleas will soon be extracting blood from pets and people.

Control of fleas starts with good housekeeping. Clean carpets, rugs, upholstered furniture, and other items in infested rooms with a vacuum cleaner and then destroy the contents of the vacuum bag.

Then apply a surface spray containing DDT, diazinon, malathion, methoxychlor, or pyrethrins plus a synergist to limited areas, such as baseboards and cracks in the floor.

Carpets, rugs, furniture, and places in the house where the pet habitually sleeps may be treated with DDT, methoxychlor, or pyrethrum sprays or with DDT, methoxychlor, or malathion dusts.

Repeat if necessary, in 7 to 10 days.

Fleas on dogs and cats may be treated directly with a dust containing 4 or 5 percent of malathion or 10 percent of methoxychlor. The dust should be rubbed into the fur to the skin.

A dust containing 5 percent of DDT or 1 percent of lindane also may be used on dogs, but do not use lindane or DDT on cats of any age or on puppies less than 2 months old.

House flies breed outdoors on decaying organic matter, but love to explore indoors and land on people and food and so spread filth with their legs and bodies.

Good sanitation outdoors and proper screening of all doors and windows help to eliminate flies. If you have to use an insecticide inside the house, use a space or aerosol spray containing dichlorvos, malathion, pyrethrins plus a synergist, or ronnel.

Be sure the product you buy specifies its use for the control of flying insects and be careful not to get the spray on food and cooking or eating utensils.

Further control of flies can be had by applying surface sprays to outside garbage cans, door and window frames, screens, and other sites flies frequent. Malathion and ronnel are suitable for this purpose.

Millipedes and centipedes are wormlike creatures with many legs. Except for the house centipede, they normally live outdoors. But heavy rain, extreme dryness, or cold weather may drive them indoors.

Millipedes won't hurt you, but centipedes have a pair of powerful poison claws just behind the mouth that can give you a bad nip that will cause severe pain and swelling. You should therefore keep away from centipedes, especially the big ones. To kill them, apply chlordane, DDT, dieldrin, or lindane to all the places where you find them.

Mites are tiny creatures. The commonest one, the clover mite, infests houses in the fall as cold weather approaches. Some mites also come from rats, mice, and birds and their nests. Others occur in foods, such as cheese and grain.

To control mites, try to find where they are coming into the house and prevent their entry. If they are coming from rats, birds, or their nests, remove these sources of infestation. A residual spray containing malathion can be used to treat infested areas.

Mosquitoes, if around, will undoubtedly pester you as you try to go to sleep. If you reach for a space or aerosol spray, be sure it is specifically meant for flying insects. Aerosols or space sprays containing DDT, dichlorvos, malathion, or pyrethrins plus a synergist are suitable.

It will help if you apply a surface spray of DDT, fenthion, or malathion to dark and secluded spots under chairs, tables, and beds, in closets, and behind furniture. The residue may be effective for several weeks.

Pantry pests include several kinds of insects that infest dry-food products kept in pantry or kitchen cupboards. Although often called "weevils," they may actually be small beetles, moth larvae, or true weevils.

Infestations may be controlled by keeping food shelves clean; inspecting food packages for infestation; sterilizing suspected infested dry foods in your oven at about 140°F for 30 minutes; storing uninfested or heat-sterilized dry foods in clean containers with tight-fitting lids; and applying a surface spray of chlordane, DDT, lindane, or malathion to the shelves.

Remove all items from the shelves before spraying. Allow the spray to dry thoroughly before you replace them.

Scorpions normally live outdoors under lumber piles, rocks, or loose bark on trees. Sometimes, however, they enter the house, where they hide during the day in closets, attics, folded blankets, shoes, and papers. Usually they will not sting unless molested, but when they do their sting is painful and occasionally causes death in infants or young children. If one should bite you, call a doctor at once. While waiting, apply first aid as described in the article "Bites of More Poisonous Insects" in Chapter 14.

To control scorpions, use chlordane or lindane inside as well as outside the house in the places where they may hide.

Spiders cause annoyance chiefly by building webs about the house. Only three species in the United States—the black widow, a close relative, and a brown spider found in the Midwest—are known to be dangerous. (For first aid for spider bites see the reference just made under scorpions.)

Basements, eaves, porches, and under steps are places most likely to be infested. The elimination of breeding places outside the house is important in control. Spiders may be killed by chlordane, dieldrin, lindane, or malathion. Do not spray a spider directly overhead, as it may drop on you and bite.

Ticks you may find in the house are probably brown dog ticks that came in on your dog. This tick rarely bites people, but its presence is annoying. Sometimes large numbers appear around baseboards, window and door casings, curtains, under the edge of rugs, and furniture.

Control of ticks requires treatment of your dog and the infested areas of the house. A veterinarian can treat your dog, or you can do the job yourself by washing the animal with a 0.5 percent water emulsion of malathion. To make this emulsion, combine thoroughly 1½ ounces of malathion 57-percent emulsifiable concentrate with 5 quarts of water.

In areas where brown dog ticks have not developed resistance to DDT, this insecticide is suggested as a surface treatment in houses. Where resistance has been built up, use malathion or diazinon.

"Wasp" is a term applied to hornets, yellow jackets, mud daubers, and other slender-waisted flying insects. These are all beneficial insects that attack and destroy harmful insects found around homes and in gardens. They build nests in trees, under eaves, and in the ground. Some wasps enter buildings in the fall to hibernate.

The trouble with wasps is that they can attack people as well as insects. Hornets and yellow jackets may sting you if you go near their nests. Mud daubers usually will not sting unless you touch them or get them caught in your clothes. (To treat stings of wasps, see unit "Bites and Stings of Insects" in Chapter 14.)

If wasps build their nests too close to your house or in bushes where children play, you should destroy the nests.

Treat the nests at night, when there is less danger of being stung. The kind of insecticide needed depends on whether the nest is above the ground or in the ground.

Apply an emulsion or suspension spray to wasp nests that are in trees and shrubbery or in your house. You can prepare an emulsion spray by mixing a chlordane, DDT, or dieldrin emulsifiable concentrate with water; a suspension spray, by mixing a DDT or chlordane wettable powder with water. Here are the proportions to use for both types:

PROPORTIONS FOR MIXING WASP SPRAYS

INSECTICIDE AS PURCHASED (CHOOSE JUST ONE TYPE)	AMOUNT OF PURCHASED PRODUCT TO MIX WITH 1 QUART OF WATER
DDT	
25-percent emulsifiable concentrate	6 ounces
50-percent wettable powder	6 level tablespoons
Chlordane	
45-percent emulsifiable concentrate	2 ounces
40-percent wettable powder	3 level tablespoons
Dieldrin	
15-percent emulsifiable concentrate	1 ounce

Treat nests in the ground with an insecticide dust containing 5 to 10 percent of DDT, 5 to 6 percent of chlordane, or 1 percent of dieldrin. A few puffs of dust directed into the opening of the nest will usually kill the wasps within 24 hours. Apply dusts with a household hand duster. Put a shovelful of moist soil over the nest hole after the treatment to prevent the wasps from escaping.

DDT Insecticide Powder

If you want, you can dilute 100-percent DDT powder to make a dust suitable for general use. Here is a formula for a 10-percent dust:

| DDT | 2 oz |
| Powdered talc or starch | 18 oz |

Combine the two powders thoroughly by mixing and sifting. Avoid inhaling the dust. Although its toxicity to humans and animals is usually slight, some people are allergic to it.

Roach Powder

This is a traditional powder for roaches that is still one of the most effective:

Sodium fluoride	5 oz
Pyrethrum	5 oz
Talc	10 oz

Combine the talc and the pyrethrum thoroughly by stirring and sifting, then mix in the powdered sodium fluoride.

Apply with a household powder duster to all places frequented by the roaches. Repeat the treatment after about four days and once more after two weeks. In this way you will kill newly hatched roaches as well as their parents.

Caution: Sodium fluoride in its concentrated form is extremely poisonous. Wash all utensils carefully after mixing it. Keep the container out of the reach of children. Do not apply it where animals or children may accidentally come in contact with it.

Roach Bait and Poison

This effective, but less poisonous, powder may be applied where the previous one might endanger animals or children:

Salicylic acid	1 oz
Trisodium phosphate	1 oz
Borax	6 oz
Granulated sugar	4 oz
Flour	8 oz

Mix thoroughly by stirring and sifting, and apply as directed for the previous powder. It will serve as both bait and poison.

Mosquito Repellents

Oil of citronella is one of the most widely used mosquito repellents. It may be used pure or mixed with mineral oil, petroleum jelly, or lanolin in the proportion of 1 part to 5. Almost any oily preparation on the skin repels mosquitoes to some extent.

If you don't like the smell of citronella, try this mixture:

Castor oil	1 oz
Alcohol	1 oz
Oil of lavender	1 oz

Caution: Do not use ordinary *denatured* alcohol here, or in any other preparation for use on the body. Use U.S.P. 95-percent ethyl alcohol from the drugstore.

CLOTHES MOTHS AND CARPET BEETLES

The larvae of clothes moths, and of their lesser known but more abundant relatives the carpet beetles, do great damage to household materials by feeding on them. The adult moths and beetles do no damage.

Female clothes moths and carpet beetles lay soft, white eggs in clothing and household furnishings, in cracks and in other concealed places. Moths lay 100 to 300 eggs, which hatch in 4 to 8 days in summer. Beetles lay about 100 eggs, which hatch in 8 to 15 days in summer. Hatching takes longer in cooler weather.

The larvae of clothes moths and carpet beetles begin feeding as soon as they hatch. They feed on wool, mohair, hair, bristles, fur, feathers, and down. They attack clothing, blankets, rugs, carpets, drapes, pillows, hair mattresses, brushes, and upholstery.

You can rid fabrics of insects and their eggs and larvae by brushing and sunning them, or by having them drycleaned.

One of the best ways to protect clothing and blankets against clothes moths and carpet beetles is to spray them with an oil-solution insecticide containing DDT, methoxychlor, Strobane, or Perthane. You may buy these in pressurized containers, or you may buy them as a liquid to be applied with a household hand sprayer.

To apply the insecticide, hang the clothing and blankets on a clothesline and spray them lightly and uniformly until their surfaces are moist. Do not soak or saturate. Let sprayed articles dry before you wear or store them.

Spray rugs and carpets with 5-percent DDT oil solution every 12 to 18 months. Use 1½ to 2 quarts of spray on a 9-by-12 rug.

Spray furniture upholstery and drapes containing wool or mohair with any of the chemicals mentioned above. When sprayed on mattresses, pillows, or upholstered furniture, the chemicals help prevent infestation; they do not kill pests already inside the stuffing.

Note: Do not apply any of these sprays to furs.

Protection in storage. You can protect woolens and furs by placing paradichlorobenzene crystals or naphthalene flakes or balls (popularly known as moth crystals, flakes, or balls) in the container or closet in which the articles are stored.

The mere odor of these chemicals does not repel the insects and is no guarantee that the concentration of vapor is sufficient to kill them.

To be effective in holding the vapor, the container (which may be a chest, box, or garment bag) must be airtight. If you store woolens in a closet without first placing them in containers, see that the closet is tightly sealed.

In a trunk or closet, use 1 pound of crystals, flakes, or balls for each 100 cubic feet of space. As the vapors are heavier than air, the chemicals should be placed near the top of the enclosure.

Articles that are not already infested can be protected without chemicals by storing them in a paper package or a cardboard box, all edges of which are carefully sealed with paper tape.

HOW TO CONTROL MILDEW IN THE HOME

Mildew is a thin, musty-smelling growth produced on many household materials by simple plants known as fungi or molds. Though always present in the air, mildew fungi need warmth and moisture and certain types of food substances in order to grow. Given these conditions, they discolor leather, fabrics, paper, and wood. Sometimes they eat into fabrics so severely that the fabrics rot and fall to pieces. Below are measures for the prevention and removal of mildew on walls and household furnishings.

How to Prevent Mildew

1. *Keep things clean.* Soil on articles can supply enough food for mildew to grow when moisture and temperature are right. Greasy films on kitchen walls provide a feast. Most man-made fibers, when clean, will not support mildew growth. Soil on them, however, will do so.

2. *Get rid of dampness.* Take steps to prevent condensation on walls. Remove excess moisture with air conditioners and dehumidifiers. If necessary, get rid of dampness by heating the house for a short time. Use silica gel, activated alumina, or calcium chloride to absorb moisture from the air. Ventilate house, closets, drawers, and musty articles thoroughly when the outside air is drier than that inside.

3. *Get rid of musty odors.* These indicate mold growth and so should be investigated and eliminated as soon as possible. Usually they disappear if the area is well heated and dried. On cement floors and on

tiled walls and bathroom floors, get rid of mustiness by scrubbing with a solution of ordinary 5-percent sodium hypochlorite bleach (Clorox, Purex, etc.) diluted ½ to 1 cup to a gallon of water. Rinse with clear water and wipe dry. Keep windows open until surfaces are thoroughly dry. *Precaution:* Work quickly and carefully on plastic and asphalt tile to avoid spotting.

4. *Keep fabrics dry.* Never let clothing or other fabric articles lie around damp or wet. After washing, dry articles thoroughly and quickly, as slow drying encourages mold. After shampooing a rug, dry it as quickly as possible.

5. *Store with mildew inhibitor.* Certain volatile chemicals, the vapors of which inhibit mold growth (and often keep moths away as well), may be used to protect fabrics during storage. Paradichlorobenzene is one. Scatter crystals of this chemical through folds of garments to be packed in boxes, or hang bags of crystals at the top of garment bags so the heavy vapors settle on the materials being protected. Use about 1 pound of the crystals for each 100 cubic feet of air space. *Precaution:* This chemical damages some plastics. Therefore remove plastic buttons and ornaments from garments and do not use plastic clothes hangers.

6. *To protect leather goods* against mildew, sponge with a 1-percent solution of dichlorophene, hexachlorophene, salicylanilide, or thymol, in denatured or rubbing alcohol. Shoe and luggage stores may have the solutions packaged already prepared. Before sponging, test a small area where it will not show to see if it will change the color of the leather.

How to Remove Mildew

1. *From textiles.* Remove mildew spots as soon as they are discovered to prevent deterioration of the material. Brush off surface growth outdoors to prevent scattering the spores in the house. Sun and air fabrics thoroughly. If any spots remain, wash fabrics with soap and water, or dry-clean them if unwashable. Rinse well and dry in the sun. If stains persist, moisten them with a mixture of lemon juice and salt and spread the article in the sun to bleach. Or bleach them with sodium perborate bleach or sodium hypochlorite bleach from the grocery store according to directions on the package.

2. *From upholstered articles, mattresses, rugs.* First remove loose mold from outer coverings by brushing (preferably outdoors) with a broom. Draw out more mold with a vacuum cleaner (if the appliance has a disposable bag, dispose of it immediately). Dry the article by sun and air, fan, electric heater, or by any other means possible. If mildew remains on upholstered articles or mattresses, sponge lightly with thick suds of soap or detergent, and wipe with a clean damp cloth. Sponge mildewed rugs and carpets with thick suds or a rug shampoo. Then remove suds with a cloth dampened in clear water. Dry in the sun if possible.

3. *From leather goods.* Wipe with a solution of equal parts of denatured or rubbing alcohol and water. Dry in a current of air. If mildew remains, wash with thick suds of a mild soap, saddle soap, or a soap containing a germicide or fungicide. Then wipe with a damp cloth and dry in an airy place.

DISINFECTING AND DEODORIZING
WITH HOUSEHOLD BLEACH

Besides its well-known ability to bleach textiles and even to lighten the color of some kinds of wood, ordinary household sodium hypochlorite liquid bleach is also a powerful disinfectant, deodorizer, and stain-removing agent. It is highly effective against all known types of virus and most bacteria. It eliminates odors partly by killing organisms that produce them and partly by chemical combination. On hard, smooth surfaces, its own chlorine odor soon disappears.

Unlike carbolic acid and other chemicals that work primarily on microorganisms, liquid chlorine bleach also reacts with dirt and other contaminants. For strongest action of the bleach as a disinfectant, it is best, therefore, to wash the surface thoroughly before applying it.

To disinfect, deodorize and remove stains from sinks, drainboards, dishes, glassware, enamelware, bathtubs, basins, woodwork, tile, porcelain, plastic: First wash surfaces thoroughly. Then wipe with a solution of ¾ cup liquid chlorine bleach to each gallon of warm water. If stubborn stains persist, keep wet for 5 minutes with bleach solution; repeat if necessary. (Do not apply with a natural sponge, and do not use on silver, aluminum, steel, or chipped enamelware.)

To sanitize toilet bowls: Cleanse and flush. Then pour in ½ cup liquid chlorine bleach. Swish solution over all inside surfaces. Let stand 10 minutes. Flush. (*Caution:* Do not use ammonia, lye, or other toilet bowl cleaner with liquid chlorine bleach. The combination would release poisonous chlorine gas.)

To deodorize drain pipes: Flush with very hot water. Follow by 1 cup liquid chlorine bleach. Let remain 5 minutes; then flush out bleach.

To help make refrigerators hygienically clean: First wash the inside surfaces. Then wipe with solution of ¾ cup liquid chlorine bleach to each gallon of warm water. Rinse, dry, and let air for 30 minutes.

Odors of garlic, onions, cabbage, or fish can be removed from your chopping board this way: Wash board thoroughly; then soak or keep wet for 10 to 15 minutes with a solution of ¼ of cup of liquid chlorine bleach to gallon of warm water. Rinse and dry.

Sickroom dishes can be sterilized by first thoroughly washing them and then soaking them for 5 minutes in a solution of ¾ cup of liquid chlorine bleach to each gallon of hot water. Rinse with hot water and let drain dry. (Do not use the bleach on silver, aluminum, steel, chipped enamelware. Disinfect these by scalding.)

Swimming Pool Disinfection

Each time you fill the pool, use 1 quart of liquid chlorine bleach (sodium hypochlorite 5 to 6 percent solution) for every 6,000 gallons of new water. To determine volume of water in pool when filled, allow 7½ gallons of water for each cubic foot of pool capacity.

If you have a chlorinator, mix the required amount of liquid chlorine bleach with 10 parts water and feed this solution through the device into main water supply line into pool. Otherwise mix 8 ounces of liquid chlorine bleach in 5 gallons of water and scatter over a portion of the pool; repeat until the required amount of bleach has been scattered over entire surface of pool.

Usually 1 pint of liquid chlorine bleach per 6,000 gallons of water is enough for daily replenishing. If you have a pool chlorine testing set, check the water daily, adding enough chlorine bleach to maintain a reading of 0.6 to 1.0 part per million.

PURIFYING WATER IN EMERGENCIES

When away from approved water supplies while traveling or camping, or during flood or other disaster conditions at home, you must make sure that available water is safe for drinking. Dysentery, infectious hepatitis, and typhoid fever are among the diseases that can be brought on by polluted water.

The only certain way to remove danger from doubtful water is to purify it yourself. Here are several approved ways to do so:

PURIFICATION WITH HEAT

1. Strain water through a clean cloth into a container to remove sediment and floating matter.

2. Boil the water vigorously for at least 1 full minute.

3. The water is ready to use as soon as it is sufficiently cool. If desired, a pinch of salt may be added

to each quart of water to improve the taste. Pouring the water back and forth from one clean container to another several times will also do so.

PURIFICATION WITH CHEMICALS

If boiling is not possible, strain the water as in Step 1 and purify with any one of the following chemicals that is available:

• Sodium hypochlorite laundry bleach containing 5 to 6 percent available chlorine (Clorox, Purex, Rose-X, etc.). Add 2 drops of this solution to each quart of clear water or 4 drops to each quart of cloudy water. If the amount of available chlorine is not stated on the label, add 10 drops to the clear and 20 drops to the cloudy water.

1. Mix thoroughly by stirring or shaking water in container.

2. Let stand for 30 minutes.

3. A slight chlorine odor should still be detectable in the water; if not repeat the dosage and let stand for an additional 15 minutes before using.

• Tincture of iodine, 2 percent, from medicine chest or first-aid kit. Add 5 drops to each quart of clear water or 10 drops to each quart of cloudy water. Stir, and let stand for 30 minutes, after which time water is safe to use.

• Iodine or chlorine tablets from drug or sporting goods store. Follow instructions on package.

Keep water purified under any of the above methods in clean, closed containers. Use it for cooking, drinking, and for brushing teeth.

CHEMICALS IN SEPTIC TANKS

According to the U.S. Health Service, the operation of septic tanks, used by millions of homes where public sewers are not available, is not at all improved by the addition of disinfectants or other chemicals. By 1967, more than 1,200 products, many containing enzymes, had been placed on the market for use in septic tanks, and extravagant claims have been made for some of them. As far as is known, however, none has been proved of advantage in properly controlled tests.

Some proprietary products which are claimed to "clean" septic tanks contain sodium or potassium lye as the active agent. These may severely damage soil structure and cause accelerated clogging, even though some temporary relief may be experienced at first.

Frequently, however, the harmful effects of ordinary household chemicals are overemphasized. Small amounts of chlorine bleaches, added ahead of the tank, may be used for odor control without adverse effects. If septic tanks are of adequate size, the small amounts of lye or other alkaline chemicals used to clean toilets and drains won't be harmful, either. Neither will soaps, detergents, bleaches, or other household materials as ordinarily used. Moderation, though, should be the rule. Advice of responsible officials should be sought before chemicals arising from a hobby or home industry are discharged into the system.

13

Fire Prevention and Fire Fighting

HOME FIRES—CAUSES AND PREVENTION

What Starts a Fire

Properly controlled, fire is one of the most useful chemical reactions known to man. Manufacturing, transportation, food processing, heating, civilization itself depend upon it. When it gets out of hand, however, fire can be a terrifying destroyer. Fire costs the lives of more than 12,000 people and a billion and a half dollars in property damage in the United States every year.

Every ordinary fire is the result of the rapid oxidation of some burnable material. For such oxidation to take place two conditions must be met: first the material must be heated to its kindling temperature; second, there must be sufficient oxygen. If in any way we can reduce the temperature below the kindling point or cut off the oxygen, the fire will stop.

The two chief methods of fire extinguishing are, therefore, cooling and smothering. Whether one, the other, or both methods should be used depends upon the type of fire.

The oldest method of reducing the kindling temperature was to soak the blazing material with water. Even today, water is still the most effective—as well as the cheapest and most abundant—tool for putting out large fires of wood, paper, clothing, or other ordinary materials.

Water is a good fire-fighting agent for several reasons. In the first place it won't burn. In the second, water has the ability to absorb more heat from a hot body, weight for weight, than any other common substance. Thirdly, in boiling, water extracts a still greater amount of heat from the burning material. In fact it takes about six times as much heat to boil away 1 pound of water already at the boiling point as it does to bring 1 pound of cold water to that temperature.

Dry chemicals, foam, carbon dioxide, and vaporizing nonflammable liquids put out fire mostly by smothering it.

How Fire Spreads

Fire spreads from one material to another, and from one place to another, in different ways. The most obvious is by contact with the original flame. It can be conducted, however, by something like sheet metal, which by itself will not burn, but which may get hot enough to set fire to any flammable material it touches. That is why stovepipes should not be allowed to come in contact with woodwork.

Fire also can be carried by flying sparks or even drafts of hot air. Firemen often find that a fire on a lower floor has made hot air rise through stairways or elevator shafts. This superheated air gathers at the top of the building causing this part to burst into flame although there may be no fire on the floors between.

Finally, the radiation of heat from a burning building may cause a nearby building to catch fire, just as the heat from a bonfire might set your clothes afire, even though the flames didn't touch you.

How to Prevent Fire

Most accidental fires can be avoided with a little care. Firemen have a saying that "a clean building seldom burns." In other words that the majority of fires start in trashpiles, rubbish, or stored odds and ends that accumulate around the house. Closets, attics, and cellars are the main source of home fires, and ordinary good housekeeping is the first line of defense against such fires.

Check your closets, attic, and basement for cast-off articles that would burn easily. These include such things as curtains, draperies, tablecloths, bedclothes, lampshades, coats, suits, dresses, wicker and wooden furniture, rags, and linoleum.

Clean out your storage spaces. You will be surprised at how many burnable odds and ends are really useless to you.

Instead of an attic, many modern homes have an air space between the top floor ceiling and the roof. If your home has such a spot, make sure you can get into it through a trap door. Keep a ladder handy.

You won't be able to put out a fire in this space unless you can reach it quickly. Never store anything there.

Whenever you leave your home you can improve its fire resistance by shutting all doors and windows. *Closed interior doors* will confine a fire to the area of origin for some time and prevent rapid spread within the building.

Check Your Electrical Appliances

Many fires happen in homes each day because of faulty or misused electrical equipment. Circuits are overloaded by plugging in too many appliances to a single outlet. An iron is switched on and then forgotten. Flammable material is left in the focus of a radiant heater. Cords are used after the insulation has worn away. Others are stretched under rugs or stapled to baseboards and door frames. If fuses blow frequently, do not replace them with bigger ones, but check your equipment. Your wiring may be overloaded to the point where it could start a fire.

Watch Your Heating Plant

Costly fires may be started by faulty furnaces, stoves, and other heating plants. Some result from too much soot in chimneys. Others are caused by rusted or cracked pipes and fittings. These may be prevented by making sure the chimney is clean and the pipes sound.

Keep magazines, papers, and clothing off radiators and away from open fireplaces or stoves. Do not allow paper lamp shades to touch light bulbs. Enough heat may build up in each of these cases to set the material on fire.

Matches and Careless Smoking Habits

According to the National Board of Fire Underwriters, the careless discarding of lighted matches and smoking materials is responsible for about 30 percent of all fires from known causes. A burning match or tobacco debris recklessly tossed aside may start a disastrous fire taking heavy toll of lives and property.

Here are a few commonsense precautions:

1. Keep all matches out of the reach of small children.

2. Have plenty of ash trays conveniently placed —and keep them clean.

3. Anywhere—be sure your lighted matches or smokes are completely snuffed out before you discard them.

4. *Don't smoke in bed* or where *No Smoking* signs are posted.

5. Don't strike matches in closets, garages, or other places where flammable materials, dust, or vapors may be ignited.

Kerosene and Cleaning Fluids

One in ten fires of known origin is caused by the incautious use of kerosene, gasoline, or other flammable fluids, and by carelessness in handling candles, lamps, open gas jets, torches, etc. Sloshing or pouring kerosene on wood or coal fires is an example of recklessness.

Using gasoline, naphtha, and other flammable liquids in the house for cleaning causes many tragedies each year. These liquids vaporize when exposed to air and may quickly produce an explosive mixture that is readily ignited by a match, pilot light, sparking motor, or even a static spark developed from rubbing textiles together. Or the quickly spreading vapor may be exploded by a smoker or a fire in another room.

Because of the ever-present danger of fire or explosion from the vapors of flammable cleaning fluids, it is not advisable to use these indoors except in the quantities needed to remove small spots, and then only in a well-ventilated room.

Radio and Television Antennas

Fires have been caused in homes by radio and television antennas falling across power lines and causing a short circuit. If possible, install antennas where they cannot fall on such lines if they should topple over. If not, make them substantial enough so that any load of wind, snow, or ice cannot topple them. Place the lead-in conductors at least 6 feet away from any part of a lightning-rod system. Antennas should also be equipped with lightning arresters approved by Underwriters' Laboratories, and should be properly grounded.

Disposal of Oily Rags

Rags and cotton waste used with linseed or other "drying" oils, or with paint containing such oils, should be burned promptly outdoors or kept in tightly closed metal containers until they can be burned. In drying, such oils combine with oxygen. When this happens on combustible materials of large surface area and poor heat conduction, so much heat may be produced that the materials often take fire spontaneously.

Safety with Natural Gas

Practically all the gas now sold by utilities in the United States is natural gas, derived from wells in the ground. Contrary to popular notion this gas is not poisonous and it has no odor of its own. Asphyxiation from natural gas can occur only when the gas becomes so concentrated that it cuts off the minimum requirement of oxygen. What you smell when you "smell gas" is not the gas itself but a powerful odorizing chemical mixed with the gas to quickly alert you to its presence should there be a leak. Although fires from natural gas do occur, they rank only fourteenth among fires from all causes in the United States and are usually the result of misuse of equipment or damage to it from outside cause.

Natural gas will burn in air only when the concentration of the gas is between 4.5 and 14.5 percent by volume. Above and below these limits, it will neither burn nor explode. Ordinarily, however, you have no way of knowing the concentration in an emergency situation. So to be on the safe side, you must follow a few simple rules.

If you have been at home for some time and suddenly smell gas from a nearby source, perhaps a pot has boiled over on the range and put out the flame under it or the hose on a portable burner has sprung a leak or has become detached. In such a case there is little or no danger. Just turn off the gas and open the windows to let the gas diffuse into the outside air. If the gas comes from a leak in a faulty pipe or appliance that you can't turn off, telephone your gas company at once, explain the condition and follow the advice you are given.

If, on the other hand, your first smell of gas comes to you from a distant room or the floor below, or, after being out for some time you get a strong smell of gas on entering the house, take care! Everything may still be perfectly safe, but you have no way of telling. If you are alone in the house, leave the house at once and telephone the gas company from the nearest neighbor's phone. If there are others in the house, first get them to leave. Do nothing in the house that might cause a flame or spark. Don't light a match or cigarette lighter. Don't turn on or off electric lights or appliances! Don't ring an electric bell! Don't use the home telephone! When gas company experts arrive they will know what to do. In the meantime, the gas will remain harmless unless some careless person ignites it.

Ventilate Properly for LP Gas

A leak in any system using flammable gases presents a fire hazard. Special precautions must be taken with "LP"—liquefied petroleum or "bottled" gas—however, because it is heavier than air and so tends to settle to the floor instead of rising, contrary to the more familiar behavior of manufactured or natural gas.

Because of this difference, reduction of hazard with LP gas begins with the proper installation and ventilation of equipment. As it would be difficult to drain away any possible leakage from basements that are wholly underground, LP gas containers should be outdoors and at least 3 feet from basement wall openings.

Drainage for LP gas may be provided by leaving a 2- or 3-inch opening across the top and bottom of the doors to the outside. The floor of the furnace or boiler room must be higher than the surrounding grade, otherwise the gas may accumulate near the floor of this room like water behind a dam. A more positive way to remove the gas is to use forced ventilation. The exhaust duct should take the air from a point within 2 inches of the lowest part of the floor.

WHAT TO DO IF A FIRE STARTS

Big fires in homes usually start from little ones: a match in a wastebasket, blazing grease in an oven or frying pan, a smoldering ironing board cover from a forgotten iron. If you are present when a little fire starts, and act quickly and sensibly enough, you should easily be able to put it out before it can spread farther. The main thing to remember is to work fast but to keep your head.

The very first thing to do if you discover a fire is to quickly size it up. If the fire is so small you are dead sure you can put it out in a few moments, get at it at once. If you have the slightest doubt that it might get out of hand, however, call the fire department immediately—or, better yet, if possible, have someone else call. Give the operator your name, address, location of the fire, and the type of fire—whether trash, flammable liquids, wood, and so on.

If the fire still seems manageable, decide what method to use and try to put it out yourself.

Putting Out Fires by Emergency Methods

Although it is recommended that every home have at least one all-purpose fire extinguisher, your home may not and so you must rely on materials at hand. If papers, rags, wood, or similar materials are burning, plain water is probably the handiest and most effective extinguishing agent. Wet the material thoroughly by any means you can find. Pots of water will do, but a quickly rigged garden hose—if you have one and facilities for connecting it—adjusted to a spray rather than a solid stream might wet and smother the fire more quickly. Incidentally, a length of garden hose long enough to reach from an inside faucet to any part of the house might be a more effective safeguard than a small fire extinguisher in this type of fire.

When paint, gasoline, grease in the frying pan, or oil in the engine of your car starts blazing, however, forget all you know about water as a good extinguishing agent. Water won't mix with oily things. Because it is heavier than most of them, it sinks, causes them to overflow, and thus spreads the flames.

Oil fires must be put out by smothering. Where oil is confined, such as in a pail, a can, or a pan on the stove, this may be done merely by covering the utensil with a pie tin, can cover, or almost anything that is flat and large enough to cover the opening. Even a sheet of cardboard, if slid over the opening deftly enough, can put out an oil fire that looks terrifying.

For smothering larger oil fires, or oil fires that are not confined, carbon-dioxide gas or foam, or dry chemicals that liberate carbon dioxide, are the most effective agents. If you have no fire extinguishers containing these, and the fire is not too large, you can get almost as good an effect by scattering ordinary bicarbonate of soda (baking soda) over the flames by the handful. For more information about bicarbonate as a fire extinguisher, see unit on "Baking Soda" in Chapter 8, Common Products with Many Uses.

When Clothing Catches Fire

Do not run. If indoors where there are rugs, drop to the floor and roll a rug over yourself. If there are no rugs, use whatever heavy article may be handy—a heavy coat or a heavy blanket. If outdoors, roll on the ground. To remain in a standing position allows the flame to burn upward over the face. Running would fan the flame and accelerate burning. Use of some heavy article wrapped around the body cuts off the oxygen and more quickly puts out the fire. It also keeps the extent of body injury to a minimum.

If Fire Gets Out of Control

If you can't control a fire, get yourself and all others in the building away from it before you are trapped. If you have to go through thick smoke to get out of your burning home, tie a handkerchief or cloth, preferably wet, over your mouth and nose. Crawl on your hands and knees.

Find a wall and follow it around to the door. Keep away from the center of the floor. It is likely to cave in first if there is a fire below. If someone else is in the room and can't find his way out, shout to him from the door. You may be able to guide him to you.

Be careful of stairs in a burning building. Keep close to the wall and tread lightly. Don't run. Feel with a foot for each step to make sure it will bear your weight before you step on it.

If you can't get down the stairs, you may have to drop from a window. You can cut your fall by about 7 feet if you lower yourself out of a window as far as you can before letting go.

If you are caught on a second or third floor, tie sheets or blankets together with square knots. Tie one end of your improvised rope to a heavy piece of furniture. Drop the other end out the window, and climb down hand over hand. Your makeshift rope may not reach the ground, but it will get you that much closer to it. You can then drop the rest of the way with less chance of hurting yourself.

If you decide that you can't escape by yourself, shut the door and call for help from a window. A closed door will hold back heat and flame for some time. Stuff a folded towel under the door to keep out smoke.

Rescue Tips

Leave rescue work to properly trained and equipped firemen, if they are present. If they are not, take someone with you when you search a burning building. Teamwork is always better. You can search more quickly and thoroughly and you can help each other if necessary. Try to search from the top downward. People who are confused or frightened, especially children, often hide under beds or in closets. Look in every room and in every hiding place you can think of.

If a door is hot to the touch, you can expect to find fire when you open it, so be careful. If the door opens toward you, brace your foot against it and turn the knob gently. An explosive back draft may occur when you open the door. If the door opens away from you, turn the knob, push, and duck to one side until you can see whether flames are going to lash out through it.

Inside a smoke-filled room, keep close to the wall and feel under and on the beds, inside closets, and over large pieces of furniture. If you think the floor won't collapse, cross the room from one corner to another to make sure no one is lying in the center.

If you find an unconscious person, put him on the floor if he isn't already there. Turn him on his back and quickly tie his wrists together. A handkerchief will do. Kneel astride him and put your head between his tied wrists. You can then crawl forward, dragging him beneath you, even though he is much heavier than you are.

To move an unconscious person downstairs, place him on his back with his head toward the stairs. Put your hands under his armpits so that his head rests on the crook of your arm. Then back down the stairs yourself, letting his feet trail.

FIRE EXTINGUISHERS

The first few minutes of a fire largely determine the amount of damage it will do. In that short time, a portable fire extinguisher may be able to make the difference between a minor annoyance and disaster.

But each class of fire calls for specialized action. By using the wrong method or the wrong extinguisher you may do more harm that good.

Classes of Fires

For purposes of fire fighting, fires are classified into four groups:

Class A: These are the ordinary penetrating fires in paper, wood, textiles, and so on that call for cooling and quenching by water or the insulating and smothering action of certain dry chemicals.

Class B: Burning liquids, such as gasoline, oils, paints, and cooking fats, where smothering action is required. Applying water here would only spread the fire.

Class C: Fires in live electrical equipment—motors, switches, appliances, and so on. A nonconducting extinguishing agent must be used on these to prevent injury or even death to the operator. (If burning electrical apparatus can be unplugged, or the switch pulled, a Class C fire can usually be treated as Class A.)

Class D: This is a new classification that would rarely, if ever, apply to fires in homes. It includes fires in combustible metals such as magnesium, sodium, and potassium. Neither water nor any ordinary fire extinguisher should be used on these. Special powdered chemicals have been developed which seal the burning surface and smother the fire.

Types of Extinguishers

Portable fire extinguishers come in seven general types, and in sizes that range from hand units about the size of a can of soda to wheeled containers weighing several hundred pounds. Here is a brief rundown of the types and how they work:

Water extinguishers include three sub-types:

1. Soda-acid, one of the oldest and most familiar types of extinguisher, contains a solution of bicarbonate of soda and a vial of sulfuric acid. When inverted, the chemicals mix, producing carbon dioxide gas which forces out the solution in a 30- to 40-foot stream. Comes in sizes from 1¼ to 40 gallons, the 2½-gallon size being standard.

2. Pressurized water extinguisher forces out its contents up to 45 feet by means of compressd air. Comes in 1¼- and 2½-gallon sizes. Pressure is restored by connecting to compressed-air line.

3. Pump tank shoots plain water or a special antifreeze mixture from 30 to 40 feet by means of a hand pump. Comes in 1½- to 5-gallon sizes and may be refilled during operation or shut down at any time.

Loaded stream extinguisher works the same as pressurized type but contains a dissolved chemical that makes it effective on Class B as well as on Class A fires.

Foam extinguisher contains a water solution of sodium bicarbonate to which a foam stabilizer has been added. An inner container holds an aluminum sulfate solution. When the extinguisher is inverted, the chemicals mix and generate carbon dioxide gas which, in turn, produces foam and forces it out in a 30- to 40-foot stream. The foam coats the burning substance with an insulating and smothering blanket of carbon dioxide bubbles. Comes in 1¼- to 40-gallon sizes.

Vaporizing liquid extinguisher that depends on the smothering effect of carbon tetrachloride or other non-flammable liquid was for many years the most popular extinguisher for small Class B and C fires. Because the vapors from these liquids have been found to be more toxic than at first suspected, however, extinguishers using them are no longer recommended for any type of fire.

Carbon dioxide extinguisher, consisting of high-pressure cylinder of liquified carbon dioxide gas, is suitable for only the smallest of Class A fires but is excellent for Class B and C. Its special advantage is that it leaves no residue and does no damage to materials on which it is used. It comes in capacities of from 2 to 50 pounds of liquid gas.

Ordinary dry chemical extinguisher consists of a container of powdered bicarbonate of soda or bicarbonate of potassium and a pressure container of carbon dioxide or of compressed nitrogen. The contents are expelled by gas pressure when a valve on a nozzle is opened. Charges range from 1 pound to 350 pounds (the latter on a wheeled cart). The 2¾- and 5-pound sizes of good make are approved by the U.S. Coast Guard for marine use. The one disadvantage of this type of extinguisher is that it leaves a large amount of powder that must be cleaned up after use.

ABC general purpose dry chemical extinguisher is the first to be satisfactory on all classes of fires. In addition to sodium or potassium bicarbonate, this contains other chemicals which provide a fire-retardant blanket on materials of Class A fires, acting to smother the fire and to prevent rekindling. Available in sizes from 1 to 20 pounds, the 2½- and 5-pound sizes of good make again being approved by the U.S.C.G. for marine use. If you are to have only one fire extinguisher, this type is probably the best choice. Because of its fire-retarding deposit, however, it leaves a clean-up problem even greater than that left by the ordinary powder extinguisher.

How Extinguishers Are Rated

Since the prices for the same type and size of extinguisher may vary considerably, it is wise to be governed by the UL ratings carried on the label of every extinguisher listed by the Underwriters' Laboratories. After the classification by type (carbon dioxide, dry chemical, etc.) you will find a combination of numbers and letters. The letters indicate the class or classes of fire for which the extinguisher is suitable; the numbers indicate the size of the UL test fire the

extinguisher can put out. A "2B:C" extinguisher, for
example, will put out a Class B and a Class C fire
the size of a standard No. 2 test fire for these
classes; a "4B:C" should put out a fire twice as big,
and so on.

About 1¼ gallons of water (either from a bucket,
a hose, or an extinguisher) will ordinarily put out the
smallest UL test fire in the A class—a fire in a panel
of wood, 8 feet square, soaked with a gallon of fuel.
Because it would take 6 pounds of dry chemical to
put out such a fire, no dry powder extinguisher containing less than this amount is given a Class A rating.
Smaller dry powder extinguishers would, however,
be useful in putting out smaller Class A fires.

Which Extinguisher for What Fire?

To help choose an extinguisher best suited to
your particular needs, see table on pages 490-491.

Making Fabrics Flame Resistant

Many home fires that cause crippling burns and
loss of life and property start when clothing and
other fabrics are accidentally ignited. This hazard is
reduced when fabrics are treated to make them flame
resistant.

Curtains and draperies for recreation and children's rooms, children's clothing, cloth toys and party
decorations, ironing-board covers, and scenery for
amateur theatricals are among many items that can
be rendered less hazardous by simple treatments you
can apply yourself. The items so treated will not be
fire*proof*. They will char and possibly glow, but

WHICH EXTINGUISHER

CLASS OF FIRE

TYPE OF
EXTINGUISHER

A

Water (soda-acid,
pump tank,
pressurized)

EXCELLENT
Water saturates
material and prevents
rekindling.

Loaded stream

EXCELLENT
Saturates material,
prevents rekindling.

Foam

EXCELLENT
Foam has both
smothering and
wetting action.

Carbon dioxide

Small surface
fires only.

Ordinary dry
chemical

Small surface
fires only.

ABC
General purpose
dry chemical

EXCELLENT
Fire-retardant
blanket prevents
reflash.

FOR WHAT FIRE?

CLASS OF FIRE

B	**C**
NO Water will spread fire, not put it out.	NO Water, a conductor, should never be used on live electrical equipment.
YES Provides smothering action, cools and quenches.	NO Liquid is a conductor and should not be used on live electrical equipment.
EXCELLENT Smothering blanket does not dissipate, floats on top of spilled liquids.	NO Foam is a conductor and should not be used on live electrical equipment.
EXCELLENT Carbon dioxide leaves no residue, does not affect equipment or food-stuffs.	EXCELLENT Carbon dioxide is a nonconductor, leaves no residue, will not damage equipment.
EXCELLENT Chemical smothers fire.	EXCELLENT Chemical is a nonconductor; screen of dry chemical shields operator from heat.
EXCELLENT Provides smothering action.	EXCELLENT Chemical is a nonconductor; screen of dry chemical shields operator from heat.

they will not burst into flame and spread the fire to surrounding objects.

The following formulas and methods of application, suggested by the National Bureau of Standards and the U.S. Department of Agriculture, are effective on cotton, linen, and viscose rayon fabrics. The solutions are suitable only for materials protected from outdoor weather. Because the chemicals are water soluble, the treatment must be renewed after each laundering.

Applying solutions. You can apply flame-retardant solutions by dipping, spraying, or sprinkling. Resin-treated fabrics, and some unused fabrics, resist wetting. To overcome this, add about 1 teaspoon of a wetting agent (any liquid dishwashing detergent will do) to each gallon of solution. Materials must be dry before treatment. Completely wet them with the solution. Do not apply solutions to materials that water would injure. If in doubt, test a small area of the material before treating it.

Preparing solutions. Four solutions are described. Choose the one best suited to the material you wish to treat. Commercial grades of the chemicals will give as good results as the more expensive reagent or pharmaceutical grades.

FORMULA 1

Borax	7 oz
Boric acid	3 oz
Hot water	2 qt

Dissolve boric acid by making a paste with a small quantity of water. Add this and the borax to water. Stir until the solution is clear. Warm the solution if it becomes cloudy or jellylike from standing.

Fabrics treated with Formula 1 do not flame when exposed to fire. Glow lasts about 30 seconds. Materials treated with it may lose their flame resistance in time. Re-treat within a year.

Do not use Formula 1 on rayon or resin-treated cotton—sometimes called crushproof, wrinkleproof, or wash-and-wear. For the latter, use Formula 3.

FORMULA 2

Borax	6 oz
Diammonium phosphate	6 oz
Water	2 qt

Add chemical to water. Stir until solution is clear. This formula is less flame retardant than Formula 1, but is more glow retardant. It slightly reduces the strength of treated fabrics if not washed out within 3 or 4 months.

FORMULA 3

Diammonium phosphate	12 oz
Water	2 qt

Add chemical to water. Stir until solution is clear. Use this formula for resin-treated cotton or rayon fabrics. This formula is less flame retardant than Formula 1, but has good glow retardant priperties. It has a greater tendency than Formulas 1 or 2 to weaken a treated fabric if the fabric is stored for long periods.

Formula 4

Ammonium sulfate	13 oz
Water	2 qt
Household ammonia	small amount

Add ammonium sulfate to water. Stir until solution is clear. Then add enough ammonia to give a faint odor. If fertilizer-grade ammonium sulfate is used, the solution may not be clear. In this case, strain through a cloth before using.

This formula has good glow-retardant properties, but is less flame retardant than Formula 1. It slightly reduces the strength of treated fabrics.

Ironing treated fabrics. After applying the solution, allow the fabrics to become nearly dry before ironing. Do not redampen with water. Use a moderately hot iron. If the fabric is wet, or the iron is too hot, the solution may stick to the iron. If it does, wipe the iron with a damp cloth.

FLAMEPROOFING PAPER AND PAPERBOARD

To flameproof paper and paper products in which afterglow may be a problem, the National Bureau of Standards suggests formulas containing ammonium phosphate, a chemical which has superior glow-inhibiting qualities. Here is a suitable formula devised by the Army Quartermaster Corps:

Borax	7 lb or 7 parts by weight
Boric acid	3 lb or 3 parts by weight
Diammonium phosphate	5 lb or 5 parts by weight
Water	13.2 gal or 110 parts by weight

Heat the water and dissolve the chemicals in it by stirring continuously as they are added. Cool it to lukewarm temperature before application. The addition of about 1/10 part of a wetting agent (liquid dishwashing detergent will do) will help it penetrate the paper. Application may be made by immersion, brush, or spray methods. Enough should be applied, however, so that the weight of the material when dry will have increased about 15 percent. Colors are not ordinarily affected by this solution more than they are by wetting with water, but it is best to test for color fastness before applying it.

The following formula is also effective for paper products:

Diammonium phosphate	10 lb or 10 parts by weight
Ammonium sulfate	5 lb or 5 parts by weight
Water	12 gal or 100 parts by weight

Mix, cool, add wetting agent, and apply as suggested for the formula above. In humid locations, it may be advisable to include 4 or 5 parts of a soluble mildew inhibitor, such as sodium benzoate, sodium propionate, or one of the proprietary fungicides.

TREATING CHRISTMAS TREES

Although natural Christmas trees cannot be made absolutely fireproof, they can be made flame resistant by several methods.

According to the Forest Products Laboratory of the Department of Agriculture, the most practical, satisfactory, and convenient method of those it has tried is to keep the tree moist, and its needles from discoloring and falling, by standing it in water. The procedure is as follows:

1. Obtain a tree that has been cut as recently as possible.

2. Cut off the end of the trunk diagonally at least 1 inch above the original cut end. Stand the tree at once in a container of water and keep the water level above the cut surface during the entire time the tree is in the house. If the tree is not set up for several days, it should be kept standing in water meanwhile in a cool place.

If started in time, this treatment not only will prevent the needles from drying out and so becoming flammable, but it will also keep them fresh and green. It will, in addition, retard the fall of needles of such species as spruce, which loses needles very easily in contrast to balsam fir, which retains its needles even after the branches have become dry.

Keeping Trees Moist and Green

A slightly more complex treatment that requires, in addition to water, several household products plus a trade brand of natural horticultural iron, is claimed by the developers to keep Christmas trees greener and moist longer than water alone. Here is the formula:

Green Garde micronized iron	¼ cup
Hot water	1 gal
Light corn syrup (Karo, etc.)	2 cups
Sodium hypochlorite solution (Clorox, Purex, Rose-X)	4 tsp

Stir micronized iron (obtainable at florists, garden supply, and hardware stores) into the hot water. Mix in corn syrup and bleach (the latter helps prevent the formation of algae). Saw about 1 inch from the bottom of the tree trunk to remove clotted resins and to level the base. Pound the base of the trunk with a hammer or axe to crush the fibers. Stand the tree in a holder that holds at least a gallon and pour in the solution. Add tap water daily to keep it filled.

Fire-Retardant Coatings

Additional protection against fire can be provided by the use of fire-retardant coatings if the retention of the natural color of the foliage is unimportant. Here are formulations for three simple ones:

1. (Produces a shiny transparent colorless coating)

	Parts by volume
Sodium silicate (water glass)	9
Water, containing a wetting agent, such as Dreft or Vel, or some liquid dishwashing detergent (1 tsp per quart)	1

2. (Produces a cream-colored coating. May be tinted with household dyes.)

	Parts by weight
Sodium silicate (water glass)	31
China clay	41
Water (containing wetting agent as in formula 1)	28

3. (Produces a frosty white coating. May be tinted with household dyes.)

	Parts by weight
Sodium alginate	1
Monoamminium phosphate	25
China clay	4
Water	70

To prepare this formula, heat the water to about 180° F, add the sodium alginate, and stir until a uniform gel is obtained. Then add the monoammonium phosphate, heating gently and stirring occasionally until it has dissolved. Finally add the china clay wet with a little water to a thick paste, and stir until it is uniformly distributed throughout the gel.

Applying the Coatings

To appreciably reduce the fire hazard, any of the foregoing coatings must be applied heavily. One coat of these formulations will greatly reduce the tendency for flames to spread; two coats are even more effective. Coatings may be applied either by dipping or by spraying. It may be necessary to thin the first formula for spray application, in which case more applications are necessary.

Silver effects can be had by spraying an aluminum paint on trees coated with either formula 2 or 3.

Extra Fire Precautions

In addition to these treatments, all possible precautions against fire should be taken around the Christmas tree, including the elimination of defective electrical connections and the avoidance of the accumulation of combustible decorations on or beneath the tree. The tree should also be placed so that its accidental burning would not ignite curtains or other combustible furnishings nor trap the occupants of a room or building.

FIRE-RETARDING COATINGS FOR WOOD

Many coating materials protect wood against fire in varying degree. The amount of protection provided depends on the amount and thoroughness of the application and the severity of fire exposure. Most preparations are of value primarily for interior use and are not durable when exposed to weather.

The following are among those which have shown good results in laboratory tests:

	Parts by weight
Basic carbonate white lead	41
Borax	32
Raw linseed oil	22.8
Turpentine	3.6
Japan drier	0.6

First work the white lead into part of the oil. Then add the rest of the oil and the other ingredients and stir in thoroughly.

Three or four thick coats, or approximately 1 gallon per 125 square feet of surface, are needed for good protection.

Here is a water-base paint that blisters under fire to produce a nonburning insulating coating:

	Parts by weight
Sodium silicate solution (40-42° Baumé)	11
Kaolin	15
Water	10

Again, 3 or 4 thick coats are necessary with 4 coats covering about 100 square feet.

FIRE-RESISTING PAINT

No paint can make a surface absolutely fireproof, but this one has proved useful in retarding fire:

Powdered asbestos	2 lb
Sodium aluminate	½ lb
Hydrated lime	½ lb
Sodium silicate, granular	1½ lb

The sodium silicate should be in the form of the granular metasilicate. Dissolve this, along with the aluminate and the lime, by stirring in the smallest possible amount of water. Then stir in the asbestos and add enough more water to make the paint easy to apply. Dry color may be added if desired. Apply at least 2 coats.

14

First Aid and Safety

PRINCIPLES OF FIRST AID

In cases of minor injury, such as a small cut, a bruise, or a splinter in the finger, first aid treatment may be all that is needed. In more serious cases, first aid is the emergency care you can provide until professional medical help arrives. What you do, or know enough *not to do,* in the first few minutes after a person is injured or suddenly becomes ill, may relieve pain, counteract shock, prevent further injury, or even save his life.

Serious Injury or Illness

In the case of a person seriously injured or taken suddenly sick, take the following steps:

1. Assess the condition thoroughly but quickly. Seconds are important if there is severe bleeding; if breathing has stopped; if the person has swallowed poison.

2. In any of the cases just mentioned, treat the person in this order, immediately:

Stop profuse bleeding.

Give artificial respiration if breathing has stopped.

Give antidote for poison.

Treat for shock.

3. Send for medical help.

4. Give nothing to eat or drink to an unconscious or internally injured person.

5. After giving first aid, make the person as comfortable as possible. Keep him warm by covering with a coat or blanket.

6. If the person has been seriously injured, do not move him unless absolutely necessary. Moving him may increase the severity of the injury, especially if head, neck, or back has been hurt, or if there are internal injuries. If possible, get professional help before attempting to move the injured person.

Moving an Injured Person

In some cases, such as in fires or highway accidents, it may, however, be necessary to move a person at once. In these cases, try not to change the person's position. Move him lengthwise rather than sidewise. If possible, slip a blanket, coat, wide board, or door under him; then pull on the end of it.

A stretcher can be improvised by using poles and a blanket, a buttoned coat, and so on. A chair tilted backward, so the person is in a half-sitting, half-lying position, is a good device for moving him if nothing flat is available.

If you must lift the person, several people should do it together. Have them stand on opposite sides of him, lifting the body parallel with the ground and supporting all parts of the body. If you must move a person by yourself, avoid doubling him up.

To Stop Serious Bleeding

There are four forms of bleeding: 1) Internal, 2) Arterial (blood is bright red, comes in spurts), 3) Venous (blood is dark red, flows rather than spurts), and 4) Capillary (light in color, oozes rather than flows).

Internal bleeding is the most serious, for first aid cannot treat it. Capillary bleeding is the least serious, and also the most common.

A normal adult has from five to six quarts of blood in his system. A loss of two or more pints is serious.

Internal bleeding is visible only as blood appears from body openings: nose, mouth, ears, etc. Except in the case of ordinary nosebleed, surgery is usually required to stop it. If internal bleeding is evident, get the person to a hospital as soon as possible, being careful while moving him not to increase the severity of the bleeding.

To stop all other forms of bleeding, press clean gauze, a sterile compress, or a clean towel against the wound with the fingers or heel of the hand. If the dressing becomes bloodsoaked, do not remove it but apply a clean compress directly over the old one. In almost all cases, this direct pressure is preferable to and effective as using a tourniquet. Except in expert hands, a tourniquet may cause severe damage to tissue by completely cutting off the blood supply to the limb below the pressure point.

Breathing Stopped—Artificial Respiration

If a person's breathing has stopped, whether from drowning, asphyxiation, chemical fumes, electric shock, choking, or other cause, you should apply artificial respiration immediately. If the cause is electric shock, first make sure that contact with the current is broken before you attempt artificial respiration; otherwise you may become an electric shock casualty yourself. If the victim is in a gas-filled room, get him into fresh air before starting artificial respiration.

Mouth-to-mouth method. This, or the mouth-to-nose, technique is now considered to be the best. It is the most practical method for emergency ventilation of a person of any age who has stopped breathing, in the absence of equipment or of help from a second person, regardless of the cause of cessation of breathing.

Here is what you do:

1. Place the victim on his back; tilt his head back so that his jaw juts out. Hold his head in this position with one hand.

2. Check victim's mouth to see that nothing—chewing gum, candy, tongue—is blocking his throat. If you see anything, wipe it out quickly.

3. Open your mouth wide and place it tightly over the victim's mouth. At the same time pinch the victim's nostrils shut or close the nostrils with your cheek. Or close the victim's mouth and place your mouth over his nose. Then (depending on which method you have chosen) blow into the victim's mouth or nose. Blow until you feel the lungs expand, see the chest rise.

4. Remove your mouth and listen for the passive exhalation. Next, take another deep breath and repeat the cycle. For an adult, blow vigorously at the rate of about 12 breaths per minute. For a child, take relatively shallow breaths appropriate for the child's size, at the rate of about 20 per minute. If you notice any resistance to your breathing, check the victim's mouth again.

5. Do not give up if results are not immediate. Many victims are revived only after prolonged effort.

Shock

Shock—or "traumatic shock"—is a depressed state of all body functions caused by injury. Unless treated, the condition may result in death, although the injury that caused it might not itself have been fatal. Causes of shock are many, loss of blood and severe pain being the most common. A person in shock appears weak. His pulse will be rapid, but may be very weak. He may break out with perspiration, vomit, or complain of nausea.

Keep the person lying down. Raise legs 12 to 18 inches unless head is injured or chest punctured. Cover him to keep his body temperature normal, but do not use hot-water bottles or any other methods to raise his temperature or cause him to perspire. If the person is conscious and not nauseated, give him half a cup of warm water, milk, tea, or coffee. If he retains this, and medical help is not expected for some time, give him more in half-cup doses as he desires it. If the ingredients are handy, substitute half-cup doses of water to which has been added ½ level teaspoon of table salt and ½ level teaspoon of baking soda (bicarbonate of soda) per quart.

FIRST AID FOR POISONS

The following suggestions are for the immediate treatment of acute poisoning that should be undertaken before a doctor arrives. Acute poisoning is caused by taking an overdose of any drug or other toxic agent, and usually occurs promptly after its ingestion.

If poison has been taken by mouth:

1. Send for a doctor immediately.
2. Keep patient warm.
3. Dilute the poison by giving 4 glasses of milk or water as quickly as possible if the person is conscious. Never give anything by mouth to an unconscious person.
4. Unless the person has taken a strong acid, alkali, or other corrosive substance, or a petroleum product such as napththa or gasoline, bring about vomiting by:
   a. placing the index finger far back on tongue and stroking from side to side.
   b. giving ½ glass of water containing 1 teaspoon powdered mustard.
   c. giving 2 or 3 glasses of lukewarm water containing 1 tablespoon salt per glass.
5. Repeat above procedure until vomited fluid is clear.
6. While giving first aid, try to identify the poison and give further treatment appropriate to that poison. If you can find the container suspected to have held the poisin, use the antidote suggested on its label. If you can identify the poison, but can't find the container, use instructions in the list below. If

you can't identify the poison, give repeated doses of a teaspoon of the following mixture stirred in water to make a thin paste:

UNIVERSAL ANTIDOTE

Powdered charcoal	2 parts
Tannic acid	1 part
Magnesium oxide	1 part

This combination, well mixed, should be prepared before needed and kept in all medicine cabinets. It is called "universal" because the charcoal will absorb phenol and strychnine; tannic acid will precipitate alkaloids, certain glucosides, and many metals; magnesium oxide will neutralize acids.

ACIDS

1. Give 2 to 3 glasses of milk or give 1 ounce milk of magnesia in large quantity of water.

Do NOT give chalk or sodium bicarbonate, as these react with the acid to produce too much gas.

Do NOT cause vomiting.

ALCOHOL

1. Give 1 to 2 glasses of milk.

2. Cause vomiting.

3. Give tablespoon sodium bicarbonate in 1 quart warm water.

AMMONIA

1. For household ammonia give 2 tablespoons vinegar, lemon juice, or grapefruit juice in 2 glasses of water. For stronger ammonia give large amount of water containing 2 tablespoons of the above weak acids per glass.

2. Give 2 ounces of olive oil or whites of 2 raw eggs.

Do NOT cause vomiting.

ARSENIC COMPOUNDS

1. Give "universal antidote" above.
2. Cause vomiting.
3. After stomach has been emptied, give whites of eggs in water or milk, milk alone, or thin gruel made from soft cereals.

ASPIRIN

1. Give 1 to 2 glasses of milk.
2. Cause vomiting.
3. Give tablespoon sodium bicarbonate in quart warm water.

BARBITURATES

1. Cause vomiting.
2. Give 2 tablespoons epsom salts in 2 glasses water.
3. Give large quantities of hot coffee or strong tea.

BELLADONNA

1. Cause vomiting.
2. Give glass of milk or "universal antidote."
3. Give artificial respiration if needed.
Keep patient quiet.

BROMIDES

1. Cause vomiting.
2. Give 2 tablespoons epsom salts in 2 glasses water.

Chlorine bleach or disinfectant
1. Cause vomiting.
2. Give 1 to 2 glasses of milk.

Codeine
1. Give glass of milk or "universal antidote."
2. Give 2 tablespoons epsom salts in 2 glasses water.

Keep patient awake.

Cold remedies
1. Give 1 to 2 glasses milk.
2. Cause vomiting.
3. Give tablespoon sodium bicarbonate in quart warm water.

Copper compounds
1. Give whites of eggs beaten with water or milk before attempting to cause vomiting or even if vomiting has occurred.
2. Cause vomiting. Repeat several times.
3. Give 1 ounce epsom salts in 1 pint water.
4. Give milk or thin gruel.

Disinfectant with carbolic acid
1. Induce vomiting.
2. Give 2 ounces olive or castor oil.
3. Give glass of milk or white of 2 raw eggs.

Gasoline, benzine, naphtha, kerosene
1. Give 2 ounces vegetable oil.
2. Give water or milk.
Do NOT cause vomiting.

INSECT & RAT POISONS WITH ARSENIC

See arsenic compounds, above.

With sodium fluoride

1. Give 2 glasses milk.
2. Cause vomiting.
3. Give 2 tablespoons milk of magnesia.

With phosphorus

1. Give 4 ounces of *mineral* oil.
2. Cause vomiting.
3. Give "universal antidote."

Do NOT give milk or white of egg. Positively do NOT give any vegetable or animal oil, as these dissolve and spread the poison.

With DDT

1. Give 2 glasses of milk.
2. Cause vomiting.
3. Give 2 tablespoons epsom salts in 2 glasses of water.

With strychnine

1. Give 2 glasses of milk.
2. Cause vomiting.
3. Give glass of milk or "universal antidote."
4. Give artificial respiration if needed.
Keep patient quiet.

IODINE TINCTURE

1. Give 2 ounces of thick starch paste, made by mixing cornstarch or flour with water.
2. Cause vomiting.
3. Give 2 ounces of salt in quart of warm water. Drink until vomit fluid is clear.
4. Give glass of milk.

LEAD COMPOUNDS
Same as arsenic compounds.

LYE (sodium hydroxide)
1. Give large drink of water containing 2 tablespoons of vinegar, lemon juice, or grapefruit juice per glass.
2. Give white of 2 raw eggs or 2 ounces of olive oil.

Do NOT cause vomiting.

MERCURY COMPOUNDS
Same as copper compounds.

MORPHINE, OPIUM, OR PAREGORIC
1. Give glass of milk or "universal antidote."
2. Give 2 tablespoons epsom salts in 2 glasses of water.

Keep person awake.

OIL OF WINTERGREEN
1. Give 1 or 2 glasses of milk or "universal antidote."
2. Cause vomiting.
3. Give tablespoon of sodium bicarbonate in quart of warm water.

"PEP" PILLS AND MEDICINES
1. Give 1 to 2 glasses of milk.
2. Cause vomiting.
3. Give glass of milk or "universal antidote."

PINE OIL
1. Give 2 to 3 glasses of water or milk.
2. Give 2 ounces of vegetable oil.

Do NOT cause vomiting.

SLEEPING PILLS
    See barbiturates.

TURPENTINE
    1. Give 4 ounces of vegetable oil.
    2. Cause vomiting.
    3. Give 2 to 3 glasses of water or milk.

WASHING SODA
    1. Give 2 tablespoons of vinegar, lemon juice, or grapefruit juice in 2 glasses of water.
    2. Give 2 ounces of olive oil or white of 2 raw eggs.

Bites and Stings of Insects

Few of the insects that bite or sting are poisonous in the sense that their bite or sting can cause serious symptoms of itself. However, there are insects that do transmit diseases where the insects act as hosts to an organism or virus of those diseases. For example, certain types of mosquitoes transmit malaria, yellow fever, and other diseases; certain types of ticks transmit spotted or Rocky Mountain fever; and certain types of biting flies transmit tularemia or rabbit fever.

The stings of bees, wasps, yellow jackets, and hornets, and the bites of mosquitoes, ticks, fleas, and bedbugs usually cause only local irritation and pain in the region stung or bitten. Moderate swelling and redness may occur, and some itching, burning, and pain may be present.

TREATMENT
    1. If a sting is left in the wound withdraw it.
    2. Apply a weak solution of ammonia, or a paste made of sodium bicarbonate and water, using a gauze compress.

3. If swelling and pain persist and other symptoms develop, see a doctor. This condition may occur if the insects have been feeding on or in contact with poisonous substances, and have transferred the poison through their bite or sting.

Bites of More Poisonous Insects

The effects of stings and bites of spiders, centipedes, tarantulas, and scorpions are in some cases much more severe than those of the insects previously mentioned. They may cause alarming symptoms but, except for bites of tarantulas and black-widow spiders, seldom prove fatal.

The black widow is a moderately large, glossy, black spider with very fine hairs over its body, giving it a silky appearance. On the underside of its abdomen is a red marking in the form of an hour glass. The female only is poisonous; the male, which is much smaller, is harmless.

SYMPTOMS

The symptoms of the more poisonous insects' stings or bites are 1 or 2 pinpoint punctures of the skin, local swelling and redness with a smarting, burning pain. The swelling, redness, and pain increase rapidly; prostration, sweating, nausea, and pain in the back, shoulders, chest, and limbs develop within a few hours. In most cases the constitutional symptoms are mild and subside within 6 to 12 hours. Occasionally, however, they are severe and end in collapse.

TREATMENT

1. Treat as for the less poisonous bites or stings of insects.

2. Where the swelling and pain are rapid and severe, secure medical aid as soon as possible. In the meantime take these measures:

a. If the bite is on a finger or toe, apply at the base a tight, narrow constricting band. If the bite is higher, use a wider band above the bite on the side nearer the heart. Remove the band after 5 minutes.

b. Pack the area in ice for 2 hours, keeping the affected extremity lower than the rest of the body during this time.

c. Keep the patient lying down, quiet, and warm. If the bite does not involve arms or legs, applications of ice are the only local first aid measure.

Contact Poison from Poison Ivy

The skin irritant of poison ivy, poison oak, and poison sumac is a nonvolatile phenolic substance called urushiol, found in all parts of the plant, including roots and fruit. It occurs in great abundance in the plant sap. The danger of poisoning is greatest in spring and summer when sap is abundant and least in late fall or winter.

Poisoning is usually caused by contact with some part of the plant. A very small amount of the poisonous substance can produce severe inflammation of the skin and is easily transferred from one object to another. Clothing may become contaminated and is often the source of prolonged infection. Dogs and cats frequently carry the poison to children or other unsuspecting persons.

Poison ivy protection

If it is necessary to work among poisonous plants, some measure of prevention can be gained by wearing protective clothing. Some protection also may be obtained by using protective creams or lotions. Here is one:

Ferric chloride	1 oz
Glycerin	5 oz
Ethyl rubbing alcohol	7 oz
Water	8 oz

Dissolve the ferric chloride in the water and then mix in thoroughly the alcohol and glycerin.

This lotion applied to the exposed skin before contact with poisonous plants will usually give effective protection. (Don't get it on your clothing or it may produce an iron stain.) After contact, wash off the lotion thoroughly with soap and water.

Contaminated clothing and tools should also be well washed with soap and water to prevent spreading the poison. Car door handles and steering wheels that have touched poison ivy or the hands of people who have touched it should similarly be washed.

Treatment for ivy poisoning

A 5-percent solution of ferric chloride in a mixture of 50 parts ethyl rubbing alcohol and 20 parts water, applied 4 or 5 times a day, usually dries the eruption. A solution of 1 tablespoon of sodium thiosulfate to 1 pint of water, applied similarly, should do the same. Apply with pads of cotton, and allow to dry on skin. Blisters may be opened with a sterile needle and the serum or pus absorbed on pads of cotton. Be sure to apply one of the solutions to the part before the blisters are opened and immediately thereafter, to prevent spreading the disease.

FIRST-AID FOR OTHER INJURIES AND AILMENTS

Bruises

These include "black eyes" and "black-and-blue" marks.

Apply ice, an ice bag, or cold compresses improvised from towels soaked in ice water and wrung out. Elevate the injured part. This treatment will reduce the swelling and pain and also the underskin bleeding, the cause of the discoloration.

Burns, Chemical

Flush the burned area well with water to dilute and remove the chemical. Do not try to neutralize acid with alkali or alkali with acid. This may do more harm than good.

If the chemical has gotten into a person's eye, flush the eye gently but thoroughly with water for at least 20 minutes. Do not use an eye cup. Cover the eye with a sterile compress and have the person see a doctor immediately.

Burns, Heat

Heat burns are given three classifications: 1) first-degree burns, in which the skin is reddened, 2) second-degree burns, in which skin is reddened and blistered, 3) third-degree burns, in which the skin and sometimes the underlying tissue is cooked or charred.

The danger to the body does not depend so much on the degree as on the extensiveness of a burn. A mild burn over a large area is more dangerous than a second-degree burn of small size. Shock is usually severe in burns over a large area. As a general rule, the first aid treatment of burns involves relief of pain and the treatment of shock. If the burn is large, call a doctor immediately.

If the burn is small, apply cold water to it until the pain is relieved. If the skin is not broken or blistered, apply a coating of petrolatum (petroleum jelly or Vaseline) or heavy mineral oil and cover the burn with several sterile gauze pads, piled one on the other, and held in place by a lightly applied bandage. If the skin is blistered, apply the gauze pads without the petrolatum or any other medication and without attempting to break the blisters.

If the burn is large, and especially if the skin is charred, take extra care. Keep the person quiet and lying down, to reduce chances of shock. Cut away clothing from burned area. To prevent contamination, wash your hands thoroughly with soap and water. Don't apply oil, ointment, antiseptic, or any other medication. Cover the burned area with half a dozen or more layers of sterile dry gauze. Or cover it with a single layer of thin plastic food-wrapping film (such as Saran Wrap), which will not stick to the wound. Treat for shock, if it occurs. Get a doctor as soon as possible.

Sunburn

Severe sunburn can be just as painful—and often just as serious—as heat burns. If blistering occurs, cover the area with sterile dressings soaked in a baking soda solution (2 tablespoons of soda to 1 quart of water). For nausea, vomiting, or fever, see a doctor.

If there is redness only, cover the burned area with a sunburn ointment, a vegetable oil, mineral oil, or baby oil. Give as much liquid as possible. Aspirin will help relieve the pain.

Cuts, Scratches

These are probably the most frequent home injury. No matter how superficial they may appear, they are potentially dangerous—germs may easily enter the body through the broken skin. They should be treated right away.

Before treating a cut or a scratch, wash your hands thoroughly. Using sterile gauze or a freshly laundered handkerchief or towel, wash the area around the cut or scratch with soap and water (soap containing hexachlorophene is particularly effective). Wash outward from the cut. Then wash the cut itself, using soap, water, and sterile gauze. Try to get as much dirt out of the wound as you can. Then cover the wound with a sterile compress and fasten in place with a bandage. On very small cuts and scratches, a combined compress and adhesive band, such as a Band-Aid, will do.

If a cut or scratch has been properly treated, it should not become infected. Infection, however, may possibly show up several days later. Any of these signs is evidence: a reddened, painful area around the wound; pus and red streaks; swelling in the wounded area, chills and fever in the patient.

See a doctor right away if any of these signs appear.

Electric Shock

Symptoms of electric shock are unconsciousness, no breathing, face and lips blue, flushed or pale, pulse weak or absent. There may also be burns in the area of contact.

If the person is still in contact with the current, the thing to do immediately is to break that contact without endangering yourself. If a switch or plug is near at hand, open the switch or pull the plug. If you can't do this quickly enough, remove the wire, move the person with a dry wooden pole, rope or other nonconducting object.

Begin artificial respiration immediately if breathing has stopped. After breathing has been restored, keep the person warm and quiet until professional help arrives. Treat for burns, if necessary, and watch out for traumatic shock, treating it if it occurs.

Eye Irritation

Don't try to remove anything more than a wind-blown object such as dust, dirt, or a small insect. If a particle does not come out readily, let a doctor do it.

First, try to flush out the particle with warm water (have the person lie on his back and pour plenty of water into the eye; *don't use an eyecup!*). Blinking during this bath may help. If this doesn't work, pull the eyelid away from the eyeball. With moist sterile gauze or cotton, lift out the particle.

Fainting

Hunger, shock, fatigue, poor ventilation—even seeing or hearing something unpleasant—can cause fainting.

To revive a person who has fainted, place him on his back with his head lower than the rest of his body. Loosen all tight clothing and apply cold compresses to his face and forehead. If someone feels faint, have him sit down and put his head between his knees. Have him breathe deeply.

Heat Exhaustion

Heat exhaustion and heatstroke are different ills and must be treated differently. In heat exhaustion the person is cold and should be warmed; in heatstroke the person is hot and should be cooled off.

Early symptoms of heat exhaustion—which can be produced by exposure to heat either indoors or outdoors—are weariness, fatigue, and a feeling of faintness. Later the person may break out in profuse, but cold, perspiration; he may turn almost white; his temperature will be normal or below normal; he may lose consciousness.

Remove the person to a cool place, have him lie down, and loosen his clothing. Cover him with a light blanket. Let him sniff aromatic spirits of ammonia. If he is conscious, give him a saltwater solution (½ teaspoon of water in ½ glass of water) every 15 minutes. Call a doctor immediately.

Heatstroke

Heatstroke, or sunstroke as it is often called, is more serious than heat exhaustion. It demands immediate medical treatment.

The victim of heatstroke will have a fever up to 105°, or even higher. He is dizzy and nauseated. His face is flushed and his skin is hot and dry. He may even lose consciousness.

Get person out of the sun and into a cooler area immediately. Have him lie on back with head and shoulders raised and as much clothing as possible removed. Apply cold to head. Cool body by wrapping in a sheet and pouring cold water on small portions at a time, or use cold cloths and ice bags. If a tub is available, place person in a tub of cold water. If the person is conscious, give him cool drinks, but do not give him stimulants. Call the doctor.

Nosebleeds

These may occur spontaneously as well as following injury to the nose. Children often have nosebleeds as the result of strenuous exercise, a cold, or high altitudes. In most cases the bleeding is more annoying than serious.

Often, sitting quietly with the head tilted back is enough to stop the bleeding. If this doesn't do it, blow the nose gently to remove all clots of blood. Then insert into the bleeding nostril a wedge of cotton, or a roll of gauze or paper napkin, moistened with water, and press firmly on the outside of the nostril. If the bleeding stops, leave the packing in place for a while.

Splinters

Most splinters lie close to the surface and are therefore not too difficult to remove. If the splinter is deeply imbedded, removal should be done by a professional.

Wash the area well with soap and water. Sterilize tweezers by passing the tips through a flame until they glow. If you can see the splinter protruding, or just under the skin, grasp it with tweezers and remove.

15

Household Chemistry

INVISIBLE INKS

Invisible or *sympathetic* inks consist of chemical solutions that are colorless when applied, but which become visible when heated or treated with other chemicals. They can be used in performing feats of chemical magic and for writing secret letters to your friends.

An invisible ink that comes ready-made is plain lemon juice. Using a clean pen, write or draw with this on ordinary unsized white paper. When dry, this "ink" can't be seen. Hold the paper over heat, however, and the writing magically appears.

Another, and one that gives better results, can be made by adding 10 drops of concentrated sulfuric acid to 1 ounce of water (*Caution:* Handle the concentrated acid carefully; it is extremely corrosive. In mixing, always add the acid to the water, and not vice versa). When heated, this ink, previously invisible, turns a deep black.

When gently heated, writing done with a solution of cobalt chloride turns blue.

If sprayed or brushed with a solution of potassium ferrocyanide, writing made with a solution of copper nitrate will become brown.

Writing made with an oxalic acid solution, if similarly treated with a solution of cobalt nitrate, will turn blue.

Writing made with a potassium thiocyanate solution, treated with a solution of ferric chloride, will turn red.

Universal Developer for Invisible Inks

If you have access to a home or school laboratory, you can compound a universal developer that will make almost any secret writing visible. Prepare it by dissolving the following chemicals in 50 milliliters of water:

Potassium iodide	4 grams
Iodine crystals	1/10 gram
Sodium chloride	5 grams
Aluminum chloride crystals (do not use anhydrous aluminum chloride)	4 grams

Apply this solution sparingly to the paper by means of a small wad of cotton dampened with it.

Erasable Ink

Here is a trick ink that you can get rid of instantly in case you don't like what you've written. Just give it a swish with a cloth and it's gone! However, it is quite useless except to astonish friends.

To make it just add 12 drops of tincture of iodine to 3 teaspoons of water, and then stir in a teaspoon of corn starch. The iodine reacts with the starch to form a deep blue-black color.

Write with a clean pen. Although this ink stands out distinctly, the starch keeps it from penetrating the paper. As soon as it is dry it can be removed with the above-mentioned swish.

TESTS FOR CHEMICALS, METALS, TEXTILES

Kitchen Tests for Acids and Alkalis

The juice of the chokecherry can be used instead of phenolphthalein solution as an indicator for bases and acids. A water infusion of the berries will turn green when you add an alkali to it and light red when you add an acid. To make the infusion, crush the berries, pour boiling water over them and, with occasional stirring, let stand for half an hour. Then filter or strain out the berries and use the clear liquid.

An infusion of the leaves of purple cabbage, made the same way, can also be used as an indicator. In this case the liquid is red when acid, purple when neutral, and blue turning to dark green as it becomes alkaline.

Test for Gold

The common method used to tell whether an article of jewelry is gold or brass is to touch it with a drop of concentrated nitric acid on the tip of a glass rod. If brass or other yellow metal alloy, or if the gold plating has worn off to expose the alloy, the acid will form copper nitrate. If this occurs, the metal and acid will turn blue and a reddish gas will be evolved. If the metal is solid gold, or plated with gold with its coating intact, there will be no reaction at all. *(Caution:* Handle nitric acid carefully. It is extremely corrosive.)

Test for Silver

Sterling silver, silver plate that is intact, and silver coins may be identified positively by means of a test solution suggested by the U.S. Secret Service. It consists simply of 10 grains of silver nitrate and 20 drops of concentrated nitric acid dissolved in 1 ounce of distilled water. *(Caution:* Handle these chemicals with care. Silver nitrate makes black stains on skin and clothing; nitric acid is extremely corrosive.) If you haven't the materials for making this, it can be put up cheaply by a druggist.

To make the test, scrape a small spot on the object to clean it and apply a drop of the solution. If the coin is real, or the object is of sterling silver or plate in good condition, the acid will not change its appearance. If the coin or object is not silver, the solution will blacken it.

Test for White Metals

Many "white" metals, such as ordinary steel, nickel, Monel metal, chromium stainless steel, and "18-8" chromium-nickel stainless steel look very much alike but vary widely in composition and price and perform quite differently in use. If you want to make sure the metal in your new equipment is what you need and paid for, you can quickly find out with a simple testing kit you can put together for a few cents.

For chemicals, all you need is a few ounces of concentrated nitric acid *(Careful!* Very corrosive poison), a like amount of distilled water, and a solution of ¼ ounce of cupric chloride in 2½ ounces of water. For apparatus, you need only three medicine droppers (one for each reagent), a few iron or steel nails, and a small bar or horseshoe magnet.

With this simple equipment you can make a quick and positive identification of eight different metals and alloys, as shown in the accompanying table.

Methods of carrying out the tests are as simple as the equipment. The first test is for magnetic properties, which can be determined by suspending the magnet on a string so it is free to turn, and then bringing the metal to be tested toward it. Monel metal is usually slightly magnetic at room temperatures, but if this quality does not show at once, a bath in ice water or a freezing mixture will cause it to be revealed.

Follow this test with the nitric acid test. Clean the spot where it is to be made with a solution of washing soda or trisodium phosphate and then rinse. Apply one or two drops of concentrated nitric acid, and wait a few minutes to note the reaction. Then dilute the acid with three or four drops of distilled water, one drop at a time. If the solution turns green or blue, proceed with the nail test for copper. (*Note:* Between tests, lay the droppers and nails in a clean glass dish, out of contact with each other.)

Keeping the nail in contact with the metal, rub the end of it in the spot of diluted nitric acid. If copper is present in the alloy being tested, it will be deposited either on the nail or on the surface of the metal, under the acid solution.

The purpose of the fourth test is to distinguish Inconel—an alloy containing 80 percent nickel, 14 percent chromium, and 6 percent iron from the "18-8" stainless steel which contains 18 percent chromium and 8 percent nickel.

A drop of the cupric chloride in hydrochloric acid is applied, and allowed to remain for two minutes. Then add slowly three or four drops of distilled water, and finally wash off all solution.

If the sample is "18-8" stainless steel, copper from the cupric chloride solution will be deposited on the metal surface. If the metal is Inconel, copper will not deposit. Only a white spot will indicate where the solution has been applied.

Chemical Humidity Indicator

Artificial flowers and dolls' dresses, impregnated with a chemical that changes color with the humidity, have long been used to indicate the relative amount of moisture in the air. Today, moisture absorbing agents, such as silica gel, treated with the same chemical are packed in salt-shaker caps and canister tops to keep salt and cookies dry. When these agents get too damp, the chemical notifies you by changing color.

The secret of all these devices is cobalt chloride, a chemical whose crystals lose water and turn blue when they are perfectly dry, and combine with water and turn pink when they are moist. Merely soak paper towelling, filter paper, or undyed cotton cloth in a strong solution of cobalt chloride in water and let dry, to make your indicator.

You can also use cobalt chloride to work a neat bit of chemical magic. Soak a handkerchief in a *dilute* solution, and dry. Warm the handkerchief and it becomes bright blue; breathe on it, and it becomes pale pink or colorless!

QUALITATIVE TESTS FOR IDENTIFYING SOME COMMON WHITE METALS AND ALLOYS

MAGNETIC TEST	NITRIC ACID TEST			Iron Nail Test for Copper	Drop Test with Cupric Chloride in Hydrochloric Acid	Material Probably Is
Reaction to Magnet	Reaction to Conc. Acid	Reaction to Acid after Dilution	Color of the Solution			
Magnetic	Reacts Slowly	Reacts Slowly	Pale Green	No Copper Plates out	Not required	Nickel
Magnetic (slightly)	Reacts	Reacts Slowly	Greenish Blue	Copper Plates out	Not required	Monel
Non-magnetic	Reacts	Reacts	Bluish Green	Copper Plates out	Not required	Copper-Nickel Alloy containing less than 60% Nickel, e.g. Nickel-Silver
Magnetic	Reacts Slowly	Reacts	Brown to Black	Not required	Not required	Steel or Cast Iron
Non-magnetic	Reacts Slowly	Reacts	Brown to Black	Not required	Not required	"Ni-Resist"
Magnetic	No Reaction	No Reaction	Colorless	Not required	Not required	Straight Chromium Stainless Steel
Non-magnetic	No Reaction	No Reaction	Colorless	Not required	Copper deposits when drop is diluted	Chromium-Nickel Stainless Steels e.g. "18-8"
Non-magnetic	No Reaction	No Reaction	Colorless	Not required	No deposition of copper occurs	Inconel

The Meaning of pH

The term "pH" is used commonly in testing soils and aquarium water, in processing foods, in chemical analysis, and in medicine. What does it mean? It is simply the symbol of a scale, numbered from 0 to 14, that rates water solutions according to their acidity or alkalinity, thus:

pH RELATIONSHIPS

pH value		Relative Acidity or Alkalinity
0	acidity	10,000,000
1		1,000,000
2		100,000
3		10,000
4		1,000
5		100
6		10
7	neutral (pure water)	1
8		10
9		100
10		1,000
11		10,000
12		100,000
13		1,000,000
14	alkalinity	10,000,000

Pure water is given the number 7—right in the middle of the scale—because it contains an equal number of acidic and basic ions and is therefore neutral. As the alkalinity of a solution increases, the pH value goes up; as the acidity increases, the pH goes down. Each step represents an increase or decrease by a factor of 10.

On this scale, the most acid substance is hydrochloric acid, which, in proper concentration, is rated at 0, or 10 million times as *acid* as water. At the other end of the scale is a solution of sodium hydroxide, rated at 14, or 10 million times as *alkaline* as water. Solutions of other substances take their places in between. Here are a few examples:

pH OF COMMON THINGS

	pH
Hydrochloric acid, normal	0.1
Sulfuric acid, normal	0.3
Oxalic acid, 0.1 normal	1.6
Limes	1.8–2.0
Ginger ale	2.0–4.0
Lemons	2.2–2.4
Swamp peats	2.7–3.4
Apples	2.9–3.3
Grapefruit	3.0–3.3
Bananas	4.5–4.7
Average garden soils	4.5–7.0
Boric acid, 0.1 normal	5.2
Best pH for most plants	6.0–7.0
Cow's milk	6.3–6.6
Drinking water	6.5–6.8
Pure water	7.0
Human blood plasma	7.3–7.5
Sodium bicarbonate, 0.1 normal	8.4

Desert soils	9.0–11.0
Calcium carbonate, saturated	9.4
Ammonia	10.6–11.6
Trisodium phosphate, 0.1 normal	12.0
Sodium metasilicate, 0.1 normal	12.6
Sodium hydroxide, normal	14.0

Approximate measurement of pH may be done with test papers or solutions that change color with different acidity or alkalinity. For instance, familiar litmus paper turns red in solutions of pH less than 7, and turns blue in solutions of more than 7. Phenolphthalein turns red in solutions more alkaline than approximately 9. Chemical supply houses and garden and aquarium stores can sell you other test papers and solutions that change color at different portions of the scale, also some "universal" papers and solutions that will give color changes for almost the entire scale.

Battery Polarity Tests

Immerse the bare ends of the leads from the battery about ½ inch apart in a strong solution of salt water. (If the battery is more than about 45 volts, place them farther apart and *be sure the parts of the wires you hold are well insulated!*) The current will decompose the salt water and in doing so will produce more bubbles about the negative wire than about the positive.

You can also test polarity with a homemade color-changing paper. To a strong salt solution add a few drops of phenolphthalein test solution. Soak strips of paper towel or filter paper in this solution and then let the strips dry. When ready to make a test, moisten a strip of the prepared paper and touch the terminal wires to it, again about ½ inch apart (and observing the precautions mentioned above!). A pink spot will form around the negative terminal.

Burning Test for Textiles

When nearly all textiles were made of the natural materials wool, cotton, linen, or silk, it was not hard for the housewife to tell by looks and feel just what her clothing, blankets, draperies, and linens were made of. Today, with dozens of new test-tube fibers competing with those original products, determination is far more complex.

A few simple tests, however, can often help solve the mystery. So long as the fibers in a fabric are not so mixed that you can't separate them, the burning test should help you identify eight or more different types of textiles. To perform it, you touch the end of a small sample to a match flame; then you note the appearance of the burning, the smell, and the nature of the ash.

Cotton and linen, as well as viscose and cuprammonium rayon (the types most commonly used) all burn rapidly with the familiar odor of "burning rags" or paper. The ash is small, and after the flame goes out a glowing coal may creep along the unburned material. Because these materials are so similar chemically, further differentiation must be made by appearance or other physical tests. You can distinguish between cotton and rayon by wetting a strand; on pulling, cotton is relatively strong, while rayon breaks easily.

Wool and hair burn more slowly and give off an odor of burnt hair or feathers. Their ash is knobby and cokelike, and the flame stops as soon as the match is removed.

Pure silk burns slowly, with a smell similar to that of wool, and leaves a row of cokelike beads along the edge of the fabric.

Weighted silk (silk made heavier by treatment with metallic salts) is readily discovered by the burning test. Only the silk fibers burn. A skeleton of black ash is left behind which retains the structure of the weave.

Acetate (Acele, Arnel) flames and melts, producing a black ball at the burning edge which hardens when cold.

Nylon doesn't really burn at all, although combustible dyes or finishes may cause it to flame slightly. It melts, though, leaving a brown mass at the edge of the material.

Modacrylic (Dynel, Verel) is hard to ignite and goes out by itself. It leaves an irregular, hard black bead. Dynel softens if treated with acetone.

Polyester (Dacron, Fortrel, Kodel, Vycron) is also hard to ignite and is self-extinguishing. It leaves a round and shiny hard black bead, rather than an irregular one, and gives off a pungent odor.

Acrylic (Orlon, Creslan, Acrilan, Zefran) burn readily with a yellow flame having a purple base and orange tip. The flame does not go out by itself. It gives off an acrid odor and leaves a hard black bead.

Glass fibers do not burn, but become red hot and may melt into tiny beads if kept in a hot flame.

Lye Test for Wool

The boiling lye test is the classic method for detecting, and determining the amount of, an adulteration of what is supposed to be pure wool.

Count the threads in a small square of the cloth and then immerse it for exactly 10 minutes in a gently boiling, 5-percent solution of lye. (*Caution:* Handle lye with care; it is extremely caustic. Prepare and boil the solution in a glass, iron, or stainless steel pot, as it attacks other metals.)

At the end of the 10 minutes, remove what is left of the square of cloth from the solution, rinse it in plain water, and count the remaining threads. As wool is the only common textile fiber that is dissolved by boiling lye, what is left is cotton or linen, or some other fiber.

Acid Test for Wool

If you are still in doubt concerning a material that appears to be only part wool, give it the "acid test." Mix two drops of concentrated sulfuric acid (*Caution:* Do not spill on clothes or skin) with 100 drops of water and put a drop or two of this 2-percent acid on a piece of the cloth to be tested, allowing it to penetrate the fabric completely. Then place the sample between two sheets of paper and press with a hot iron for 1 minute. If the material contains cotton, the spot where the acid was placed becomes charred. When you rub the charred spot gently between your thumb and forefinger, the cotton falls away and leaves behind it whatever wool the material contains.

Test for Water in Gasoline

When you buy gasoline for your car or solvents for oil paints and varnishes are you getting 100 percent of what you expect, or is there water mixed with it? With the help of a powder you can make easily, you can find out in an instant.

Put an ounce or so of copper sulfate crystals in a small glass baking dish and place the dish in an oven heated to about 490°F. The heat drives the water out of the blue crystals. When all has gone, what remains is anhydrous (waterless) copper sulfate—a pale gray powder. When the powder has cooled, put it in a small bottle having a tight stopper, for use as needed.

To make a test, put a little of the powder into a test tube or small vial and add some of the suspected liquid. Then stopper the tube and give it a few shakes. If the liquid contains water, the copper sulfate will take back the water it lost and once more turn blue. If the liquid is free of water, the powder will remain gray.

Coloring Fireplace Flames

By soaking fireplace logs in water solutions of certain chemicals and then drying them, or merely by sprinkling the powdered chemicals on the flames, you can conjure up brilliant colors to suit your whim.

Here is a list of some of the chemicals and of the colors they produce:

Strontium nitrate	Red
Common salt	Yellow
Borax	Green
Barium nitrate	Apple green
Copper nitrate	Emerald green

Copper chloride	Bluish green
Calcium chloride	Orange
Lithium chloride	Purple

HEAT AND COLD FROM CHEMICALS

Chemical Heating Bottles

Bottles that become warm when water is added to them operate on well-known physical or chemical principles. Most of these contain iron filings or borings and some salt which becomes chemically active by the addition of water.

One composition that produces mild heat when water is added is:

Iron filings	40 parts
Manganese dioxide	5 parts
Common salt	3 parts

Another:

Iron filings	4 parts
Calcium chloride	2 parts
Powdered sulfur	1 part
Common salt	1 part

One that gives more heat:

Iron filings	24 parts
Copper chloride	10 parts
Ammonium chloride	1 part

Mix the above thoroughly and add about 16 parts of water when ready to start the reaction.

Degrease the iron filings or borings in the above mixtures before using them by washing them with gasoline or painter's naphtha.

Cold from Chemicals

Chemicals that react chemically with water when going into solution cause the water to heat up. Those that merely dissolve absorb heat from the water in doing so and cool it down. You can give a practical demonstration of cold from chemicals by cooling a bottle of soda on a picnic, in a household emergency, or as a party surprise.

All you need is a large fruit-juice can, a turkish bath towel, 1 pound of common photographic hypo, water, and a couple of rubber bands. Fold the towel and wrap it around the sides and bottom of the can for insulation. Then pour in 1 quart of the coldest water you can get, dissolve the hypo in it by rapid stirring, and put in the bottle to be cooled. The temperature of the bottle should go down about 30°F. (The hypo solution need not be wasted. Bottle it and use it for preparing photographic fixing baths.)

A mixture of 50 parts of ammonium chloride and 50 parts potassium nitrate, dissolved in 160 parts water, will produce even greater cold. If the ingredients are originally at moderate room temperature, solution will cause a drop to below 32°F.

Freezing Mixtures

The following, from the Smithsonian Tables, are other mixtures that can produce low temperatures for many processes. The figure in column A is the number of parts of the substance named in the first column to be added to the parts of the substance in column B. The next column gives the original temperature of the ingredients, and the last one the final temperature after they are mixed.

Substance	A	B		Initial Temp. °C	Resulting Temp. °C
Sodium acetate, crystals	85	Water	100	10.7	— 4.7
Ammonium chloride	30	"	100	13.3	— 5.1
Sodium nitrate	75	"	100	13.2	— 5.3
Sodium thiosulfate (hypo)	110	"	100	10.7	— 8.0
Potassium iodide	140	"	100	10.8	—11.7
Ammonium nitrate	60	"	100	13.6	—13.6
Calcium chloride	30	Snow	100*	—1	—10.9
Ammonium chloride	25	"	100	—1	—15.4
Ammonium nitrate	45	"	100	—1	—16.75
Sodium nitrate	50	"	100	—1	—17.75
Sodium chloride (salt)	33	"	100	—1	—21.3
	1	"	.49	0	—19.7
	1	"	.61	0	—39.0
	1	"	.70	0	—54.9
Calcium chloride, hexahydrate	1	"	.81	0	—40.3
	1	"	1.23	0	—21.5
	1	"	2.46	0	— 9.0
	1	"	4.92	0	— 4.0
		"	73.00	0	—30.0
Alcohol at 4°C	77	Dry ice**			—72.0
Chloroform		Dry ice			—77.0
	1	Water	0.94	20	— 4.0
	1	Snow	0.94*	0	— 4.0
Ammonium nitrate	1	Water	1.20	10	—14.0
	1	Snow	1.20*	0	—14.0
	1	Water	1.31	10	—17.5
	1	Snow	1.31*	0	—17.5

*Finely shaved ice may be used in place of the snow.
Dry ice should be broken into small lumps and made into a mush with the alcohol or chloroform. (Caution:** Don't handle dry ice with your hands; it may freeze your fingers. Use tongs or wear thick gloves. To break it up, put larger pieces in a cloth bag and pound it with a hammer or ice-breaking mallet.)

THE CHEMICAL ACTIVITY OF METALS

By means of elaborate tests, chemists have arranged all metals in a list according to the ease with which they enter into chemical reactions. This list is variously called the "activity series," the "electromotive series," the "electrochemical series," or the "displacement series," depending upon the use for which it is intended. Starting with the most active, here is the order for the commonest metals:

Li	lithium
K	potassium
C	calcium
Na	sodium
Mg	magnesium
Al	aluminum
Zn	zinc
Cr	chromium
Fe	iron
Ni	nickel
Sn	tin
Pb	lead
H	HYDROGEN
Bi	bismuth
Cu	copper
Hg	mercury
Ag	silver
Au	gold

Because it acts much the same as a metal in displacement reactions, hydrogen is included as a guidepost. Any metal above hydrogen is more active than hydrogen, and so will displace this gas from such acids as sulfuric and hydrochloric. Metals below hydrogen cannot displace it from any of the acids.

Metallic plating and the darkening of kitchen pots. This difference in the activity of metals explains many reactions in everyday chemistry. For example, it explains the plating of one metal on another without outside current, described in the chapter on metals. When any metal is placed in a solution of a salt of a metal that stands below it, the first metal is dissolved and the second is thrown out of solution in metallic form.

Aluminum pots and pans in the kitchen are often darkened by this swapping of metals. If you cook oatmeal, spinach, or other iron-containing food in an aluminum pot, some of the aluminum changes place with some of the iron, the latter being deposited as a dark coating inside the pot. Although the tidy housewife may scour away this deposit, she needn't do so, for the iron will be removed chemically if some acid food such as tomatoes, rhubarb, or sauerkraut is later cooked in the pot. The iron thus regained is not only harmless but is also a valuable food mineral.

Metals give up electrons differently. A more specific way to express the activity of metals is to say that they vary in their ability to ionize, or give up electrons. Metals at the top of the list give up electrons more easily than those at the bottom. This difference makes electric batteries possible and explains corrosion and electrolytic action between touching metals.

If two metals of different activity are immersed in a suitable solution and then connected by a wire, electrons will flow through the wire from the more active metal. The farther apart the metals in the series, the greater will be the electromotive force or voltage.

Electrical activity explains corrosion. A similar electrical effect accounts for the accelerated corrosion that often takes place when two metals are in contact in the presence of moisture. This explains why the iron in "tin cans" corrodes more rapidly when the tin plating is broken than if it were not plated at all. It also explains why the iron in zinc-plated, or "galvanized," iron is protected when the zinc coating is damaged. In the latter case, the zinc dissolves, and in so doing forms a protective coating over the iron.

16

Miscellaneous Hints And Formulas

To Clean High-Fidelity Records

Your hi-fi records that have become very dirty may be effectively cleaned by washing them in a solution of Joy, or other mild liquid dishwashing detergent. Using lukewarm water, make a solution a trifle weaker than that recommended for dishes. Dip the record part way into the solution and wipe gently in the direction of the grooves, using a soft cloth or a cellulose sponge and being careful to avoid the label. Then rinse under running lukewarm water and prop up on edge to dry without wiping. This treatment will remove fingermarks, dust, and grease imbedded in the grooves, and will not leave any deposit of its own to collect further dust.

Anti-Static Fluid for Records

One of the best anti-static fluids with which to moisten the dust brushes used to clean the grooves of high-fidelity records can be made by mixing 20 parts of ethylene glycol with 80 parts of water. Applied sparingly, this fluid coats the record with a thin film of moisture which permits the static electricity to leak off.

To Prevent Candles from Dripping

When the water in the following solution evaporates, the solids left behind will form a protective film around the candle.

Epsom salt	2 oz
Dextrin	2 oz
Water	13 oz

Dissolve the Epsom salt and the dextrin in the water. Dip the candles in the solution and then let them dry.

To Make Cut Flowers Last Longer

A pinch of salt in the water in which the flowers are placed is one of the oldest methods. A crushed aspirin tablet is another. Both work by retarding the growth of harmful bacteria.

A less-known method is the use of liquid chlorine bleach. This also disinfects the water and keeps it sweet-smelling. In addition, it has definite beneficial effects on certain flowers. It tends, for instance, to intensify the color of orchids and chrysanthemums and prevents fading which occurs when asters are kept in plain water. Also, while roses in plain water open rapidly and begin to drop their petals, roses in liquid chlorine-bleach solution remain in bud much longer. (This treatment is not recommended, however, for gardenias.)

Make the solution by thoroughly mixing 1 teaspoon of the bleach (Clorox, Rose-X, Purex, etc.) in each gallon of cold water. Then pour into vases.

Dustproofing Tennis Courts

Tennis courts, running tracks, and other bare-earth recreational areas can be made dustproof by sprinkling them with powdered calcium chloride. This chemical absorbs moisture from the air and by doing so acts as a dirt stabilizer.

Fire Starters

As campfire, outdoor grill, and fireplace starters, short pieces of kindling that have been dipped in melted paraffin wax and allowed to cool are excellent. To be on the safe side, always melt the paraffin in a double boiler, never over an open fire.

Make Your Own Yogurt

If you like yogurt, but find it expensive, why not make it yourself at about one-third of the cost of the ready-made product?

Dating back to the beginnings of recorded history, yogurt is a solid or semisolid milk product that has become that way chiefly through the action of *Lactobacillus bulgaricus* or other similar friendly bacteria. The noted Russian zoologist and bacteriologist, Metchnikoff, stimulated modern interest in it early in this century with the theory that the regular use of yogurt might improve health and prolong life by controlling harmful bacteria in the intestines. This idea no longer makes sense, but yogurt still carries on as a tasty, easily digested variation of milk that retains all of milk's food value.

Most commercial yogurt is made from whole milk from which part of the cream has been removed and replaced by dry skim milk. You can make it from whole milk, skim milk, or a combination. For a thicker product, use whole milk with 3 or 4 heaping teaspoons of dry skim milk added to each quart.

To make the first batch of yogurt, you will need a "starter" of 2 or 3 tablespoons of the ready-made unflavored variety for each quart of milk. To kill unwanted bacteria in it, first heat the milk to the boiling point in the top of a double boiler. As soon as the milk has cooled to a lukewarm temperature of about 110 to 115°F, stir in the yogurt until it is mixed thoroughly. Then either leave the mixture in the top of the double boiler or pour it into glasses or jars that have been prewarmed and which are then placed in a pan of warm water up to their necks. In either case, cover the mixture, and keep the water at lukewarm temperature. As soon as the milk has solidified (which should take about 2 hours), put it in the refrigerator. When cold, it is ready for use.

Subsequent batches of yogurt can be made by using yogurt from the previous batch as a starter. This process can be repeated for perhaps a month, or until the strain of bacteria gets too weak. Then you will have to start all over again with a little of the ready-made variety.

Saving Money on Lighter Fluid

Cigarette lighter fluid is often simply V.M.&P. naphtha—a high-grade benzine used for thinning paint and for dry cleaning—put up in small containers with a dispensing spout and sold at from four to eight times the price you would pay for the naphtha under its own name in a supermarket or paint store. For greater convenience in filling a lighter with naphtha, pour some from its original can into a smaller bottle or other container and use a medicine dropper.

Inexpensive Lubricating Oil

A good lubricating oil for household, office, and small shop appliances that costs only a fraction of so-called "machine oil" can be made by blending medicinal mineral oil or 10-SAE automobile oil with a little kerosene to lower its viscosity. Do not, however, use this (or indeed any ordinary machine oil) on watches or fine clocks. These require special oils that do not gum up even after years of service. For motors of ¼-horsepower and larger, use 20-SAE automobile oil just as it comes.

Dry Lubricant for Wood

Melt ordinary paraffin wax in the top of a double boiler and stir in as much fine flake or powdered graphite as can be easily wet by the liquid wax. Remove from heat, pour into a square pan, and before the mixture has completely hardened cut into sticks of convenient size.

This lubricant is particularly effective on wood or other nonmetallic substances. Rub it on both of the surfaces that come in contact.

Care of Oilstones

Soak a new stone in oil for several days before using, unless it is of the oil-filled variety. Keep it in a box with a closed cover or wrap it with household plastic wrap and leave a few drops of fresh clean oil on it.

To preserve the flat even surface, sharpen tools on the entire stone surface, turning the entire stone end for end occasionally. A half-and-half mixture of machine oil and kerosene works well on most stones, although a special oil may be bought for the purpose. Some stones, such as those made from natural rock, give best results with water.

With an old cloth, wipe off dirty oil right after using the stone. If the stone gums up or becomes glazed, its cutting qualities can usually be restored with gasoline or petroleum naphtha. Scouring the stone with loose abrasive powder or with sandpaper fastened to a smooth board will sometimes help.

If a silicon-carbide stone becomes clogged, it can be renovated by heating in an oven or over a fire. Place it in an old pan to catch the oil and dirt that will ooze out. Wipe the stone dry while it is hot, then resoak in oil.

If a stone becomes uneven, its flat surface can be restored by grinding on the side of a grindstone, or rubbing down with sandstone.

Porous stones may be tempered in their cutting by filling the surface with wax or petroleum jelly.

To Clean Files

Immerse the files for several minutes in a dilute solution of sulfuric acid made by adding about 1 ounce of the concentrated acid to 4 ounces of water. (To prevent violent spattering, be sure to add the acid to the water and not vice versa! Wear rubber gloves and use a glass dish or pan.) This treatment will etch the imbedded iron and steel particles so they may readily be removed by a stiff wire brush. Next wash the files well in plain water and then coat them slightly with machine oil or penetrating oil diluted slightly with gasoline. Wipe off the excess.

Lead and brass filings lodged in the teeth can best be removed with a stiff brush.

Aluminum filings can be removed quite easily by soaking the files in a warm lye solution. The aluminum is eaten away by this, while the hydrogen gas generated in the process helps to throw out the metal particles. When using lye, again wear rubber gloves and do not spill any on your clothes or surroundings as this chemical and its solution are very caustic. After treatment, wash the files well and oil as before.

Improvised Metal Polishes

Portland cement mixed with motor oil makes a cheap and effective polish suited to rough work.

Rottenstone, mixed with household mineral oil or any other nonacid oil to a creamy consistency, also makes a good polish. Finish the job with a final rubbing of dry rottenstone or whiting.

Filling Cracks in Wood

Cracks in furniture and other woodwork, if not too extensive, can be filled with wood sawdust or file dust mixed with thin liquid glue or shellac. Mix the wood dust with the liquid until a thick paste is formed, and press into the crack with a putty knife. Let the mixture harden slightly and then rub the spot with fine sandpaper. This covers the repair with fine dust, which is held by the soft filler and conceals the defect.

Medium for Grinding Glass

Glycerin may be used instead of the usual mixture of turpentine and camphor as a medium in which to suspend emery powder in grinding glass. Glycerin has sufficient body and viscosity to carry the emery well. Because it is water soluble, it is easily washed away when the job is finished.

To Clean Wallpaper

If not too great, soil may be removed from wallpaper by rubbing it with a slice of rye bread. This does not seem so strange when we remember that many regular wallpaper-cleaning preparations are made largely from rye flour. It's the gluten in rye flour that does the trick.

Tricks in Cutting Glass

Cutting sheet glass and tubing need not be a shattering experience if you follow a few simple rules of the experts. Actually a glass cutter does not cut glass; it splits it. If the wheel is sharp and it is drawn over the glass at the right speed and pressure, it makes a fine score or groove by slightly crushing or pulverizing the glass under the edge of the wheel. The beveled sides of the wheel act as wedges which push against the sides of the groove and pry the glass apart so that the crack is started. If a crack fails to start in the cutting, tap the scratch with the ball end of the glass cutter to start a crack. Break off a narrow strip along the edges by placing the strip into a notch in the cutter and using the handle as a lever to break off the narrow strip. Glass tubing or rod is cut by nicking the surface with a triangular file.

HOW TO CUT WINDOW OR PICTURE-FRAME GLASS

1. Place several layers of newspaper or a piece of carpet on a firm level surface and place the glass pane upon this padding.

2. Make certain the glass is clean—dirty glass does not cut well and dulls the cutter.

3. Brush turpentine directly along the line to be cut. This keeps the cutter bearings from gumming and keeps the cutter sharp longer.

4. To make a straight cut, use a straightedge to guide the cutter. A wooden yardstick is ideal, since the wood will not slip as easily on glass as would metal.

5. Lubricate cutting wheel with a drop of light machine oil, and remove excess.

6. Hold the guide with one hand against the glass and hold the cutter in a vertical position in the other hand. Your forefinger should be extended along the back of the cutter with the tip of the finger down near the wheel.

7. Start the groove at the far end of the guide and draw the cutter toward you. The correct pressure is important, since too much pressure may crack the pane and both too little or too much pressure may make an unsatisfactory groove. If the correct pressure is applied and the cutter is drawn toward you at the right speed, the wheel will make a scratching sound. If the wheel is dull, or too much pressure is applied, the sound will be more like crunching than scratching. (If you doubt your judgment of this point, practice on a piece of scrap glass until you can distinguish the difference.)

8. Draw the cutter over the line once only. If it becomes necessary to correct an imperfect groove, do

not use a new cutter for this purpose—use an old one. Drawing a sharp cutter over a groove the second time dulls it.

9. Make a continuous mark all the way from one edge to the other. If made properly, a slight crack will be visible the complete length of the mark. It is best seen from the side opposite the mark.

10. To part the glass, slide the pane over to the edge of the bench or table so the score mark is parallel to and projecting about ⅛ inch beyond the edge. Holding down the portion resting on the table with one hand, grasp the projecting end between the fingertips and palm of the other hand. Apply a light pressure and the glass will part.

How to cut plate glass

Proceed as above, trying particularly to start a continuous crack along the bottom of the groove or the scratch. A sharp cutter and the right pressure will usually start this crack when the groove is scored. If the crack does not appear then, it can generally be started by turning the pane over and tapping against the unscored surface with the end of the cutter handle, directly over the line scored on the other side. A crack which is not continuous can be extended all the way along the groove by such tapping.

How to cut safety glass

This is a sandwich made of a sheet of tough plastic between two sheets of tempered regular glass. To cut it, follow these steps:

1. Score the glass along one surface in the usual way with a glass cutter.

2. Lay the glass on a table with the scored line on top, directly above and parallel with the table edge.

3. While holding down the part of the glass that is on the table with one hand, grasp the overhanging part with the other hand and press down until you see or hear the glass crack along the cut. Or you can secure the part on the table with a board held by two C-clamps, and press on the overhanging part with both hands.

4. Turn the glass over and score a second line exactly opposite the first.

5. Repeat steps 2 and 3 to break the layer of glass on the second side.

6. Work the glass back and forth to break the plastic sheet between the glass sheets. If it doesn't part readily, lay the glass over a small stick or rod, weight down the two sections to spread the cut, and separate the plastic sheet with a razor blade.

How to cut glass tubing and rod

Cut small-diameter glass tubing by first giving it a single sharp nick, at the place desired, with one corner of a triangular file. Then hold the tubing with one hand on each side of the nick, with the nick on the surface directly away from you, and apply pressure as if to bend the ends of the tube toward you. The tube will crack apart at the nick. Cut small-diameter glass rods in the same manner. To cut large-diameter tubing or rods, make a continuous scratch with the file around the entire diameter. (*Caution:* Better wear heavy gloves or wrap your hands with rags when applying pressure to prevent injury if the glass should break in the wrong place.)

Solutions for Hydroponics, or Gardening without Soil

Raising plants from solutions of chemicals in water has been practiced experimentally for more than a century. Chemiculture on a commercial scale, however, did not begin until 1929, when Dr. William F. Gericke of the University of California first made the suggestion and began the actual promotion. Previously investigators had used distilled water and expensive laboratory-pure chemicals for their experiments. Gericke proved that tap water and cheap technical and fertilizer-grade chemicals would work just as well; that indeed sometimes they would work even better because of impurities that were themselves beneficial to plant growth. He also coined the now-popular term "hydroponics," and gave impetus to a hobby that rapidly spread.

Since then an extensive investigation of hydroponics has been carried on by the U.S. Department of Agriculture, the agricultural experiment stations of many states and foreign countries, and by commercial growers. The technique has proved especially suited to growing plants in greenhouses and in arid regions where many plants will grow only poorly or not at all. As a hobby, either pure hydroponics or sand culture is ideal. It can be practiced indoors as well as out, and with little more equipment to begin with than a glass or plastic container, a single young plant, and the required solution.

If you want to try it, better first read a book on the subject, as different plants, different climate, and water of different composition may require a variation in technique. Here is a formula for a typical nutrient solution:

Ammonium phosphate, monobasic	½ oz
Potassium nitrate	2½ oz
Calcium nitrate	2½ oz
Magnesium sulfate (Epsom salts)	1½ oz

These are the amounts of major nutrients needed to make 25 gallons of solution. The ammonium phosphate and magnesium sulfate may be of technical grade and the potassium and calcium nitrates of fertilizer grade.

In addition, plants require for their growth small amounts of manganese, boron, and iron.

To make a manganese and boron solution dissolve ⅛ teaspoon of pure manganese sulfate or manganese chloride and 1 teaspoon of drugstore powdered boric acid in 1 gallon of water. Add about 4 teaspoons of this solution to each 1 gallon of the main nutrient solution as you use it.

Make an iron solution by dissolving 1 teaspoon of iron sulfate or iron citrate in 1 quart of water. Add this about twice a week to the nutrient solution in use, at the rate of 1 teaspoon to the gallon.

The following formula has been recommended for making 25 gallons of solution for use in sand culture. It may be improved by adding small amounts of manganese, boron, and iron, as above, as the solution is used.

Ammonium sulfate	½ oz
Potassium phosphate, monobasic	1 oz
Magnesium sulfate	2 oz
Calcium nitrate	8 oz

How to Make Fertilizer by Composting

The purpose of a compost box or heap is to produce fertilizer or plant food through the decay of garbage, weeds, leaves, lawn clippings, sod, manure, or other similar matter. Properly made compost not only enriches the soil chemically, but improves its physical condition. When mixed with clay soil, for instance, it makes it looser and more crumbly, permitting better air circulation and water drainage. When applied to sandy soil, it increases the water-holding capacity.

Make a compost heap by alternating layers of manure or vegetable matter with soil. To hasten decay, scatter a mixture of garden fertilizer and lime, or 2 parts superphosphate, 2 parts hydrated lime, and 1 part ammonium sulfate on each layer of vegetable matter, using about 10 pounds of this mixture for each 100 pounds of material to be treated. When the pile is completed, wet thoroughly with water and cover with soil. The soil is used to absorb the ammonia, which would otherwise escape. Decay proceeds most rapidly when the weather is warm.

Some home gardeners prefer a compost box. This is usually built square, with dimensions large enough to hold all the material to be composted. A box 6 feet square and 4 or 5 feet high should be large enough in most cases. The layers of soil, manure or other matter, and chemicals are built up in the same way as suggested for the heap.

Sterilizing Aquariums

After cleaning a fish tank, or beginning the use of a second-hand one, it is best to sterlize the tank before refilling it. One way to do this is to rub all the inside surfaces thoroughly with a damp cloth covered with table salt. Another is to swish around in it for a few minutes a solution of brine, made by dissolving a pound of table salt in about a quart and a half of warm water. Pour or siphon out the brine before filling with fresh water. A little remaining salt won't hurt most fish.

A third way is to fill the tank with warm water and add ¾ cup of household liquid chlorine bleach to each gallon. Immerse equipment in aquarium for 5 minutes. Then pour or siphon out this solution and rinse aquarium and equipment well with plain water. Let air for about 30 minutes before refilling with fresh water.

Salt for Sick Fish

Common table salt—the noniodized variety—is an inexpensive and effective remedy for a number of ills of freshwater fish. The salt treatment must be given in a bare tank, however, as a salt solution strong enough to cure fish ailments will kill most aquarium plants.

One of the commonest diseases of fish that responds to salt is caused by a fungus called *Saprolegnia*. It takes the form of a whitish scum, and often appears after the first stages of the disease *Ichthyophthirius*, popularly known as "Ich."

Begin the treatment by putting the fish in a tank or enameled pan containing a salt solution in the proportion of 2 level teaspoons of salt to the gallon of seasoned water. During the next 24 hours, gradually increase the salt concentration to double this amount. If the fish have not visibly improved by the next day, gradually add another 2 teaspoons of salt to the gallon. When the treatment is finished, gradually add fresh water until the salt concentration is quite low before putting the fish back in their regular tank.

Leeches will generally detach themselves from fish if you place the fish in a solution of 3 ounces of noniodized salt in a gallon of water. Leave them for about 30 minutes. Then pick off any remaining leeches with tweezers and paint the sore spots on the fish with Mercurochrome.

Removing Chlorine from Aquarium Water

If chlorine in tap water is strong enough to taste or smell, it is harmful to fish. Chlorine can be removed, however, in a number of ways. If you can wait, the cheapest and best way is to let the water stand in open containers for a day or two, thus letting the chlorine diffuse naturally into the air. You can hasten this process to a few minutes by heating the water to about 110°F (don't heat it higher, however, or you may produce undesirable changes in the water). As soon as the water has cooled to 75 or 80 degrees, it is ready for use.

Removing Chlorine with "Hypo"

You can de-chlorinate aquarium water almost instantly by stirring into it a little sodium thiosulfate, or photographer's "hypo." About ½ grain of this chemical will remove the chlorine from 1 to 6 gallons of water, depending on the concentration of the gas.

This amount of thiosulfate, dissolved in 1 ounce of water, may cost about 35 cents at an aquarium supply store. At a photographic supply store, however, you can buy a whole pound (or 14,000 times as much) of the crystalline chemical for the same price!

Don't get acid fixing powder, but just plain sodium thiosulphate or plain "hypo." Kodak puts it up in 1-pound packages.

The amount to add to the water is not critical, but don't add more than necessary. A few crystals equivalent in bulk to a 5-grain aspirin tablet should de-chlorinate at least 10 gallons of water. Dissolve them in a glass of water and then stir this solution into the bulk of the water until it is thoroughly mixed. If you can still smell chlorine, stir in a little more.

Although you may never be able to use a whole pound of hypo for de-chlorinating the water in a small aquarium, you can always share it with your fish-fancier friends, use it for removing iodine stains (see Chapter 7), or use it in various photographic processes (see Chapter 10).

Saving Money on Other Aquarium Chemicals

Tropical-fish clubs and individuals with many or large tanks can also save money by mixing their own solutions of other chemicals used for treating aquarium water or ailing fish. Books on fish care tell you what chemicals to use and in what amounts. Although aquarium stores once supplied the required solid chemicals, you may now have to hunt them down in chemical or photographic supply houses or in a friendly neighborhood drugstore.

To find out whether you would save or not by making your own solutions, just figure out how much of a given chemical you might need in a reasonable time and then compare the cost of the required amount of the chemical as contained in a prepared solution with that of the solid chemical. As a help in doing this, remember that 1 ounce of a 1 percent solution contains about 4½ grains of solid; that there are 437½ grains to an ounce, and 7,000 grains to a pound.

In figuring costs, don't let technical terminology mislead you into believing that common and cheap chemicals are rare and expensive ones. "Sodium chloride," for instance, is just common salt; "sodium bicarbonate" is ordinary baking soda; "sodium thiosulfate" is photographic "hypo"; "calcium sulfate" is gypsum or plaster of Paris; "magnesium sulfate" is Epsom salt; while "inert ingredients" generally means either plain water or common salt.

Potassium permanganate, a mild and multipurpose antiseptic used for clearing green water and treating fungus and parasitic diseases of fish, is one chemical on which you can save money by mixing your own solutions. For clearing aquarium water of bacteria and algae the usual concentration is about 1 grain of permanganate for each 8 gallons of water. To treat fungus disease, you need a stronger solution— the sick fish is held in a net for 1 minute in a solution of 1 grain of the chemical in 1 quart of water.

In a typical prepared solution, you will get just this 1 grain, dissolved in 1 ounce of water, for about 35 cents. If you bought much permanganate at this price, the cost would soon be enormous. By buying potassium permanganate in crystal form and mixing your own solutions, however, its long-term cost is negligible. From a chemical or photographic supply house (the latter can order it for you if it doesn't carry it in stock), you can get 1 pound (7,000 grains) of the crystalline chemical for about two dollars, or 4 ounces

(1,750 grains) for about one dollar. If you use a lot, either is a bargain. What you don't use in treating aquarium water and sick fish, you can use in making photographic reducers and tray-cleaning solutions (see Chapter 10).

As permanganate solutions work better when freshly made, store this chemical in dry form and mix solutions only when needed. Never, however, add the crystals directly to the tank water. First dissolve them completely in a few ounces of water in a glass and then stir the resulting solution thoroughly into the water in the tank.

Methylene blue, malachite green, and potassium dichromate are other solutions you can mix economically. Methylene blue should be of medicinal or USP grade, and malachite green should be zinc-free and not the type ordinarily used for dyeing. Both may be bought from chemical supply houses or drugstores. These are more expensive than potassium permanganate, and you don't need much, so just buy an ounce or less, if possible. Potassium dichromate can be bought at a photographic supply house for about a dollar a pound.

For convenience in use, make 5-percent stock solutions of each of these chemicals by dissolving 22 grains of dry chemical per ounce of water.

Gordon's Tropical Fish Formula

This formula, devised by the late Dr. Myron Gordon, noted geneticist of the New York Zoological Society, makes a nourishing between-live-food snack and is said to be suited to all but very small fish:

Calf's liver	1 lb
Pablum or Ceravim	14 level tablespoons
Wheat germ	6 level tablespoons
Salt	1 level tablespoon
Water	1 pint

Cut the liver into ½-inch chunks and remove all the sinewy material. Add to the water and grind to a mash, using a kitchen blender if you have one. Then drain through a fine sieve. Next add the Pablum or Ceravim and the wheat germ gradually to the mashed liver to make a thick, lumpless paste, blending in the salt at the same time.

For better keeping, package the food in small screw-top glass jars. After filling, and with the covers loosely in place, stand the jars in a pan of water and bring the water to a boil. Then turn off the heat, screw down the caps, and let the jars cool with the water. When cool, put the jars in the refrigerator, where they may be kept for a month or so.

Health Grit for Birds

This combination of calcium and carbon is a necessary staple in the diet of all caged birds. You can buy it already prepared, or you can make it from egg shells and wood charcoal.

Dry several egg shells in the oven until they are light brown. Crush them into a powder by rolling a bottle over them on a flat surface. Powder an equal amount of wood charcoal by the same method and mix the two thoroughly. Place in a bottle cap or a small feeding dish in the bird's cage.

To Remove Odor from Cats and Dogs

When your dog smells "doggy" or your cat smells "catty," bathe him with a solution of ½ cup of liquid chlorine bleach to each gallon of lukewarm suds. Rinse and dry. This antiseptic bath aids in ridding animals of odors and helps prevent the spread of infection.

Dog and Cat Repellent Powder

Place the following ingredients in a box or bag and shake together for several minutes. Be careful not to inhale the dust or get it in your eyes. Sprinkle where desired.

Cayenne pepper	1 oz
Powdered mustard	1½ oz
Flour	2½ oz

Dog and Cat Repellent Spray

To keep dogs and cats from outdoor structures of wood, concrete, or stone, spray these with a concentrated solution of moth flakes (naphthalene or paradichlorobenzene) in mineral spirits or painter's naphtha. The solvent will evaporate, leaving crystals of the moth repellent in the structure. For a long time these will give off vapors that are distasteful to animals as well as to moths.

To Prolong the Shelf Life of Dry Cells

Even when not being used, dry cells will deteriorate with time. What is called the "shelf life" of a battery is the length of time the battery can be stored at room temperature (70°F) and still retain approximately 90 percent of its original capacity.

In general, a dry battery will operate more efficiently at higher temperatures. Its shelf life, however, will be extended if the battery is stored at lower temperatures. This is because the chemical reactions that cause deterioration slow down as temperature is decreased.

Tests made by the Naval Ordnance Laboratory, the National Bureau of Standards, and the military and scientific laboratories of a number of European countries bear this out. According to these tests, unused dry cells lose about 21 percent of their capacity in a year when stored at 70°F. Sealed in moisture-proof plastic bags, there was a loss of 11 percent when stored at 40°F, 7 percent at 10°F, and a mere 2.5 percent when stored in a deep freeze at 30 below zero.

To keep dry cells for a long time at peak capacity, wrap them tightly in polyethylene film (heat-sealing the joints, if possible) and store them at temperatures of 0°F or below in a freezer. While the cells are frozen, avoid unnecessary handling as this might crack the internal and external seals, which become brittle at low temperatures. Before using them, allow the cells to warm up to room temperature in their wrappings.

For shorter periods of storage, wrap the cells similarly and keep them in the household refrigerator. In this case, they need not be warmed up before use.

Determining the Charge of Car Batteries

The relative state of charge of a car storage battery can be determined either by measuring the specific gravity of the electrolyte in its cells with a hydrometer, or by measuring their voltage. As a battery hydrometer is considerably cheaper than a sufficiently accurate voltmeter, the hydrometer method is the one generally used.

The hydrometer is a simple glass barrel syringe enclosing a calibrated float. When a sample of the electrolyte from a battery cell is drawn up by the syringe, the stem of the float projects above the level of the liquid to a degree depending on the liquid's density. The specific gravity is then read directly on a scale inside the steam. (For more about hydrometers and specific gravity, see the next chapter.)

The specific gravity of a typical fully charged automobile battery is approximately 1.260. In other words, its acid content makes the electrolyte 1.26 times as heavy as plain water. As the battery is discharged, more and more of the acid combines with the plates, diluting the electrolyte and so causing it to become lighter. At the same time, voltage drops.

To help you check the state of charge of your battery, here are specific gravity and open-circuit voltage readings for a standard battery at 80°F and various states of charge:

State of charge	Specific gravity	Open circuit cell voltage*
100%	1.260	2.10
75%	1.230	2.07
50%	1.200	2.04
25%	1.170	2.01
Discharged	1.110	1.95

*This voltage is given to the nearest hundredth of a volt, and should be taken when a battery is not on charge and is not being discharged. The battery also should not have been charged during the previous 16 hours, as charging produces a higher voltage which may persist for about that length of time.

As specific gravity is also affected by expansion and contraction of the electrolyte caused by changes in temperature, the following corrections should be applied to obtain precise readings:

Above 80°F—Add .004 to the hydrometer reading for each 10° that the electrolyte temperature exceeds 80°F.

Below 80°F—Subtract .004 from the hydrometer reading for each 10° that the electrolyte temperature is below 80°F.

How to Measure Relative Humidity

When we complain about the "humidity," we generally mean the high relative humidity often suffered in hot summer weather. Relative humidity is simply the relationship between the amount of moisture in the air to the amount it can hold. As hot air can hold more moisture than cold air, one way to reduce the relative humidity is to pass it through the cooling system of an air conditioner or a dehumidifier.

For the sake of health and comfort, however, it is also important to *add* moisture to hot indoor air in winter. For cold outdoor air, even when saturated, becomes drier than the air over the Sahara when brought indoors and heated to 70 or 80 degrees.

For greatest comfort at ordinary indoor temperatures, the relative humidity should be kept somewhere between about 30 and 45 percent.

The most reliable indicator of relative humidity for home use (the dial type that comes with thermometer and barometer sets is usually notoriously inaccurate) is the wet-and-dry-bulb type. This consists simply of a pair of thermometers, mounted vertically side by side, one of which has a piece of wet cloth wrapped around its bulb. When fanned strongly, either by hand or by an electric fan, evaporation of moisture from the cloth on the wet bulb causes the temperature on that thermometer to read lower than that on the dry-bulb thermometer. To find the relative humidity from these readings, merely subtract the wet-bulb temperature from the dry-bulb temperature and refer to the accompanying table.

Or if you don't have a ready-made wet-and-dry-bulb thermometer, you can improvise one from any two household or chemical thermometers, one of which has an uncovered bulb. Wet a small square of muslin thoroughly with water and wrap it about one and a half times around this bulb, tying it in place at top and bottom with thread. Place both thermometers in the breeze of a fan and read both after a minute or so. Then find the relative humidity as described above.

Temperature-Humidity Index—THI

With a ready-made or homemade wet-and-dry-bulb thermometer, you can also determine the THI or temperature humidity index. The purpose of the THI is to measure or predict human discomfort in the summertime resulting from the combined effects of temperature and humidity. To calculate the THI, add wet-bulb and dry-bulb thermometer readings, multiply the sum by 0.4 and add 15. The theory behind this measurement is that more than half the people will be uncomfortable when the THI passes 75. Practically everybody will be uncomfortable

HOW TO MEASURE RELATIVE HUMIDITY

Dry-bulb temp. °F	Depression of the wet bulb, °F									
	2	4	6	8	10	12	14	16	20	24
	Relative humidity (per cent)									
60	89	78	68	58	48	39	30	21	5	
62	89	79	69	59	50	41	32	24	8	
64	90	79	70	60	51	43	34	26	11	
66	90	80	71	61	53	44	36	29	14	
68	90	80	71	62	54	46	38	31	16	3
70	90	81	72	64	55	48	40	33	19	6
72	91	82	73	65	57	49	42	43	21	9
74	91	82	74	65	58	50	43	36	23	11
76	91	82	74	66	59	51	44	38	25	13
78	91	83	75	67	60	53	46	39	27	16
80	91	83	75	68	61	54	47	41	29	18
82	92	84	76	69	61	55	48	42	30	20
84	92	84	76	69	62	56	49	43	32	21
86	92	84	77	70	63	57	50	44	33	23
88	92	85	77	70	64	57	51	46	35	25
90	92	85	78	71	65	58	52	47	36	26
92	92	85	78	72	65	59	53	48	37	28
94	93	85	79	72	66	60	54	49	38	29
96	93	86	79	73	66	61	55	50	39	30
98	93	86	79	73	67	61	56	50	40	32
100	93	86	80	73	68	62	56	51	41	33

when it reaches 80 or above.

Cooling Capacity of Air Conditioners

The earliest home air conditioners were rated in terms of tons of refrigeration—1 ton of refrigeration being the cooling capacity of 1 ton of ice melting in 24 hours. Today air conditioners are generally rated in terms of British thermal units of heat removed per hour (Btuh or Btu/hr). One ton of refrigeration is equal to 12,000 Btu/hr.

On a clear day at noon, solar energy received by 1 square foot of horizontal area is about 290 Btu/hr.

Sandpaper to Fit the Job

Modern "sandpapers," now called "coated abrasives," are available in a number of different types, in several different coatings, and in literally hundreds of different shapes, sizes, and grades of grit. In choosing sandpaper, it is of first importance to choose the right coating and appropriate fineness of grit.

Flint, the old timer, is a soft, yellowish quartz mineral that looks much like sand. It is the cheapest material but cuts slowly and wears out quickly. Its chief usefulness today is for cleaning painted, resinous, or waxy surfaces which would clog any paper and require frequent replacement.

Garnet is the hardest of natural abrasives. Although it is more than twice as expensive as flint paper, it cuts better and lasts five times as long. It is a favorite with woodworkers for fine sanding.

Aluminum oxide is a hard, tough synthetic mineral made in the electric furnace. Made in the form of sheets, belts, and disks, aluminum oxide paper is fast becoming the most widely-used all-around paper.

Silicon carbide, another product of the electric furnace, is the hardest of all common abrasives. Materials coated with it are used in finishing metals, stone, and plastics. The finest grades are used either dry, or mixed with water or rubbing oil, for polishing varnish, shellac, and lacquer finishes.

What grit size to use? Modern abrasives come in grits as fine as baby powder and as coarse as gravel. The old grading system, using arbitrary numbers from an ultra-coarse 4 up to a super-fine 10/0, is inadequate for the wide range of present abrasives and is being replaced by a system based on mesh sizes that grains must pass through. Leaving out sizes too coarse for smoothing purposes, the accompanying table shows the corresponding numbers for all classifications.

GRIT AND GRADE NUMBERS OF ABRASIVES

	Flint	Garnet	Aluminum oxide	Silicon carbide
			12/0 — 600	600
			11/0 — 500	500
			10/0 — 400	400
			9/0 — 320	320
Extra fine		8/0 — 280	8/0 — 280	280
	5/0	7/0 — 240	7/0 — 240	240
Very fine	4/0	6/0 — 220	6/0 — 220	220
	3/0	5/0 — 180	5/0 — 180	180
	2/0	4/0 — 150	4/0 — 150	150
Fine	1/0	3/0 — 120	3/0 — 120	120
	½	2/0 — 100	2/0 — 100	100
Medium	1	1/0 — 80	1/0 — 80	80
	1½	½ — 60	½ — 60	60
Coarse	2	1 — 50	1 — 50	50

In finishing wood, you might use 60 grit for coarse sanding, 80 for smoothing, and 120 to 220 for finishing. On metals you would probably use no coarser grit than 80 and, in some cases, run up to the very finest.

Smoothing paints or other fine finishes, on wood or metal, will require very fine grits. The first coat might be smoothed with 220 grit, the second with 320, and the third with 400. You might use light oil with the last rubbing.

At the other extreme is floor sanding, where 30 grit may be used for removing the old finish, 40 or 50 for smoothing, and 80 or 100 for final sanding.

Coated abrasives can also be used for sharpening tools. For average sharpening, the grit sizes will be about the same as the grinding wheels used for the same purpose, say 40 or 50 grit for rough sharpening and 100 or 120 for finishing.

For work on specialized materials such as glass, marble, gems, and plastics, it would be best to consult a textbook on the proper grits for each particular substance.

Closed or open coating? Abrasive papers come in two types of coatings. Closed-coat papers have tightly packed grains that cover the entire surface; opencoat papers have grains that cover only 50 to 70 percent of the surface. The closed-coat cuts faster, but is more apt to become clogged when used on soft materials. Use open-coat on soft or gummy woods, paint, and other finishes, and on some soft metals and plastics.

Which abrasive for what? The object here is to choose the one that cuts fastest and most efficiently with a given material. With some materials, not all experts agree. The accompanying chart (Selecting an Abrasive), however, will serve as a guide.

Trade names of different abrasives. Flint and garnet papers are so marked on the back, but the synthetic abrasives may carry only trade names. Here are a few. For *aluminum oxide:* Adalox, Luminite, Luminox, Metalite, Three-M-ite, Alundum, Jewelox, Aloxite. For *silicon carbide:* Tri-M-ite, Carborundum, Durite, Crystolon, Jewlite, Amunite.

SELECTING AN ABRASIVE FOR DIFFERENT MATERIALS

	Aluminum oxide	Silicon carbide	Garnet
Ceramics (to shape and sand)		x	
Floors (to sand)		x	
Gems (to cut and shape)		x	
Glass (to shape and sand)		x	
Leather (to shape and sand)	x	x	
Metals, hard (to shape and sand)	x		
Metals, soft (to shape and sand)	x	x	
Metals, hard (to polish)	x		
Metals (to remove rust and dirt)	x		
Paint (to smooth)	x	x	
Plastics (to shape and sand)		x	
Wood (to hand-shape and sand)			x
Wood (to power-shape and sand)	x		x
Tools (to sharpen)	x		

Other Finishing Abrasives

Steel wool in rolls or pads from the local grocery store is familiar to everyone as an aid in cleaning food from pots and pans, rust from tools, and paint and varnish from anything in paint removal jobs. Pads of finer grade are sold in hardware, paint, and craft stores for the final finishing of wood. They are graded No. 0 as Fine, 2/0 Very Fine, 3/0 Extra Fine, and 4/0 as Finest. When using 3/0 or 4/0, better wear gloves to keep from getting steel "splinters" in your fingers.

Pumice is a time-honored abrasive powder of volcanic origin used for rubbing down the final finish coat. It comes in four grades, with 4/0 the finest and 0 the coarsest. Lubricate it with water or oil.

Rottenstone, a decomposed siliceous limestone, is still softer and finer than pumice and is sometimes used after it to give a higher sheen.

17

Calculations
and Conversions

HOW TO COMPUTE CIRCUMFERENCE,
AREA, AND VOLUME

All dimensions should be expressed in terms of the same unit—say in inches or centimeters. The computed areas will then be in terms of square inches or square centimeters, and the volumes in terms of cubic inches or cubic centimeters, and so on depending on the unit used.

Circumference
Circumference of a circle: Diameter times 3.1416.

Area
Triangle: Multiply length of base by height and divide by 2.

Square: Square the length of one side.

Rectangle: Multiply the length of the base by the height.

Regular polygons

> *Pentagon (5 sides):* Square length of one side and multiply by 1.720.

> *Hexagon (6 sides):* Square length of one side and multiply by 2.598.

> *Octagon (8 sides):* Square length of one side and multiply by 4.828.

Circle: Multiply the square of the radius by 3.1416.

Ellipse: Multiply long diameter by short diameter by 0.7854.

Sphere: Multiply square of the diameter by 3.1416.

Cylinder: Add area of both ends to the circumference times height.

Cube: Square length of one side and multiply by 6.

Volume

Pyramid: Multiply area of the base by the height and divide by 3.

Cube: Cube the length of one edge.

Rectangular solid: Multiply length by width by height.

Cylinder: Multiply the square of the radius of the base by 3.1416, then multiply by the height.

Sphere: Multiply the cube of the radius by 3.1416, then multiply by 4 and divide by 3.

Cone: Multiply the square of the radius of the base by 3.1416, then multiply by the height and divide by 3.

WATER WEIGHTS AND MEASUREMENTS

A gallon of water weighs 8.336 pounds and contains 231 cubic inches.

A cubic foot of water contains 7½ gallons, 1728 cubic inches and weighs 62.4 pounds.

To find the pressure in pounds per square inch at the base of a column of water, multiply the height of the column in feet by 0.433.

TEMPERATURE CONVERSIONS

Temperature in everyday usage may be stated either in degrees Fahrenheit (°F) or in degrees Celsius or centigrade (°C). (Although the term "centigrade" is still often used in the United States, it was recommended by the International Committee on Weights and Measures and the National Bureau of Standards in 1948 that the term be officially changed to "Celsius," after Anders Celsius, the Swedish astronomer who invented the scale.)

Both scales are based on two fixed temperature points, the melting point of ice and the boiling point of water at normal atmospheric pressure.

On the Fahrenheit scale (named after Gabriel Daniel Fahrenheit, who devised it in 1714) the ice point is 32°, and the steam point is 212°. The interval between these points is divided into 180 parts or degrees.

On the Celsius scale (commonly used in most of the rest of the world, and for scientific work in the United States), the ice point is 0 and the steam point is 100, with the interval between divided into 100 parts or degrees.

By extending their scales beyond the ice point and the boiling point, both systems may be carried down to *absolute zero*, the temperature at which molecular motion ceases, and upward indefinitely as no upper limit to temperature is known.

On the Celsius scale, absolute zero is —273.16 degrees.

On the Fahrenheit scale, absolute zero is —459.69 degrees.

Fahrenheit to Celsius (or Centigrade)

To convert from degrees Fahrenheit to degrees Celsius, first subtract 32 from the number of degrees F, then multiply the remainder by 5/9 (or 0.556).

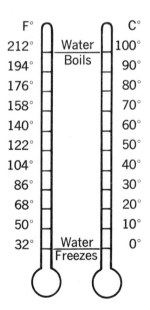

Comparison between Fahrenheit and Celsius scales, showing boiling and freezing point of water.

F°		C°
212°	Water Boils	100°
194°		90°
176°		80°
158°		70°
140°		60°
122°		50°
104°		40°
86°		30°
68°		20°
50°		10°
32°	Water Freezes	0°

Celsius to Fahrenheit

To convert from degrees Celsius to degrees Fahrenheit, multiply the number of degrees C by 9/5 (or 1.8) and add 32.

Two-way Temperature Conversion Table

Find the temperature you want to convert—either Fahrenheit or Celsius (Centigrade)—among the boldface numbers in the center column. Then look to the appropriate column to the left or right to find the temperature you want to convert to.

°C		°F
—273.16	—459.69	
—184	—300	
—169	—273	—459.4
—157	—250	—418
—129	—200	—328
—101	—150	—238
—73.3	—100	—148
—45.6	—50	—58
—40.0	—40	—40
—34.4	—30	—22
—28.9	—20	—4
—23.3	—10	14
—17.8	0	32
—12.2	10	50
—6.67	20	68
—1.11	30	86
4.44	40	104
10.0	50	122

°C		°F
15.6	60	140
21.1	70	158
23.9	75	167
26.7	80	176
29.4	85	185
32.2	90	194
35.0	95	203
36.7	98	208.4
37.8	100	212
43	110	230
49	120	248
54	130	266
60	140	284
66	150	302
93	200	392
121	250	482
149	300	572

The Kelvin Scale

There is a third temperature scale that you may often read about but which—unless you are a physicist—you may never have occasion to use. It is an absolute temperature scale called the Kelvin scale, after William Thomson, Lord Kelvin. This uses the Celsius unit for its degree but places its 0 at absolute zero. The ice point then becomes 273.16°K and the boiling point 373.16°K. To convert Celsius to Kelvin, just add 273.16 degrees to the Celsius reading.

PERCENTAGE SOLUTIONS

Ordinarily percentage solutions may be made by dissolving an "X" amount of a chemical in enough water or some other solvent to make 100 parts. It becomes more complicated, however, when you have to dilute a solution of less than 100 percent to make another percent. In such a case, this simple criss-cross method will help:

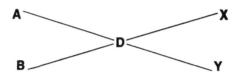

To figure dilutions by this method:
1. Place the percentage strength of the solution to be diluted at A.
2. Place the percentage of the diluting solution at B. (Water should be entered as zero.)
3. Place the percentage desired at D.
4. Subtract D from A and place the answer at Y.
5. Substract B from D and place at X.

Then mix X parts of A with Y parts of B to make the percent solution at D.

For example, to dilute 28-percent ammonium hydroxide to make a 5-percent solution:

Just add 5 parts of 28-percent ammonium hydroxide to 23 parts of water.

HOUSEHOLD WEIGHTS AND MEASURES

Weighing with Coins

Lack small weights for your balance? U.S. coins will serve quite well as substitutes. Here are their approximate values:

Dime	40 grains or	2½ grams
Cent	50 grains or	3⅛ grams
Nickel	80 grains or	5 grams
Quarter	100 grains or	6¼ grams
Half-dollar	200 grains or	12½ grams

An ounce equals 437.5 grains, therefore 2 half-dollars and a dime combined are near enough to serve as a 1-ounce weight.

Measuring with Coins

Ever caught without a ruler when you needed to know the thickness of a board? Money will help. The diameter of a U. S. cent is ¾ inch. Hold a penny against the edge of the stock and you can judge its thickness: ⅝, ¾ inch or whatever.

Coins are also handy for determining the nominal sizes of steel water pipe. If the inside diameter of a pipe is about half the diameter of a quarter, it is nominal ⅜-inch pipe. If it is somewhat smaller than a dime, it is ½-inch pipe. If a penny fits inside loosely, you have ¾-inch pipe. In 1-inch pipe a quarter will fit loosely, but a half-dollar won't go. If the opening is twice the diameter of a dime, the pipe is 1¼ inches. Combined diameters of a nickel and a penny approximately equal the inside diameter of 1½-inch pipe. A half-dollar and a nickel add up to 2-inch pipe.

Approximate Household Measures

The following will be more accurate if you use standard measuring cups and measuring spoons.

1 teaspoon	1/6 fluid ounce
1 teaspoon	1.33 fluid drams
1 teaspoon	5 milliliters
1 teaspoon	5 medicine droppers
1 teaspoon	75 to 100 drops
1 tablespoon	½ fluid ounce
1 tablespoon	4 fluid drams
1 tablespoon	14.5 milliliters
1 tablespoon	3 teaspoons
1 cup	8 fluid ounces
1 cup	64 fluid drams
1 cup	237 milliliters
1 cup	48 teaspoons
1 cup	16 tablespoons
1 pint (liquid)	16 fluid ounces
1 pint	128 fluid drams
1 pint	473 milliliters
1 pint	96 teaspoons
1 pint	32 tablespoons
1 pint	2 cups
1 medicine dropper	about 20 drops
1 medicine dropper	1 milliliter (approx.)
1 grain	1 drop (approx.)
1 ounce	437.5 grains
1 ounce	28.35 grams
1 fluid ounce	8 fluid drams

1 fluid ounce	30 milliliters
1 fluid ounce	2 tablespoons
1 fluid ounce	6 teaspoons
1 quart (liquid)	0.946 liter
1 liter	1.056 quarts
1 gallon	8.33 pounds of water
1 gallon	231 cubic inches
1 gallon	0.1337 cubic foot
1 cubic foot of water	7.5 gallons

FRACTIONS OF AN INCH WITH DECIMAL AND METRIC EQUIVALENTS

	Fractions of an inch		Decimals of an inch	Millimeters
		1/64	0.0156	0.379
	1/32		0.0313	0.794
		3/64	0.0469	1.191
	1/16		0.0625	1.588
		5/64	0.0781	1.984
	3/32		0.0938	2.381
		7/64	0.1094	2.778
⅛			0.1250	3.175
		9/64	0.1406	3.572
	5/32		0.1563	3.969
		11/64	0.1719	4.366
	3/16		0.1875	4.763
		13/64	0.2031	5.159
	7/32		0.2188	5.556
		15/64	0.2344	5.933
¼			0.2500	6.350
		17/64	0.2656	6.747
	9/32		0.2813	7.144
		19/64	0.2969	7.541
	5/16		0.3125	7.938
		21/64	0.3281	8.334
	11/32		0.3438	8.731
		23/64	0.3594	9.128

	Fractions of an inch		Decimals of an inch	Millimeters
3/8			0.3750	9.525
		25/64	0.3906	9.922
	13/32		0.4063	10.319
		27/64	0.4219	10.716
	7/16		0.4375	11.113
		29/64	0.4531	11.509
	15/32		0.4688	11.906
		31/64	0.4844	12.303
1/2			0.5000	12.700
		33/64	0.5156	13.097
	17/32		0.5313	13.494
		35/64	0.5469	13.891
	9/16		0.5625	14.288
		37/64	0.5781	14.684
	19/32		0.5938	15.081
		39/64	0.6094	15.478
5/8			0.6250	15.875
		41/64	0.6406	16.272
	21/32		0.6563	16.669
		43/64	0.6719	17.066
	11/16		0.6875	17.463
		45/64	0.7031	17.859
	23/32		0.7188	18.256
		47/64	0.7344	18.653
3/4			0.7500	19.050
		49/64	0.7656	19.447
	25/32		0.7813	19.844
		51/64	0.7969	20.241
	13/16		0.8125	20.638
		53/64	0.8281	20.034
	27/32		0.8438	21.431
		55/64	0.8594	21.828
7/8			0.8750	22.225
		57/64	0.8906	22.622
	29/32		0.9063	23.019
		59/64	0.9219	23.416
	15/16		0.9375	23.813
		61/64	0.9531	24.209
	31/32		0.9688	24.606
		63/64	0.9844	25.003
			1.0000	25.400

SHORTCUT CALCULATIONS FOR HOME AND SHOP PROBLEMS

How much paint? When painting the exterior of a house, figure the number of square feet of area to be covered. Subtract floor and window areas. Add 10 percent to any area covered by narrow lap siding, 20 percent to any that is unusually rough or porous, 30 percent if corrugated. For the first coat on concrete blocks add 50 percent.

Multiply your final figure by the number of coats you intend to put on, then divide by the manufacturer's square-feet-per-gallon coverage figure. When this figure isn't available, divide by 500 to get the minimum gallons you'll need.

How much wallpaper? Although wallpaper is calculated on the basis of single rolls, it is actually sold by what are called double rolls 16 yards long and 18 inches wide.

For a quick figure on the number of rolls needed for a room, measure the distance around the room in yards and multiply by 2 to get the number of strips needed. Then measure the strip length you'll need and divide 16 yards by this to see how many strips you can get from a roll. Divide the total number of strips by this to find out how many rolls you will need. Savings at doors and windows usually allow for wastage.

How many concrete blocks? Find out the easy way. If they are standard 8-by-8-by-16 blocks, multiply the wall height by the length. Multiply the result by 1.2. Your answer is the number of blocks required.

For example, to find out how many blocks to buy for a wall 16 feet long by 8 feet high: 16 x 8 x 1.2 gives 154 blocks, approximately.

Estimating cedar shingles. The standard unit of packing for cedar shingles is a "square"—which means 100 square feet of roof when used in a particular way. Four bunches of 16-inch shingles make a square—or cover 100 square feet when exposed 5 inches to the weather. A four-bunch square of 18-inch shingles covers 100 square feet, 5½ inches to the weather. A three-bunch square of 24-inch shingles covers 100 square feet, 10 inches to the weather.

Floor-tile count. How many standard 9-by-9 floor tiles do you need to cover a given space? Estimate the requirement this way: Multiply the floor length by the width, and then multiply the product by 1.8.

The answer includes roughly 5 percent waste allowance, depending on the size of the floor. For example, a floor 18 by 12 feet: 18 times 12 is 216. Then 216 by 1.8 gives 389 tiles.

To determine pipe size from outside dimension, remember the fraction 5/16 inch. In the nominal sizes from ⅛ through 1 inch, standard, extra-strong, and double-extra-strong pipe measures approximately 5/16 inch larger on the outside than its nominal size specification (or so close that the pipe cannot be confused for another size). Simply measure the outside diameter and subtract 5/16 inch. Example, if pipe outside diameter measures about 1-5/16": 1-5/16 minus 5/16 gives 1 inch nominal size.

Water capacity of pipes. How much flow a water pipe will deliver depends upon more than its inside diameter. (Pressure, pipe length, and lift are also involved.) But you can quickly compare the capacities of any two pipe sizes if you remember that they vary as the squares of the diameters. That's why pipe with a 1½-inch opening will deliver more than twice as much water as one with a 1-inch opening.

Nail sizes. These are pretty arbitrary, but the smaller nails fall into a pattern that can take the strain off your memory. Divide the penny size of a nail by 4 and add ½ inch to get its length in inches. Or subtract ½ inch from the inch length of a nail and multiply by 4 to get its size. Thus an 8-penny (8-d) nail is 2½ inches long (8 divided by 4 gives 2; 2 plus ½ gives 2½).

But remember this works only for nails up to 10-penny (10-d) or 3 inches.

What pulley size? When stepping up or reducing speed with pulleys, you are dealing with four factors: motor speed, drive-pulley diameter, and driven-pulley diameter. You know three of these factors and you want to find the fourth.

This is the way to figure it: Take the pulley of known diameter and speed (this may be actual or desired speed). Multiply speed by diameter and divide the result by the known diameter *or* speed (again actual or desired) of the other pulley. The result is the missing figure.

For instance: Your joiner has a 2½-inch pulley and you want it to turn at about 4,200 rpm. What

size pulley should you put on your 1,725-rpm motor
to run the joiner at that speed?

Multiply 4,200 by 2½, then divide by 1,725 and
you get just over 6. Using a 6-inch pulley on the
motor shaft will do the trick for you.

Surface speed of sander. Revolutions per minute
often must be converted into surface feet per minute
to give you the recommended speed for a sanding
drum or sanding belt (too high a speed will scorch
the material being sanded). Knowing the desired surface feet per minute, you can determine the required
rpm for the drum or the driven drum on a belt
sander. Divide the surface-feet-per-minute figure by
the drum diameter in inches multiplied by .262. Once
you have the rpm figure, use the preceding pulley
formula to get the required belt-driven ratio.

Surface feet of work in lathe in feet per minute
for a given spindle speed and work (or tool) diameter
can be determined by multiplying ¼ of the speed
by the work or tool diameter. For example: a lathe
running 400 rpm, 3-inch work diameter, what sfm or
surface feet per minute? Here's how: ¼ of 400 rpm
equals 100. 100 times 3 inches gives 300 sfm.

When you want to select a speed to give a desired surface speed, divide desired sfm by work or tool
diameter and then multiply by 4. Example: You want
300 sfm for 3-inch work diameter. Find machine
speed required this way: 300 divided by 3 inches
gives 100. 100 times 4 gives 400 rpm.

These mental calculations are accurate to something like 4 percent.

Beam stiffness. Stiffness refers to how much a beam will bend under a given weight. The formula for determining it is: width multiplied by the cube of the depth.

Comparing a full 2-by-10 with a full 4-by-6, you have 2 x 10 x 10 x 10 versus 4 x 6 x 6 x 6, giving a ratio of 2,000 to 846. So although the 4-by-6 contains more lumber and costs more, it will sag 2⅓ times as much as the 2-by-10 beam when it is carrying the same load.

Beam strength. Comparing the cross-sectional area of two beams does not necessarily give you their relative strength. For example: A full 2-by-10 joist will take about a 39-percent greater load than a full 4-by-6, although it weighs and costs one-sixth less. Use the following formula for determining the load-bearing strength: Square the dimension in the direction of the stress, and multiply that figure by the other dimension. In the case of joists the direction of stress is, of course, through the greater dimension of the beams. With the 2-by-10 you therefore get 10 x 10 x 2, or 200, as against 6 x 6 x 4, or 144 for the 4-by-6. The difference in strength between dressed lumber and its nominal size is so slight that for practical purposes it can be ignored.

Cylindrical tank capacity. Remember that a circle has approximately three-fourths the area of a square drawn around it, plus 5 percent of this figure. Multiply this total by the height or length of the tank in like units of measurement to get the volume. Convert to cubic feet and multiply the resulting figure by 7½, which is the approximate number of gallons to the cubic foot.

Spherical tank capacity. A sphere has approximately half the volume of a cube drawn around it, plus 5 percent of the figure arrived at. Again, multiply the cubic footage by 7½ to get gallons.

WEIGHT OF MATERIALS

Weight of Liquids

The old axiom "a pint's a pound the world around" is a good rule-of-thumb on which to estimate the weights of liquids. Actually a pint of water weighs just a fraction of an ounce over a pound. Pints of most watery fluids will tip the scale at about a pound. Alcohol, oil, gasoline, turpentine, and similar fluids weigh a little less. Other liquids, like carbon tetrachloride and glycerin, weigh a little more.

For an approximation of the weight in pounds of a pint of the following liquids, multiply by the first number given. The second number tells you directly the number of pounds per cubic foot.

	Specific gravity	Pounds per cubic foot
Acetone	0.792	49.4
Alcohol, ethyl	0.791	49.4
Alcohol, methyl	0.810	50.5
Benzene	0.899	56.1
Carbon tetrachloride	1.595	99.6
Ether	0.736	45.9

	Specific gravity	Pounds per cubic foot
Gasoline	0.66-0.69	41-43
Glycerin	1.26	78.6
Kerosene	0.82	51.2
Linseed oil	0.942	58.8
Mercury	13.6	849
Milk	1.028-0.1035	64.2-64.6
Sea water	0.125	63.99
Turpentine	0.87	54.3
Water	1.0	62.4

The Meaning of Specific Gravity

The number you multiply with in the above table is labeled "specific gravity" (abbreviated sp. gr.). This is simply the ratio of the weight of a substance to that of an equal volume of water at the same temperature. It can also be considered to be the *density* of a substance in terms of grams per milliliter (or cubic centimeter), for in its densest state (at 3.98°C) 1 milliliter of pure water weighs exactly 1 gram.

Knowing the specific gravity of a substance can be useful in many ways. For instance, it can help you to figure out how much of a particular substance you can fit in a bottle, or a packing case, or the trunk of your car; or, turning things around, how much a certain volume of a given substance will weigh. Then again you can often tell one pure liquid from another just by determining its specific gravity. By the same means, you can also determine the concentration of certain acids and salt solutions, the percentage of alcohol in liquors and anti-freeze, and even the charge on the battery in your car.

Determining Density with a Hydrometer

Measurement of the specific gravity of liquids is conveniently done with a *hydrometer*, a simple device of glass that is floated in a sample of the liquid to be tested. The calibrated stem of the hydrometer projects at a height out of the liquid depending upon the liquid's density.

Hydrometers are made with special scales for testing alcohol, milk and oils, sugar solutions, and the relative condition of battery charge. Most hydrometers, however, read either directly in specific gravity or in degrees Baumé (Bé). The latter system of units was devised in 1768 by the French chemist Antoine Baumé in an attempt to provide a simpler scale. In fact, he devised two scales—one for liquids lighter than water, and one for those heavier. Because the Baumé hydrometer, with its uniformly spaced divisions, was easy to make and easy to read, it caught on quickly and is used for some purposes to this day. The Baumé scale is, though, purely arbitrary, and so you often have to convert it into specific gravity to con tinue your calculations. To help you in this, here is the relationship between the two systems:

DEGREES BAUMÉ (AMERICAN)—SPECIFIC GRAVITY CONVERSION TABLE READINGS AT 60°F (15.55°C)

Specific gravity	Light Baumé degrees	Heavy Baumé degrees	Pounds per gallon	Gallons per pound
0.6600	82		5.50	0.1818
0.6731	78		5.60	0.1786
0.6863	74		5.72	0.1748
0.7000	70		5.83	0.1715
0.7071	68		5.89	0.1698
0.7216	64		6.01	0.1664
0.7368	60		6.14	0.1629
0.7527	56		6.27	0.1595
0.7692	52		6.41	0.1560
0.7685	48		6.55	0.1527
0.8046	44		6.70	0.1493
0.8235	40		6.86	0.1458
0.8434	36		7.03	0.1422
0.8642	32		7.20	0.1389
0.8861	28		7.38	0.1355
0.9091	24		7.57	0.1321
0.9333	20		7.78	0.1285
0.9589	16		7.99	0.1252
0.9722	14		8.10	0.1235
0.9859	12		8.21	0.1218
1.000	10	0	8.33	0.1200
1.007		1	8.38	0.1193
1.014		2	8.46	0.1182
1.021		3	8.50	0.1176
1.028		4	8.56	0.1168
1.043		6	8.69	0.1151
1.058		8	8.81	0.1135
1.074		10	8.94	0.1119
1.090		12	9.08	0.1101
1.107		14	9.21	0.1086
1.124		16	9.36	0.1068
1.142		18	9.51	0.1052
1.160		20	9.67	0.1034

Specific gravity	Light Baumé degrees	Heavy Baumé degrees	Pounds per gallon	Gallons per pound
1.198		24	9.99	0.1001
1.239		28	10.32	0.0969
1.283		32	10.69	0.0935
1.330		36	11.09	0.0902
1.381		40	11.51	0.0869
1.436		44	11.96	0.0836
1.495		48	12.45	0.0800
1.559		52	12.99	0.0769
1.629		56	13.57	0.0737
1.706		60	14.21	0.0704

SPECIFIC GRAVITY AND WEIGHT
OF COMMON SOLIDS

Substance	Specific gravity	Weight in pounds per cubic foot
Acrylic plastics	1.18	74
Aluminum, hard-drawn	2.7	168
Asbestos	2.0-2.8	125-175
Asphalt	1.1-1.5	69-94
Basalt	2.4-3.1	150-190
Beeswax	0.96-0.97	60-61
Brass	8.2-8.7	511-543
Brick	1.4-2.2	87-137
Bronze	8.74-8.89	545-554
Cement, portland	1.5	94
Cement, set	2.7-3.0	170-190
Chalk	1.9-2.8	118-175
Clay	1.8-2.6	112-162
Coal, anthracite	1.4-1.8	87-112
Coal, anthracite, piled		47-58
Coal, bituminous	1.2-1.5	75-94
Coal, bituminous, piled		40-54
Concrete	2.3	145

Substance	Specific gravity	Weight in pounds per cubic foot
Copper, hard-drawn	8.89	555
Cork	0.22-0.26	14-16
Earth, dry, loose		65-88
Earth, moist, compacted		95-135
Glass, common	2.4-2.8	150-175
Glass, flint	2.9-5.9	180-370
Gold, wrought	19.33	1207
Granite	2.46-2.76	165-172
Gravel, damp, loose		82-125
Gravel, dry, compacted		90-145
Gypsum	2.31-2.33	144-145
Ice	0.917	57
Iron, cast gray	7.03-7.13	439-445
Iron, wrought	7.8-7.9	487-492
Ivory	1.83-1.92	114-120
Lead	11.0	687
Lime	0.87-1.2	53-75
Magnesium	1.74	109
Marble	2.6-2.8	160-177
Nickel	8.6-8.9	537-556
Paraffin	0.87-0.91	54-57
Phenolic plastic, cast	1.27-1.31	79-82
Platinum	21.37	1334
Polyethylene	0.92	57
Sand, dry, compacted		110
Sand, damp, loose		94
Sandstone	2.14-2.35	134-147
Silver, wrought	10.6	662
Snow, fresh fallen		5-12
Snow, wet, compact		15-20
Steel	7.83	489
Styrene plastic	1.06	66
Tar	1.02	64
Tin	7.29	455
Vinyl plastic	1.4	87
Zinc	7.1	443

SPECIFIC GRAVITY AND WEIGHT
OF WOODS

Wood, seasoned	Specific gravity	Weight in pounds per cubic foot
Apple	0.66-0.84	41-52
Ash	0.65-0.85	40-53
Balsa	0.11-0.14	7-9
Basswood	0.32-0.39	20-37
Beech	0.70-0.90	43-56
Birch	0.51-0.77	32-48
Blue gum	1.00	62
Box	0.95-1.16	59-72
Butternut	0.38	24
Ebony	1.11-1.33	69-83
Greenheart (British Guiana)	1.06-1.23	66-77
Hickory	0.60-0.93	37-58
Ironwood, black	1.08	67
Lignum vitae	1.17-1.33	73-83
Mahogany, Honduras	0.66	41
Mahogany, Spanish	0.85	53
Maple	0.62-0.75	39-47
Oak	0.60-0.90	37-56
Pine, pitch	0.83-0.85	52-53
Pine, white	0.35-0.50	22-31
Pine, yellow	0.37-0.60	23-37
Redwood	0.44	27
Satinwood	0.95	59
Spruce	0.48-0.70	30-44
Teak, Indian	0.66-0.88	41-55
Teak, African	0.98	61
Walnut	0.64-0.70	40-43
Willow	0.40-0.60	24-37

SPECIFIC GRAVITY AND WEIGHT
OF GASES

The specific gravity of gases and vapors listed below is based on a system in which the specific gravity of air is 1, the atmospheric pressure normal, and the temperature 32°F or 0°C.

Gas	Weight in pounds per cubic foot	Specific gravity
Acetylene	0.0732	0.907
Air	.0807	1.000
Ammonia	.04813	0.540
Butane, iso	.1669	2.067
Carbon dioxide	.123	1.529
Carbon monoxide	.07806	0.967
Chlorine	.2006	2.486
Ether vapor	.2088	2.586
Ethylene	.07868	0.975
Helium	.01114	0.318
Hydrogen	.00561	0.070
Mercury vapor	.56013	6.940
Methane	.04475	0.554
Nitrogen	.07807	0.967
Oxygen	.08921	1.105
Propane	.1254	1.554
Sulfur doxide	.1827	2.264
Water vapor	.05028	0.623

Multiplier Prefixes for the Metric
or International System

By combining the following prefixes with such basic unit names as meter, gram, liter, volt, ampere, or ohm, you can indicate the multiples and submultiples of the Metric or International System. For example, by combining the prefix "kilo" with "volt," you get "kilovolt," meaning "1,000 volts"; by combining "Milli" with it, you get "millivolt," or "0.001 volt."

Prefix	Abbreviation	Multiplier
tera	T	10^{12} or 1,000,000,000,000
giga	G	10^9 or 1,000,000,000
mega	M	10^6 or 1,000,000
kilo	k	10^3 or 1,000
hecto	h	10^2 or 100
deka	da	10 or 10
deci	d	10^{-1} or .1
centi	c	10^{-2} or .01
milli	m	10^{-3} or .001
micro	μ	10^{-6} or .000001
nano	n	10^{-9} or .000000001
pico	p	10^{-12} or .000000000001
femto	f	10^{-15} or .000000000000001
atto	a	10^{-18} or .000000000000000001

MISCELLANEOUS UNITS OF MEASUREMENT

AGATE: A size of type of about 5½ point. Also a printing measure of 1/14 inch used for measuring column length in periodical advertising.

ANGSTROM (A or λ): .0001 micron or 1 ten-billionth of a meter. Used in measuring the length of light waves.

ASTRONOMICAL UNIT (A.U.): A unit used in astronomy equal to the mean distance of the earth from the sun, or about 93 million miles.

BARREL (bbl): For liquids except petroleum, 31½ U.S. gallons; for petroleum, 42 gallons. For dry products except cranberries, 105 dry quarts or 7056 cubic inches; for cranberries, 5826 cubic inches. An English beer barrel holds 43.23 U.S. gallons.

BOARD FOOT (fbm): Designates lumber 12 inches by 12 inches by 1 inch, or 144 cubic inches.

BOLT: For measuring cloth, it is 40 yards. For measuring wallpaper, the bolt equals 16 yards.

CABLE'S LENGTH: At sea, 100 to 120 fathoms, or 200 to 240 yards.

CARAT (c): 200 milligrams or 3.086 grains troy. Named from the seed of the carob plant that was once used as a weight in the Mediterranean countries. Used for weighing precious stones. When spelled karat or K or KT, the term means a twenty-fourth part in expressing the proportion of fineness of a gold alloy. For example, a gold alloy containing 18/24 by weight of gold is 18 karats fine.

CHAIN (ch): The length of an actual chain used by surveyors. It is 66 feet, or 1/80 mile long, and is divided into 100 parts called links.

CUBIT: Used thousands of years ago by the Babylonians and Egyptians, the cubit was the first unit of measurement recorded in history. It represented the distance between the elbow and the tip of the extended middle finger. A modified Egyptian cubit —the Olympic cubit—was later used by the Greeks and Romans and was equal to our 18.24 inches. In English measure, the cubit became 18 inches.

ELL: The English ell is 45 inches. In the past and in different communities the value of the ell has ranged from 24.7 to 48 inches. At present in the Netherlands, the ell is the meter, or 39.37 inches. It is used for measuring cloth.

FATHOM (fath): Originally the distance to which a man could stretch his arms. Now standardized as

6 feet. Used chiefly for measuring cables and depth of water.

FURLONG: In Anglo-Saxon times, the furlong meant what its name said—a furrow's length, or the length of an average furrow plowed by a farmer. Today it means 40 rods or 220 yards.

HAND: Derived from the width of the hand, this measurement is now 4 inches or 10.16 centimeters. Used for measuring the height of horses.

HOGSHEAD (hhd): A wine and other liquid measure, once quite variable but now standardized at 63 U.S. gallons or 238.5 liters.

KNOT: This is not a unit of distance, but a rate of speed of 1 nautical mile an hour. It is therefore not correct to say a ship travels "at 28 knots *an hour*"; she travels simply "at 28 knots."

LEAGUE: A unit used in different countries and at different times to mean distances varying from about 2.4 to 4.6 miles. In English-speaking countries it now usually means 3 miles—either nautical or statute—but is generally used vaguely or poetically.

LIGHT-YEAR: Nearly 6 trillion miles, the distance light travels in a year at the rate of more than 186,000 miles a second. Used for measuring distances in interstellar space.

LINK: One-hundredth part of a chain, or 7.92 inches. Used by surveyors.

MAGNUM: Wine or spirit bottle holding about 2/5 gallon, or the amount such a bottle will hold.

MICRON (μ): One thousandth of a millimeter. Used for scientific measurements.

MIL: One thousandth of an inch. Used especially for measuring the diameter of wire. A *circular mil* represents the area of a circle 1 mil in diameter. The area of a cross-section of wire is generally expressed in circular mils.

NAUTICAL MILE: Theoretically equal to 1 minute or 1/21600 part of a great circle of the earth, or roughly 1-1/6 land miles. As the earth is not a perfect circle, various lengths have been assigned to it in different times and places. The British *Admiralty mile*, for instance, is equal to 6,080 feet or 1,853.2 meters. A U.S. unit no longer officially used, is 6,080.2 feet or 1,853.248 meters. An international unit equal to 6,076.115 feet or 1,852 meters has been used officially by the U.S. since 1959. The nautical mile is used in both sea and air navigation.

PICA: One-sixth inch or 12 points. Used for measurements in printing and as the name for 12-point type.

PIPE: Wine measure equal to 2 hogsheads.

POINT: Approximately 1/72 inch or 1/12 pica. Used for measuring type size.

QUIRE: Measure for paper quantity—originally 24 sheets, but now usually 25. Twenty quires make a ream.

REAM: Measure for paper quantity—originally 480 sheets, but now usually 500.

ROD: Today a rod equals 5½ yards or 16½ feet. This measure was originally determined in the 16th century by lining up 16 men, left-foot-to-left-foot, as they left church on Sunday morning.

SPAN: An English unit equal to 9 inches or 22.86 centimeters. Derived from the distance between the tip of thumb and the tip of the little finger when both are outstretched.

STONE: A varying unit of weight that in the past has ranged from 4 to 26 pounds avoirdupois. In Great Britain it today has a legal value of 14 pounds.

TOWNSHIP: A division of territory in surveys of U.S. public land, measuring almost 36 square miles. The south, east, and west borders are each 6 miles long. As the latter two follow the meridians of the earth, the north border is a little shorter. Often these geological townships have later become also political townships.

TUN: The capacity of a large cask by the same name —2 pipes, 4 hogsheads, or 252 old English wine gallons (which are the same as U.S. gallons).

How Long is a Meter?

You are taught in school that the meter, the unit of length in the Metric System, is roughly 39.37 inches. Scientists who set the standards, however, have to be more precise.

As originally proposed, the meter was to be equal to one 10-millionth part of the quarter-meridian (the distance from the North Pole to the Equator) passing through Paris. To try to find out how long the quarter-meridian really was, two engineer-surveyors spent six years surveying the land between Barcelona and Dunkirk. They calculated the rest. In 1799, based on this work, a standard meter was constructed.

In 1960 the Eleventh General (International) Conference on Weights and Measures redefined the meter in terms of measurements of modern science. Today the standard meter is a unit of length equal to 1,650,763.73 wavelengths in a vacuum of the orange-red radiation of krypton 86 corresponding to the unperturbed transition between the $2p_{10}$ and $5d_5$ levels. No need now to travel to the North Pole to check your meter stick!

CONVERSIONS OF COMMON UNITS

The following table has been compiled especially for this book in the hope that it might make conversions from one measurement unit to another faster and simpler. In it common units of weight, area, volume, power, velocity, and so on are not separated into categories as is often done, but are listed in straight alphabetical order. To use it, just find in the left column the unit you want to convert, then in the middle column the one you want to convert to. Convert merely by multiplying the number of original units by the number you find directly to the right of the second unit.

To convert from such units as spoons, cups, and other household utensils, see earlier section "Approximate Household Measures," and to convert from specialized units and others not commonly used, see "Miscellaneous Units of Measurement."

Unless otherwise mentioned, all weight units are avoirdupois, and all volume units (pints, bushels, gallons, etc.) are U.S. Customary units.

CONVERSIONS OF COMMON UNITS

To convert from	to	multiply by
Acres	square feet	43,560
	square yards	4840
	square miles	0.00156
	square meters	4046.856
	hectares	0.40468
Atmospheres	pounds per sq inch	14.697
	feet of water @ 4°C	33.90
	inches of mercury @ 0°C	29.92
	millimeters mercury @ 0°C	760
Btu	calories (large)	0.252
	horsepower-hours	0.000393
	kilowatt-hours	0.000293
Btu per hour	horsepower	0.000393
	kilowatts	0.000293
Bushels	dry pints	64
	dry quarts	32
	pecks	4
	cubic feet	1.24445
	liters	35.239
	cubic yard	0.04609
Calories (large)	Btu	3.968
	watt-hours	1.1619
Candles per sq cm	Lamberts	3.142
Candles per sq inch	Lamberts	0.4869
Centimeters	inches	0.3937
	feet	0.0328
Chains (surveyor's)	feet	66
	rods	4
Cubic centimeters	cubic inches	0.06102
Cubic feet	cubic inches	1728
	cubic meters	0.028317
	cubic yards	0.037037
	gallons	7.48
	liters	28.32
Cubic feet of water	pounds @ 60°F	62.37
	gallons	7.481

To convert from	to	multiply by
Cubic inches	fluid ounces	0.554113
	quarts	0.017316
	gallons	0.004329
	milliliters	16.387064
Cubic meters	cubic feet	35.3145
	cubic yards	1.30795
Cubic yards	cubic feet	27
	cubic meters	0.76456
Drams	grains	27.34375
	drams (troy or apothecary)	0.45573
	ounces	0.0625
	ounces (troy or apothecary)	0.05697
	grams	1.771845
Drams (troy or apothecary)	grains	60
	drams (avoirdupois)	2.194286
	ounces (avoirdupois)	0.13714
	ounces (troy or apothecary)	0.125 or ⅛
	grams	3.88794
Drams (US fluid)	minims	60
	fluid ounces	0.125 or ⅛
	cubic inches	0.22559
	milliliters	3.6966
Fathoms	feet	6
Feet	centimeters	30.48
	fathoms	0.16667
	miles	0.00019
	kilometers	0.0003
Feet of water	pounds per square foot	62.42
	pounds per square inch	0.4335
	inches of mercury @ 0°C	0.88265
Feet per minute	feet per second	0.01667
Feet per second	miles per hour	0.68182
Gallons	milliliters	3785
	cubic inches	231
	cubic feet	0.1337
	cubic yards	0.00495
	cubic meters	0.00379
	fluid ounces	128
	quarts	4
	liters	3.7853
	British gallons	0.8327

To convert from	to	multiply by
Gallons of water	pounds of water @ 60°F	8.3453
Gallons (British)	pounds of water @ 62°F	10
	US gallons	1.201
Grains	ounces	0.00229
	ounces (troy or apothecary)	0.00208
	grams	0.0648
Grains per gallon	parts per million (ppm)	17.118
	grams per liter	0.01714
Grams	grains	15.432
	drams	0.56438
	drams (troy or apothecary)	0.25721
	ounces	0.03527
	ounces (troy or apothecary)	0.03215
	pound	0.0022
	pound (troy or apothecary)	0.00268
Grams per liter	grains per gallon	58.418
Hectares	square meters	10,000
	acres	2.471
Horsepower	foot-pounds per minute	33,000
	Btu per minute	42.42
	Btu per hour	2546
	metric horsepower	1.014
	kilowatts	0.7457
Inches	feet	0.08333
	yards	0.02778
	centimeters	2.54
	meters	0.0254
Inches of mercury @ 0°C	pounds per square inch	0.4912
	inches of water	13.6
Inches of water @ 4°C	ounces per square inch	0.582
	inches of mercury	0.0735
Kilograms	grains	15,432.36
	drams	564.3834
	drams (troy or apothecary)	257.21
	ounces	35.27396
	ounces (troy or apothecary)	32.15075
	pounds	2.20462
	pounds (troy or apothecary)	2.67923
	short tons	0.0011
	long tons	0.00098
	metric tons (tonnes)	0.001

To convert from	to	multiply by
Kilometers	feet	3280.8
	miles	0.62137
Kilowatts	Btu per minute	56.90
	horsepower	1.341
	metric horsepower	1.397
Kilowatt-hours	Btu	3413
Knots	nautical miles per hour	1
	miles per hour	1.1508
Lamberts	candles per sq centimeter	0.3183
	candles per sq inch	2.054
Leagues	miles	3
Links (surveyor's)	feet	0.66
	inches	7.92
	chain	0.01
	rod	0.04
Liters	fluid ounces	33.814
	quarts	1.05669
	gallons	0.2642
	British gallons	0.21998
	cubic inches	61.02374
	cubic feet	0.03531
	cubic meters	0.001
	cubic yards	0.00131
Lumens per sq foot	foot-candles	1
Lux	foot-candles	0.0929
Meters	inches	39.37
	feet	3.2808
	yards	1.094
Miles	nautical miles	0.869
	feet	5280
	yards	1760
	meters	1609.344
Miles (nautical)	statute miles	1.1508
Miles per hour	knots	0.8684
	miles per minute	0.016667
	feet per second	1.467
Miles per minute	knots	52.104
	feet per second	88
Milliliters	minims	16.231
	fluid drams	0.2705
	fluid ounces	0.0338
	cubic inches	0.061

To convert from	to	multiply by
Millimeters	inches	0.03937
Minims	fluid drams	0.016667
	fluid ounces	0.002
	milliliters	0.0616
Ounces	grains	437.5
	drams	16
	drams (troy or apothecary)	7.292
	ounces (troy or apothecary)	0.9146
	pounds	0.0625
	pounds (troy or apothecary)	0.07595
	grams	28.34952
	kilograms	0.02835
Ounces (troy or apothecary)	grains	480
	drams	17.55429
	drams (troy or apothecary)	8
	ounces (avoirdupois)	1.09714
	pound (troy or apothecary)	0.08333
	pound	0.06857
	grams	31.1035
	kilograms	0.0311
Ounces (fluid)	minims	480
	pints	0.0625
	quarts	0.03125
	gallons	0.00781
	cubic inches	1.80469
	cubic feet	0.00104
	milliliters	29.57353
	liters	0.02957
Ounces (fluid, British)	fluid ounces, U.S.	0.96
Ounces per square inch	pounds per square inch	0.0625
	inches of water	1.73
	inches of mercury	0.127
Parts per million (ppm)	grains per gallon	0.05835
Pecks	bushels	0.25 or ¼
Pints (dry)	pecks	0.0625
	bushels	0.01562
	cubic inches	33.60031
	cubic feet	0.01944
	liters	0.55061

To convert from	to	multiply by
Pints (fluid)	minims	7680
	fluid ounces	16
	fluid quart	0.5 or ½
	gallons	0.125 or ⅛
	cubic inches	28.875
	cubic feet	0.01671
	milliliters	473.17647
	liters	0.47318
Pounds	grains	7000
	drams	256
	drams (troy or apothecary)	116.6667
	ounces	16
	ounces (troy or apothecary)	14.58333
	pound (troy or apothecary)	1.21528
	grams	453.59237
	kilograms	0.453592
	short tons	0.0005
	long tons	0.000446
	metric tons	0.0004536
Pounds (troy or apothecary)	grains	5760
	drams (avoirdupois)	210.6514
	drams (troy or apothecary)	96
	ounces (avoirdupois)	13.16571
	ounces (troy or apothecary)	12
	pound (avoirdupois)	0.82286
	grams	373.24172
	kilograms	0.45359
Pounds of water	gallons	0.1198
Quarts (dry)	pecks	0.125 or ⅛
	bushels	0.03125
	cubic inches	67.2006
Quarts (fluid)	fluid ounces	32
	cubic inches	57.749
	cubic feet	0.033421
	milliliters	946.358
	liters	0.946333

To convert from	to	multiply by
Rods	chains	0.25 or ¼
Square centimeters	square inches	0.115
	square feet	0.00108
Square feet	square inches	144
	square yard	0.111111
	square centimeters	929
	square meters	0.0929
Square inches	square centimeters	6.452
Square meters	square feet	10.765
	square yard	1.196
Square miles	acres	640
	square kilometers	2.589998
Square yards	square meters	0.836
Tons (long)	pounds	2240
	kilograms	1016.0470
	short tons	1.12
	metric tons	1.016
Tons (short)	pounds	2000
	kilograms	907.185
	long tons	0.89286
	metric tons	0.907185
Tons (metric, tonnes)	pounds	2204.62
	kilograms	1000
	long tons	0.984206
	short tons	1.10231
Tons of refrigeration	Btu per hour	12,000
Watts	Btu per hour	3.415
	horsepower	0.00134
Watt-hours	Btu	3.413
Yards	centimeters	91.44
	meters	0.9144

18

Useful Information

COMMON NAILS REFERENCE TABLE

The 'd'' in nail sizes means "penny" and is the abbreviation for the Latin **denarius,** an ancient Roman coin. Originally, 2d, 10d, etc., referred to the cost in pennies for 100 nails. Now it refers to a definite size.

Size	Length and	Gage No.	Diameter Head	Approx. No. to Pound
2d	1″	15	11/64″	845
3d	1¼″	14	13/64″	540
4d	1½″	12½	¼″	290
5d	1¾″	12½	¼″	250
6d	2″	11½	17/64″	165
7d	2¼″	11½	17/64″	150
8d	2½″	10¼	9/32″	100
9d	2¾″	10¼	9/32″	90
10d	3″	9	5/16″	65
12d	3¼″	9	5/16″	60
16d	3½″	8	11/32″	45
20d	4″	6	13/32″	30
30d	4½″	5	7/16″	20
40d	5″	4	15/32″	17
50d	5½″	3	½″	13
60d	6″	2	17/32″	10

FINISHING NAILS REFERENCE TABLE

Size	Length and Gage No.		Diam. Head Gage	Approx. No. to Pound
3d	1¼"	15½	12½	880
4d	1½"	15	12	630
6d	2"	13	10	290
8d	2½"	12½	9½	195
10d	3"	11½	8½	125

CASING NAILS REFERENCE TABLE

Size	Length and Gage No.		Diam. Head Gage	Approx. No. to Pound
4d	1½"	14	11	490
6d	2"	12½	9½	245
8d	2½"	11½	8½	145
10d	3"	10½	7½	95
16d	3½"	10	7	72

Sizes of Iron, Steel, and Brass Pipe

Pipe sizes are generally determined by the inside diameter of the pipe. Does it confuse you, then, to find that to get a pipe about ¼ inch in diameter on the inside and ⅜ inch on the outside you must ask for "⅛-inch pipe"? The story behind this anomaly goes back to the days when materials were weaker and pipe of ⅜-inch outside diameter *did* have an inside diameter of only ⅛ inch. When materials became stronger and walls could be thinner, it was decided to keep the same *outside* diameter so that standard threading tools and fittings could still be used. The inside diameter of threaded iron, steel, and brass pipe therefore became somewhat larger than its nominal size. In the larger sizes the difference is small; in the smaller ones, though, it can confound you.

Here are the nominal and approximate actual dimensions of commonly used sizes of standard threaded pipe:

Nominal size	Approx. inside diameter	Approx. outside diameter	Threads per inch	Tap drill
$\frac{1}{8}$"	$\frac{1}{4}$"	$\frac{3}{8}$"	27	$\frac{11}{32}$"
$\frac{1}{4}$"	$\frac{3}{8}$"	$\frac{17}{32}$"	18	$\frac{7}{16}$"
$\frac{3}{8}$"	$\frac{1}{2}$"	$\frac{11}{16}$"	18	$\frac{37}{64}$"
$\frac{1}{2}$"	$\frac{5}{8}$"	$\frac{13}{16}$"	14	$\frac{23}{32}$"
$\frac{3}{4}$"	$\frac{13}{16}$"	1"	14	$\frac{59}{64}$"
1"	1 $\frac{1}{16}$"	1 $\frac{5}{16}$"	11½	1 $\frac{5}{32}$"
1¼"	1 $\frac{3}{8}$"	1 $\frac{5}{8}$"	11½	1 ½"
1½"	1 $\frac{5}{8}$"	1 $\frac{7}{8}$"	11½	1 $\frac{47}{64}$"
2"	2 $\frac{1}{16}$"	2 $\frac{3}{8}$"	11½	2 $\frac{7}{32}$"
2½"	2 $\frac{9}{16}$"	2 $\frac{7}{8}$"	8	2 $\frac{5}{8}$"

SIZES OF DRILLS OR BITS TO BORE HOLES FOR WOOD SCREWS

Number (gauge) of screw	Approx. diam. of screw shank	FIRST HOLE (SHANK)		SECOND HOLE (PILOT)	
		Twist-drill size	Auger size	Twist-drill size	Auger size
1	5/64	5/64			
2	3/32	3/32		1/16	
3	3/32	7/64		1/16	
4	7/64	7/64		5/64	
5	1/8	1/8		5/64	
6	9/64	9/64		3/32	
7	5/32	5/32	3	7/64	
8	11/64	11/64	3	7/64	
9	11/64	3/16	3	1/8	
10	3/16	3/16	3	1/8	
12	7/32	7/32	3	9/64	
14	15/64	1/4	4	5/32	3
16	17/64	17/64	5	3/16	3
18	19/64	19/64	5	13/64	4

Standard auger bits are sized by sixteenths of an inch. The number stamped on the square tang represents the diameter of the bit in these units. For example, a Number 3 bit will cut a hole 3/16 inch in diameter, while a Number 4 will cut a 1/4-inch hole.

COPPER WIRE TABLE

(Brown & Sharpe or American Wire Gauge)

| AWG B&S gauge | Diameter in mils | Turns per linear inch | | Feet per pound | | Ohms per 1000 ft at 68°F |
		Enamel	Double cotton covered	Bare	Double cotton covered	
1	289.3	—	—	3.947	—	.1264
2	257.6	—	—	4.977	—	.1593
3	229.4	—	—	6.276	—	.2009
4	204.3	—	—	7.914	—	.2533
5	181.9	—	—	9.980	—	.3195
6	162.0	—	—	12.58	—	.4028
7	144.3	—	—	15.87	—	.5080
8	128.5	7.6	7.1	20.01	19.6	.6405
9	114.4	8.6	7.8	25.23	24.6	.8077
10	101.9	9.6	8.9	31.82	30.9	1.018
11	90.74	10.7	9.8	40.12	38.8	1.284
12	80.81	12.0	10.9	50.59	48.9	1.619
13	71.96	13.5	12.0	63.80	61.5	2.042
14	64.08	15.0	13.8	80.44	77.3	2.575
15	57.07	16.8	14.7	101.4	97.3	3.247
16	50.82	18.9	16.4	127.9	119	4.094
17	45.26	21.2	18.1	161.3	150	5.163
18	40.30	23.6	19.8	203.4	188	6.510
19	35.89	26.4	21.8	256.5	237	8.210
20	31.96	29.4	23.8	323.4	298	10.35
21	28.46	33.1	26.0	407.8	370	13.05
22	25.35	37.0	30.0	514.2	461	16.46
23	22.57	41.3	31.6	648.4	584	20.76
24	20.10	46.3	35.6	817.7	745	26.17
25	17.90	51.7	38.6	1031	903	33.00
26	15.94	58.0	41.8	1300	1118	41.62
27	14.20	64.9	45.0	1639	1422	52.48
28	12.64	72.7	48.5	2067	1759	66.17
29	11.26	81.6	51.8	2607	2207	83.44

| AWG B&S gauge | Diameter in mils | Turns per linear inch | | Feet per pound | | Ohms per 1000 ft at 68°F |
		Enamel	Double cotton covered	Bare	Double cotton covered	
30	10.03	90.5	55.5	3287	2534	105.2
31	8.928	101	59.2	4145	2768	132.7
32	7.950	113	62.6	5227	3137	167.3
33	7.080	127	66.3	6591	4697	211.0
34	6.305	143	70.0	8310	6168	266.0
35	5.615	158	73.5	10480	6737	335.0
36	5.000	175	77.0	13210	7877	423.0
37	4.453	198	80.3	16660	9309	533.4
38	3.965	224	83.6	21010	10666	672.6
39	3.531	248	86.6	26500	11907	848.1
40	3.145	282	89.7	33410	14222	1069

A mil is 1/1000 (one-thousandth) of an inch.

Measurements of covered wires may vary slightly with different manufacturers.

Wire of size 6 and larger is always stranded. The diameters shown here, however, are those of solid wires of equivalent cross section.

Resistance of Copper Wire

In estimating the resistance of copper wire, it may help to remember several approximate relationships:

Size wire AWG, B&S	Ohms per 1,000 feet	Feet per ohm
10	1	1,000
20	10	100
30	100	10
40	1,000	1

An increase of 1 in AWG or B&S wire size increases resistance 25%

An increase of 2 increases resistance 60%

An increase of 3 increases resistance 100%

Electrical Conductivity of Metals

With the conductivity of copper rated at 100, here are the relative conductivities of other common metals. All are measured at 68°F or 20°C.

	Relative conductivity
Aluminum	59
Brass	28
Cadmium	19
Chromium	55
Climax	1.83
Cobalt	16.3
Constantin	3.24
Copper, hard drawn	89.5
Copper, annealed	100
Everdur	6
German silver, 18%	5.3
Gold	65
Iron, pure	17.7
Iron, wrought	11.4
Lead	7
Manganin	3.7
Mercury	1.66
Molybdenum	33.2
Monel	4
Nichrome	1.45
Nickel	12-16

	Relative conductivity
Phosphor bronze	36
Platinum	15
Silver	106
Steel	3-15
Tin	13
Tungsten	28.9
Zinc	28.2

Electricity Consumed by Common Appliances

The following table may help you determine the number and capacity of electrical outlets needed in your home or shop, and to estimate the operating cost of various appliances.

Electric power is charged for by the kilowatt-hour. To find out how long it takes an appliance to use this much electricity, just divide 1,000 by the wattage of the appliance. Using this method, you find you can run a 2-watt clock for 500 hours or a 100-watt lamp for 10 hours on 1 kilowatt-hour. At the other extreme, you discover that a 5,000-watt range oven will consume the same amount of power in 1/5 hour, or 12 minutes.

	Watts
Air conditioner, room	800 to 1500
Blanket	150 to 200
Blender	250
Clock	2 to 3
Coffeemaker	600 to 1000
Deep fryer	1200 to 1650

	Watts
Dishwasher	600 to 1000
Dryer, clothes	4000 to 8700
Fan, portable	50 to 200
Food mixer	120 to 250
Freezer, home	300 to 500
Frying pan	1000 to 1200
Furnace blower	800
Garbage disposal unit	200 to 400
Grill	1000 to 1200
Heat lamp	250
Heater, portable, home	600 to 1650
Heater, portable, home, 230-volt	2800 to 5600
Heating pad	50 to 75
Hot plate, each burner	550 to 1200
Iron, hand	660 to 1200
Ironer	1200 to 1650
Lamps, incandescent	2 up
Lamps, fluorescent	15 to 60
Motors: ¼-horsepower	300 to 400
½-horsepower	450 to 600
1-horsepower	950 to 1000
Projector, movie or slide	150 to 550
Radio, transistor	6 to 12
Radio, tube	35 to 150
Range, oven and all burners	8000 to 16000
Refrigerator	150 to 300
Roaster	1200 to 1650
Rotisserie-broiler	1200 to 1650
Sewing machine	60 to 90
Shaver	8 to 12
Stereo hi-fi	100 to 400

	Watts
	Watts
Television	200 to 400
Toaster	550 to 1200
Vacuum cleaner	200 to 800
Waffle iron	600 to 1100
Washing machine	400 to 800
Water heater	2000 to 5000
Water pump	300 to 700

What Size Wire for the Circuit?

The minimum size wire to be used in electrical circuits is determined both by safety and by efficiency. In all cases, wiring installations should conform to the rules of the National Electrical Code, which is based on the recommendations of the National Fire Protection Association. This Code is concerned only with preventing electrical or thermal hazards that might electrocute somebody or start a fire. Beyond the bare requirements of safety, however, circuits should be designed so they do not waste too much electricity in the form of useless heat and that they deliver it at the end of the line at a sufficiently high voltage to properly do its job.

The following table may help you meet both requirements. The first column of wire sizes indicates the minimum National Electric Code size of copper wire for a circuit of given amperage; the second column, the minimum size for the service wire that feeds the circuit. The remaining columns indicate the sizes of wires needed to carry electricity over different distances with a drop of voltage at the far end of only 3 percent. The latter figures would, of course, apply to extension cables as well as to permanent circuits.

WIRE SIZES FOR DIFFERENT LOADS
AND DISTANCES—120 VOLTS

Load in amperes	Minimum wire size (AWG)	Service wire size (AWG)	WIRE SIZE (AWG)							
			Distance in feet to load							
			50	75	100	125	150	175	200	250
15	14	10	14	12	10	8	8	6	6	6
20	14	10	12	10	8	8	6	6	6	4
25	12	8	10	8	8	6	6	4	4	4
30	12	8	10	8	6	6	4	4	4	2
35	12	6	8	6	6	4	4	4	2	2
40	10	6	8	6	6	4	4	2	2	2
45	10	6	8	6	4	4	2	2	2	1
50	10	6	8	6	4	4	2	2	2	1
55	8	4	6	4	4	2	2	2	1	0
60	8	4	6	4	4	2	2	1	1	0
65	8	4	6	4	4	2	2	1	0	2/0
70	8	4	6	4	2	2	1	1	0	2/0
75	6	4	6	4	2	2	1	0	0	2/0
80	6	4	6	4	2	2	1	0	0	2/0
85	6	4	4	4	2	1	1	0	2/0	3/0
90	6	2	4	2	2	1	0	0	2/0	3/0
95	6	2	4	2	2	1	0	2/0	2/0	3/0
100	4	2	4	2	2	1	0	2/0	2/0	3/0

Heating Values of Various Fuels

Coal—25 million BTU per ton (average)

Wood—12½ million BTU (per cord approximately)

Oil (domestic grades)—136,000 BTU per gallon

Gas (manufactured)—500 to 550 BTU per cu ft

Gas (natural)—1,000 to 1,100 BTU per cu ft

Gas (butane)—3,200 BTU per cu ft = 100,000 BTU per gallon (liquid)

Gas (propane)—2,519 BTU per cu ft = 91,044 BTU per gallon (liquid)

Electricity—3,412 BTU per kilowatt-hour

BTU Input for Domestic Gas Appliances

	Approx. input BTU per hour
Range, free standing	65,000
Built-in oven or broiler unit	25,000
Built-in top unit	40,000
Water heater (quick recovery), automatic storage—	
30-gallon tank	30,000
40-gallon tank	38,000
50-gallon tank	50,000
Water heater, automatic instantaneous	
2 gallon per minute	142,000
4 gallon per minute	285,000
6 gallon per minute	428,400
Refrigerator	3,000
Clothes dryer	35,000
Incinerator	32,000

RUBBER STOPPER SIZES
(All measurements in millimeters)

Stopper Size No.	Fits openings	Top diameter	Bottom diameter	Length
00	10 to 13	15	10	26
0	13 to 15	17	13	26
1	15 to 17	19	15	26
2	16 to 18.5	20	16	26
3	18 to 21	24	18	26
4	20 to 23	26	20	26
5	23 to 25	27	23	26
5½	25 to 26	29	25	26
6	26 to 27	32	26	26
6½	27 to 31.5	34	27	26

Stopper Size No.	Fits openings	Top diameter	Bottom diameter	Length
7	30 to 34	37	30	26
8	33 to 37	41	33	26
9	37 to 41	45	37	26
10	42 to 46	50	42	26
10½	45 to 47	53	45	26
11	48 to 51.5	56	48	26
11½	51 to 56	60	51	26
12	54 to 59	64	54	26
13	58 to 63	67	58	26
13½	61 to 70	75	61	35
14	75 to 85	90	75	39
15	83 to 95	103	83	39

How to Buy Glass

Because of improved manufacturing techniques, today's ordinary sheet glass, or "window glass," is remarkably strong and clear and has fine visual qualities. It is made by drawing sheets directly from a bath of molten glass. Although sheet glass does not have quite the optical flatness of plate glass, it is fire-polished and transparent and will ordinarily be the choice for home windows, picture protection, and glass for hotbeds and greenhouses.

Clear plate glass is glass of practically the same chemical composition, but with its surfaces ground and polished for perfect flatness. It is made in thin sizes for mirrors and for windows and in heavy thicknesses for large openings in commercial buildings, glass doorways, partitions, showcases, bookshelves, decorative panels, and so on.

Float glass is a type of flat glass made by a new process. It is flat and parallel like polished plate and may be used for the same purposes.

Listed below are the forms and sizes in which you can buy all three types:

Type of glass	Use or quality	Thickness (inches)	Maximum size (inches)
Window glass	Photo	$\frac{1}{16}$	36 x 50
	Picture	$\frac{5}{64}$	36 x 50
	Single strength	$\frac{3}{32}$	40 x 50
	Double strength	$\frac{1}{8}$	60 x 80
	Sheet	$\frac{3}{16}$	120 x 84
		$\frac{7}{32}$	120 x 84
		$\frac{1}{4}$	120 x 84
		$\frac{3}{8}$	60 x 84
		$\frac{7}{16}$	60 x 84
	Greenhouse	$\frac{1}{8}$	20 x 24
Clear polished plate	Glazing	$\frac{1}{8}$	76 x 128
		$\frac{1}{4}$	127 x 226
	Mirrors	$\frac{1}{4}$	127 x 226
	Commercial	$\frac{5}{16}$	127 x 226
		$\frac{3}{8}$	125 x 281
		$\frac{1}{2}$	125 x 281
		$\frac{3}{4}$	120 x 280
		1	74 x 148
		$1\frac{1}{4}$	74 x 148
Float glass	Glazing, mirrors	$\frac{1}{4}$	122 x 200

Frequency Range of Voices and Instruments

If your stereo hi-fi speakers cannot reach down to 20 Hz (formerly *cycles per second*) don't worry too much. No musical instrument except a pipe organ with a 32-foot pipe can go so low. The piano comes next, with its very lowest tone at 27.5 Hz. At the other extreme, the highest fundamental tone of any ordinary musical instrument—shared by the organ, piano, and piccolo—is about 4,186 Hz.

The fundamental frequencies of the singing voice range from about 65 Hz for the lowest tone of the bass to about 1,568 Hz for the highest of the soprano. The harmonics or overtones of both instruments and voices—the extra frequencies that characterize one source of sound from another—extend to about 10,000 Hz, while frequencies in a door squeak, chirping insects, or escaping steam may go beyond 16,000 Hz. It is because of these harmonics that you need good high-frequency response in your hi-fi to get completely natural sound.

To help get a clearer idea of the frequency range of orchestral instruments and human voices, see table at right based on the American standard frequency of 440 Hz for middle A. Where two frequencies are given, the first one is for special instruments.

Useful Facts About Rope

The smallest cordage that is technically called "rope" is about ½ inch in circumference and 3/16 inch in diameter.

Manila rope is the strongest and most durable rope made of natural fibers. It is made of abaca, a relative of the banana plant, and commonly called Manila fiber because it is grown almost entirely in the Philippines and shipped chiefly from the port of Manila.

Sisal rope (made often from a related fiber, henequen) is next in importance to Manila and is about 80 percent as strong. Its fiber comes from a plant in

Instrument	Frequency in Hz (cycles per second)	
	Lower limit	Upper limit
Organ	16, 32	4186
Piano	27	4186
Contra bassoon	30	175
Harp	32	3136
Bass violin	32, 41	262
Bass tuba	41	234
Trombone	51, 82	524
Bassoon	58	623
French horn	61	699
Cello	65	880
Bass clarinet	65, 73	467
E-flat baritone saxophone	69	416
B-flat tenor saxophone	103	623
Viola	131	1318
E-flat alto saxophone	138	831
English horn	164	934
Trumpet	164	1047
Violin	195	2093
Oboe	233	1397
Flute	261	2043
Piccolo	587	4186

Voice

Bass	65	294
Baritone	98	416
Tenor	123	1174
Contralto	174	933
Soprano	261	1568

the century plant family, and was formerly exported from Sisal, Yucatán.

Nylon rope, made from synthetic fibers, is more expensive than Manila rope but about twice as strong. It also has the unique property of being able to stretch about 8 percent and then return to its original length on release of its load. This property makes it extremely useful for long tow lines, or under other conditions where a sudden strong pull might snap an ordinary rope.

Dacron rope is nearly as strong as nylon, is almost impervious to moisture, is a good electrical insulator, and does not stretch at all. It is especially useful for guy lines for antennas, for outdoor clotheslines that stay taut during dry or wet weather, and for other purposes where stretch or electrical conduction would be detrimental.

Polyethylene rope, one of the newest, is about $\frac{1}{3}$ stronger than Manila rope and is the only rope that will float indefinitely on water. Because of its latter ability, polyethylene rope is becoming standard for lifelines and for tow ropes in water skiing.

ROPE SIZES AND STRENGTHS
FOR 3-STRAND MANILA AND SISAL ROPE
WITH STANDARD LAY
(For safe loads, allow at least a 5 to 1 safety factor)

NOMINAL SIZE				MINIMUM BREAKING STRENGTH, POUNDS	
Threads	Circumference, inches	Diameter, inches	Weight per 100 feet, pounds	Manila	Sisal
6-fine	9/16	3/16	1.47	450	360
6	3/4	1/4	1.96	600	480
9	1	5/16	2.84	1,000	800
12	1-1/8	3/8	4.02	1,350	1,080
15	1-1/4	7/16	5.15	1,750	1,400
18	1-3/8	15/32	6.13	2,250	1,800
21	1-1/2	1/2	7.35	2,650	2,120
	1-3/4	9/16	10.20	3,450	2,760
	2	5/8	13.10	4,440	3,520
	2-1/4	3/4	16.30	5,400	4,320
	2-1/2	13/16	19.10	6,500	5,200
	2-3/4	7/8	22.00	7,700	6,160
	3	1	26.50	9,000	7,200
	3-1/4	1-1/16	30.70	10,500	8,400
	3-1/2	1-1/8	35.20	12,000	9,600
	3-3/4	1-1/4	40.80	13,500	10,800
	4	1-5/16	46.90	15,000	12,000
	4-1/2	1-1/2	58.80	18,500	14,800
	5	1-5/8	73.00	22,500	18,000
	5-1/2	1-3/4	87.70	26,500	21,200
	6	2	105.00	31,000	24,800

Mohs' Scale of Hardness

Minerals, metals, abrasive grits and other materials are still compared for hardness on the "Mohs' scale," a rating devised in 1820 by Friedrich Mohs, noted German mineralogist. In this scale, talc, the softest mineral, is rated as 1, while diamond, the hardest, is 10. Each mineral on the scale is hard enough to scratch the one below it. Here is the basic scale:

1	talc	6	feldspar
2	rocksalt or gypsum	7	quartz
3	calcite	8	topaz
4	fluorite	9	corundum
5	apatite	10	diamond

Compared with this scale, here are some values for other materials:

Agate	6-7	Iron	4-5
Aluminum	2-2.9	Kaolinite	2-2.25
Amber	2-2.5	Lead	1.5
Anthracite	2.2	Magnesium	2
Asphalt	1-2	Marble	3-4
Brass	3-4	Opal	4-6
Cadmium	2	Osmium	7
Carborundum	9-10	Platinum	4.3
Chromium	9	Pumice	6
Copper	2.5-3	Silicon	
Diatomaceous		carbide	9-10
earth	1-1.5	Silver	2.5-7
Emery	7-9	Steel	5-8.5
Flint	6.8-7	Tin	1.5-1.8
Garnet	7.5-8.5	Tourmaline	7.3

Glass	4.5-6.5	Tungsten	
Gold	2.5-3	carbide	9-10
Graphite	0.5-1	Wax, 32°F	0.2
Gypsum	1.6-2	Zinc	2.5

FREEZING POINT OF ANTI-FREEZE MIXTURES

ETHYL ALCOHOL-WATER MIXTURES			
% alcohol by volume	Specific gravity, 60°F	Freezing point	
		°C	°F
3.1	0.9954	− 1.0	30.2
8.5	0.9884	− 3.0	26.6
14.0	0.9822	− 5.0	23.0
20.0	0.9761	− 7.5	18.5
25.0	0.9710	−10.5	13.0
29.5	0.9660	−14.0	6.8
32.5	0.9624	−16.0	3.2
36.0	0.9577	−18.8	− 2.0
40.5	0.9511	−23.6	−10.5
46.3	0.9413	−28.7	−19.7

ETHYLENE GLYCOL (PRESTONE)-WATER MIXTURES			
% alcohol by volume	Specific gravity, 60°F	Freezing point	
		°C	°F
12.5	1.019	− 3.9	25
17.0	1.026	− 6.7	20
25.0	1.038	−12.2	10
32.5	1.048	−17.8	0
38.5	1.056	−23.3	−10
44.0	1.063	−28.9	−20
49.0	1.069	−34.4	−30
52.5	1.073	−40.0	−40

TEMPERATURES USEFUL TO KNOW

DEGREES CELSIUS (CENTIGRADE)	DEGREES FAHRENHEIT	
—273	—459.4	Absolute zero
—130	—202	Alcohol freezes
—78.5	—109.3	Dry ice sublimes
—38.9	—38	Mercury freezes
0	32	Ice melts
34.5	94.1	Ether boils
37	98.6	Temperature of human body
60	140	Wood's metal melts
78.5	173.3	Alcohol boils
100	212	Water boils
160	320	Sugar melts
232	450	Tin melts
327	621	Lead melts
658	1,216	Aluminum melts
700	1,292	Dull red heat
800	1,472	Pyrex glass begins to soften
1,000	1,832	Bright red heat
1,083	1,980	Copper melts
1,400	2,552	White heat
1,500	2,732	Temperature of Bunsen flame
1,530	2,786	Iron melts
1,773	3,223	Platinum melts
4,000	7,232	Temperature of electric furnace
6,000	10,800	Temperature of sun's surface

CHEMICAL ELEMENTS

NAME	SYMBOL	ATOMIC WEIGHT	ATOMIC NUMBER
Actinuium	Ac	227	89
Aluminum	Al	26.98	13
Americium	Am	243	95
Antimony, stibium	Sb	121.76	51
Argon	Ar	39.944	18
Arsenic	As	74.92	33
Astatine	At	210	85
Barium	Ba	137.36	56
Berkelium	Bk	249	97
Beryllium	Be	9.013	4
Bismuth	Bi	208.99	83
Boron	B	10.82	5
Bromine	Br	79.916	35
Cadmium	Cd	112.41	48
Calcium	Ca	40.08	20
Californium	Cf	251	98
Carbon	C	12.011	6
Cerium	Ce	140.13	58
Cesium	Cs	132.91	55
Chlorine	Cl	35.457	17
Chromium	Cr	52.01	24
Cobalt	Co	58.94	27
Copper	Cu	63.54	29
Curium	Cm	247	96
Dysprosium	Dy	162.51	66
Einsteinium	E	254	99

NAME	SYMBOL	ATOMIC WEIGHT	ATOMIC NUMBER
Erbium	Er	167.27	68
Europium	Eu	152	63
Fermium	Fm	253	100
Fluorine	F	19	9
Francium	Fr	223	87
Gadolinium	Gd	157.26	64
Gallium	Ga	69.72	31
Germanium	Ge	72.60	32
Gold, aurum	Au	197	79
Hafnium	Hf	178.50	72
Helium	He	4.003	2
Holmium	Ho	164.94	67
Hydrogen	H	1.008	1
Indium	In	114.82	49
Iodine	I	126.91	53
Iridium	Ir	192.2	77
Iron, ferrum	Fe	55.85	26
Krypton	Kr	83.80	36
Lanthanum	La	138.92	57
Lawrencium	Lw	257	103
Lead, plumbum	Pb	207.21	82
Lithium	Li	6.940	3
Lutetium	Lu	174.99	71
Magnesium	Mg	24.32	12
Manganese	Mn	54.94	25
Mendelevium	Mv	256	101
Mercury, hydrargyrum	Hg	200.61	80
Molybdenum	Mo	95.95	42

NAME	SYMBOL	ATOMIC WEIGHT	ATOMIC NUMBER
Neodymium	Nd	144.27	60
Neon	Ne	20.183	10
Neptunium	Np	237	93
Nickel	Ni	58.71	28
Niobium (columbium)	Nb	92.91	41
Nitrogen	N	14.008	7
Nobelium	No	254	102
Osmium	Os	190.2	76
Oxygen	O	16	8
Palladium	Pd	106.4	46
Phosphorus	P	30.975	15
Platinum	Pt	195.09	78
Plutonium	Pu	242	94
Polonium	Po	210	84
Potassium, kalium	K	39.1	19
Praseodymium	Pr	140.92	59
Promethium	Pm	147	61
Protactinium	Pa	321	91
Radium	Ra	226	88
Radon	Rn	222	86
Rhenium	Re	186.22	75
Rhodium	Rh	102.91	45
Rubidium	Rb	85.48	37
Ruthenium	Ru	101.1	44
Samarium	Sm	150.35	62
Scandium	Sc	44.96	21
Selenium	Se	78.96	34
Silicon	Si	28.09	14

NAME	SYMBOL	ATOMIC WEIGHT	ATOMIC NUMBER
Silver, argentum	Ag	107.873	47
Sodium, natrium	Na	22.991	11
Strontium	Sr	87.63	38
Sulfur	S	32.066	16
Tantalum	Ta	180.95	73
Technetium	Te	99	43
Tellurium	Te	127.61	52
Terbium	Tb	158.93	65
Thalium	Tl	204.39	81
Thorium	Th	232	90
Thulium	Tm	168.94	69
Tin, stannum	Sn	118.7	50
Titanium	Ti	47.90	22
Tungsten, wolfram	W	183.86	74
Uranium	U	238.07	92
Vanadium	V	50.95	23
Xenon	Xe	131.30	54
Ytterbium	Yb	173.04	70
Yttrium	Y	88.91	39
Zinc	Zn	65.38	30
Zirconium	Zr	91.22	40

POPULAR AND SCIENTIFIC NAMES FOR CHEMICALS

POPULAR NAME	CHEMICAL NAME	FORMULA
Alcohol, grain	Ethyl alcohol	C_2H_5OH
Alcohol, wood	Methyl alcohol	CH_3OH
Alum, common	Aluminum potassium sulfate	$AlK(SO_4)_2 \cdot 12H_2O$
Alumina	Aluminum oxide	Al_2O_3
Alundum	Fused aluminum oxide	Al_2O_3

POPULAR NAME	CHEMICAL NAME	FORMULA
Antichlor	Sodium thiosulfate	$Na_2S_2O_3 \bullet 5H_2O$
Aqua ammonia	Ammonium hydroxide solution	$NH_4OH + H_2O$
Aqua fortis	Nitric acid	HNO_3
Aqua regia	Nitric and hydrochloric acids	$HNO_3 + HCl$
Aromatic spirits of ammonia	Ammonia gas in alcohol	
Asbestos	Magnesium silicate	$Mg_3Si_2O_7 \bullet 2H_2O$
Aspirin	Acetylsalicylic acid	$C_2H_3O_2C_6H_4CO_2H$
Baking soda	Sodium bicarbonate	$NaHCO_3$
Banana oil	Amyl acetate	$CH_3CO_2C_5H_{11}$
Baryta	Barium oxide	BaO
Bauxite	Impure aluminum oxide	Al_2O_3
Benzol	Benzene	C_6H_6
Bichloride of mercury	Mercuric chloride	$HgCl_2$
Black lead	Graphite	C
Black oxide of copper	Cupric oxide	CuO
Black oxide of mercury	Mercurous oxide	Hg_2O
Bleaching powder	Calcium hypochlorite	$CaOCl_2$
Bluestone	Copper sulfate	$CuSO_4 \bullet 5H_2O$
Blue vitriol	Copper sulfate	$CuSO_4 \bullet 5H_2O$
Boracic acid	Boric acid	H_3BO_3
Borax	Sodium borate	$Na_2B_4O_7 \bullet 10H_2O$
Brimstone	Sulfur	S
Brine	Strong sodium chloride solution	$NaCl\ H_2O$
"Butter of"	Chloride or trichloride of	
Caliche	Impure sodium nitrate	$NaNO_3$
Calomel	Mercurous chloride	Hg_2Cl_2
Carbolic acid	Phenol	C_6H_5OH
Carbonic acid gas	Carbon dioxide	CO_2
Caustic potash	Potassium hydroxide	KOH
Caustic soda	Sodium hydroxide	$NaOH$
Chalk	Calcium carbonate	$CaCO_3$
Chile saltpeter	Sodium nitrate	$NaNO_3$
Chloroform	Trichloromethane	$CHCl_3$

POPULAR NAME	CHEMICAL NAME	FORMULA
Chrome alum	Chromium potassium sulfate	$CrK(SO_4)_2 \cdot 12H_2O$
Chrome yellow	Lead chromate	$PbCrO_4$
Copperas	Ferrous sulfate	$FeSO_4 \cdot 7H_2O$
Corrosive sublimate	Mercuric chloride	$HgCl_2$
Cream of tartar	Potassium bitartrate	$KHC_4H_4O_6$
Crocus powder	Ferric oxide	Fe_2O_3
DDT	Dichlorodiphenyl-trichloroethane	$(C_6H) \cdot Cl_2 \cdot CH \cdot CCl_3$
Dry ice	Solid carbon dioxide	CO_2
Dutch liquid	Ethylene dichloride	$CH_2Cl \cdot CH_2Cl$
Emery powder	Impure aluminum oxide	Al_2O_3
Epsom salts	Magnesium sulfate	$MgSO_4 \cdot 7H_2O$
Ethanol	Ethyl alcohol	C_2H_5OH
Ether	Ethyl ether	$(C_2H_5)_2O$
Fluorspar	Natural calcium fluoride	CaF_2
Formalin	Formaldehyde	$HCOH$
French chalk	Natural magnesium silicate	$H_2Mg_3(SiO_3)_4$
Galena	Natural lead sulfide	PbS
Glauber's salt	Sodium sulfate	$Na_2SO_4 \cdot 10H_2O$
Green vitriol	Ferrous sulfate	$FeSO_4 \cdot 7H_2O$
Gypsum	Natural calcium sulfate	$CaSO_4 \cdot 2H_2O$
Hypo	Sodium thiosulfate	$Na_2S_2O_3 \cdot 5H_2O$
Javelle water	Originally potassium hypochlorite solution,	$KOCl + H_2O$
	now usually sodium hypochlorite solution	$NaOCl + H_2O$
Labarraque's solution	Sodium hypochlorite solution	$NaOCl + H_2O$
Lime, unslaked	Calcium oxide	CaO
Limewater	Calcium hydroxide solution	$Ca(OH)_2 + H_2O$
Litharge	Lead oxide	PbO
Lithopone	Zinc sulfide plus barium sulfate	$ZnS + BaSO_4$
Magnesia	Magnesium oxide	MgO
Magnesite	Magnesium carbonate	$MgCO_3$
Marble	Calcium carbonate	$CaCO_3$

POPULAR NAME	CHEMICAL NAME	FORMULA
Marsh gas	Methane	CH_4
Methanol	Methyl alcohol	CH_3OH
Methylated spirits	Methyl alcohol	CH_3OH
Milk of magnesia	Magnesium hydroxide in water	$Mg(OH)_2$
Minium	Lead tetroxide	Pb_3O_4
"Muriate of"	Chloride of	
Muriatic acid	Hydrochloric acid	HCl
Natural gas	Mostly methane	CH_4
Niter	Potassium nitrate	KNO_3
Oil of bitter almonds (artificial)	Benzaldehyde	C_6H_5CHO
Oil of mirbane	Nitrobenzene	$C_6H_5NO_3$
Oil of vitriol	Sulfuric acid	H_2SO_4
Oil of wintergreen (artificial)	Methyl salicylate	$C_6H_4OHCOOCH_3$
Oleum	Fuming sulfuric acid	$H_2SO_4SO_3$
Orpiment	Arsenic trisulfide	As_2S_3
Paris green	Copper aceto-arsenite	$3Cu(AsO_2)_2 \cdot Cu(C_2H_3O_2)_2$
Pearl ash	Potassium carbonate	K_2CO_3
Peroxide	Peroxide of hydrogen solution	$H_2O_2 + H_2O$
Phosgene	Carbonyl chloride	$COCl_2$
Plaster of Paris	Calcium sulfate	$(CaSO_4)_2 \cdot H_2O$
Plumbago	Graphite	C
Potash	Potassium carbonate	K_2CO_3
Prussic acid	Hydrocyanic acid	HCN
Pyro	Pyrogallic acid	$C_6H_3(OH)_3$
Quicklime	Calcium oxide	CaO
Quicksilver	Mercury	Hg
Red lead	Lead tetroxide	Pb_3O_4
Red oxide of copper	Cuprous oxide	Cu_2O
Red oxide of mercury	Mercuric oxide	HgO
Red prussiate of potash	Potassium ferricyanide	$K_3Fe(CN)_6$
Rochelle salt	Potassium sodium tartrate	$KNaC_4H_4O_6 \cdot 4H_2O$

POPULAR NAME	CHEMICAL NAME	FORMULA
Rouge	Ferric oxide	Fe_2O_3
Sal ammoniac	Ammonium chloride	NH_4Cl
Saleratus	Sodium bicarbonate	$NaHCO_3$
Sal soda	Crystalline sodium carbonate	$NaHCO_3$
Salt	Sodium chloride	$NaCl$
Salt cake	Impure sodium sulfate	Na_2SO_4
Saltpeter	Potassium nitrate	KNO_3
Saltpeter (Chile)	Impure sodium nitrate	$NaNO_3$
Salt of lemon	Potassium binoxalate	$KHC_2O_4 \cdot H_2O$
Salts of tartar	Potassium carbonate	K_2CO_3
Silica	Silicon dioxide	SiO_2
Slaked lime	Calcium hydroxide	$Ca(OH)_2$
Soapstone	Impure magnesium silicate	$H_2Mg_3(SiO_3)_4$
Soda ash	Dry sodium carbonate	Na_2CO_3
Spirit of hartshorn	Ammonia gas in alcohol	
Spirits of salt	Hydrochloric acid	HCl
Spirits of wine	Ethyl alcohol	C_2H_5OH
Sugar of lead	Lead acetate	$Pb(C_2H_3O_2)_2 \cdot 3H_2O$
Sulfuric ether	Ethyl ether	$(C_2H_5)_2O$
Talc	Magnesium silicate	$H_2Mg_3(SiO_3)_4$
TNT	Trinitrotoluene	$C_6H_2CH_3(NO_3)_3$
Toluol	Toluene	$C_6H_5CH_3$
Vinegar	Dilute and impure acetic acid	CH_3COOH
Washing soda	Crystalline sodium carbonate	$NaHCO_3$
Water glass	Sodium silicate	Na_2SiO_3
White arsenic	Arsenic trioxide	As_2O_3
White lead	Basic lead carbonate	$(PbCO_3)_2 \cdot Pb(OH)_2$
White vitriol	Zinc sulfate	$ZnSO_4 \cdot 7H_2O$
Whiting	Powdered calcium carbonate	$CaCO_3$
Wood alcohol	Methyl alcohol	CH_3OH
Xylol	Xylene	$C_6H_4(CH_3)_2$
Zinc white	Zinc oxide	ZnO

THE GREEK ALPHABET

Lower-case Letter	Capital Letter	Name of Letter	English Equivalent
α	A	alpha	a
β	B	beta	b
γ	Γ	gamma	g
δ	Δ	delta	d
ϵ	E	epsilon	e
ζ	Z	zeta	z
η	H	eta	$\bar{e}$
θ	Θ	theta	th
ι	I	iota	i
$\varkappa$	K	kappa	k
λ	Λ	lambda	l
μ	M	mu	m
ν	N	nu	n
ξ	Ξ	xi	x
o	O	omicron	o
π	Π	pi	p
ρ	P	rho	r
σ	Σ	sigma	s
τ	T	tau	t
υ	Υ	upsilon	u
ϕ	Φ	phi	ph
χ	X	chi	ch
ψ	Ψ	psi	ps
ω	Ω	omega	$\bar{o}$

Sources Of Materials

As mentioned in the Introduction, many chemicals and other raw materials that were once easy to get at the local grocery, paint, hardware, or drugstore may now require a little scouting after.

To save the cost of packing and shipping, it is best first to try to find your materials nearby. The Yellow Pages of your local telephone directory may give you a good start. Look under dealers of chemicals, building materials, industrial hardware, janitor's, photographic, artist's supplies, and so on, depending on the product you need and the field in which it is apt to be used. Sometimes a friendly druggist, or hardware or paint dealer may be willing to refer you to sources of raw materials he used to carry but doesn't any more. Larger photographic dealers may order for you any of a long list of photographic chemicals of a manufacturer they deal with, but which they may not ordinarily stock.

Materials you cannot get locally, you can usually order by mail. In this case, a minimum order is generally required and you must, of course, pay for shipping.

General lists of manufacturers and suppliers of chemicals and related raw materials can be found in the following two annual publications, available in many large libraries:

Oil, Paint, and Drug Reporter, Buyer's Directory, Schnell Publishing Company, N.Y.

Chemical Week, Buyer's Guide, McGraw-Hill Publications, N.Y.

Present sources of a number of hard-to-find materials are mentioned with the materials where they occur in the book. Here are some additional suggestions, along with the names of a few specific dealers, that may help you find more.

GENERAL CHEMICALS

Fisher Scientific Company, 711 Forbes Ave., Pittsburgh, Pa. 15219. Branches with complete stocks are maintained in many other major cities in the U.S. and Canada. This is one of the largest suppliers of laboratory chemicals and laboratory equipment in the world, and carries a complete line. Try it for rarer chemicals when you can't find them locally. Deals almost entirely by mail.

Amend Drug and Chemical Company, Inc., 117 E. 24th St., N.Y. 10010. Carries a wide stock of laboratory and industrial chemicals. Convenient for anyone in the New York City area.

Ward's Natural Science Establishment, Inc., P.O. Box 1712, Rochester, N.Y. 14603. Also Ward's of California, P.O. Box 1749, Monterey, Calif. 93942. This long-established company carries a stock of general chemicals, as well as all kinds of specimens and equipment for the study of biology and earth sciences.

Berg Chemical Company, Inc., 441 W. 37th St., N.Y. 10018. A good source for all sorts of industrial chemicals, including synthetic solvents and detergents, quaternary compounds, pesticides, clays, alcohols, acids and alkalies, Stoddard solvent, and wetting agents.

Mallinckrodt Chemical Works, 2nd & Mallinckrodt Sts., St. Louis, Mo. Large manufacturing chemists, with branches in New York and Los Angeles. Usually sell through local dealers. Has a considerable line of chemicals used in the photography and graphic arts industries. This includes nitric, sulfuric, acetic, oxalic, salicylic, and glacial acetic acids, ethyl acetate, formaldehyde, glycerine, sodium silicate, thiourea, potassium permanganate, as well as the usual developing and fixing chemicals. Any of these may be ordered through a photographic dealer that handles this company's products.

Eastman Kodak Company, Rochester, N.Y. 14650. Many of the photographic chemicals made by Mallinckrodt are also made by Eastman, and may be similarly bought or ordered through Kodak dealers.

The following dealers generally sell chemicals and laboratory apparatus in smaller quantities to schools, student, and home chemistry hobbyists. The first four have catalogs.

Hagenow Laboratories, Inc., 2810 Wollmer St., Manitowoc, Wis. 54220.

Tracey Scientific Laboratories, Inc., P.O. Box 615, Evanston, Ill.

Biological Supply Company, 1176 Mt. Hope Ave., Rochester, N.Y. 14620.

National Scientific Company, 13 S. Park Ave., Lombard, Ill. 60148.

Harry Ross, 61 Reade St., N.Y. 10007. This pioneer dealer in used microscopes and other laboratory equipment carries a modest line of chemicals for schools and students, and is one of the very few dealers in N.Y.C. that still sells chemicals over the counter.

MISCELLANEOUS RAW MATERIALS

H. Behlen & Bro., Inc., 10 Christopher St., N.Y. 10014, founded in 1888, is one of the last big manufacturer-dealers in the country to carry a complete line of raw materials for the paint, varnish, and wood-finishing trades. Besides the expected pigments, stains, dyes, solvents, waxes, coated abrasive, and polishing powders, Behlen sells an amazing assortment of often elusive industrial chemicals and other basic products that should be a delight to the do-it-yourself formula compounder. These include acids and alkalies, bronze powders, clays, dextrin, fibers, fuller's earth, gelatins, all kinds of dry glues, lacquer sticks, litharge, lithopone, red and white lead, metal leafs, resins, silex, sodium silicate, iron and copper sulfates, sodium silicate, potassium permanganate, and trisodium phosphate. Sells over the counter and by mail. A catalog of major items costs 35 cents.

WOOD-FINISHING SUPPLIES

For wood-finishing supplies alone, try hardware and paint stores, lumberyards and suppliers of building materials. Craft supply stores that include woodworking are also good sources.

Albert Constantine and Son, Inc., 2050 Eastchester Road, Bronx, N.Y. 10461—its parent company dating back to 1812—carries a complete line of such materials as well as a wide inventory of fine and rare woods for craft work and furniture making. Sells by mail and over the counter. Minimum mail order $4.75. Catalog 25 cents.

PIGMENTS, STAINS, AND DYES

First try local paint and hardware stores.

Founded in 1853, Fezandie & Sperrle, Inc., 103 Lafayette St., N.Y. 10013, probably carries anything you need in this line: dry colors, aniline dyes, stains for wood and for leather, lime-proof colors for cement, food, drug, and cosmetic colors—even tattoo colors! It also sells such specialties as dextrin, glues, gums, and waxes, collapsible tubes for containing home-ground artist's paints, and casein. Will supply price lists. Minimum mail order $3.50.

Another venerable company, Pylam Products Company, Inc., 95-10 218th St., Queens Village, N.Y. 11429, makes and sells certified food, drug, and cosmetic colors, as well as alcohol, water, wax, and solvent-soluble dyes for coloring candles, soaps, detergents and all sorts of consumer products. Has list for each type of color. Minimum mail order $5.00.

Murray-Williams Color & Chemical Co., 353-361 Boyden Ave., Maplewood, N.J. 07040, makes and sells dry pigments, cement colors, aniline colors, and sundry products such as silex, pumice, dextrin, powdered rosin, and zinc and copper sulfates. Will send price lists. Sells both through retail paint and hardware stores and by mail.

Landers-Segal Color Company, 78 Delavan St., Brooklyn, N.Y. 11231, makes and sells the same general line of colors and chemical specialties as Murray-Williams. Packages 1-ounce envelopes of aniline colors (dry wood stains), and 1-pound and 5-pound packages of dry colors and chemical specialties. Has price lists. Sells usually through retail paint and hardware stores throughout the country.

Playhouse Colors, 771 Ninth Ave., N.Y. 10019, specializes in color materials for professional and amateur stage "props" and scenery. These include dry colors, fluorescent colors, casein paints, water-soluble dyes, glues, pastes, dextrin, and all the equipment needed to apply the colors. Such paints can also, of course, be used for all sorts of decorative work (or "pop art") inside the house, where an inexpensive, brilliant, water-based paint is desired, or the ingredients can be used separately wherever such materials are needed. A catalog is available.

WAXES

Beeswax is still used by leather workers to wax thread, finish belt edges, and so on, and is available from art-and-craft supply stores. This and other waxes —such as carnauba, candelilla, ceresine, ozokerite— used widely in the commercial manufacture of polishes and floor waxes, cosmetics, lubricants, and water-repellents, will probably have to be obtained from special dealers in waxes listed in the Yellow Pages in your phone book or from one of the manufacturers listed below.

Frank B. Ross Co., Inc., Jersey City, N.J. 07304. For industrial users of wax, this company publishes a booklet, "Ross Waxes," that contains a wealth of information about the origin of the many natural and synthetic waxes and their physical characteristics and varied uses.

Cornelius Wax Refining Corporation, 1711 Elizabeth Ave. West, Linden, N.J. 07036. This company also publishes an informative booklet concerning wax characterists and applications.

M. Argueso & Co., Inc., 441 Waverly Ave. Mamaroneck, N.Y. 10543, imports, refines, and compounds waxes, and has sales representatives and stocks in principle cities throughout the country. See phone book.

PLASTICS MATERIALS

MOP (Mail Order Plastics), 58 Lispenard St., N.Y. 10013, carries a wide line of plastic boxes, cabinets, bags, bottles, tubing, sheets, cement, and laboratory ware. Has catalog.

Castolite Company, Woodstock, Ill. 60098. Liquid plastics and fiberglass for casting, molding, coating, and laminating.

Bel-Art Products Pequannock, N.J. 07440. Plastic sheets, tubes, rods, covers, containers, and laboratory ware.

Most craft supply stores also carry liquid casting plastics and a variety of solid forms.

ARTS AND CRAFTS

Besides paints, pastels, canvasses, metals, leather, and other typical arts and crafts materials, artist's and craftworker's supply stores are often a mine of general raw materials that are now often hard to find elsewhere. In larger ones you can get such things as asphaltum varnish (for etching backgrounds), beeswax, liver of sulfur, gold and aluminum leaf, bronze powders, leather dyes, jars, bottles, collapsible tubes, powdered charcoal, modeling and ceramic clays, casting plaster, etc.

If you can't find a local dealer that has what you need, you might try one of these:

Arthur Brown & Bro., Inc., 2 West 46th St., N.Y. 10036. This is probably the largest general artist's supply dealer in America. Sells over the counter and by mail from a large catalog.

Skil-Crafts, 309 Virginia Ave., Joplin, Mo. 64801. Has wide line of arts and crafts materials. Large catalog sent for 50 cents.

American Handicrafts Co. has more than 60 stores throughout the U.S. Look in the phone book of the large city nearest you and you'll probably find one. Sells by mail through a catalog and has a complete stock in each of its stores.

Economy Crafts, 47-11 Francis Lewis Blvd., Flushing, N.Y. 11361. Has wide stock, which it sells from store and by mail. Catalog 25 cents.

Allcraft Recreation Materials, Inc., 122 Main St., Hempstead, N.Y. 11550. Sells all sorts of arts and crafts materials to schools and individuals. Catalog 50 cents.

MARBLE AND MARBLE CARE

For marble to use in projects, or for materials to clean, polish, or repair marble, see section on marble dealers and importers in the Yellow Pages of your phone book, or get in touch with either of the following:

Marble Institute of America, Pennsylvania Bldg., Washington, D.C. 20004. This non-profit association of marble experts and dealers has a mark remover and polishing kit, and can give advice on marble problems.

Vermarco Supply Co., Division of Vermont Marble Co., Proctor, Vt. 05765. Has branches in many U.S. cities. Has complete line of marble cleaning, polishing, and cementing materials.

pH TEST MATERIALS

Papers and liquids that change color to give rough indications of acidity or alkalinity can be bought in garden supply stores and from chemical supply houses. More elaborate equipment for giving more accurate indications can also be bought from the latter sources.

Complete kits for all sorts of pH testing, as well as information concerning methods, can be obtained from the LaMotte Chemical Products Company, Chestertown, Md. 21620.

ELECTROPLATING SUPPLIES

The HBS Equipment Division, 3543 East 16th St., Los Angeles, Calif. 90023, carries all the materials necessary to take up electroplating as a serious lobby or as a small business. These include plating chemicals, metal anodes, tanks, electrical supply and control equipment, and materials to buff and polish the final finish. Has catalog. Minimum mail order $10.

INDEX

Glues (*continued*)
  hide (animal), 184-85, 188-91
  liquid, 185-86, 189
  natural origin, 184-86, 188-93
  resin (synthetic-resin), 186-88, 189
  solders, liquid or cold, 115
  stains on
    textiles, 273-276
    wood, 19
  thermoplastic and thermosetting, 186
Glycerin
  glass grinding, 549
  hand lotion, 410
  soap
    making, 404
  weight calculation, 589-90
Gold
  buffs and compounds, 98
  electroplating with, 109
  solders for, 115, 120, 121
  specific gravity, 594
  test for, 524-25
  weight, cubic foot, 594
Gold chloride solution, 347-48
Granite, specific gravity and cubic-foot weight, 594
Grass
  herbicides, 302-3, 438-39
  stains, textiles, 276
Gravel, specific gravity and cubic-foot weight, 594
Gravy and meat juice stains, 276
Gray stains
  indoor and furniture, 29
  outdoor, 23
Grease, on machines, cleaning, 287
  rustproofing with, 121-22
Grease and oil stains
  garage floors, 294
  marble, 229-30
  textiles, 272, 273, 280
    solvents, 269
    various, 273 ff.
Greek alphabet, 639
Greenheart, specific gravity and cubic-foot weight, 595
Greenhouses, whitewashing, 75, 76, 80
Green stains
  outdoors, 22-23

Grinding glass, 549
Grinding wheels
  abrasive quality, 136-38
  speeds, 138-39
Grit for birds, 561
Grits, coated abrasives, 568-71
Grout, shrinkage prevention, 156-57
Grubs, white, 432
Gum acacia
  hand cream, 409
  mucilage, 198-99
Gum tragacanth
  crayons, 325-27
  denture adhesive, 422
Gum wood
  properties and cost, 6
  stains, pigment oil, 27-30
  weathering, 8
Gypsum, specific gravity and cubic-foot weight, 594

Hacksaw blades, 139-40
Hair, burning test for, 533
Hammer
  handles, oiling, 307
Hands
  creams and lotions
    glycerin, 410
    lotion, 410
    protective, 409
  fingernail polish
    remover, 414
    stains, on textiles, 275
  fingernails, presoaping, 304
  odors, onion and fish, 297
  photographic materials stains, 39-95
  powders, cleaning, 407
  soaps—*see also* Soaps
Hardness, Mohs' scale of, 628-29
Hardwoods—*see also* Lumber; Woods; specific names
  lumber sizes, 2
  properties and relative costs, 6-7
  plywood—*see* Plywood
  water stains for, 31-32
  weathering, 8-9
Heat
  burns from, first aid for, 516-17
  from chemicals, 536
  exhaustion, first aid for, 520
  whitewashing to control,